THE SAGA OF TANYA THE EVIL

16

...arlo Zen
...Tojo
...obu Shinotsuki

EMPIRE (including occupied territory)
COUNTRIES AT WAR
REGIONS OF CONFLICT
NEUTRAL COUNTRIES
100 0 100 200 300
REGADONIA ENTENTE ALLIANCE
RUSSY FEDERATION
IMPERIAL NORDEN
ALBION COMMONWEALTH
IMPERIAL OSTLAND (POTENTIAL DISPUTE)
EMPIRE
UNIFIED STATES
FRANÇOIS REPUBLIC
IMPERIAL DACIA
PRINCIPALITY OF DACIA
KINGDOM OF ILDOA
WALDSTÄTTE CONFEDERACY
ISPAGNA COLLECTIVE
UNREDEEMED ILDOA (POTENTIAL DISPUTE)

Die Zeiten

DIE KRIEGSGESCHICHTE EINES KLEINEN MÄDCHEN No.016

The battle log so far...

Our protagonist, a coolheaded salaryman in contemporary Japan, dies after being pushed off a train platform by a resentful man he fired.

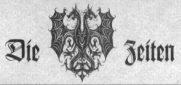

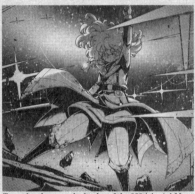

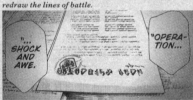

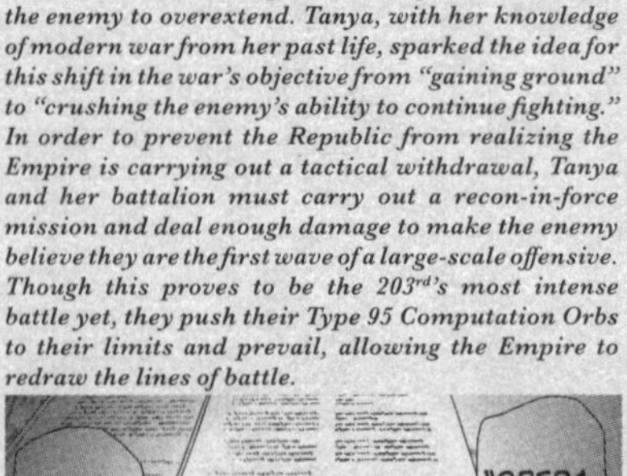

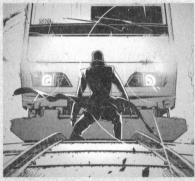

In the world beyond death, he encounters Being X, who claims to be the Creator. His lack of faith angers the being, and he is reborn in another world where gunfire and magic intermingle in combat. "You will be born into an unscientific world as a woman, come to know war, and be driven to your limits!"
In the other world, he is reincarnated as Tanya Degurechaff. Upon recognition of her magic aptitude, she is sent to the battlefield at the age of nine.

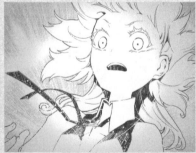

Using the knowledge from her previous life, she climbs the ranks, aiming for a safe position in the rear, but her outstanding achievements and bravery make such a good impression on her superiors that she is, on the contrary, repeatedly sent to the front lines...

Tanya has become the leader of the 203rd Aerial Mage Battalion and been stationed on the contested Rhine lines in recognition of her achievements in Dacia and Norden. Despite her efforts, not only has there been no real change in the war but the imperial supply city of Arene and its people have been reduced to ashes.
However, General von Zettour decides to break through this deadlock with a life-or-death gamble. His plan: to pull back from the lines that so much blood and steel have been expended to defend and compel the enemy to overextend. Tanya, with her knowledge of modern war from her past life, sparked the idea for this shift in the war's objective from "gaining ground" to "crushing the enemy's ability to continue fighting."
In order to prevent the Republic from realizing the Empire is carrying out a tactical withdrawal, Tanya and her battalion must carry out a recon-in-force mission and deal enough damage to make the enemy believe they are the first wave of a large-scale offensive. Though this proves to be the 203rd's most intense battle yet, they push their Type 95 Computation Orbs to their limits and prevail, allowing the Empire to redraw the lines of battle.

"OPERATION...
"...SHOCK AND AWE.

When Tanya returns to the Empire, she is met with a sealed letter containing new orders to commence Operation Shock and Awe. Its objective—to have mages board "acceleration units" and launch a direct assault on enemy headquarters.
Onward, ever onward. Zettour's plan to "escape forward," on which the fate of the Empire rests, begins.

THE SAGA OF TANYA THE EVIL

Character Introductions

Name des Paßinhabers

Tanya von Degurechaff

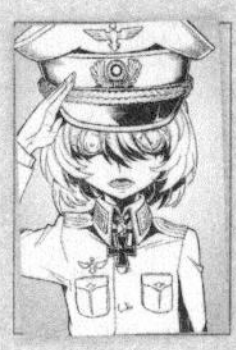

(Rufname, Familienname)

Dienstgrad	Dienststellung
MAJOR	AERIAL MAGIC OFFICER

An extremely rational little girl who was a salaryman in her previous life. Joins the army to escape life in the orphanage. Becomes a mage after her talent for magic is recognized. She couldn't care less about national defense and simply wants to live a quiet life safe in the rear. Unfortunately, misunderstanding after misunderstanding causes others to think she is a patriot full of fighting spirit.

(Angaben zur Person)

Name des Paßinhabers

Johann-Mattäus Weiss

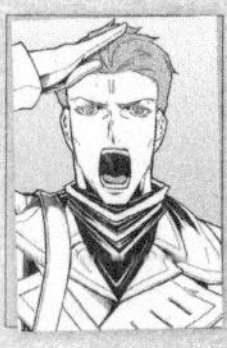

(Rufname, Familienname)

Dienstgrad	Dienststellung
FIRST LIEUTENANT	AERIAL MAGIC OFFICER

A mage in the Imperial Army and a member of Major Degurechaff's 203rd Aerial Mage Battalion. He's an earnest, outstanding soldier, but because he doesn't have much combat experience, most of his knowledge comes from textbooks. Having made it through the hellish training, it's clear his skills and fighting spirit are impeccable. That plus his talent for unit management means the army has high expectations of him.

(Angaben zur Person)

Name des Paßinhabers

Viktoriya Ivanovna Serebryakov

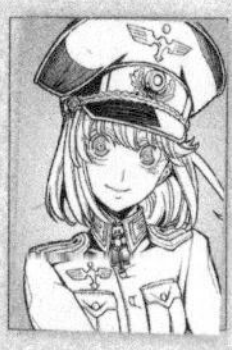

(Rufname, Familienname)

Dienstgrad	Dienststellung
SECOND LIEUTENANT	AERIAL MAGIC OFFICER

A mage in the Imperial Army. After being practically forced to enlist in the cadet corps due to her magic abilities, she is stationed in a unit on the front lines. Having proven herself capable in combat, she is recommended for the officer track. She sees Major Degurechaff as a kind, peace-loving individual and respects and supports her as her outstanding adjutant.

(Angaben zur Person)

Name des Paßinhabers

Erich von Lergen

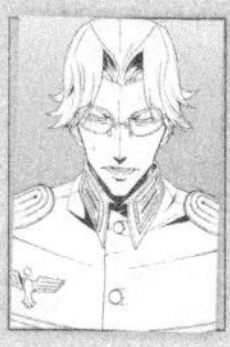

(Rufname, Familienname)

Dienstgrad	Dienststellung
MAJOR GENERAL	SENIOR STAFF OFFICER IN THE GENERAL STAFF

A sensible man whose hard work shows. The army expects great things from this General Staff officer; he is currently gaining experience in Personnel. Major Degurechaff makes him nervous because he can sense how abnormal and insane she is, but he's also forced to admit that she is right when it comes to the war, so his personal feelings and duty come into conflict.

(Angaben zur Person)

Name des Paßinhabers

Warren Grantz

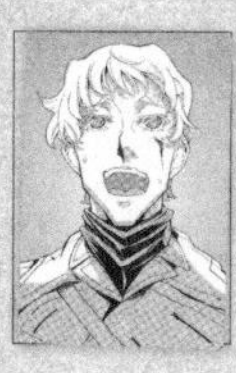

(Rufname, Familienname)

Dienstgrad	Dienststellung
SECOND LIEUTENANT	AERIAL MAGIC OFFICER

A newly commissioned officer joining the 203rd Aerial Mage Battalion as a replenishment. A fresh grad from the academy, he dreams of fighting heroically to defend his country. He's still quite green as both an officer and a mage, but he has a lot of potential, so his future seems bright.

(Angaben zur Person)

Name des Paßinhabers

Adelheid von Schugel

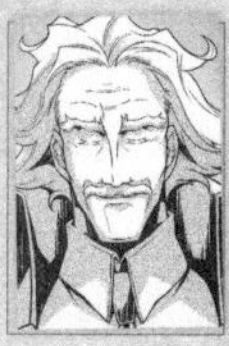

(Rufname, Familienname)

Dienstgrad	Dienststellung
——	CHIEF ENGINEER

A technical expert who researches magic technology in the Empire. He is a true "genius" of an engineer, albeit one who seemingly traded in his common sense for his talents, who heard the voice of God while developing a new orb. This revelation led to the completion of the miraculous Elinium Type 95, and since then, he has become a pious believer, though he remains a mad scientist prone to reckless behavior.

(Angaben zur Person)

Name des Paßinhabers

Hans von Zettour

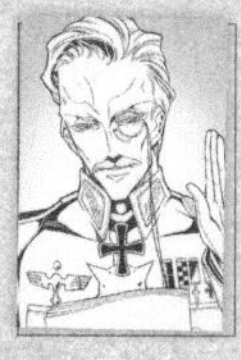

(Rufname, Familienname)

Dienstgrad	Dienststellung
MAJOR GENERAL	DEPUTY DIRECTOR OF THE SERVICE CORPS IN THE GENERAL STAFF

Employing his clear thinking and wealth of knowledge, he works on logistics and plans operations with his friend and colleague Major General Rudersdorf, the deputy director of Operations. He has a very high opinion of Major Degurechaff and does what he can to take her wishes into account. He's so far learned that in war college, evaluators had concerns that he was "too scholarly and thus not suited to becoming a general."

(Angaben zur Person)

The Saga of Tanya the Evil

16

Chapter: 44

Open Sesame I

O O 5

Chapter: 45

Open Sesame II

0 8 5

Chapter: 46

Open Sesame III

1 4 5

Original Story: Carlo Zen   Art: Chika Tojo
Character Design: Shinobu Shinotsuki

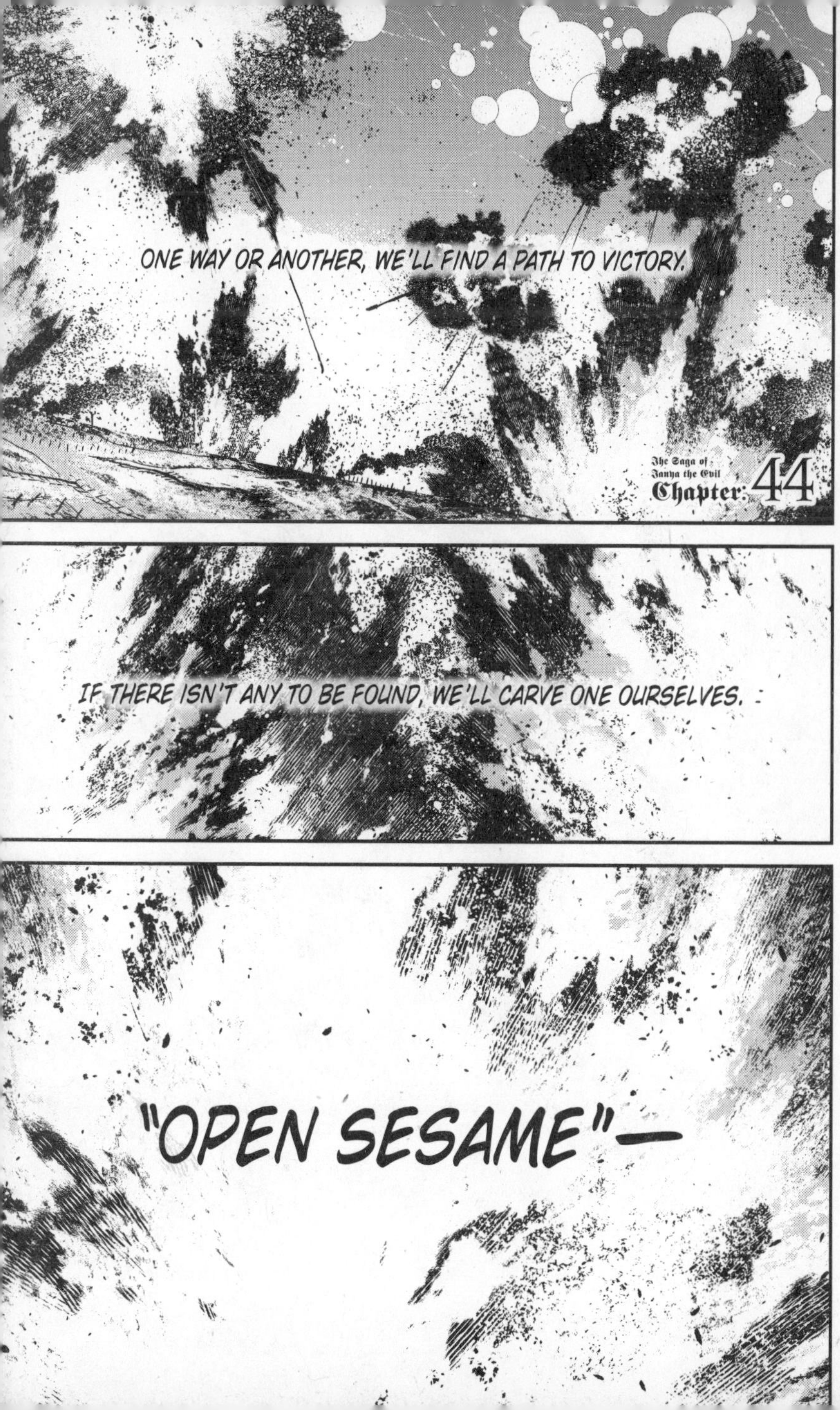
ONE WAY OR ANOTHER, WE'LL FIND A PATH TO VICTORY.
The Saga of Tanya the Evil
Chapter: 44
IF THERE ISN'T ANY TO BE FOUND, WE'LL CARVE ONE OURSELVES.
"OPEN SESAME"—

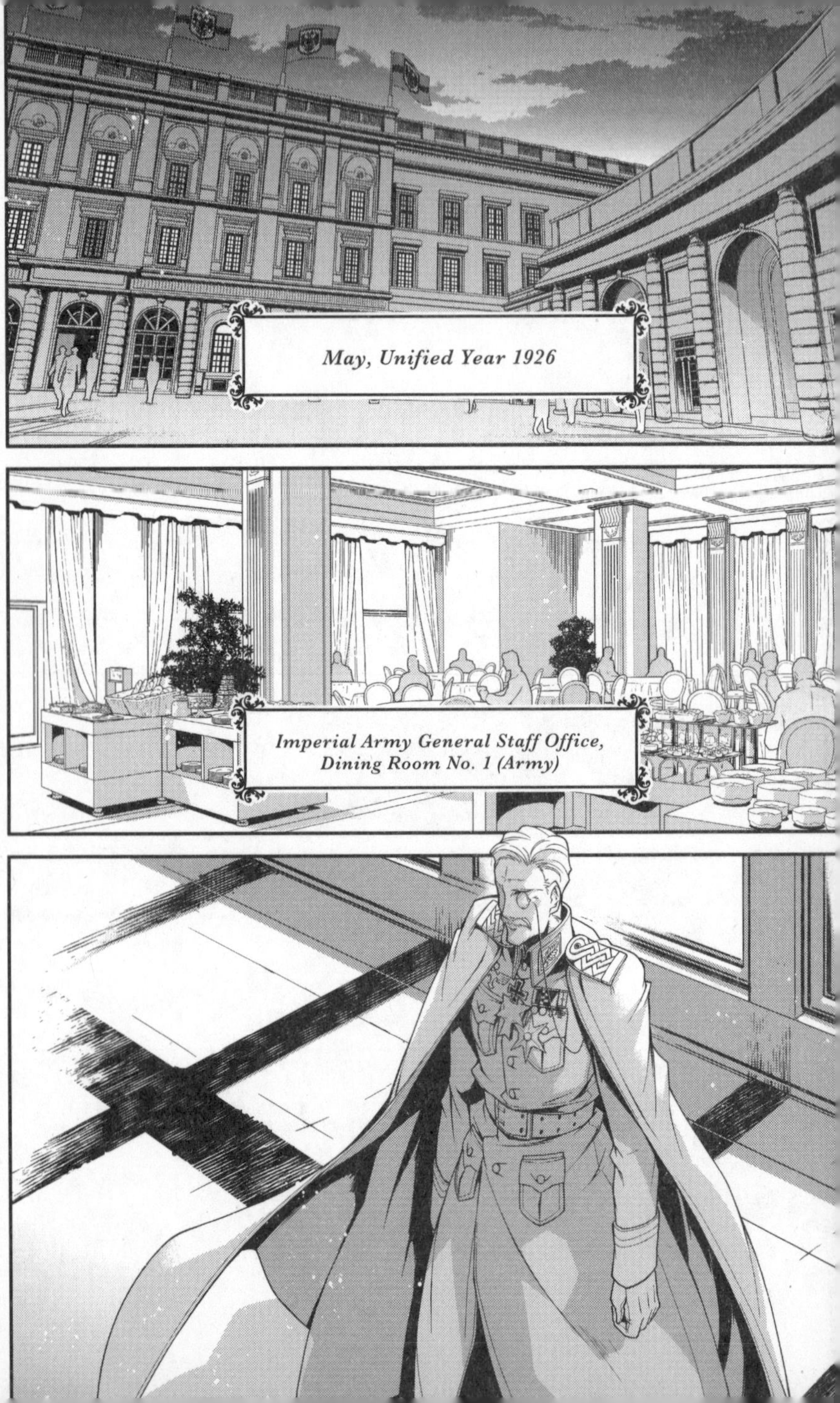
May, Unified Year 1926
Imperial Army General Staff Office,
Dining Room No. 1 (Army)

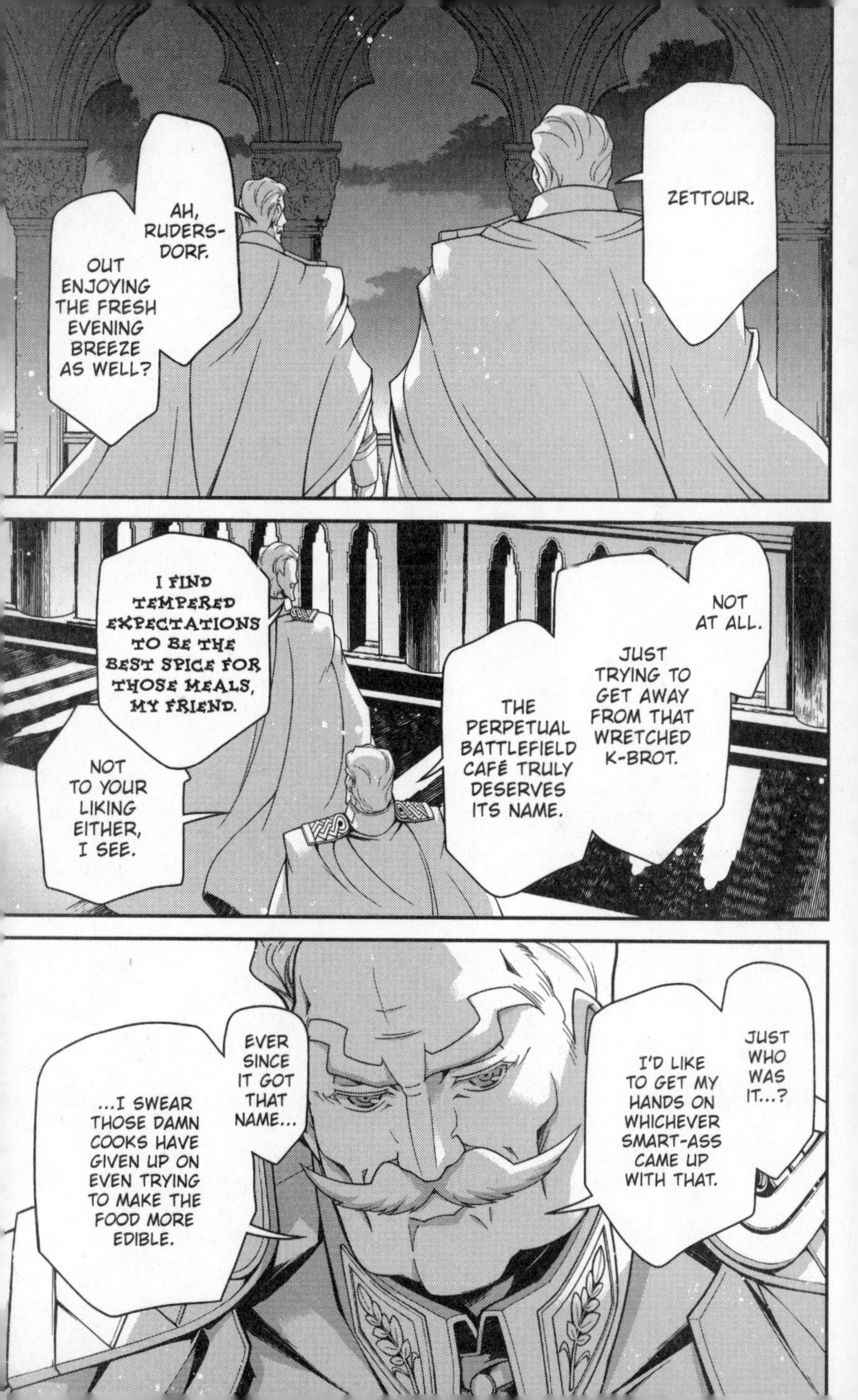
ZETTOUR.
AH, RUDERSDORF.
OUT ENJOYING THE FRESH EVENING BREEZE AS WELL?
NOT AT ALL.
JUST TRYING TO GET AWAY FROM THAT WRETCHED K-BROT.
THE PERPETUAL BATTLEFIELD CAFÉ TRULY DESERVES ITS NAME.
I FIND TEMPERED EXPECTATIONS TO BE THE BEST SPICE FOR THOSE MEALS, MY FRIEND.
NOT TO YOUR LIKING EITHER, I SEE.
JUST WHO WAS IT...?
I'D LIKE TO GET MY HANDS ON WHICHEVER SMART-ASS CAME UP WITH THAT.
EVER SINCE IT GOT THAT NAME...
...I SWEAR THOSE DAMN COOKS HAVE GIVEN UP ON EVEN TRYING TO MAKE THE FOOD MORE EDIBLE.

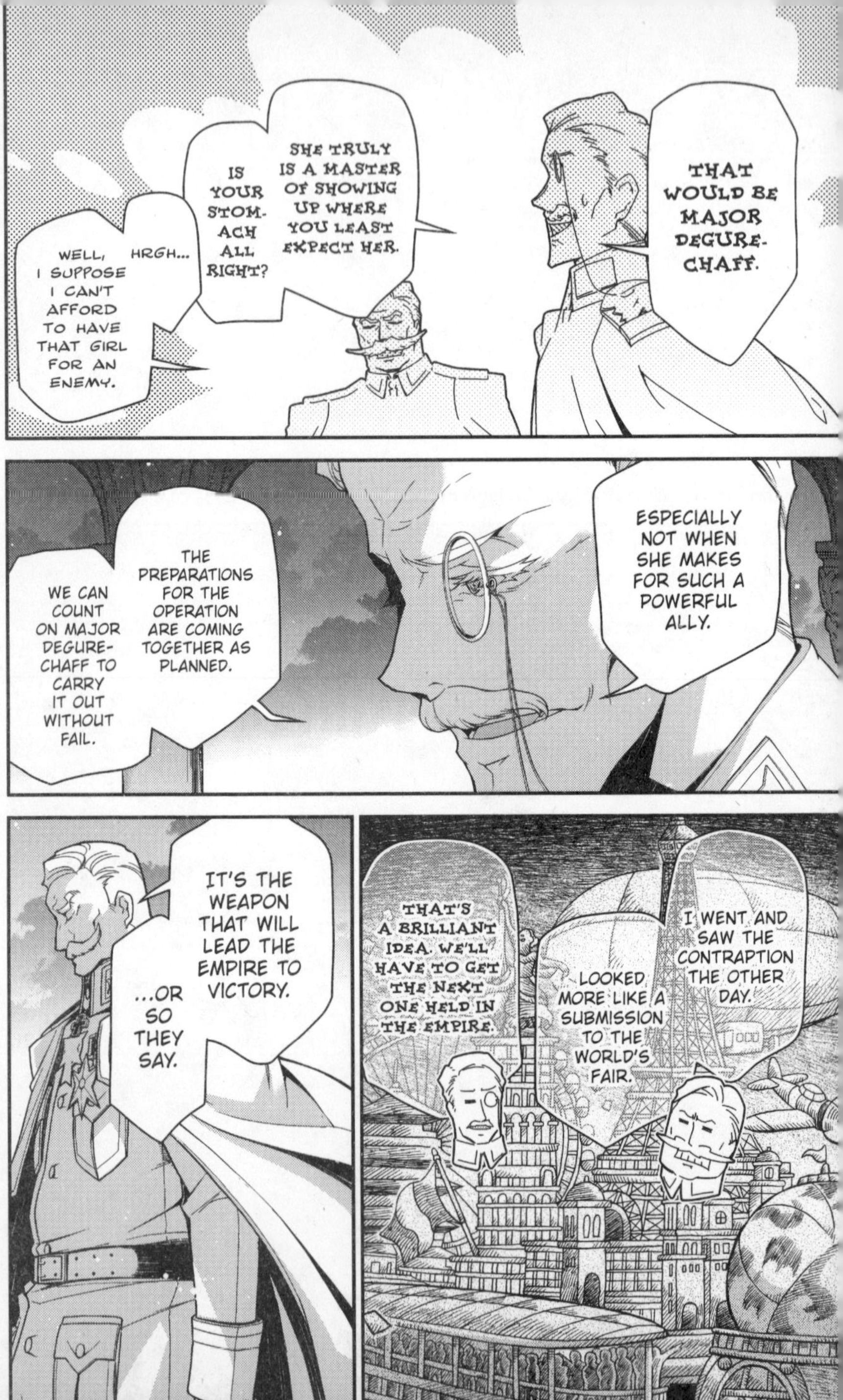
THAT WOULD BE MAJOR DEGURE-CHAFF.
SHE TRULY IS A MASTER OF SHOWING UP WHERE YOU LEAST EXPECT HER.
IS YOUR STOM-ACH ALL RIGHT?
HRGH...
WELL, I SUPPOSE I CAN'T AFFORD TO HAVE THAT GIRL FOR AN ENEMY.
ESPECIALLY NOT WHEN SHE MAKES FOR SUCH A POWERFUL ALLY.
THE PREPARATIONS FOR THE OPERATION ARE COMING TOGETHER AS PLANNED.
WE CAN COUNT ON MAJOR DEGURE-CHAFF TO CARRY IT OUT WITHOUT FAIL.
I WENT AND SAW THE CONTRAPTION THE OTHER DAY.
LOOKED MORE LIKE A SUBMISSION TO THE WORLD'S FAIR.
THAT'S A BRILLIANT IDEA. WE'LL HAVE TO GET THE NEXT ONE HELD IN THE EMPIRE.
IT'S THE WEAPON THAT WILL LEAD THE EMPIRE TO VICTORY.
...OR SO THEY SAY.

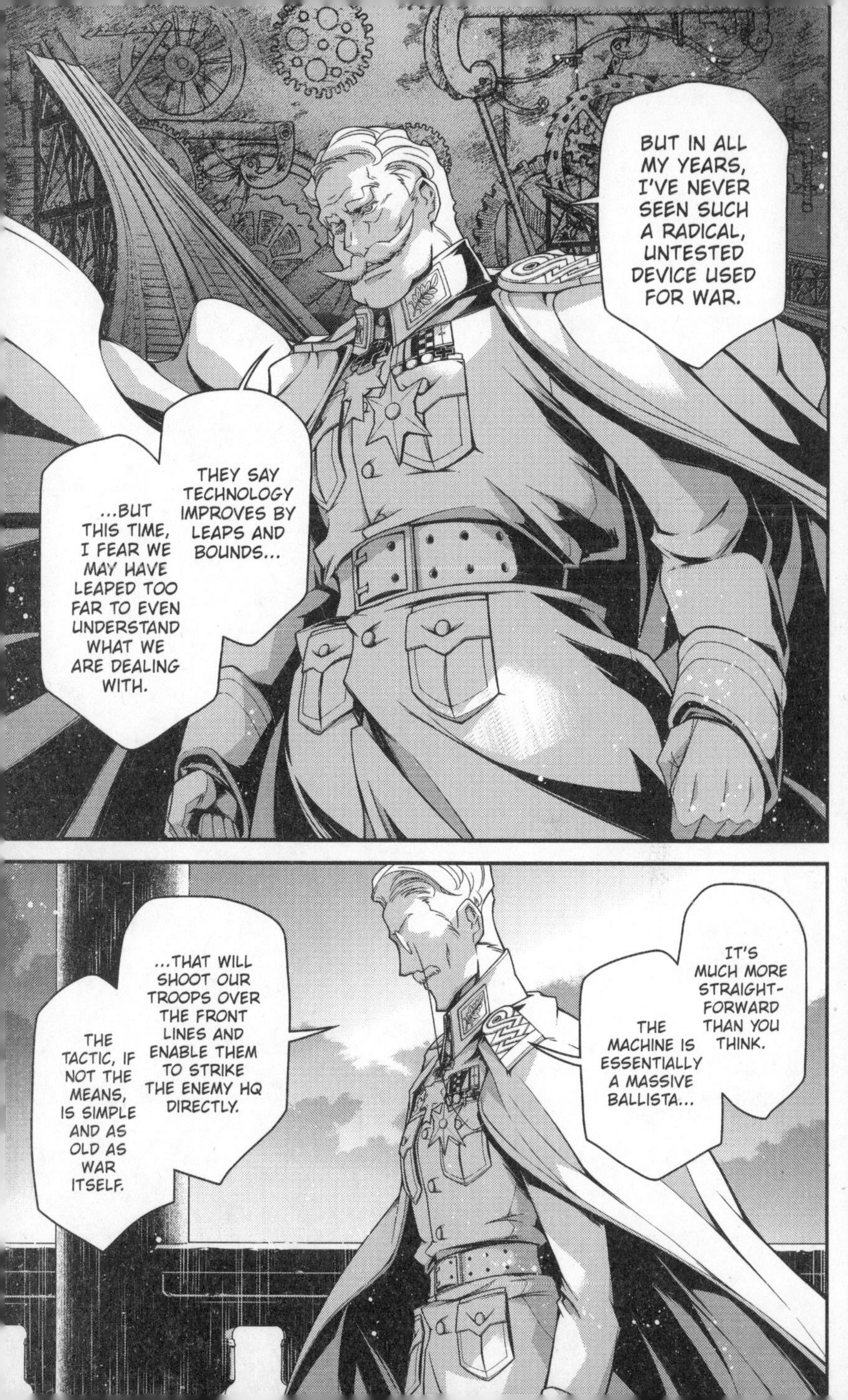
BUT IN ALL MY YEARS, I'VE NEVER SEEN SUCH A RADICAL, UNTESTED DEVICE USED FOR WAR.
THEY SAY TECHNOLOGY IMPROVES BY LEAPS AND BOUNDS...
...BUT THIS TIME, I FEAR WE MAY HAVE LEAPED TOO FAR TO EVEN UNDERSTAND WHAT WE ARE DEALING WITH.
IT'S MUCH MORE STRAIGHT-FORWARD THAN YOU THINK.
THE MACHINE IS ESSENTIALLY A MASSIVE BALLISTA...
...THAT WILL SHOOT OUR TROOPS OVER THE FRONT LINES AND ENABLE THEM TO STRIKE THE ENEMY HQ DIRECTLY.
THE TACTIC, IF NOT THE MEANS, IS SIMPLE AND AS OLD AS WAR ITSELF.

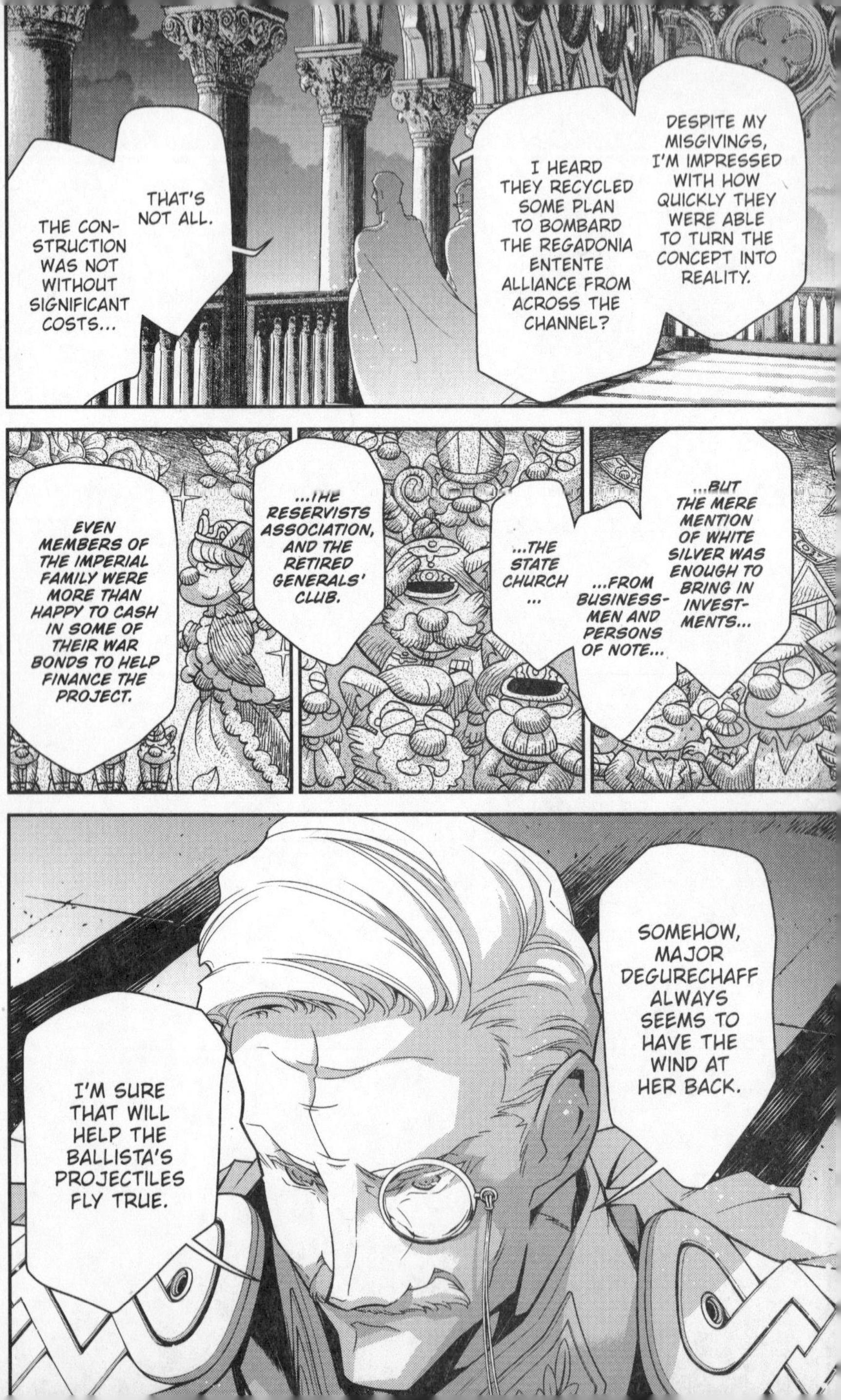
DESPITE MY MISGIVINGS, I'M IMPRESSED WITH HOW QUICKLY THEY WERE ABLE TO TURN THE CONCEPT INTO REALITY.
I HEARD THEY RECYCLED SOME PLAN TO BOMBARD THE REGADONIA ENTENTE ALLIANCE FROM ACROSS THE CHANNEL?
THAT'S NOT ALL.
THE CON-STRUCTION WAS NOT WITHOUT SIGNIFICANT COSTS...
...BUT THE MERE MENTION OF WHITE SILVER WAS ENOUGH TO BRING IN INVEST-MENTS...
...FROM BUSINESS-MEN AND PERSONS OF NOTE...
...THE STATE CHURCH ...
...THE RESERVISTS ASSOCIATION, AND THE RETIRED GENERALS' CLUB.
EVEN MEMBERS OF THE IMPERIAL FAMILY WERE MORE THAN HAPPY TO CASH IN SOME OF THEIR WAR BONDS TO HELP FINANCE THE PROJECT.
SOMEHOW, MAJOR DEGURECHAFF ALWAYS SEEMS TO HAVE THE WIND AT HER BACK.
I'M SURE THAT WILL HELP THE BALLISTA'S PROJECTILES FLY TRUE.

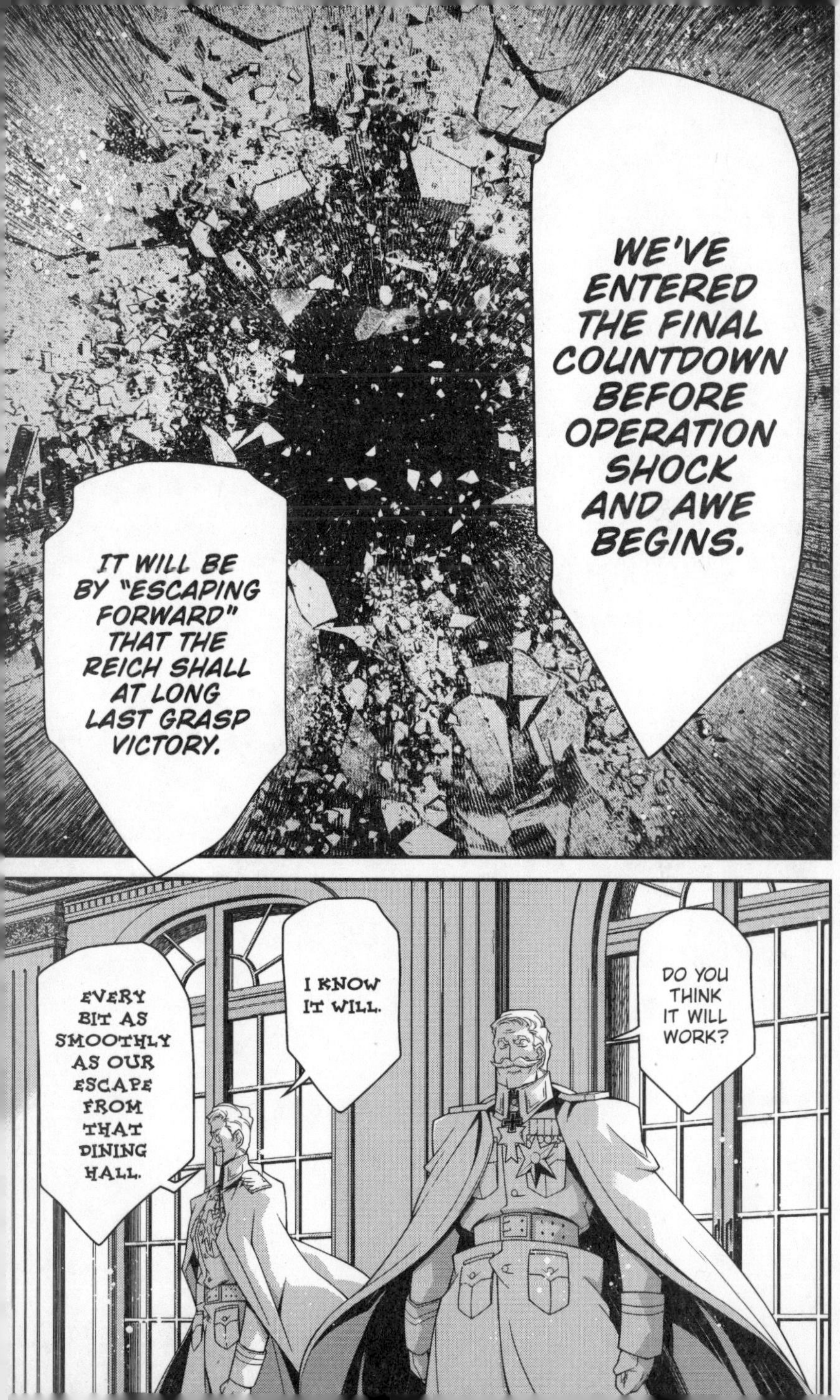
WE'VE ENTERED THE FINAL COUNTDOWN BEFORE OPERATION SHOCK AND AWE BEGINS.
IT WILL BE BY "ESCAPING FORWARD" THAT THE REICH SHALL AT LONG LAST GRASP VICTORY.
DO YOU THINK IT WILL WORK?
I KNOW IT WILL.
EVERY BIT AS SMOOTHLY AS OUR ESCAPE FROM THAT DINING HALL.

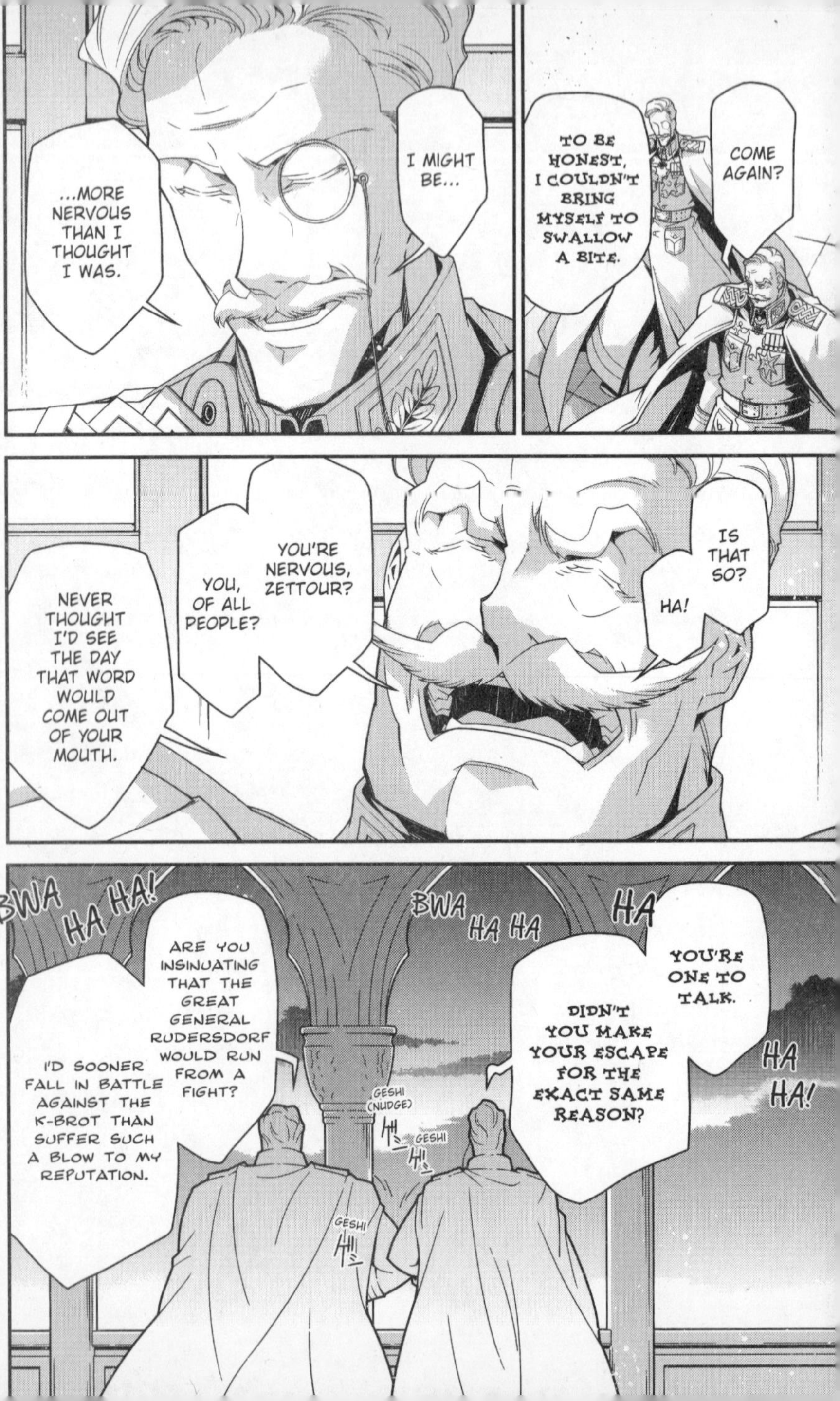
COME AGAIN?
TO BE HONEST, I COULDN'T BRING MYSELF TO SWALLOW A BITE.
I MIGHT BE...
...MORE NERVOUS THAN I THOUGHT I WAS.
IS THAT SO?
HA!
YOU'RE NERVOUS, ZETTOUR?
YOU, OF ALL PEOPLE?
NEVER THOUGHT I'D SEE THE DAY THAT WORD WOULD COME OUT OF YOUR MOUTH.
HA
YOU'RE ONE TO TALK.
DIDN'T YOU MAKE YOUR ESCAPE FOR THE EXACT SAME REASON?
HA HA!
BWA HA HA
GESHI (NUDGE)
GESHI
ARE YOU INSINUATING THAT THE GREAT GENERAL RUDERSDORF WOULD RUN FROM A FIGHT?
BWA HA HA!
I'D SOONER FALL IN BATTLE AGAINST THE K-BROT THAN SUFFER SUCH A BLOW TO MY REPUTATION.
GESHI

IT'S NO EXAGGERATION TO SAY THAT THE FATE OF THE REICH IS RIDING ON THIS LARGE-SCALE OPERATION.

SHOULD IT FAIL, ALL OUR EFFORTS UP TO THIS POINT WILL HAVE BEEN FOR NOTHING.

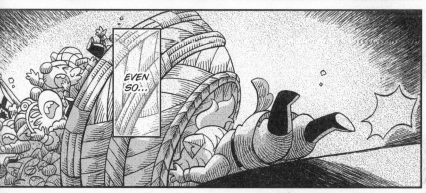

EVEN SO...

...PRESSING FORWARD IS THE EMPIRE'S ONLY PATH TO VICTORY.

NO, THAT IS NOT ENOUGH— WE MUST ADVANCE WITH ALL OUR MIGHT, AS FAST AS WE CAN.

IN WHICH CASE, WE TRULY HAVE NO CHOICE BUT TO ESCAPE FORWARD.

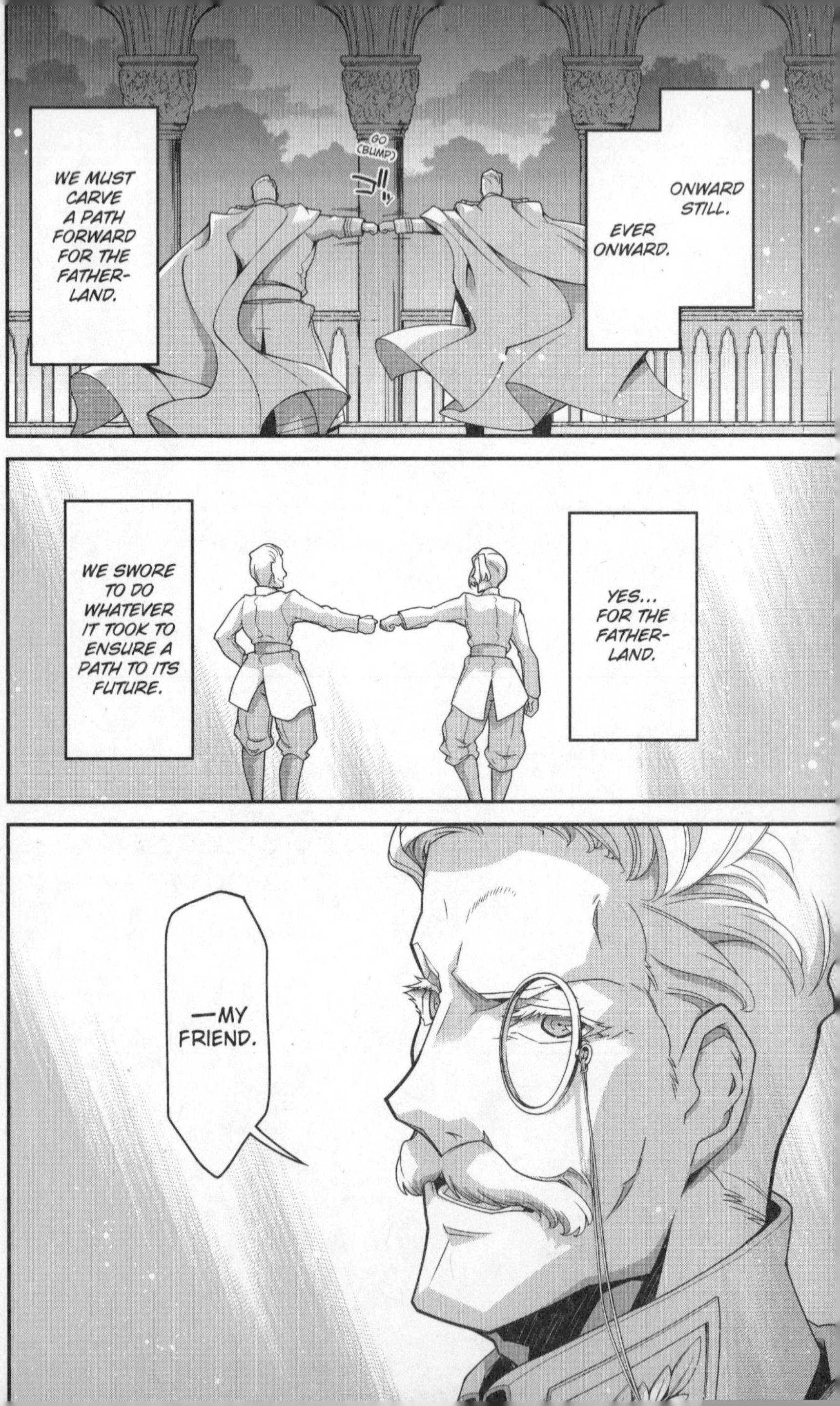
ONWARD STILL.
EVER ONWARD.
GO (BUMP)
WE MUST CARVE A PATH FORWARD FOR THE FATHER-LAND.
YES... FOR THE FATHER-LAND.
WE SWORE TO DO WHATEVER IT TOOK TO ENSURE A PATH TO ITS FUTURE.
—MY FRIEND.

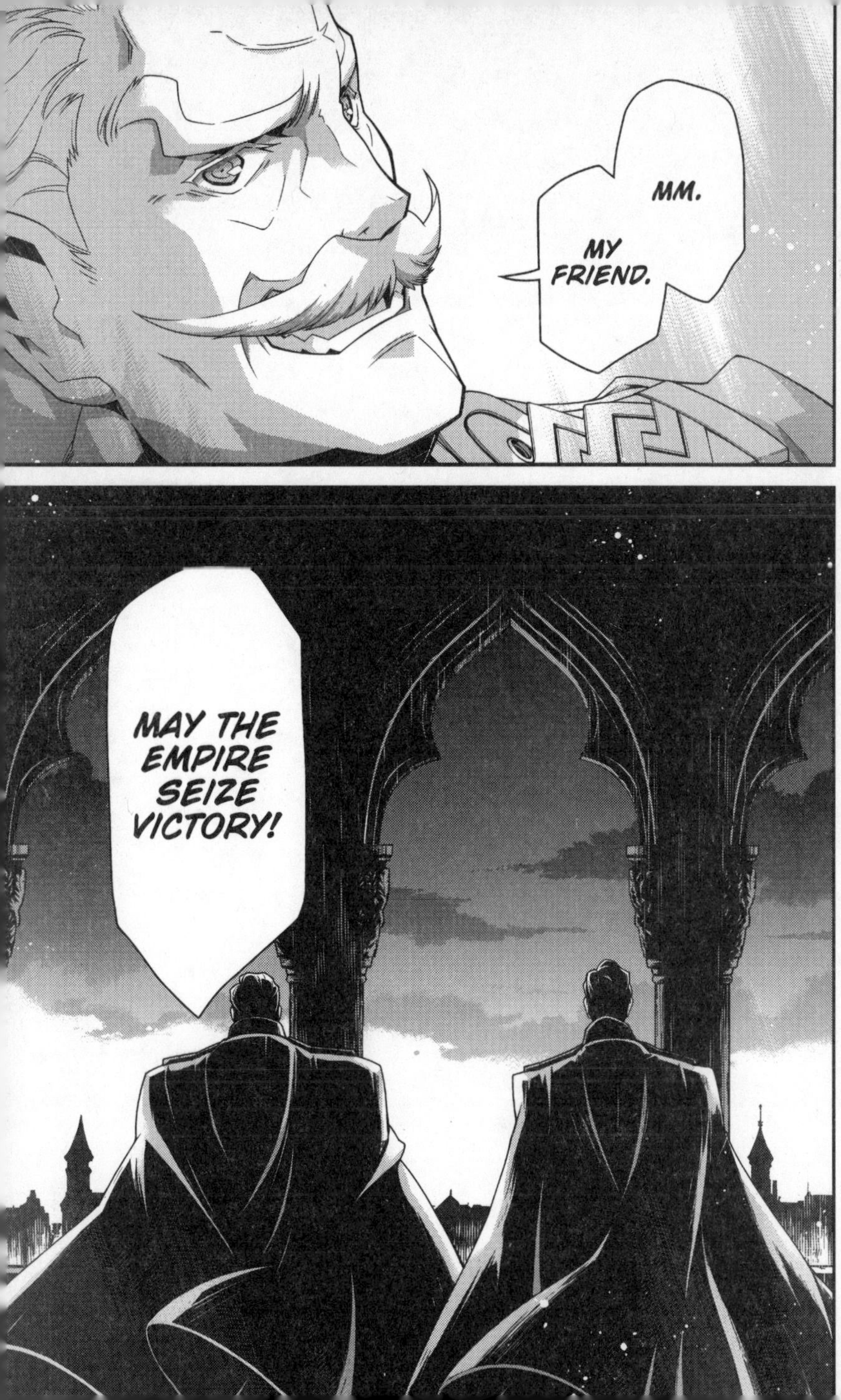
MM.
MY FRIEND.
MAY THE EMPIRE SEIZE VICTORY!

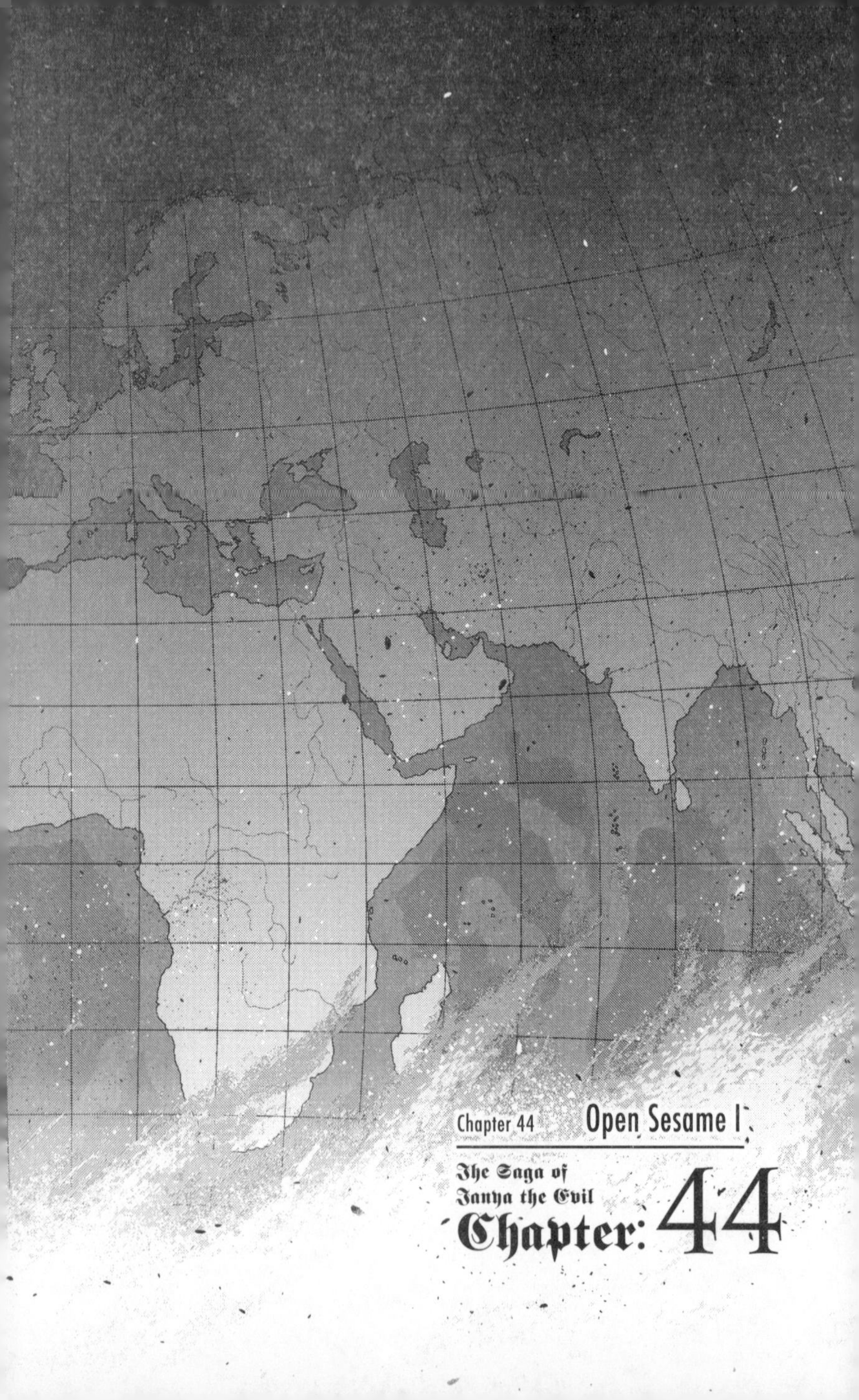

Chapter 44 Open Sesame I

The Saga of Tanya the Evil

Chapter: 44

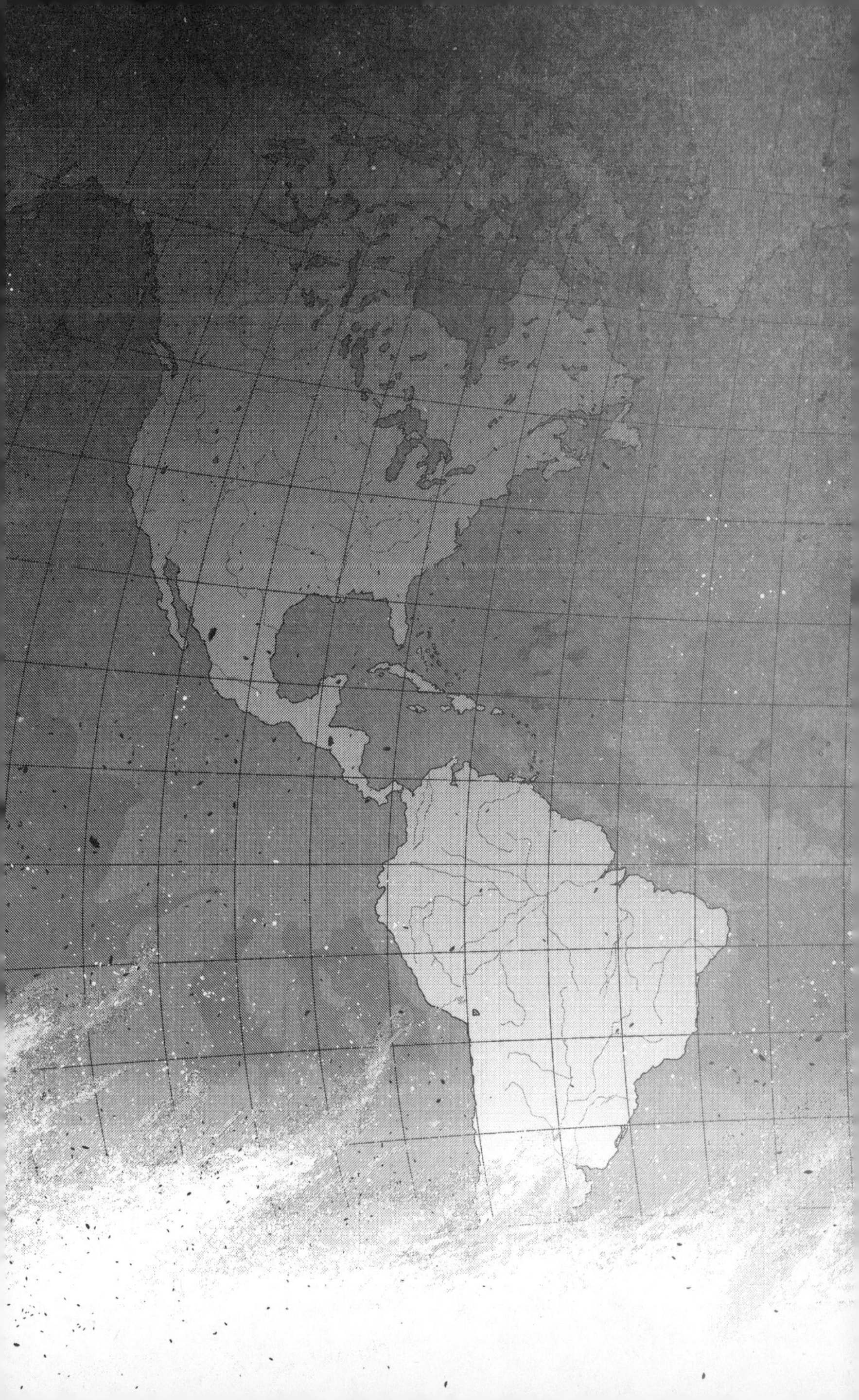

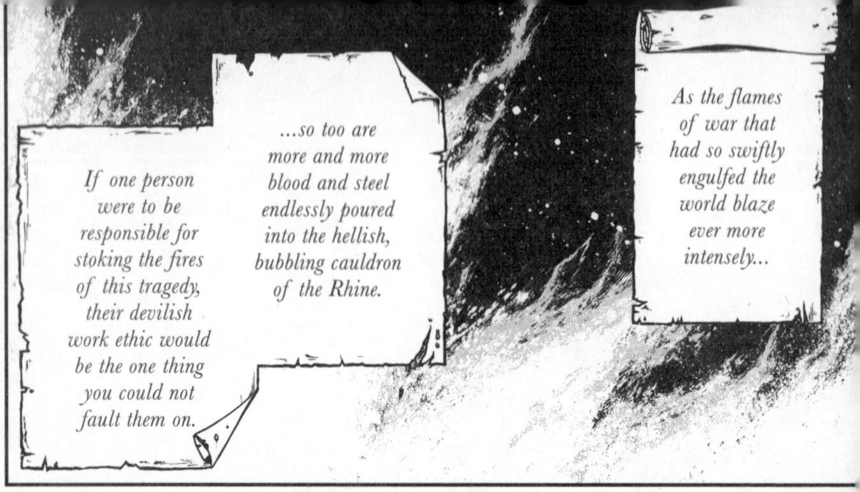
As the flames of war that had so swiftly engulfed the world blaze ever more intensely...
...so too are more and more blood and steel endlessly poured into the hellish, bubbling cauldron of the Rhine.
If one person were to be responsible for stoking the fires of this tragedy, their devilish work ethic would be the one thing you could not fault them on.

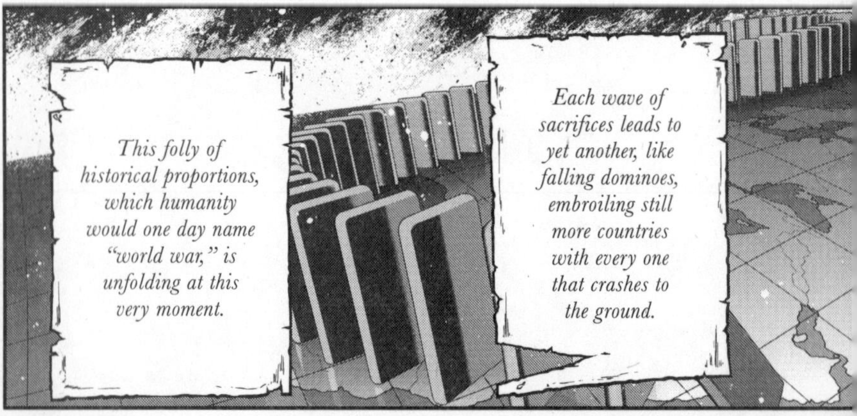
Each wave of sacrifices leads to yet another, like falling dominoes, embroiling still more countries with every one that crashes to the ground.
This folly of historical proportions, which humanity would one day name "world war," is unfolding at this very moment.

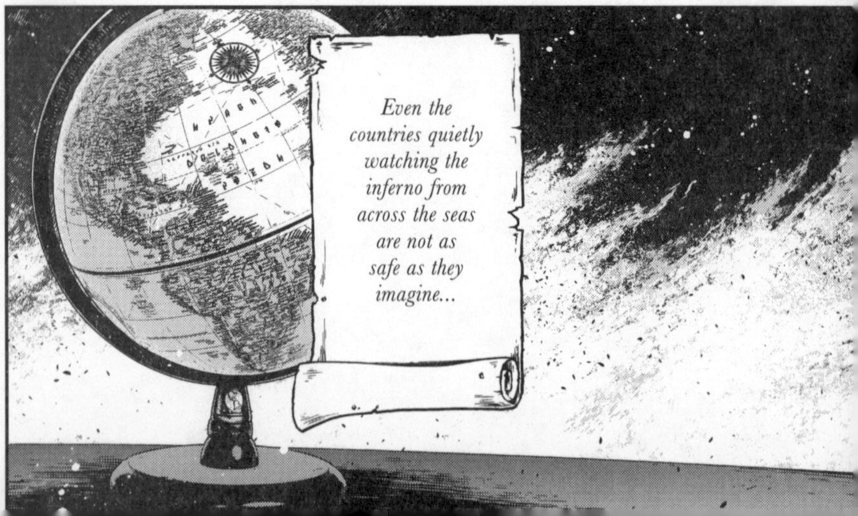
Even the countries quietly watching the inferno from across the seas are not as safe as they imagine...

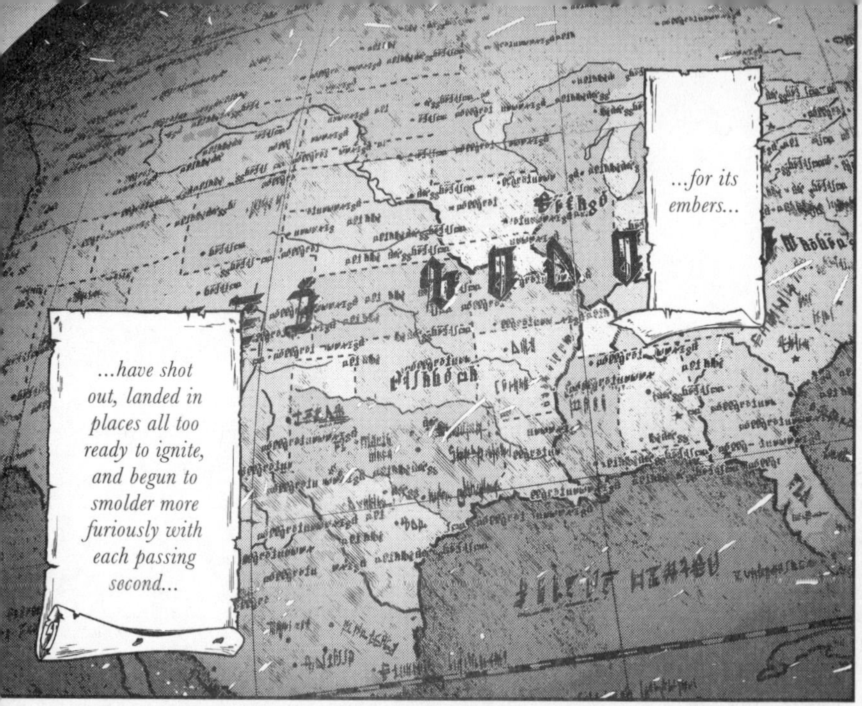
...for its embers...
...have shot out, landed in places all too ready to ignite, and begun to smolder more furiously with each passing second...
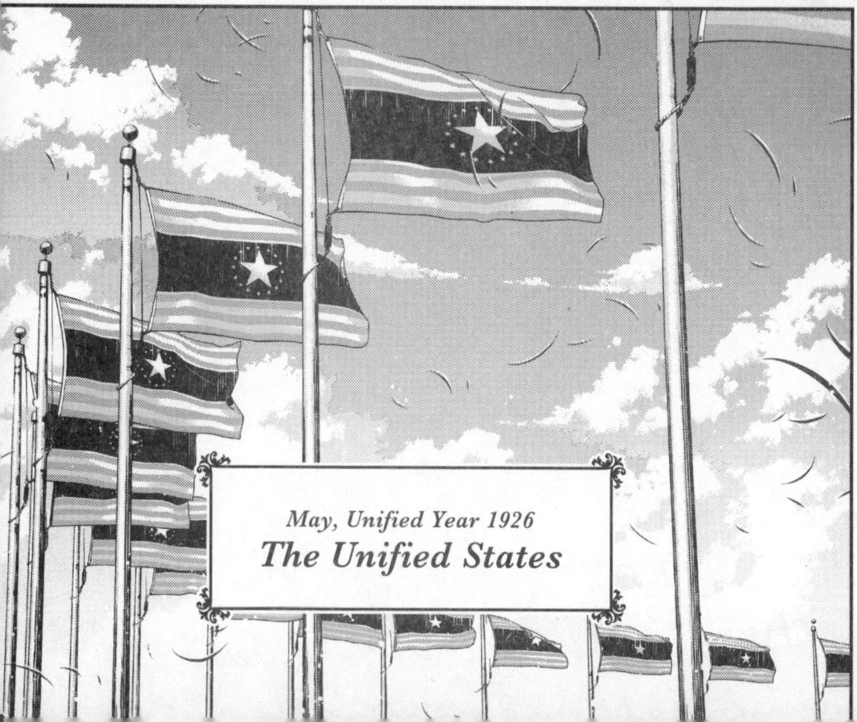
May, Unified Year 1926
The Unified States

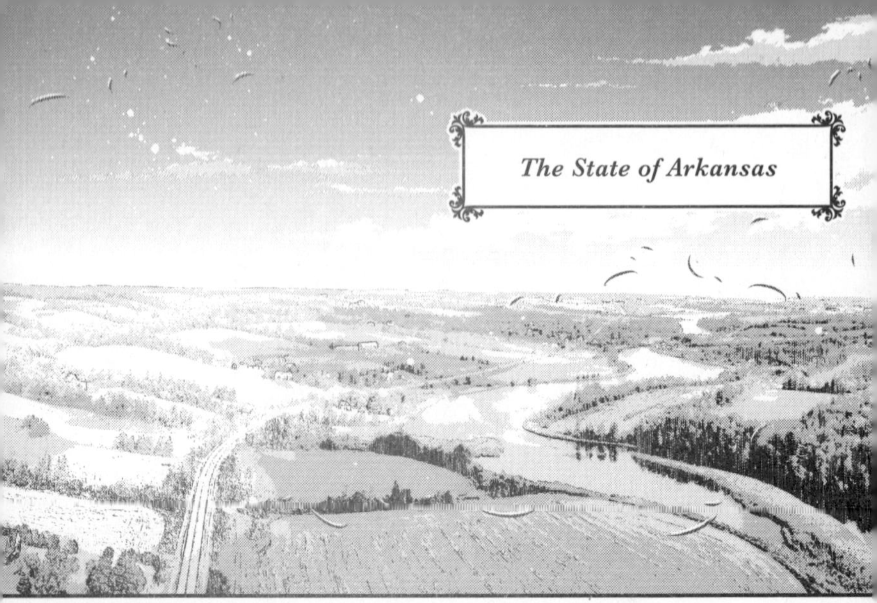
The State of Arkansas
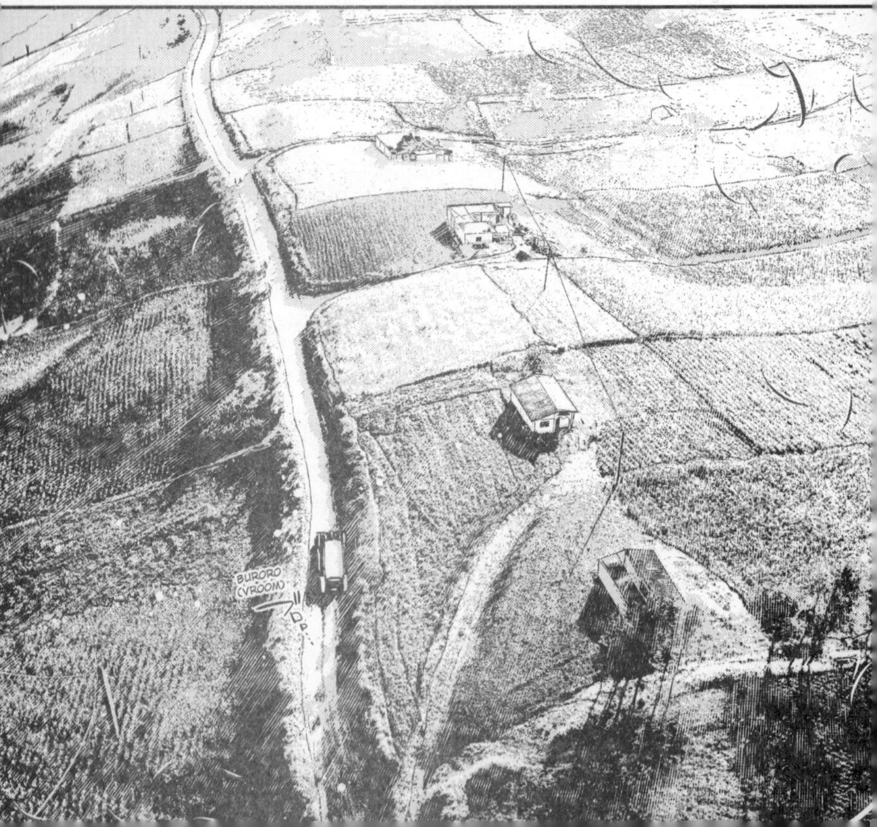
BURORO
(VROOM)

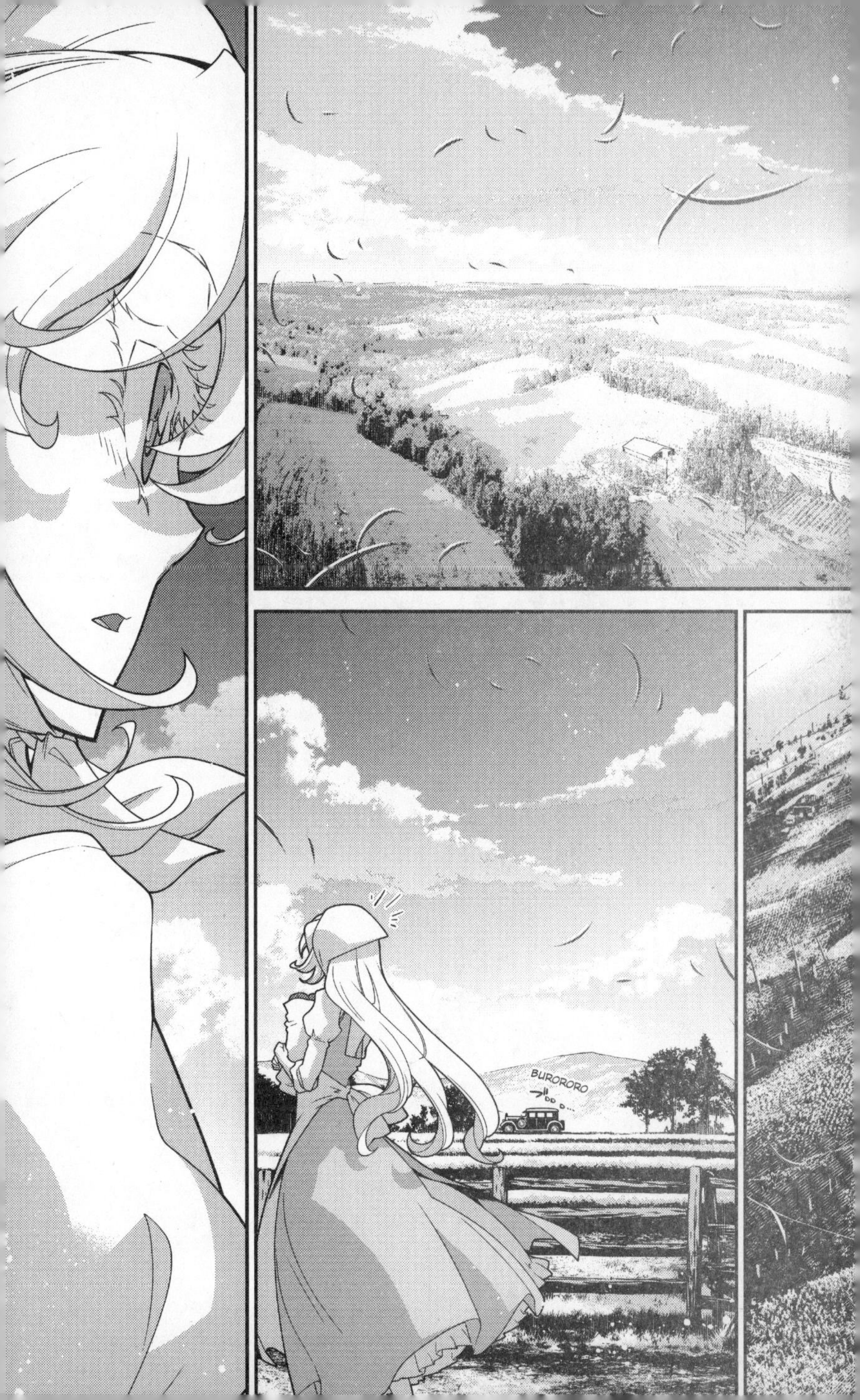
BUROROR0

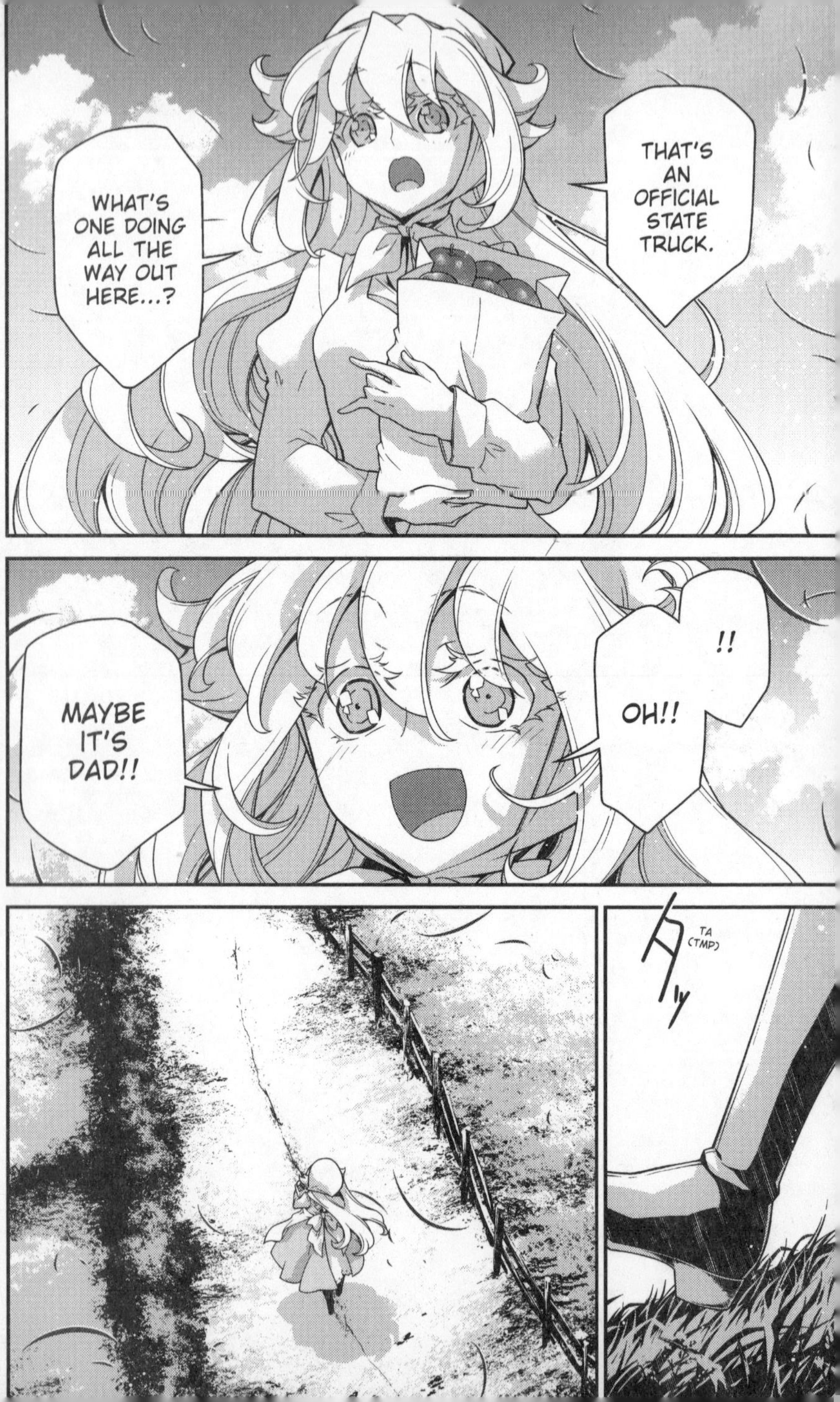
THAT'S AN OFFICIAL STATE TRUCK.
WHAT'S ONE DOING ALL THE WAY OUT HERE...?
!!
OH!!
MAYBE IT'S DAD!!
TA (TMP)

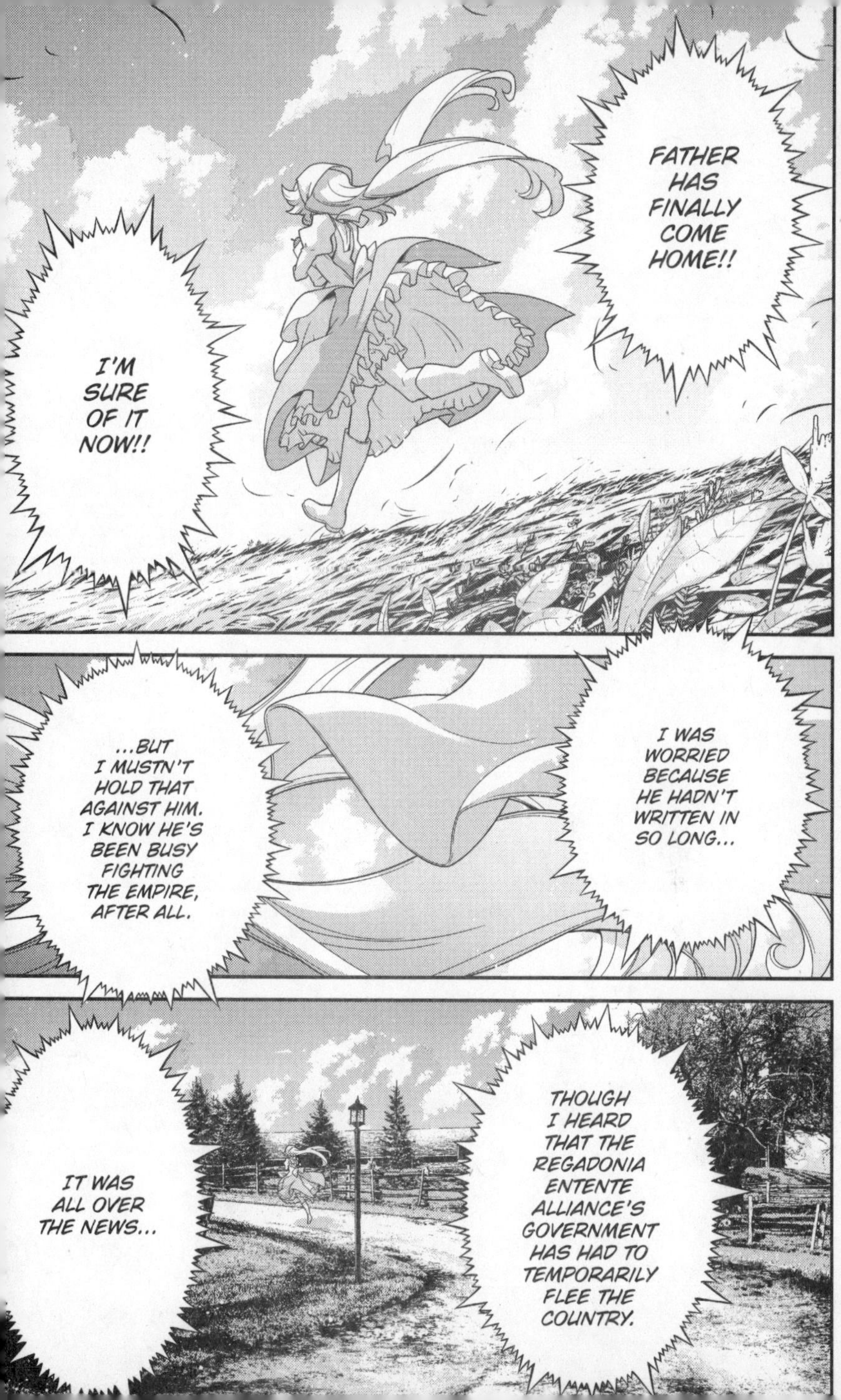
FATHER HAS FINALLY COME HOME!!
I'M SURE OF IT NOW!!
I WAS WORRIED BECAUSE HE HADN'T WRITTEN IN SO LONG...
...BUT I MUSTN'T HOLD THAT AGAINST HIM. I KNOW HE'S BEEN BUSY FIGHTING THE EMPIRE, AFTER ALL.
THOUGH I HEARD THAT THE REGADONIA ENTENTE ALLIANCE'S GOVERNMENT HAS HAD TO TEMPORARILY FLEE THE COUNTRY.
IT WAS ALL OVER THE NEWS...

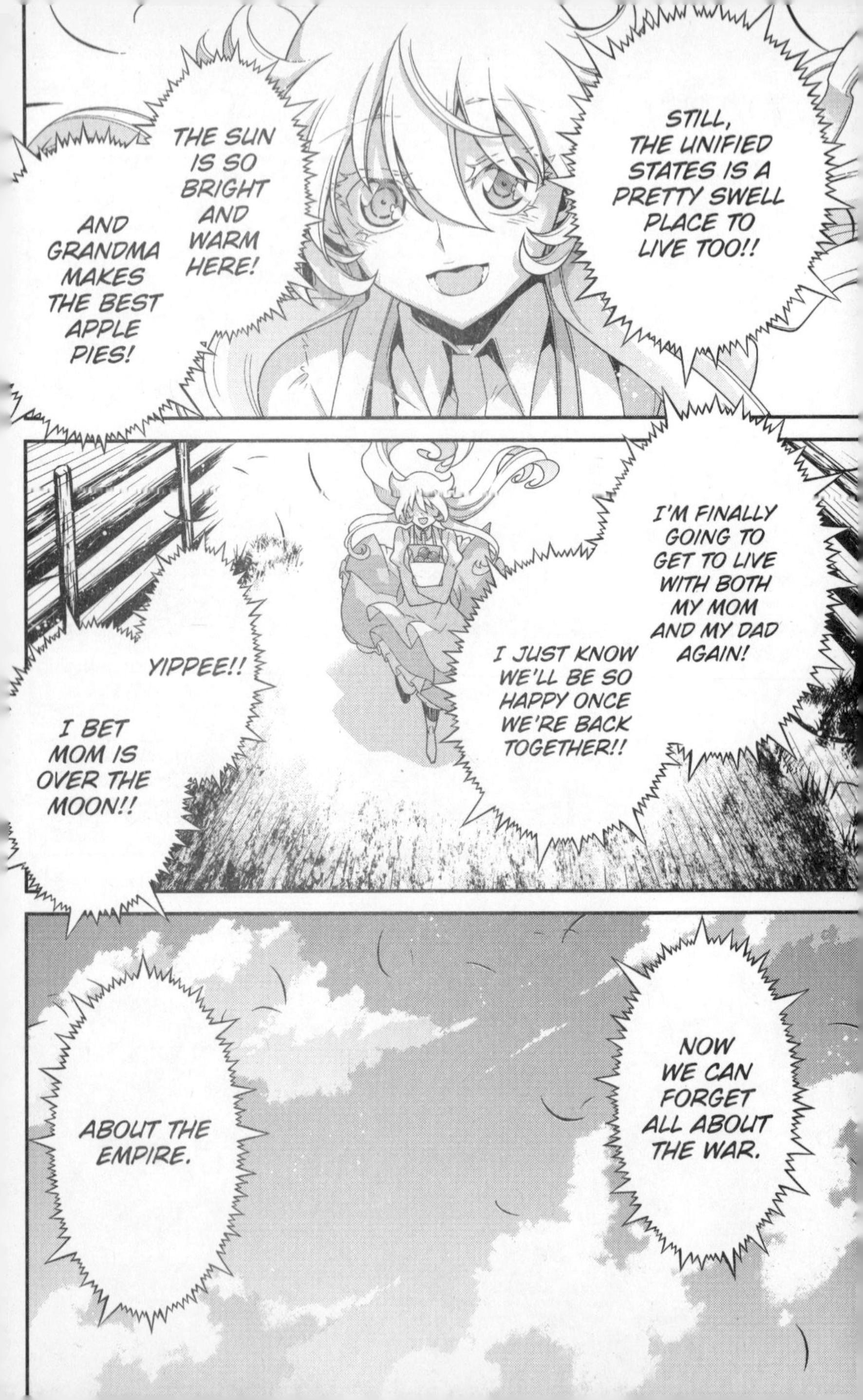
STILL, THE UNIFIED STATES IS A PRETTY SWELL PLACE TO LIVE TOO!!
THE SUN IS SO BRIGHT AND WARM HERE!
AND GRANDMA MAKES THE BEST APPLE PIES!
I'M FINALLY GOING TO GET TO LIVE WITH BOTH MY MOM AND MY DAD AGAIN!
I JUST KNOW WE'LL BE SO HAPPY ONCE WE'RE BACK TOGETHER!!
YIPPEE!!
I BET MOM IS OVER THE MOON!!
NOW WE CAN FORGET ALL ABOUT THE WAR.
ABOUT THE EMPIRE.

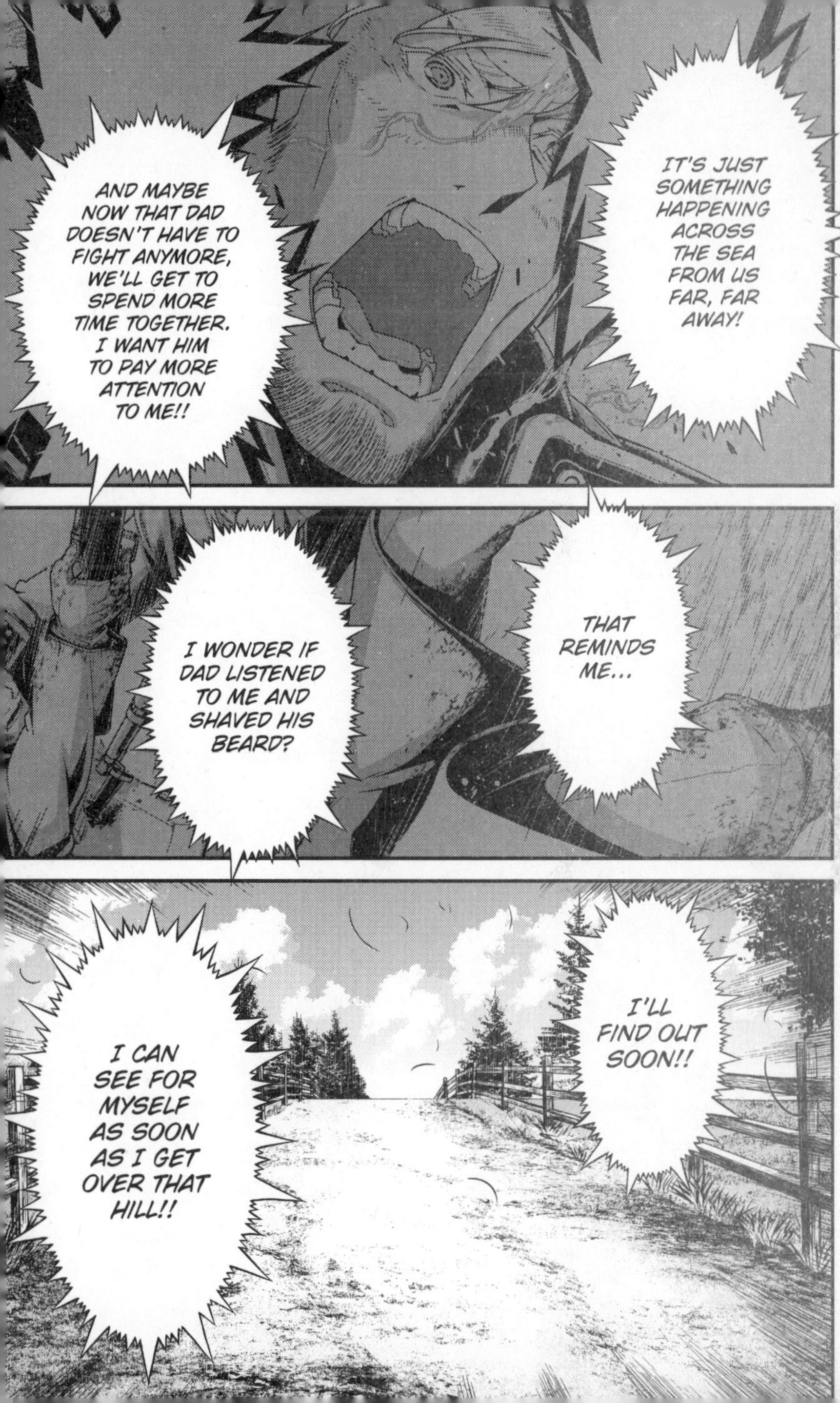
IT'S JUST SOMETHING HAPPENING ACROSS THE SEA FROM US FAR, FAR AWAY!
AND MAYBE NOW THAT DAD DOESN'T HAVE TO FIGHT ANYMORE, WE'LL GET TO SPEND MORE TIME TOGETHER. I WANT HIM TO PAY MORE ATTENTION TO ME!!
THAT REMINDS ME...
I WONDER IF DAD LISTENED TO ME AND SHAVED HIS BEARD?
I'LL FIND OUT SOON!!
I CAN SEE FOR MYSELF AS SOON AS I GET OVER THAT HILL!!

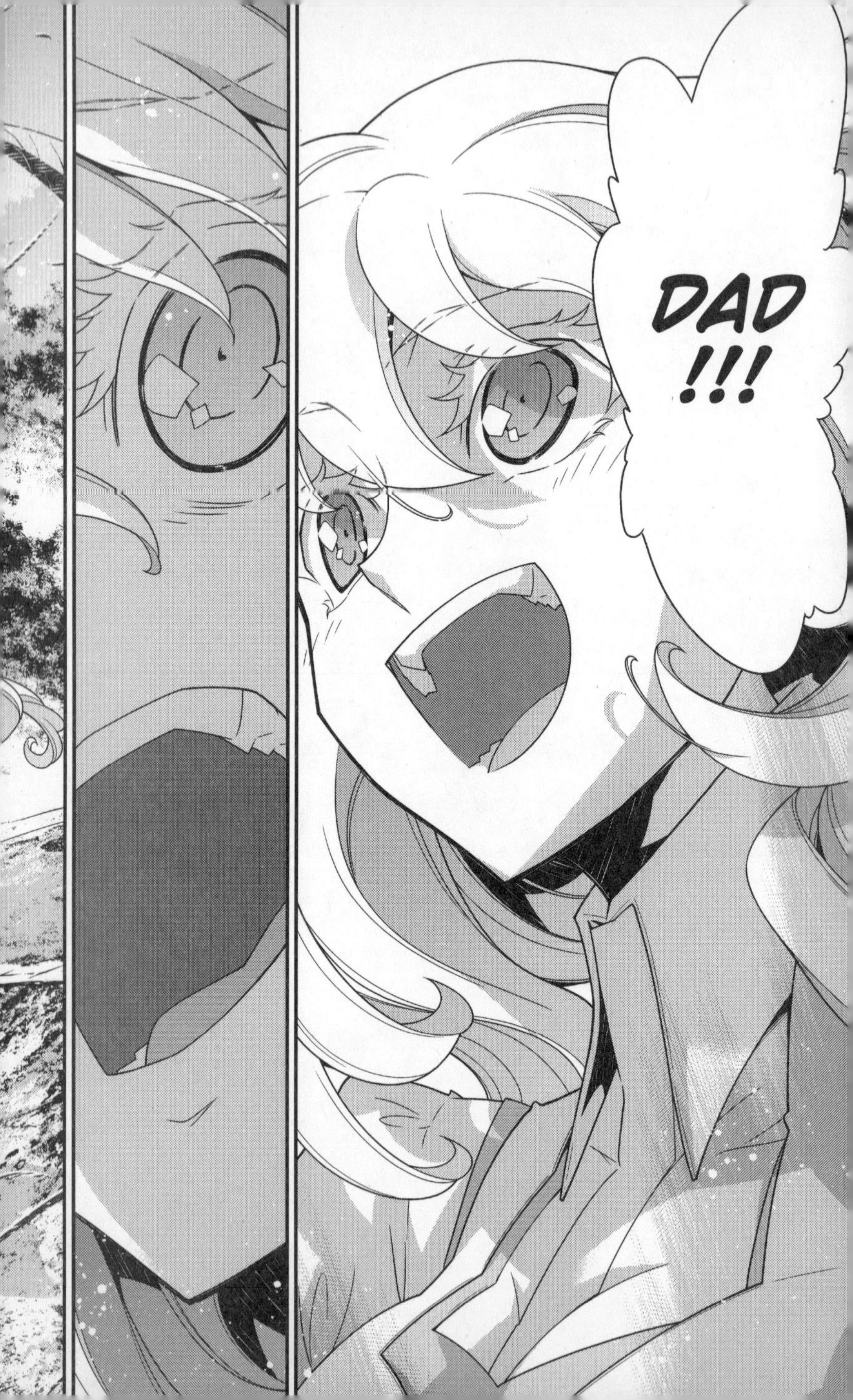
DAD!!!

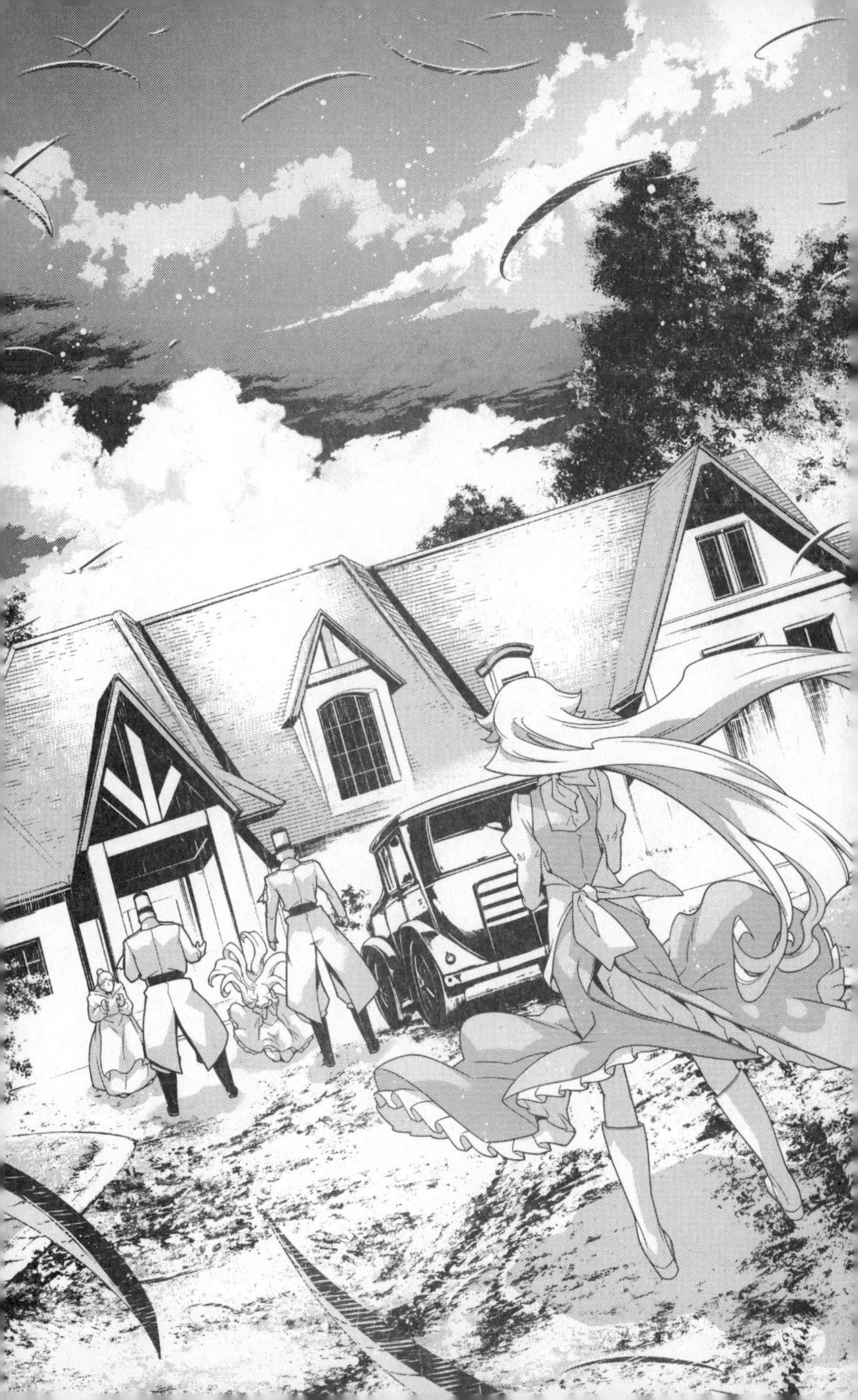

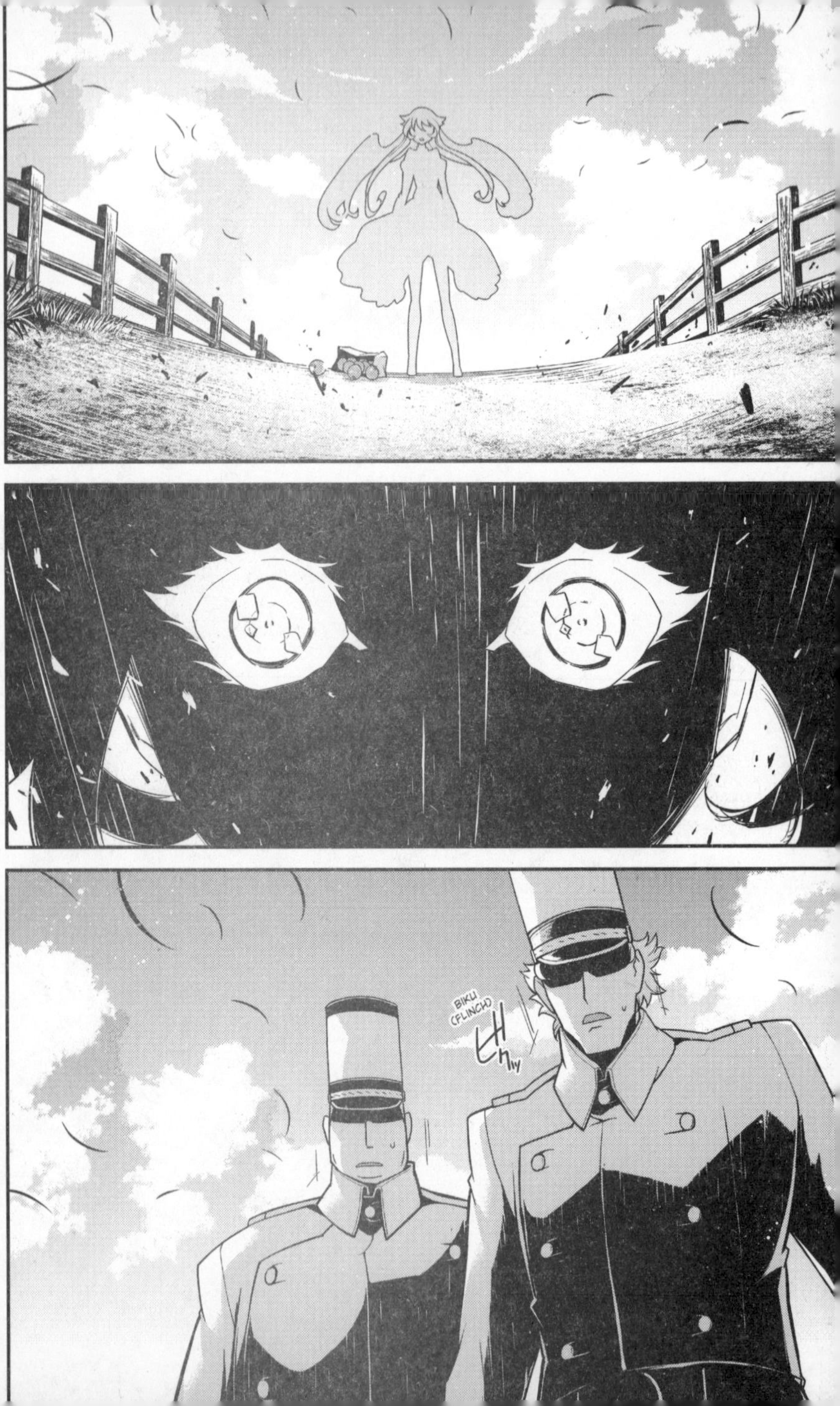
BIKU (FLINCH)

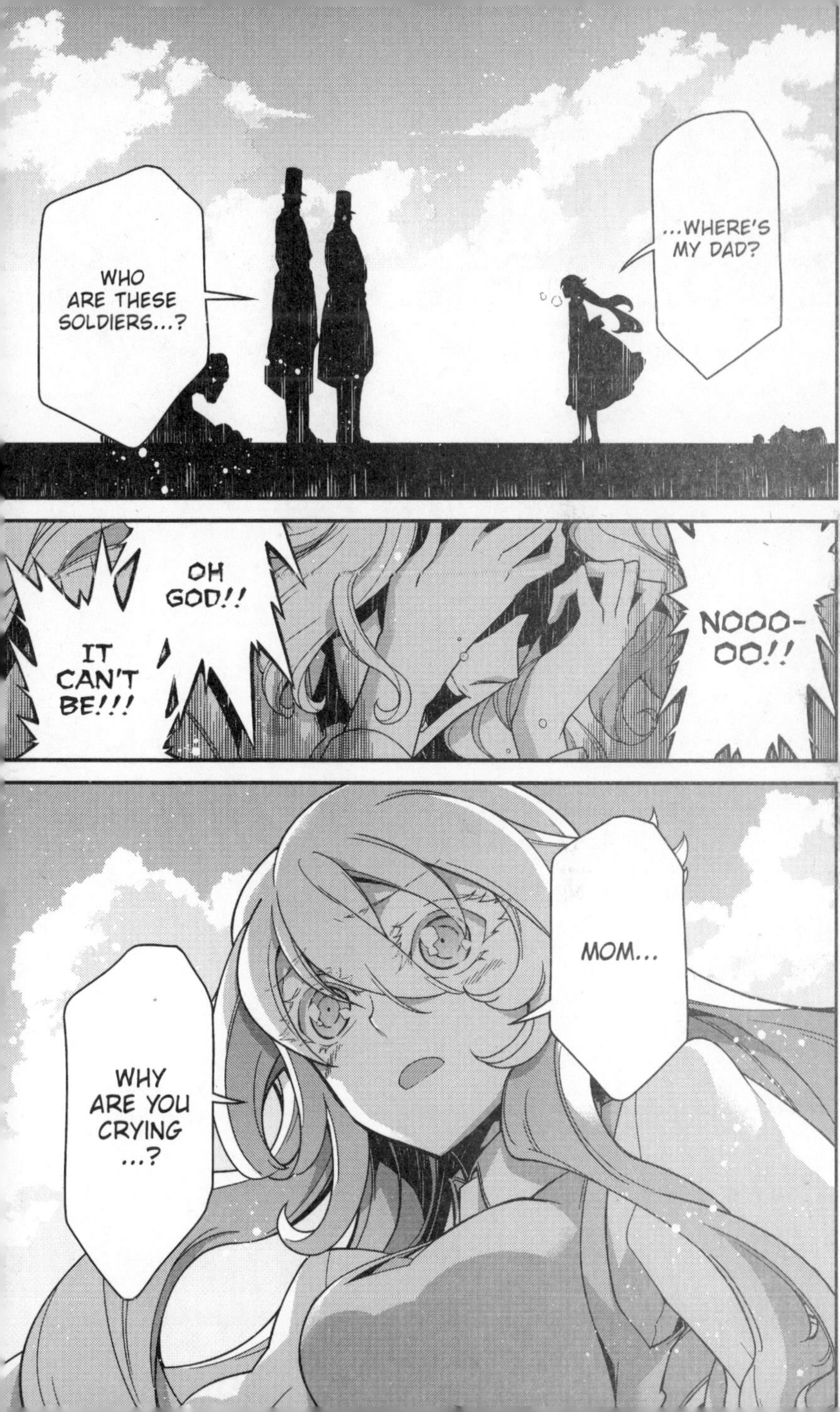
...WHERE'S MY DAD?
WHO ARE THESE SOLDIERS...?
NOOOO-OO!!
OH GOD!!
IT CAN'T BE!!!
MOM...
WHY ARE YOU CRYING...?

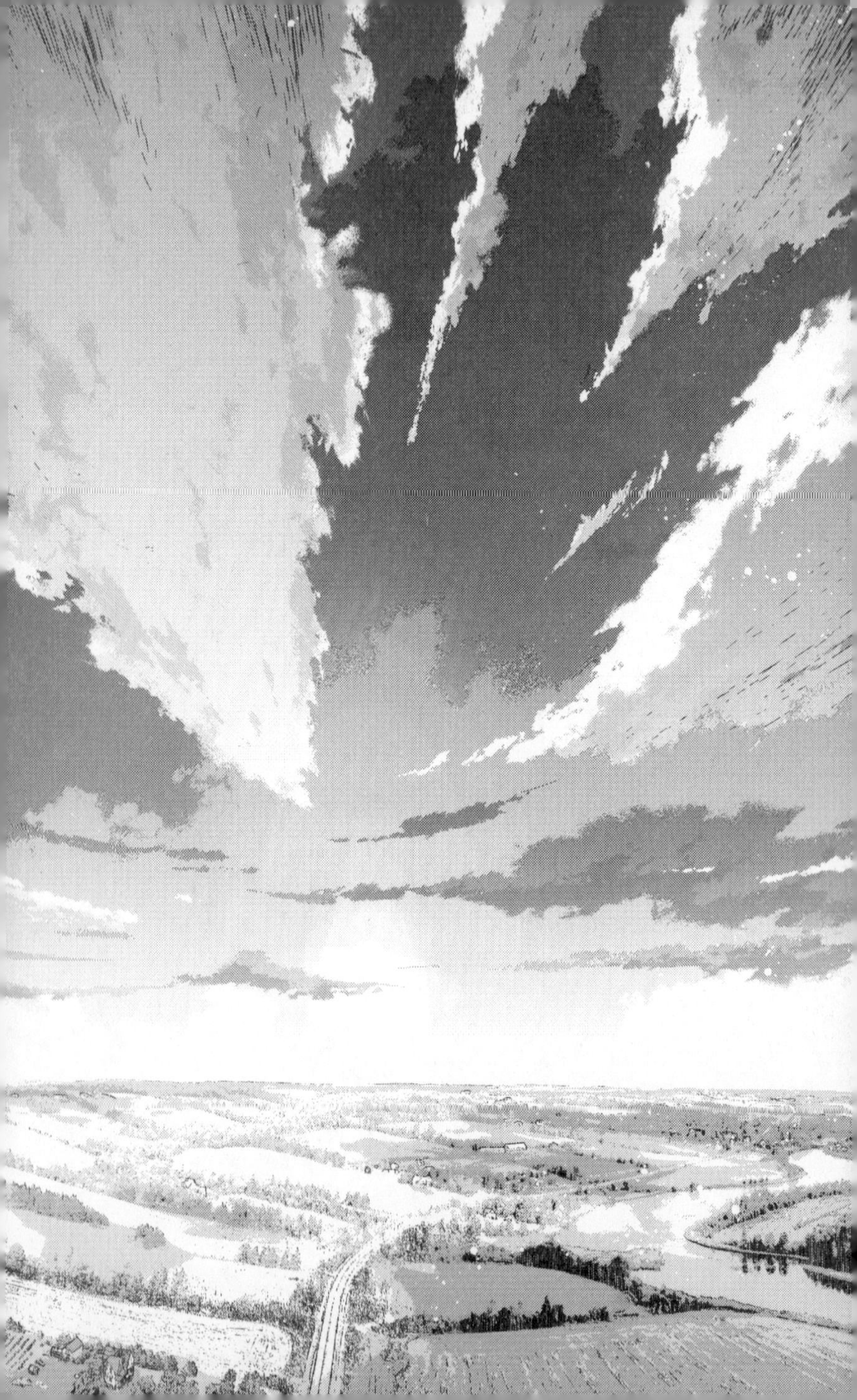

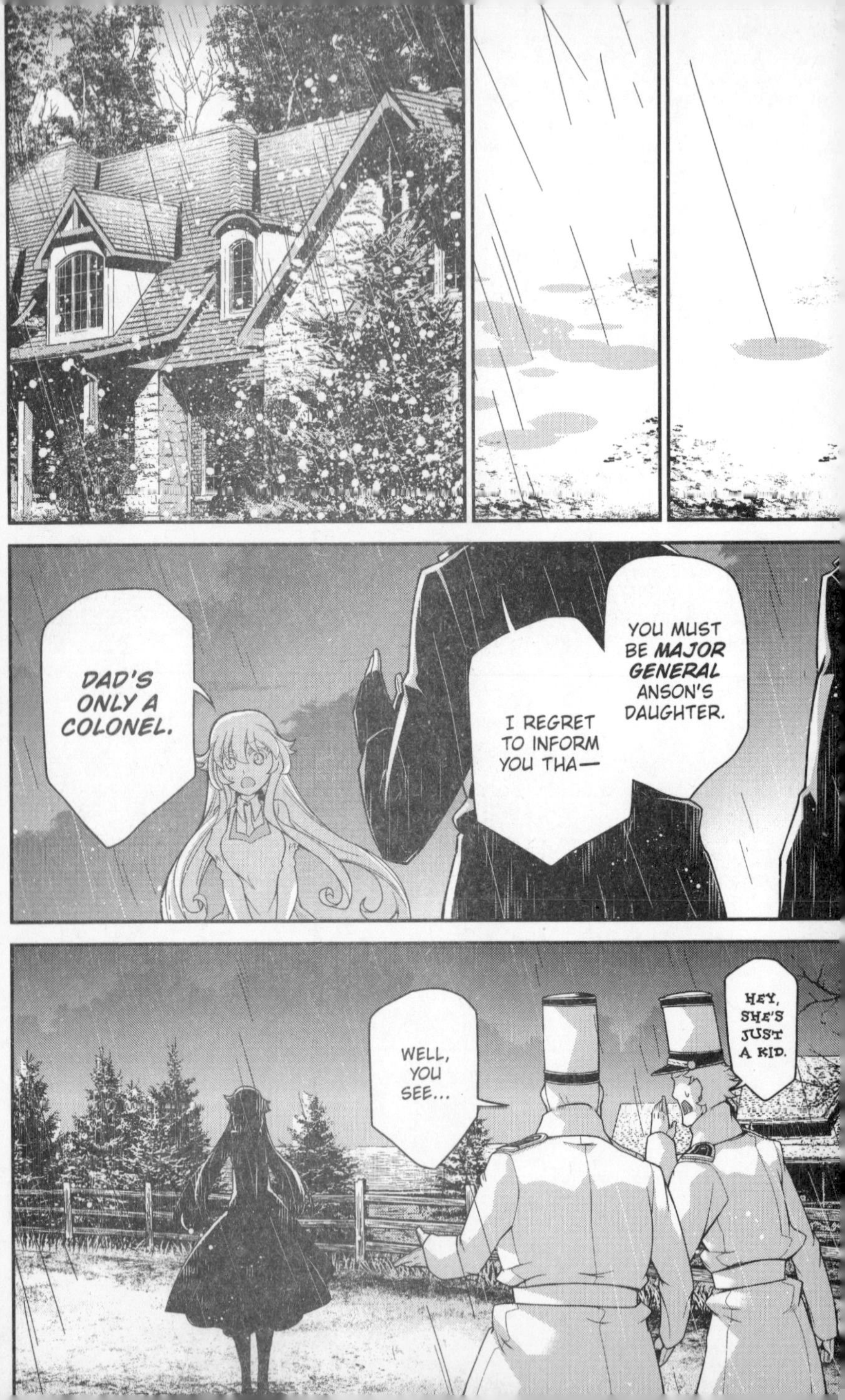
YOU MUST BE **MAJOR GENERAL** ANSON'S DAUGHTER.
I REGRET TO INFORM YOU THA—
DAD'S ONLY A COLONEL.
HEY, SHE'S JUST A KID.
WELL, YOU SEE...

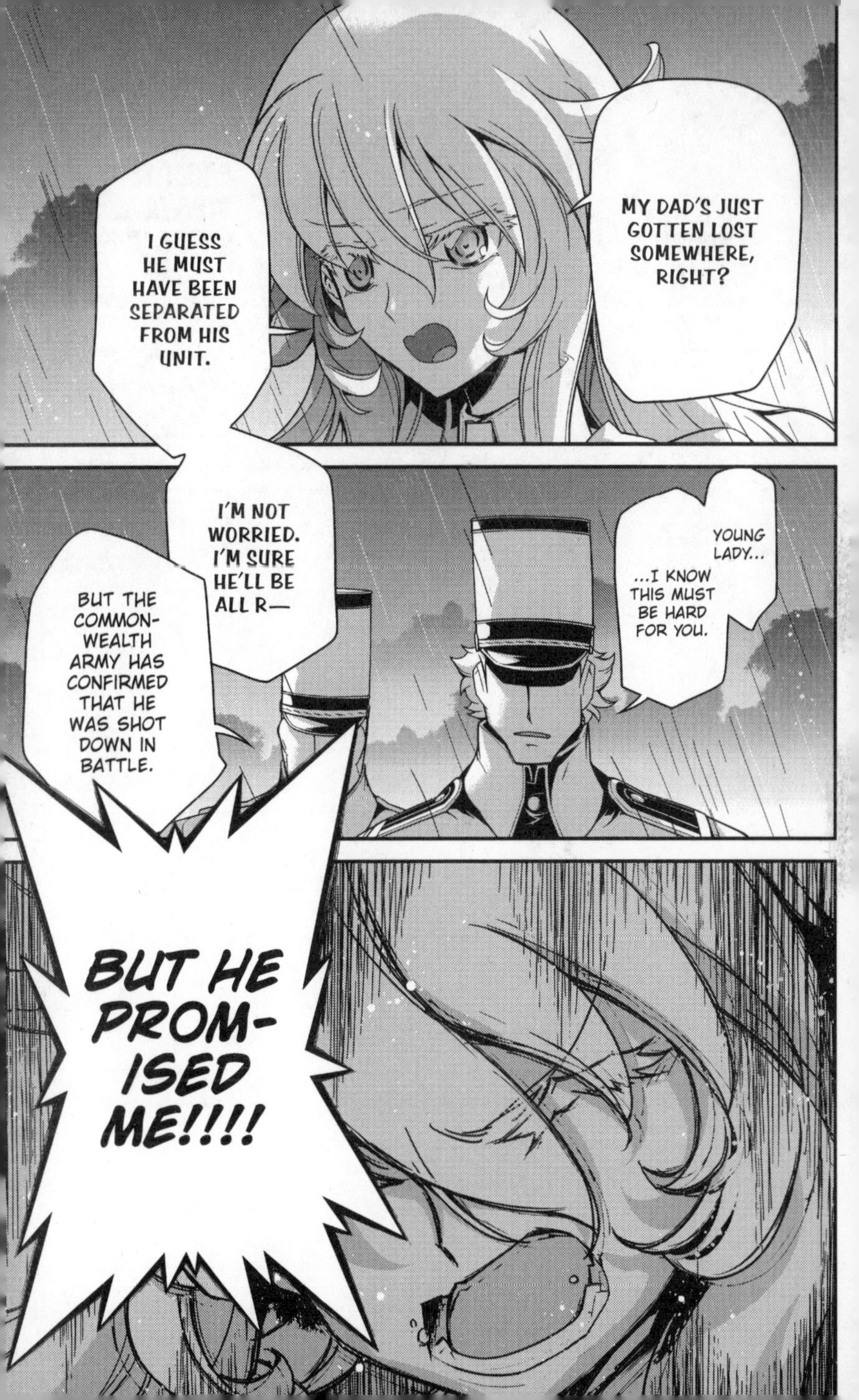
MY DAD'S JUST GOTTEN LOST SOMEWHERE, RIGHT?
I GUESS HE MUST HAVE BEEN SEPARATED FROM HIS UNIT.
I'M NOT WORRIED. I'M SURE HE'LL BE ALL R—
YOUNG LADY...
...I KNOW THIS MUST BE HARD FOR YOU.
BUT THE COMMON-WEALTH ARMY HAS CONFIRMED THAT HE WAS SHOT DOWN IN BATTLE.
BUT HE PROM-ISED ME!!!!

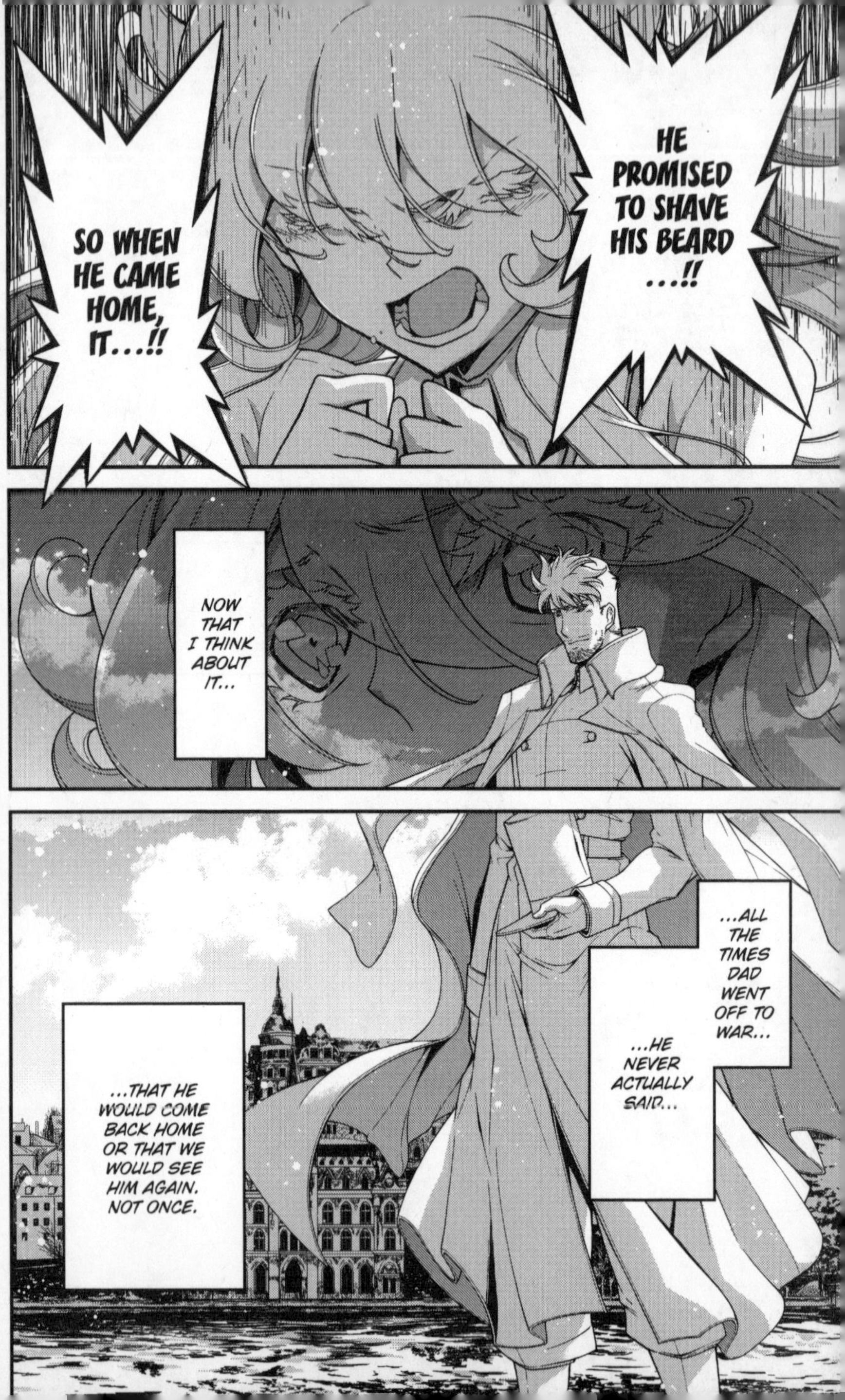
HE PROMISED TO SHAVE HIS BEARD ...!!
SO WHEN HE CAME HOME, IT...!!
NOW THAT I THINK ABOUT IT...
...ALL THE TIMES DAD WENT OFF TO WAR...
...HE NEVER ACTUALLY SAID...
...THAT HE WOULD COME BACK HOME OR THAT WE WOULD SEE HIM AGAIN. NOT ONCE.

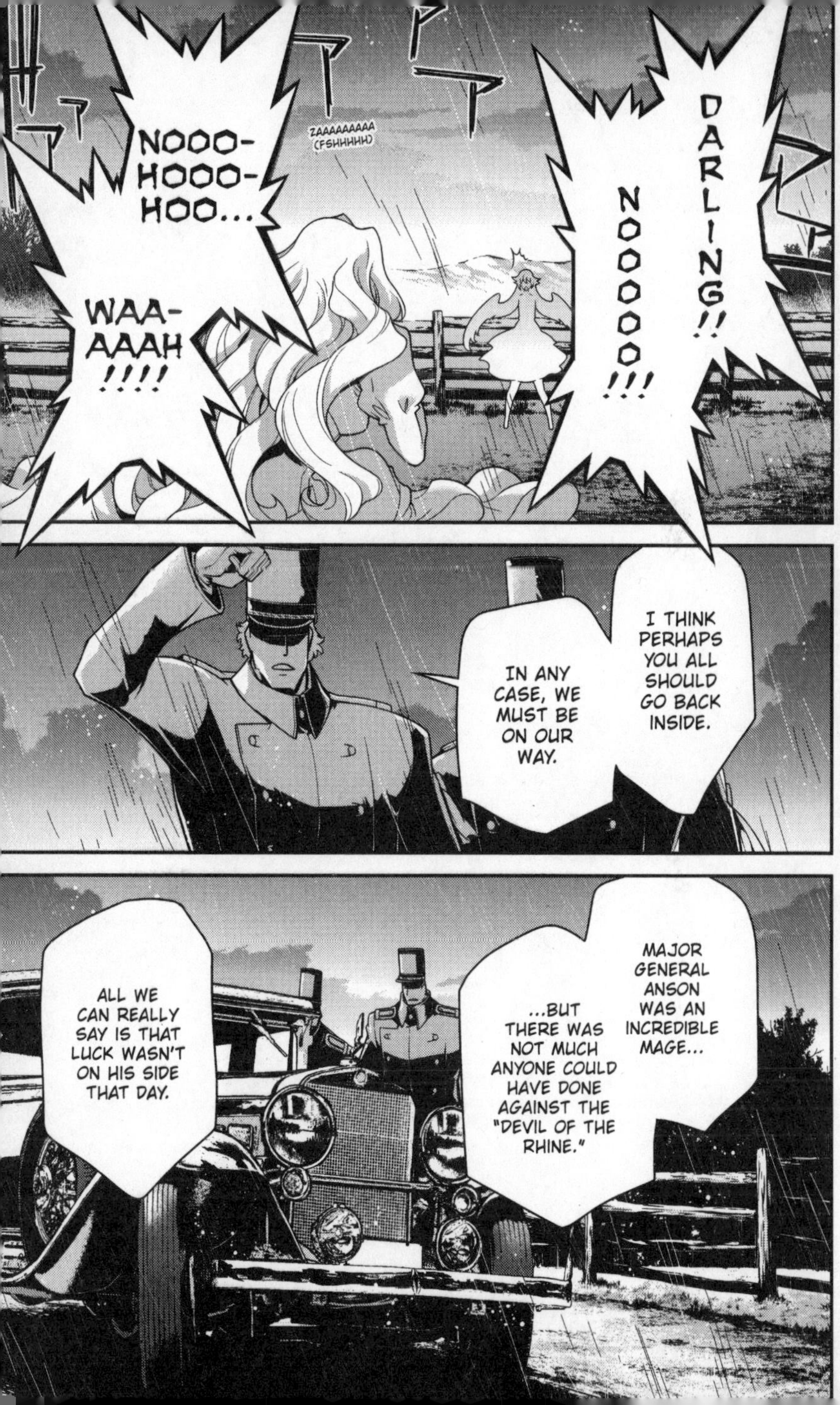
DARLING!!
NOOOOOO!!!
ZAAAAAAAAA (FSHHHHHH)
NOOO-HOOO-HOO...
WAA-AAAH!!!!
I THINK PERHAPS YOU ALL SHOULD GO BACK INSIDE.
IN ANY CASE, WE MUST BE ON OUR WAY.
MAJOR GENERAL ANSON WAS AN INCREDIBLE MAGE...
...BUT THERE WAS NOT MUCH ANYONE COULD HAVE DONE AGAINST THE "DEVIL OF THE RHINE."
ALL WE CAN REALLY SAY IS THAT LUCK WASN'T ON HIS SIDE THAT DAY.

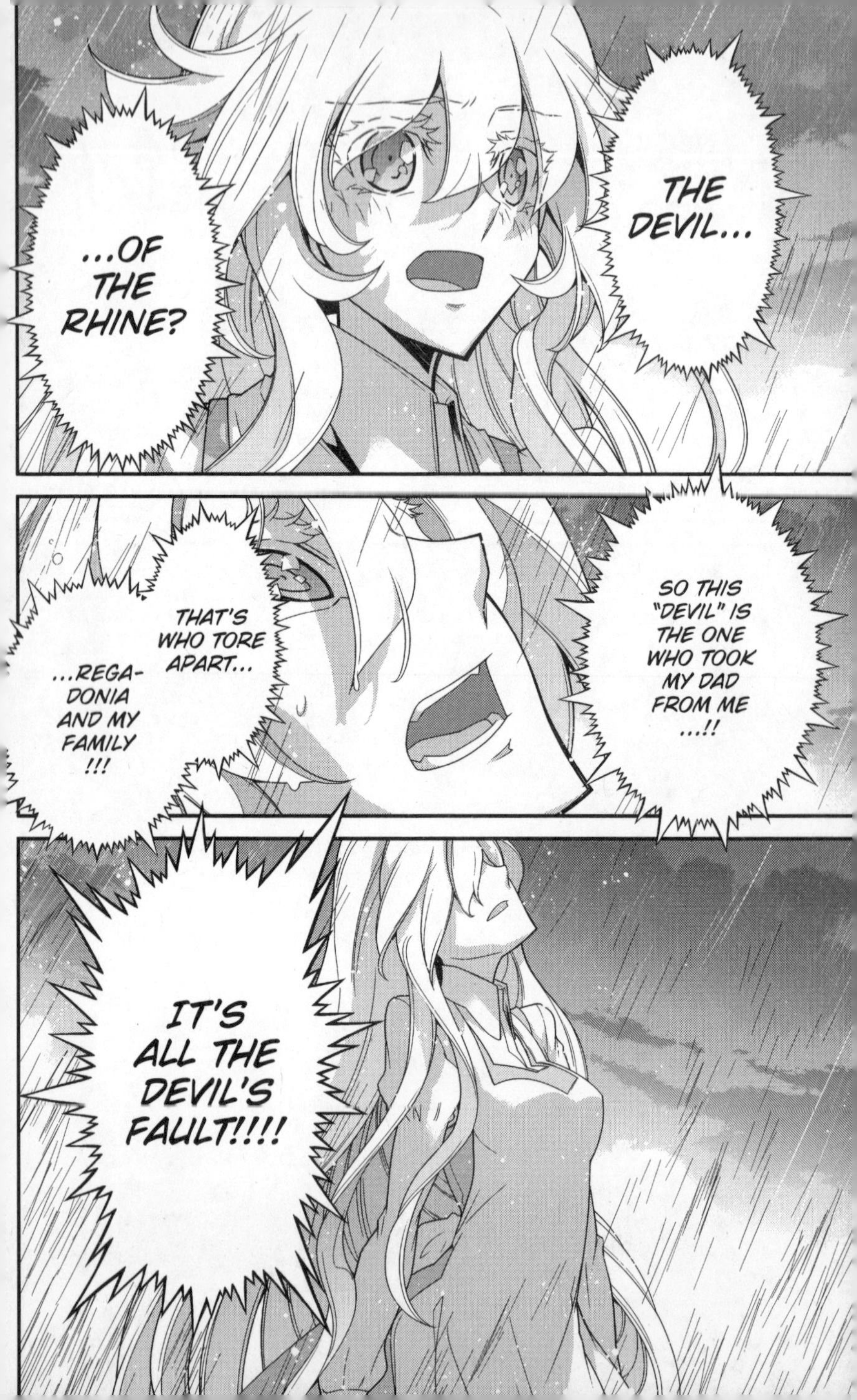
THE DEVIL...
...OF THE RHINE?
SO THIS "DEVIL" IS THE ONE WHO TOOK MY DAD FROM ME ...!!
THAT'S WHO TORE APART...
...REGA-DONIA AND MY FAMILY !!!
IT'S ALL THE DEVIL'S FAULT!!!!

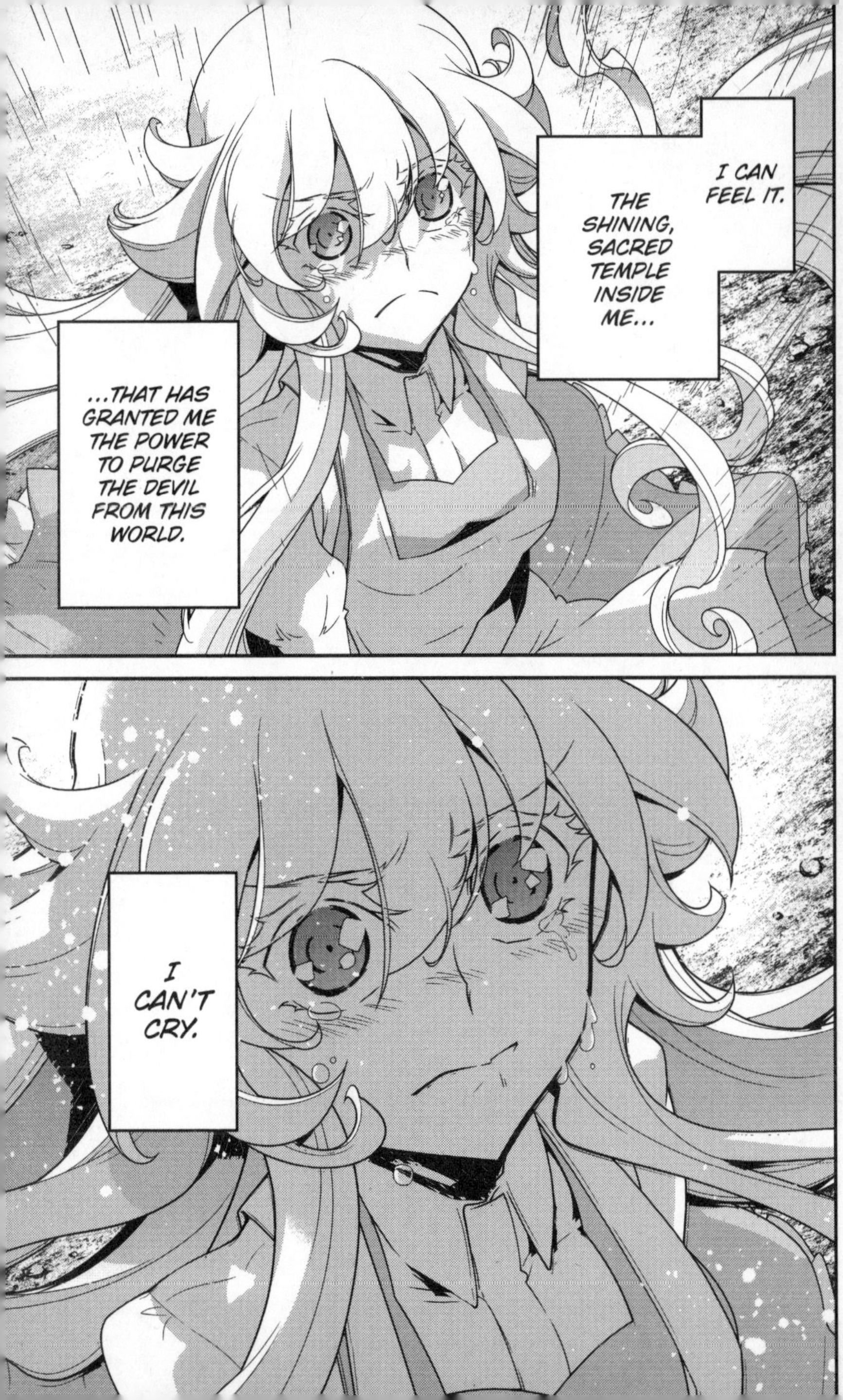
I CAN FEEL IT.
THE SHINING, SACRED TEMPLE INSIDE ME...
...THAT HAS GRANTED ME THE POWER TO PURGE THE DEVIL FROM THIS WORLD.
I CAN'T CRY.

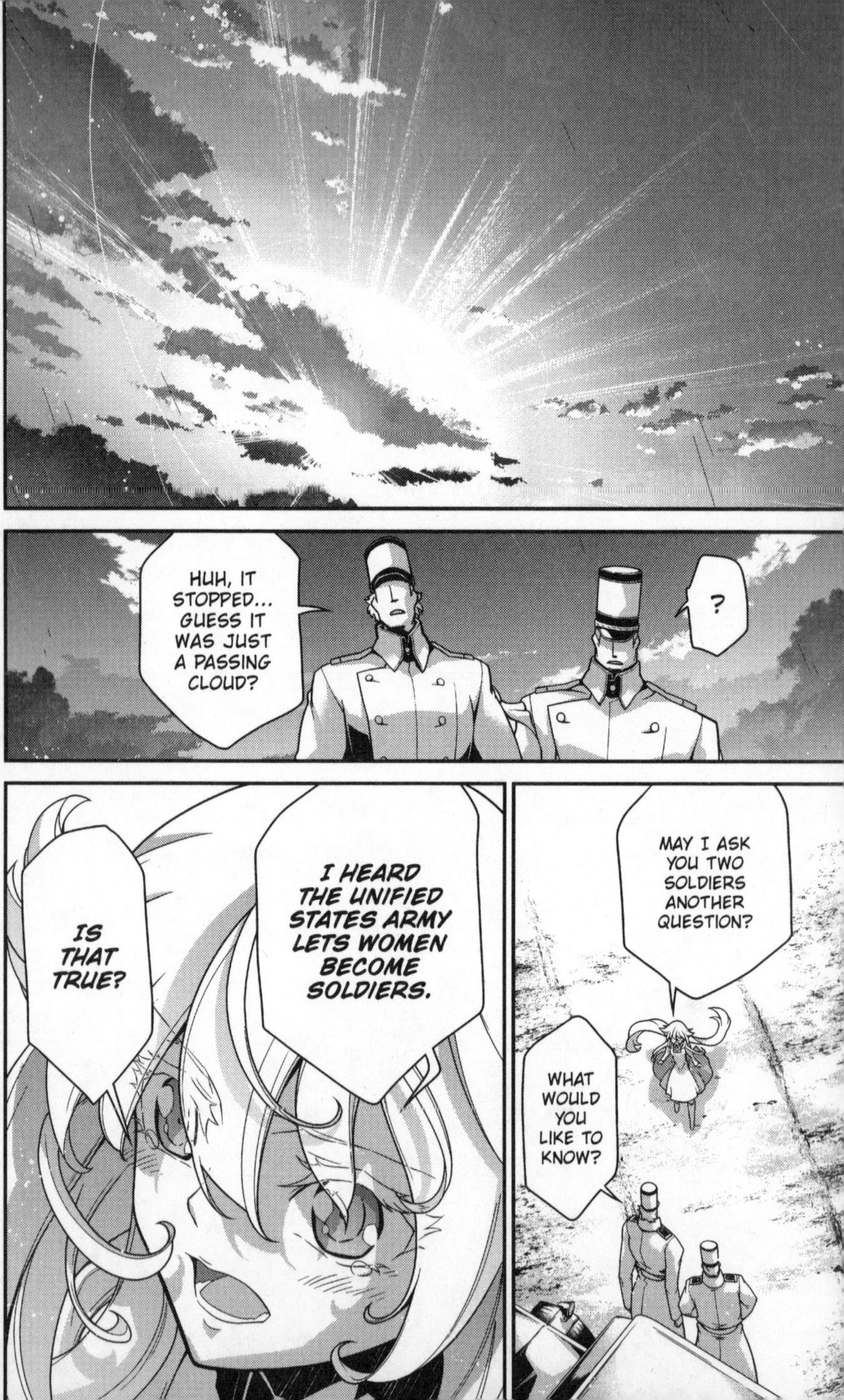
?
HUH, IT STOPPED... GUESS IT WAS JUST A PASSING CLOUD?
MAY I ASK YOU TWO SOLDIERS ANOTHER QUESTION?
WHAT WOULD YOU LIKE TO KNOW?
I HEARD THE UNIFIED STATES ARMY LETS WOMEN BECOME SOLDIERS.
IS THAT TRUE?

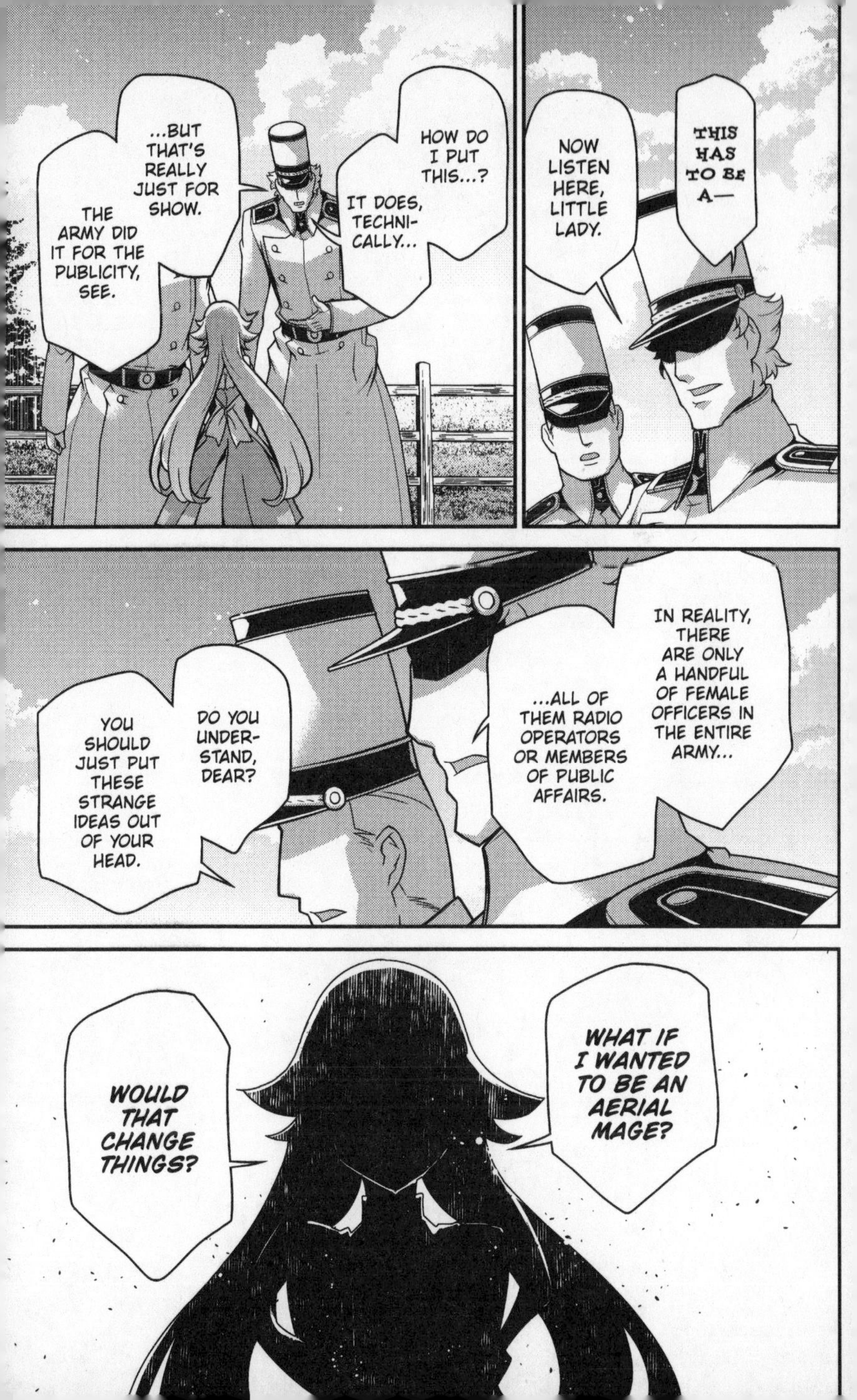
THIS HAS TO BE A—
NOW LISTEN HERE, LITTLE LADY.
HOW DO I PUT THIS...?
IT DOES, TECHNICALLY...
...BUT THAT'S REALLY JUST FOR SHOW.
THE ARMY DID IT FOR THE PUBLICITY, SEE.
IN REALITY, THERE ARE ONLY A HANDFUL OF FEMALE OFFICERS IN THE ENTIRE ARMY...
...ALL OF THEM RADIO OPERATORS OR MEMBERS OF PUBLIC AFFAIRS.
DO YOU UNDERSTAND, DEAR?
YOU SHOULD JUST PUT THESE STRANGE IDEAS OUT OF YOUR HEAD.
WHAT IF I WANTED TO BE AN AERIAL MAGE?
WOULD THAT CHANGE THINGS?

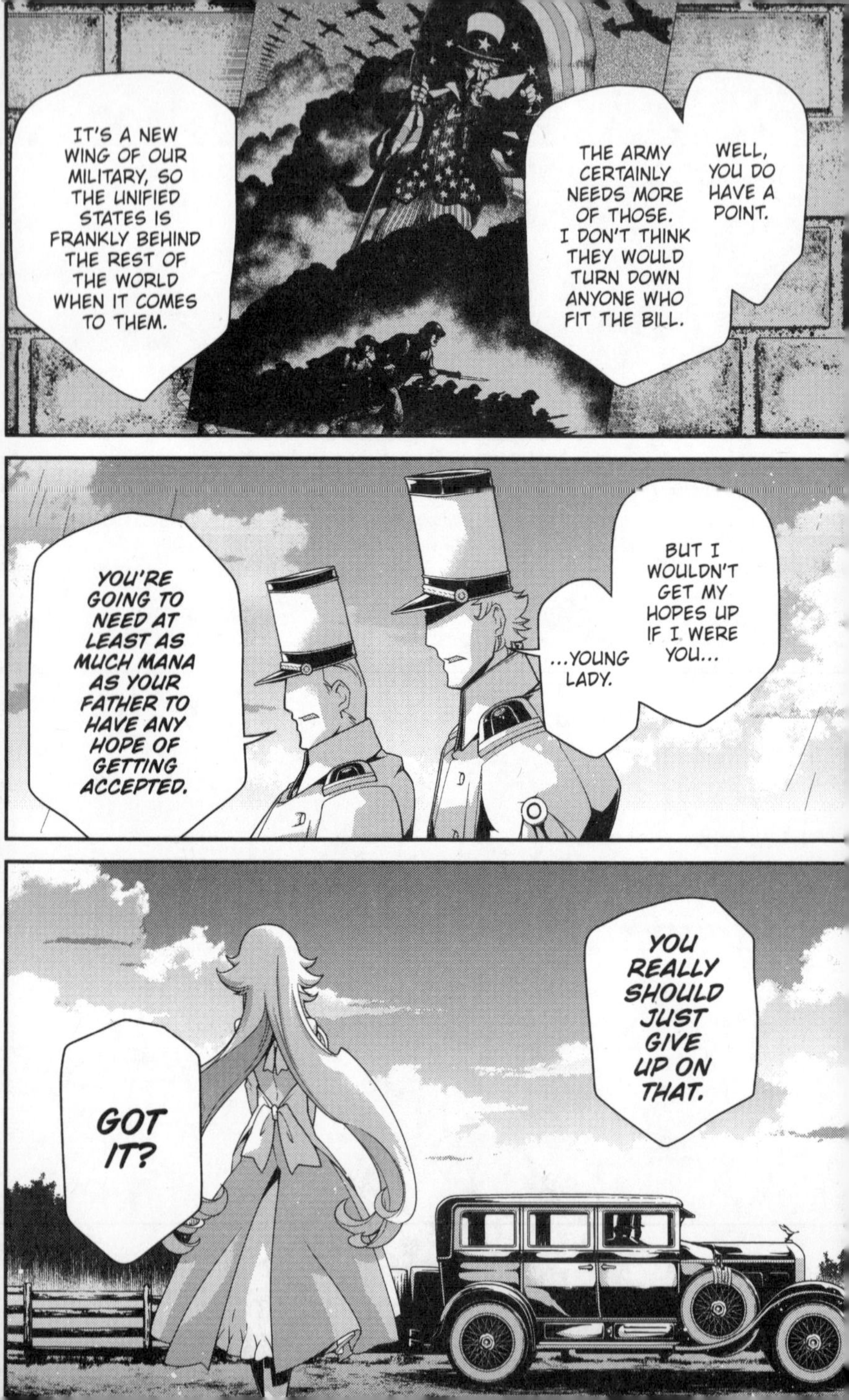
WELL, YOU DO HAVE A POINT.
THE ARMY CERTAINLY NEEDS MORE OF THOSE. I DON'T THINK THEY WOULD TURN DOWN ANYONE WHO FIT THE BILL.
IT'S A NEW WING OF OUR MILITARY, SO THE UNIFIED STATES IS FRANKLY BEHIND THE REST OF THE WORLD WHEN IT COMES TO THEM.
BUT I WOULDN'T GET MY HOPES UP IF I WERE YOU...
...YOUNG LADY.
YOU'RE GOING TO NEED AT LEAST AS MUCH MANA AS YOUR FATHER TO HAVE ANY HOPE OF GETTING ACCEPTED.
YOU REALLY SHOULD JUST GIVE UP ON THAT.
GOT IT?

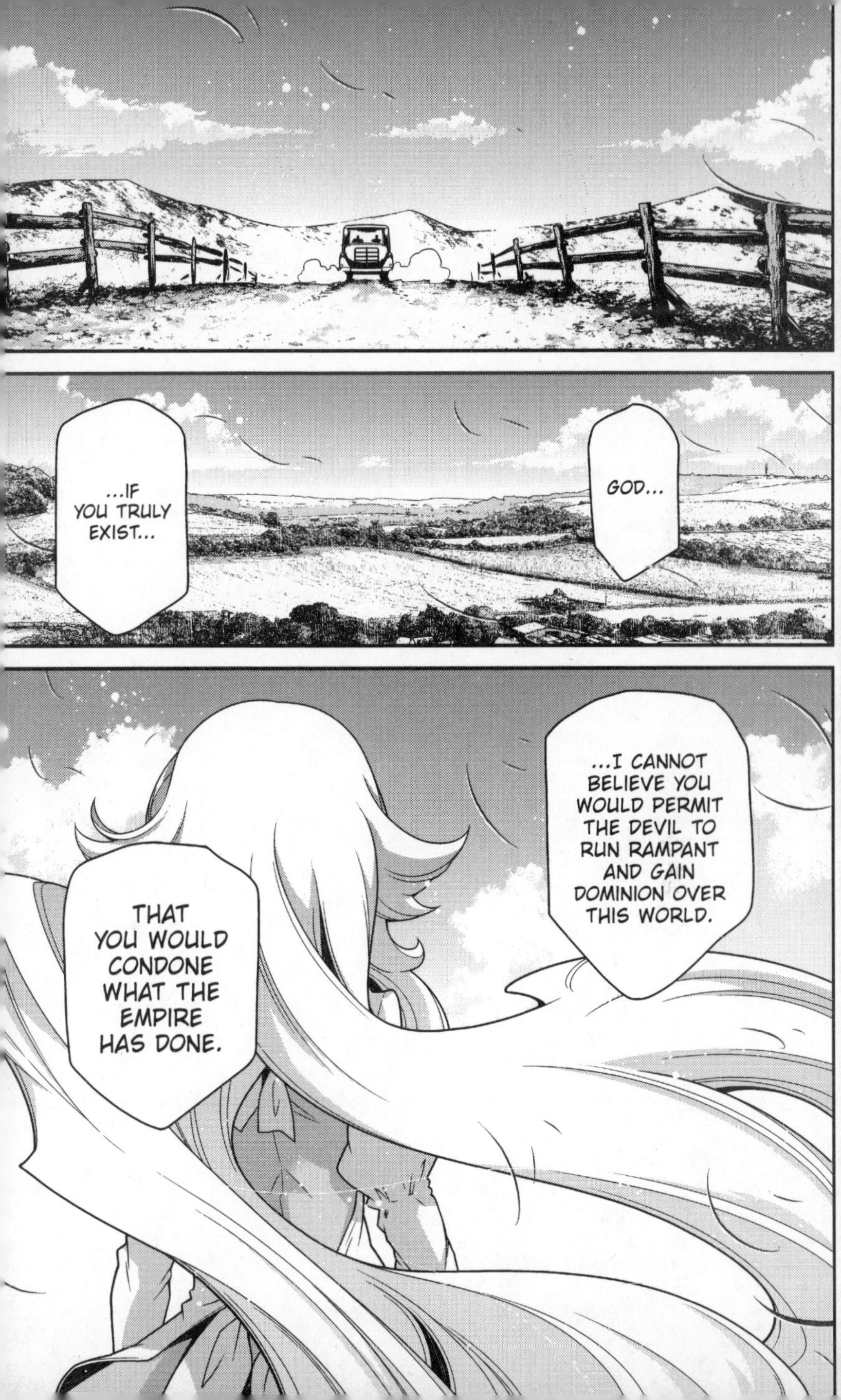
GOD...
...IF YOU TRULY EXIST...
...I CANNOT BELIEVE YOU WOULD PERMIT THE DEVIL TO RUN RAMPANT AND GAIN DOMINION OVER THIS WORLD.
THAT YOU WOULD CONDONE WHAT THE EMPIRE HAS DONE.

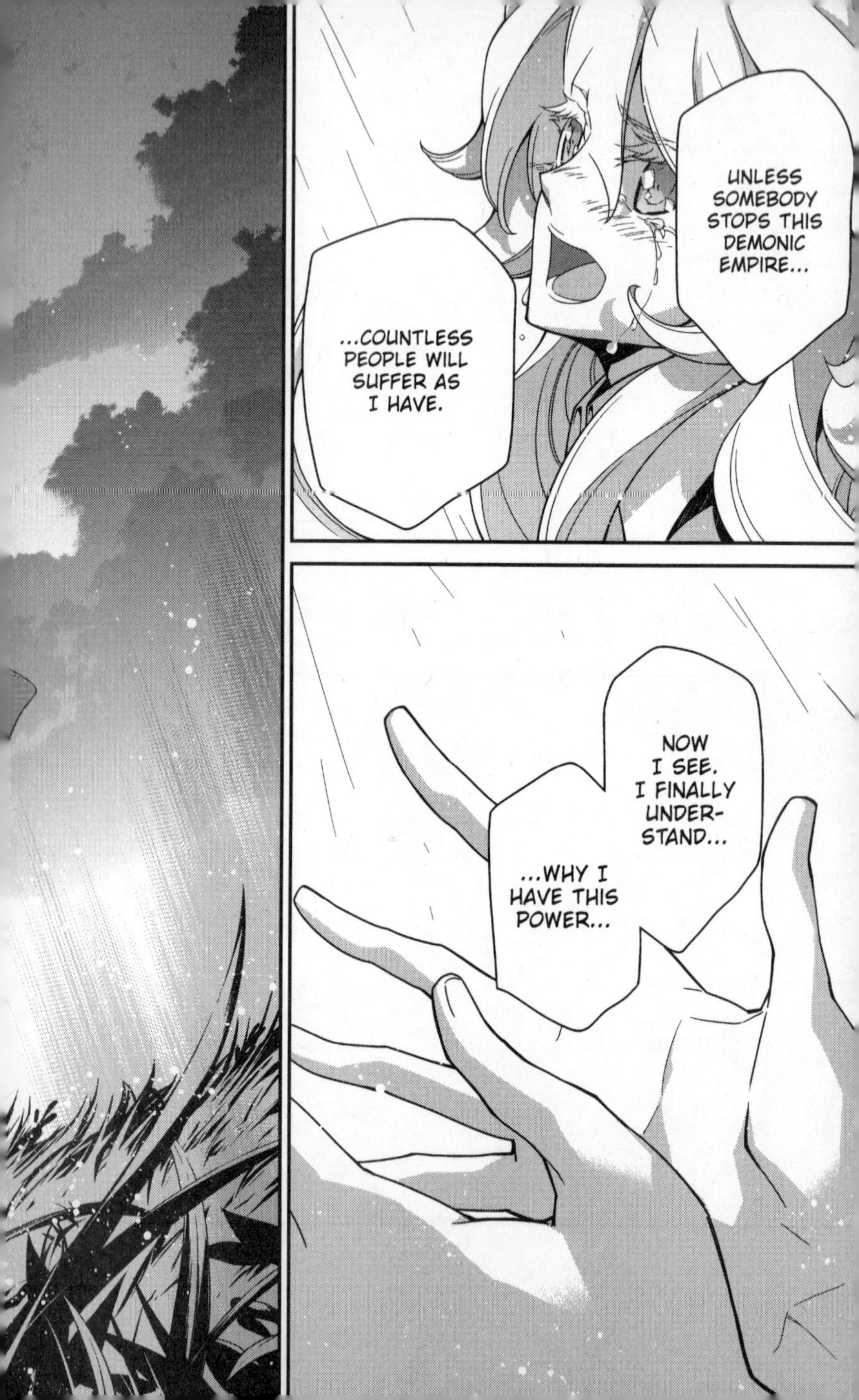
UNLESS SOMEBODY STOPS THIS DEMONIC EMPIRE...
...COUNTLESS PEOPLE WILL SUFFER AS I HAVE.
NOW I SEE. I FINALLY UNDER-STAND...
...WHY I HAVE THIS POWER...

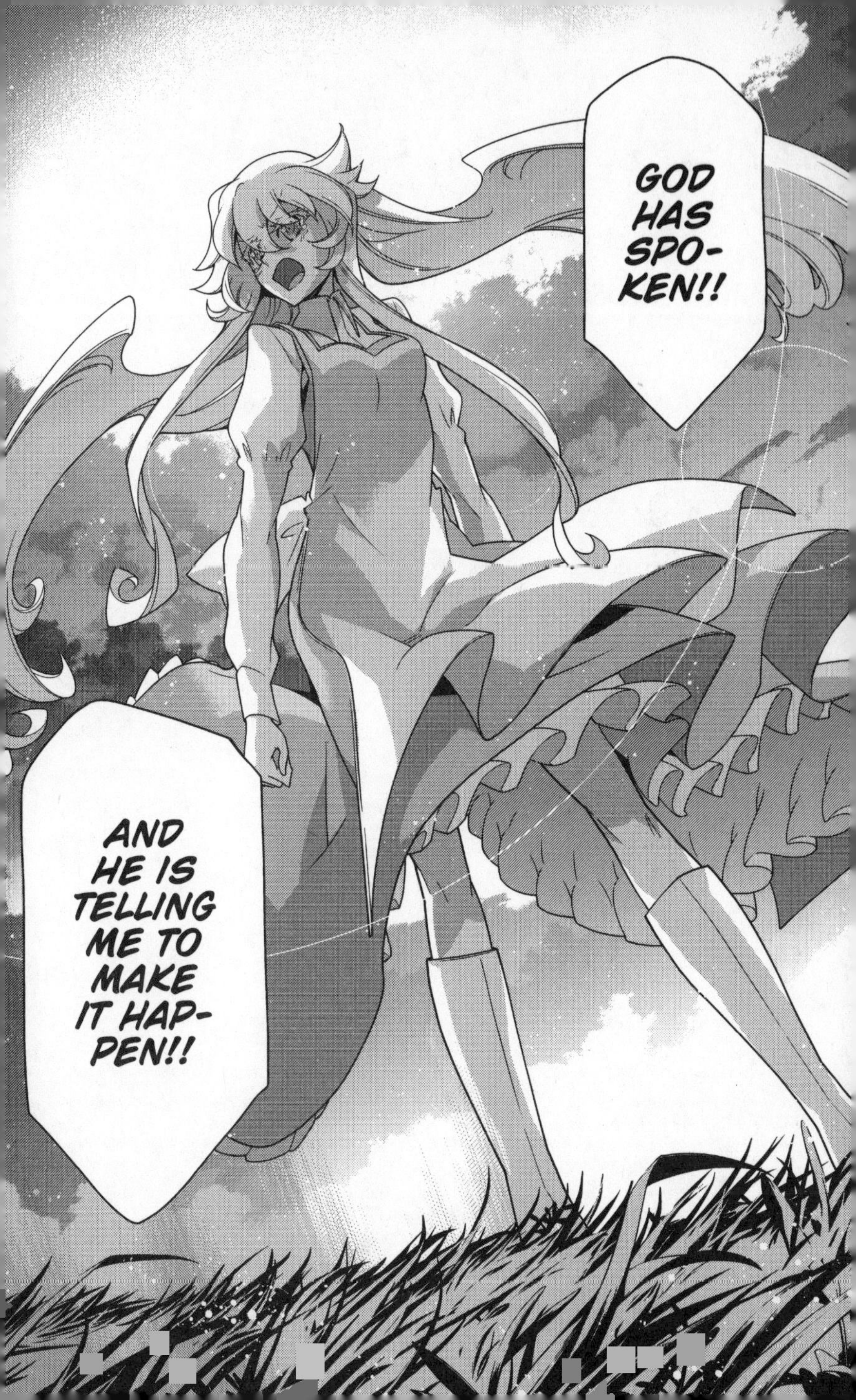
GOD HAS SPO-KEN!!
AND HE IS TELLING ME TO MAKE IT HAP-PEN!!

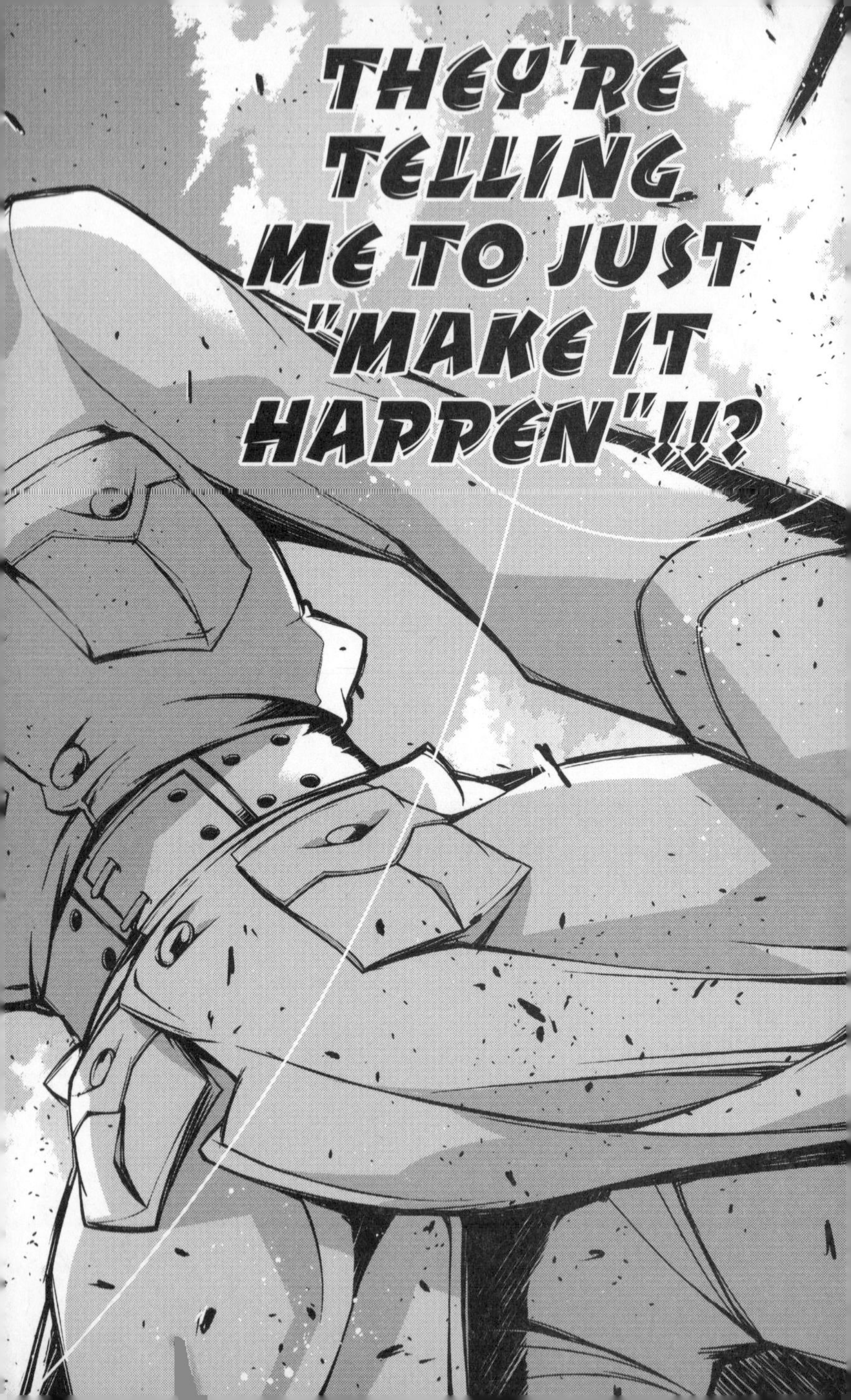
THEY'RE TELLING ME TO JUST "MAKE IT HAPPEN"!!?

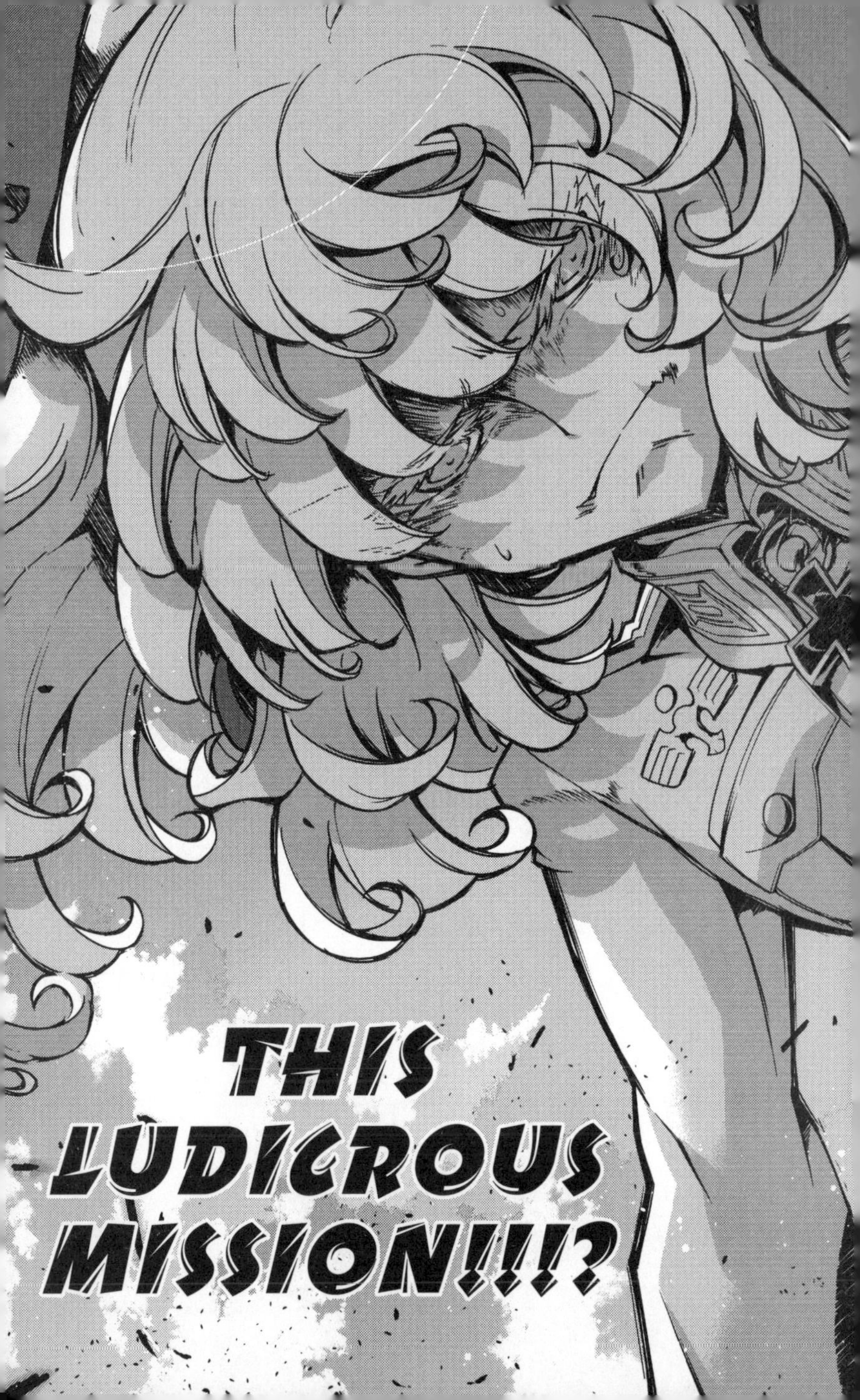
THIS LUDICROUS MISSION!!!?

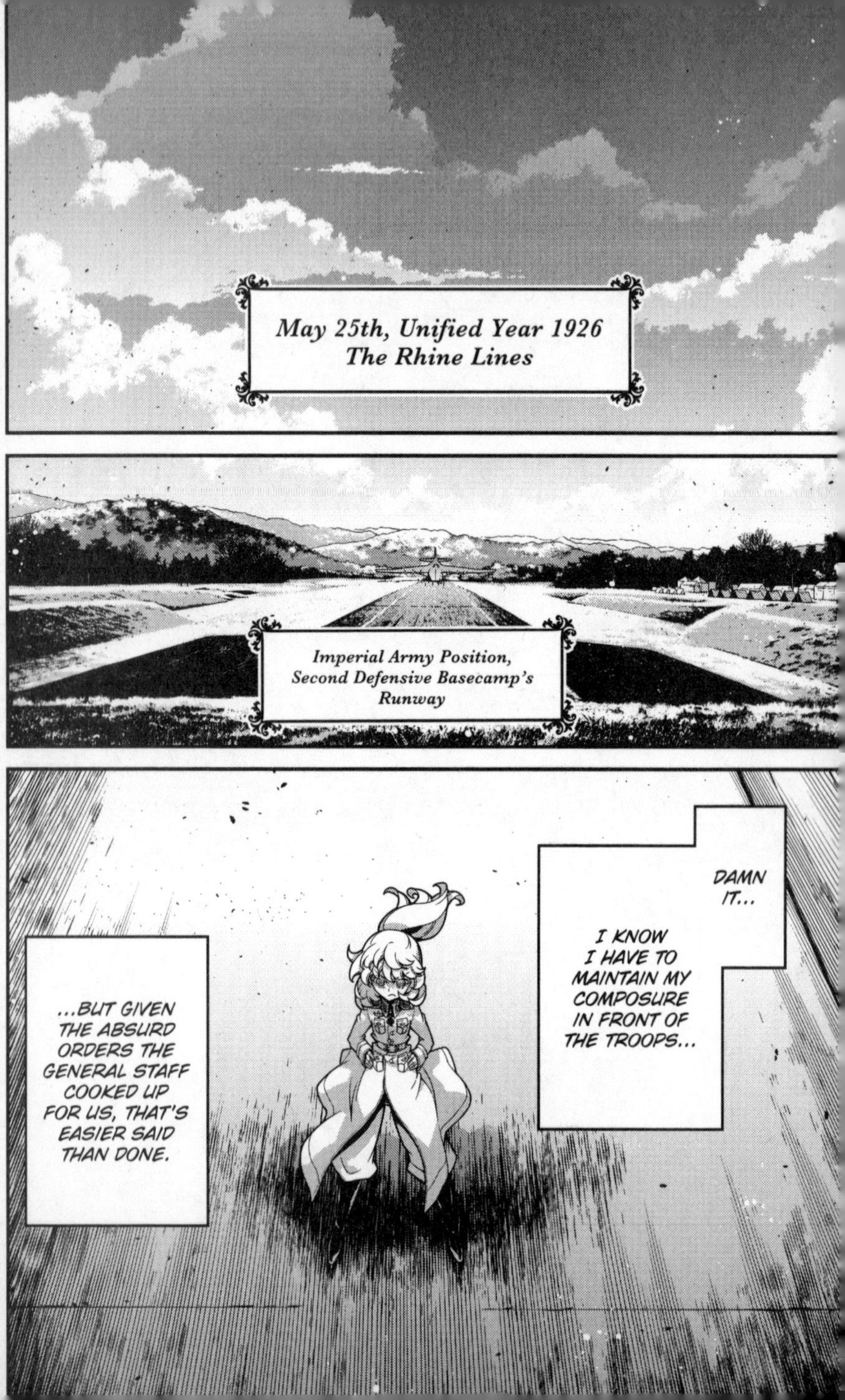
May 25th, Unified Year 1926
The Rhine Lines
Imperial Army Position, Second Defensive Basecamp's Runway
DAMN IT...
I KNOW I HAVE TO MAINTAIN MY COMPOSURE IN FRONT OF THE TROOPS...
...BUT GIVEN THE ABSURD ORDERS THE GENERAL STAFF COOKED UP FOR US, THAT'S EASIER SAID THAN DONE.

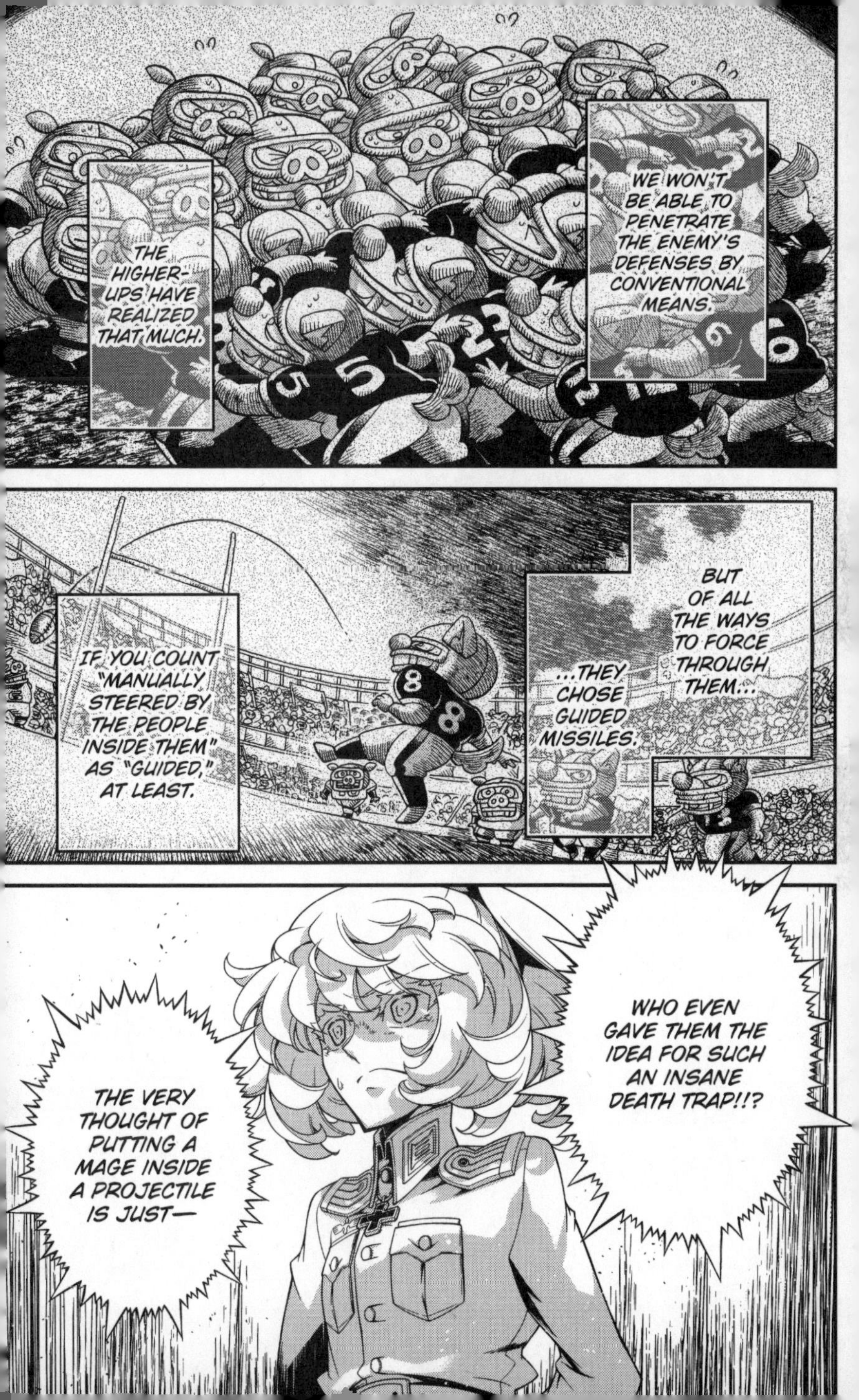
WE WON'T BE ABLE TO PENETRATE THE ENEMY'S DEFENSES BY CONVENTIONAL MEANS.
THE HIGHER-UPS HAVE REALIZED THAT MUCH.
BUT OF ALL THE WAYS TO FORCE THROUGH THEM...
...THEY CHOSE GUIDED MISSILES.
IF YOU COUNT "MANUALLY STEERED BY THE PEOPLE INSIDE THEM" AS "GUIDED," AT LEAST.
WHO EVEN GAVE THEM THE IDEA FOR SUCH AN INSANE DEATH TRAP!!?
THE VERY THOUGHT OF PUTTING A MAGE INSIDE A PROJECTILE IS JUST—

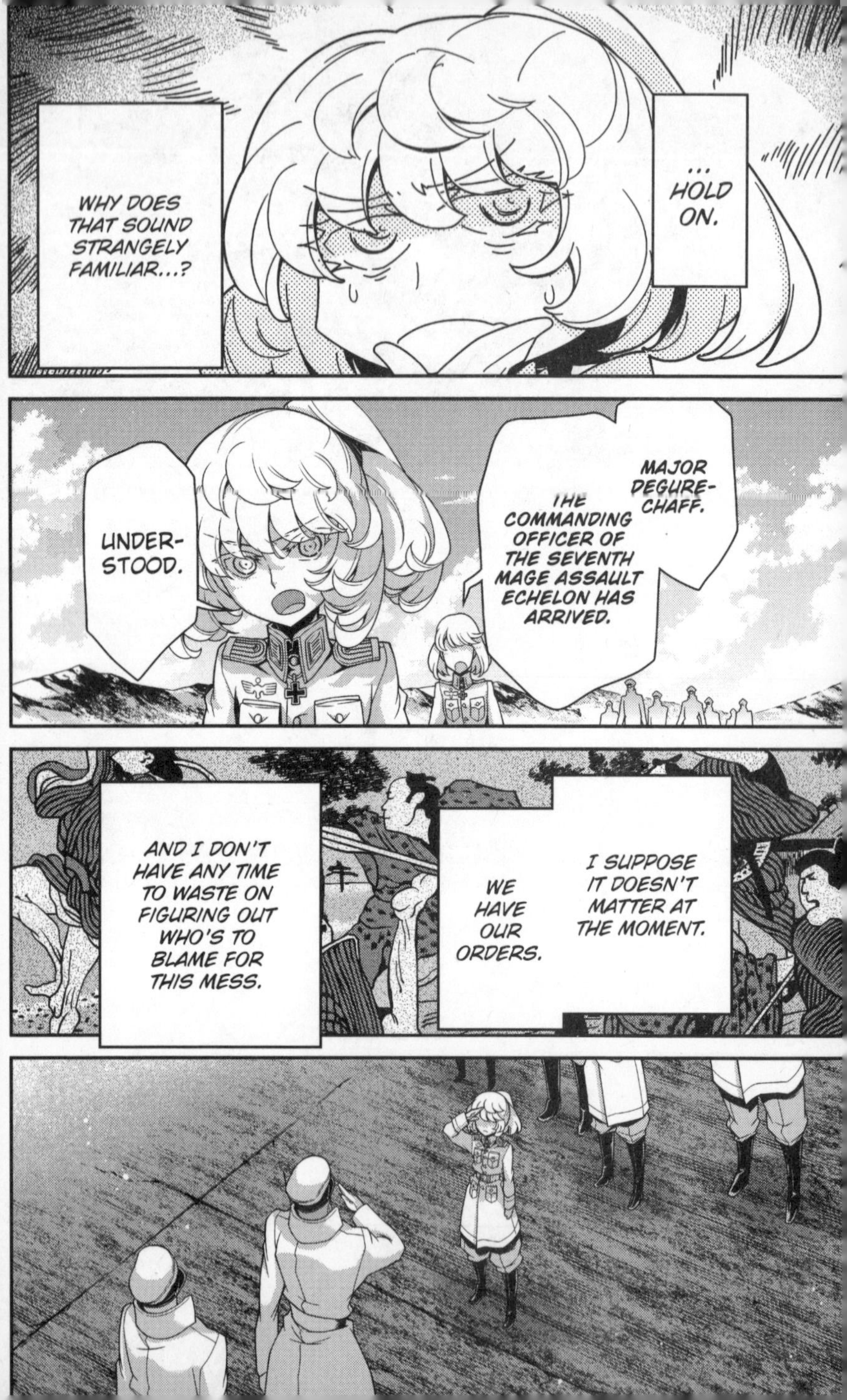
...HOLD ON.
WHY DOES THAT SOUND STRANGELY FAMILIAR...?
MAJOR DEGURE-CHAFF.
THE COMMANDING OFFICER OF THE SEVENTH MAGE ASSAULT ECHELON HAS ARRIVED.
UNDER-STOOD.
I SUPPOSE IT DOESN'T MATTER AT THE MOMENT.
WE HAVE OUR ORDERS.
AND I DON'T HAVE ANY TIME TO WASTE ON FIGURING OUT WHO'S TO BLAME FOR THIS MESS.

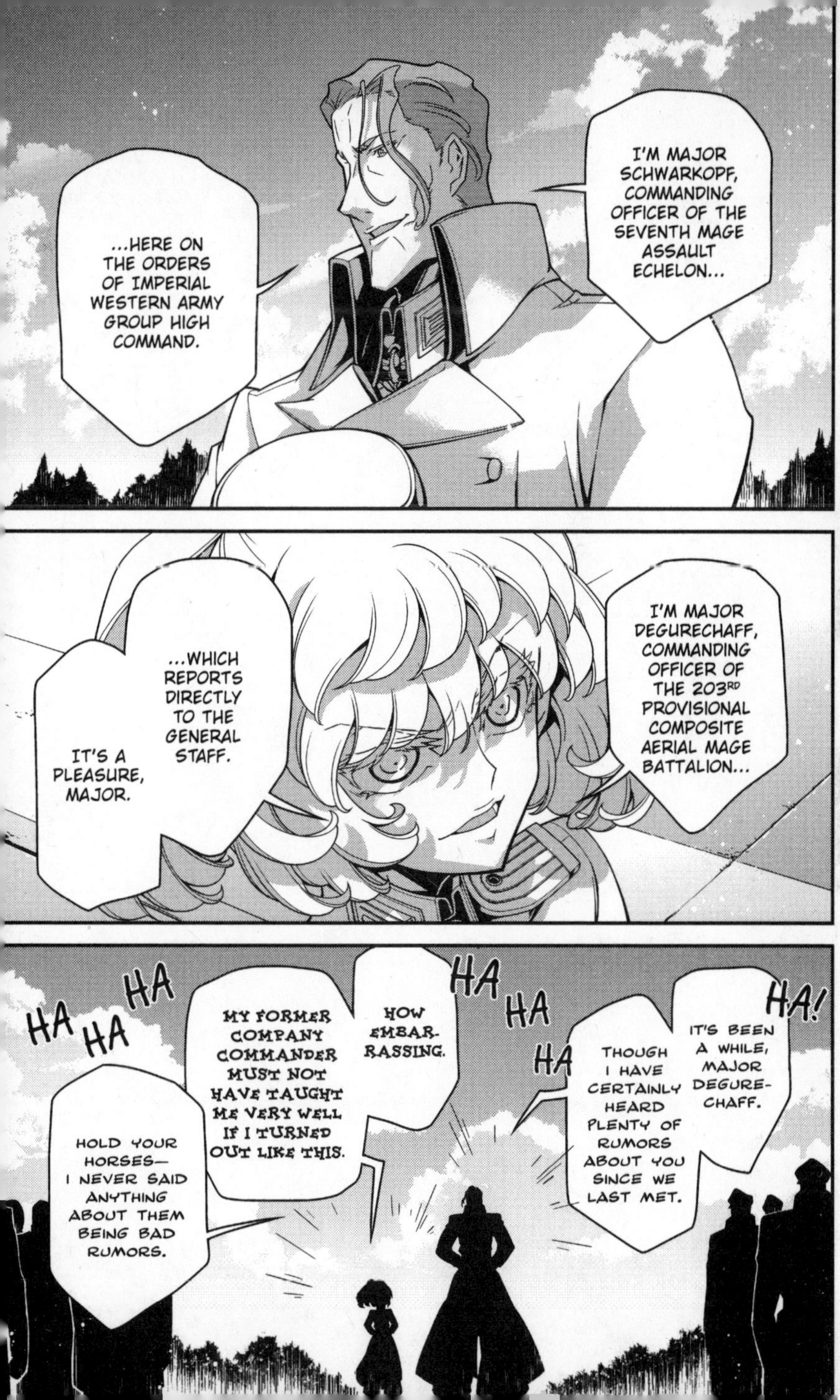
I'M MAJOR SCHWARKOPF, COMMANDING OFFICER OF THE SEVENTH MAGE ASSAULT ECHELON...
...HERE ON THE ORDERS OF IMPERIAL WESTERN ARMY GROUP HIGH COMMAND.
I'M MAJOR DEGURECHAFF, COMMANDING OFFICER OF THE 203RD PROVISIONAL COMPOSITE AERIAL MAGE BATTALION...
...WHICH REPORTS DIRECTLY TO THE GENERAL STAFF.
IT'S A PLEASURE, MAJOR.
HA!
IT'S BEEN A WHILE, MAJOR DEGURECHAFF.
THOUGH I HAVE CERTAINLY HEARD PLENTY OF RUMORS ABOUT YOU SINCE WE LAST MET.
HA HA HA HA
HOW EMBARRASSING.
MY FORMER COMPANY COMMANDER MUST NOT HAVE TAUGHT ME VERY WELL IF I TURNED OUT LIKE THIS.
HA HA HA
HOLD YOUR HORSES— I NEVER SAID ANYTHING ABOUT THEM BEING BAD RUMORS.

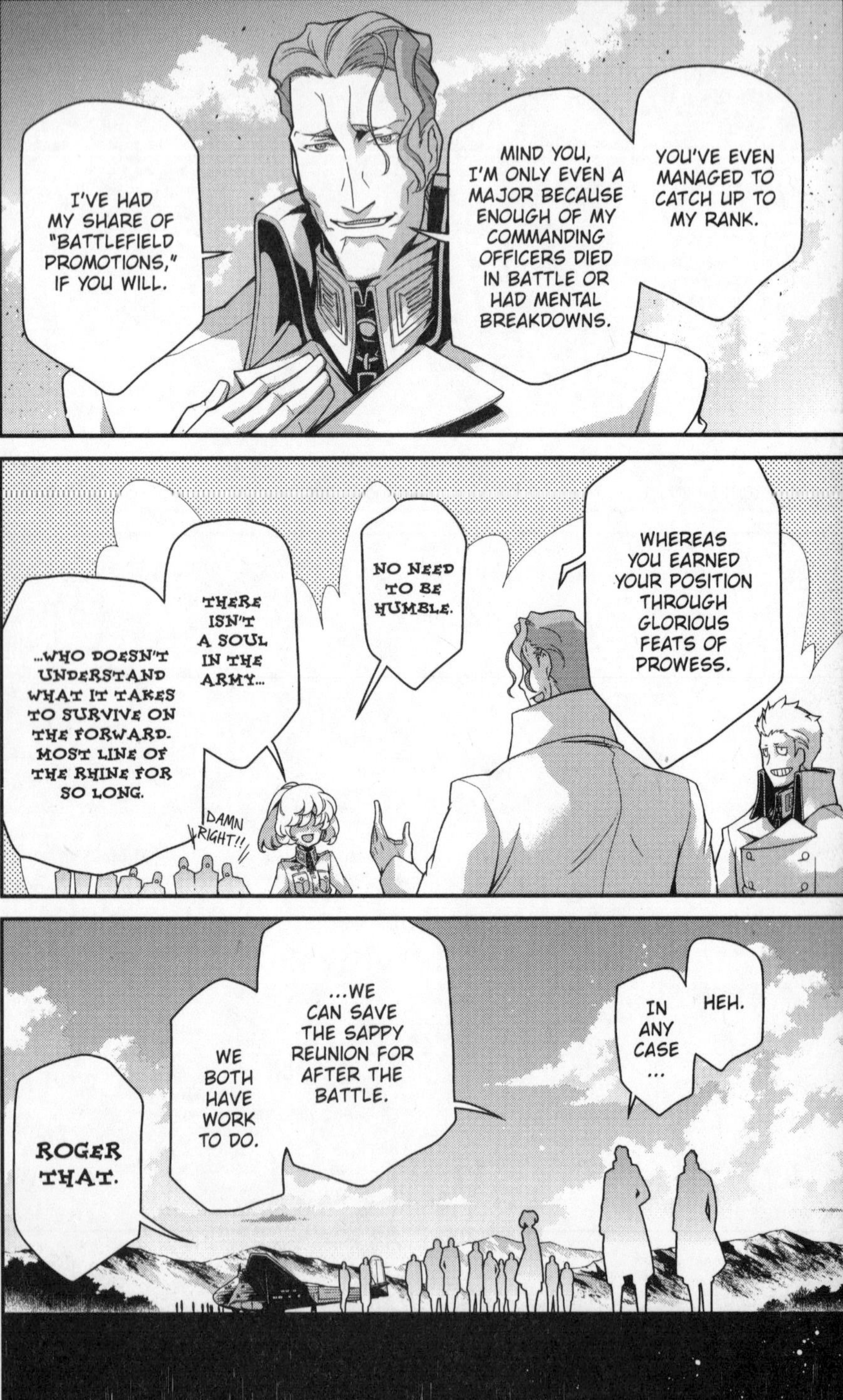
YOU'VE EVEN MANAGED TO CATCH UP TO MY RANK.
MIND YOU, I'M ONLY EVEN A MAJOR BECAUSE ENOUGH OF MY COMMANDING OFFICERS DIED IN BATTLE OR HAD MENTAL BREAKDOWNS.
I'VE HAD MY SHARE OF "BATTLEFIELD PROMOTIONS," IF YOU WILL.
WHEREAS YOU EARNED YOUR POSITION THROUGH GLORIOUS FEATS OF PROWESS.
NO NEED TO BE HUMBLE.
THERE ISN'T A SOUL IN THE ARMY...
...WHO DOESN'T UNDERSTAND WHAT IT TAKES TO SURVIVE ON THE FORWARD-MOST LINE OF THE RHINE FOR SO LONG.
DAMN RIGHT!!
HEH.
IN ANY CASE ...
...WE CAN SAVE THE SAPPY REUNION FOR AFTER THE BATTLE.
WE BOTH HAVE WORK TO DO.
ROGER THAT.

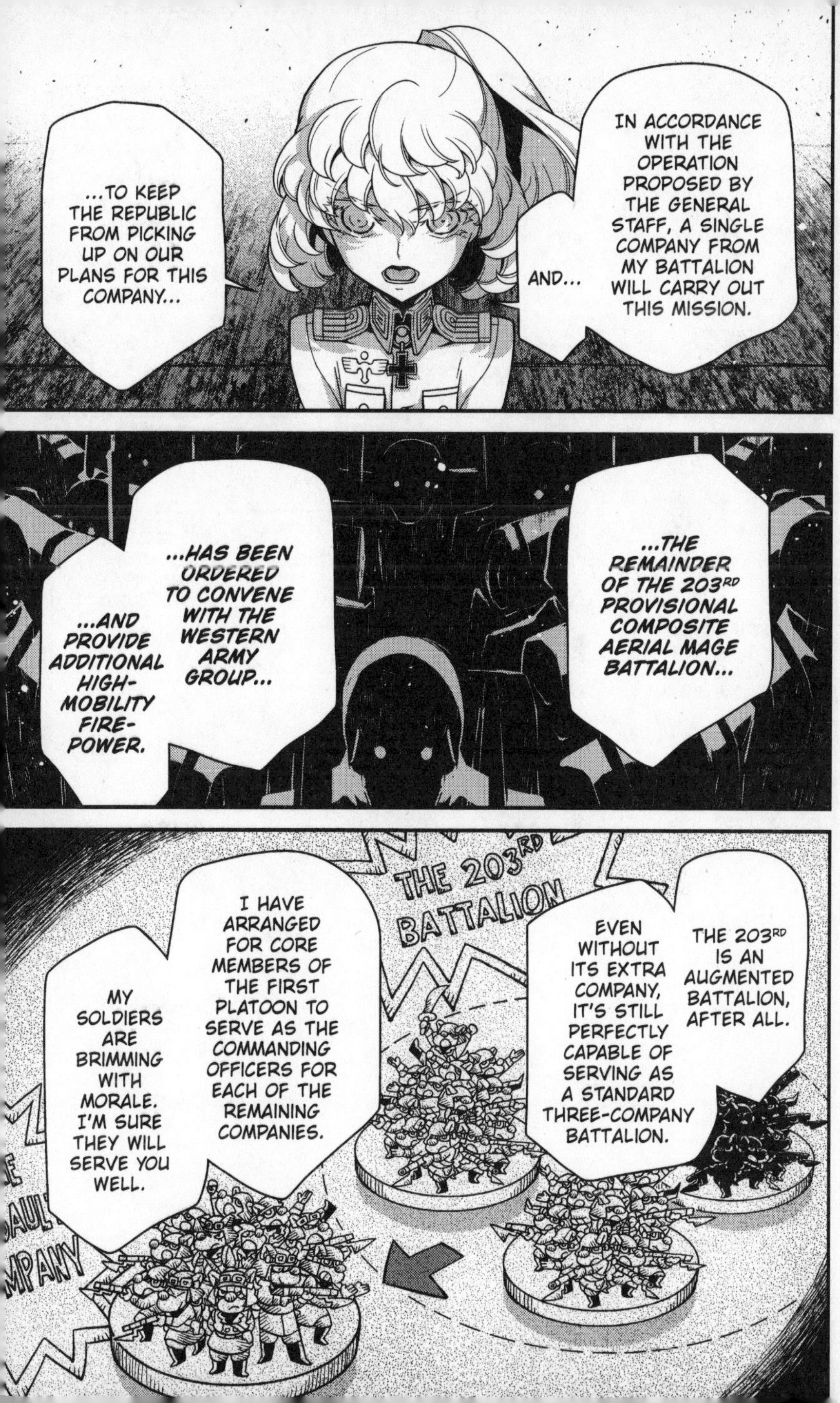
IN ACCORDANCE WITH THE OPERATION PROPOSED BY THE GENERAL STAFF, A SINGLE COMPANY FROM MY BATTALION WILL CARRY OUT THIS MISSION.
AND...
...TO KEEP THE REPUBLIC FROM PICKING UP ON OUR PLANS FOR THIS COMPANY...
...THE REMAINDER OF THE 203RD PROVISIONAL COMPOSITE AERIAL MAGE BATTALION...
...HAS BEEN ORDERED TO CONVENE WITH THE WESTERN ARMY GROUP...
...AND PROVIDE ADDITIONAL HIGH-MOBILITY FIRE-POWER.
THE 203RD IS AN AUGMENTED BATTALION, AFTER ALL.
EVEN WITHOUT ITS EXTRA COMPANY, IT'S STILL PERFECTLY CAPABLE OF SERVING AS A STANDARD THREE-COMPANY BATTALION.
THE 203RD BATTALION
I HAVE ARRANGED FOR CORE MEMBERS OF THE FIRST PLATOON TO SERVE AS THE COMMANDING OFFICERS FOR EACH OF THE REMAINING COMPANIES.
MY SOLDIERS ARE BRIMMING WITH MORALE. I'M SURE THEY WILL SERVE YOU WELL.

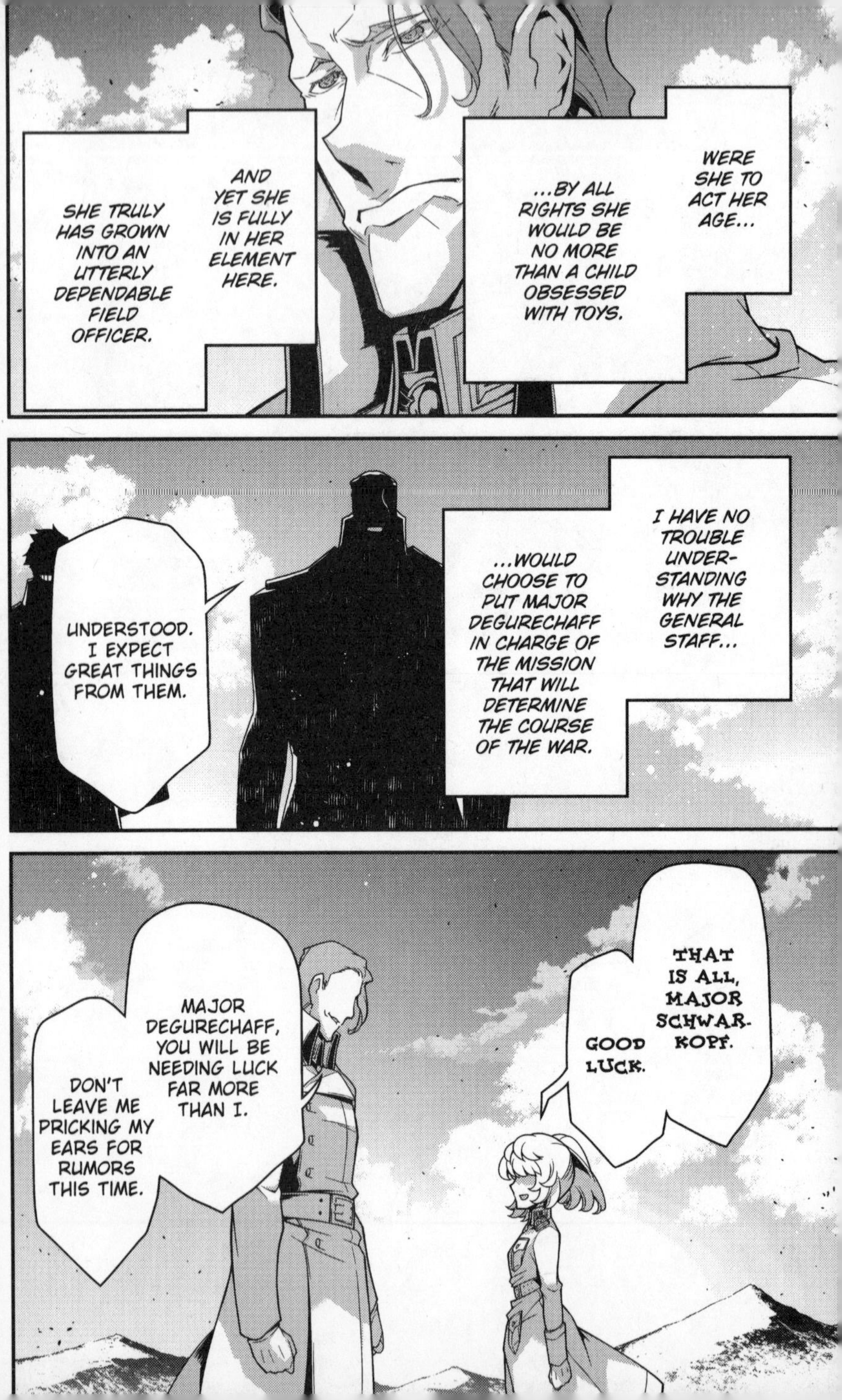
WERE SHE TO ACT HER AGE...
...BY ALL RIGHTS SHE WOULD BE NO MORE THAN A CHILD OBSESSED WITH TOYS.
AND YET SHE IS FULLY IN HER ELEMENT HERE.
SHE TRULY HAS GROWN INTO AN UTTERLY DEPENDABLE FIELD OFFICER.
I HAVE NO TROUBLE UNDER-STANDING WHY THE GENERAL STAFF...
...WOULD CHOOSE TO PUT MAJOR DEGURECHAFF IN CHARGE OF THE MISSION THAT WILL DETERMINE THE COURSE OF THE WAR.
UNDERSTOOD. I EXPECT GREAT THINGS FROM THEM.
THAT IS ALL, MAJOR SCHWAR-KOPF.
GOOD LUCK.
MAJOR DEGURECHAFF, YOU WILL BE NEEDING LUCK FAR MORE THAN I.
DON'T LEAVE ME PRICKING MY EARS FOR RUMORS THIS TIME.

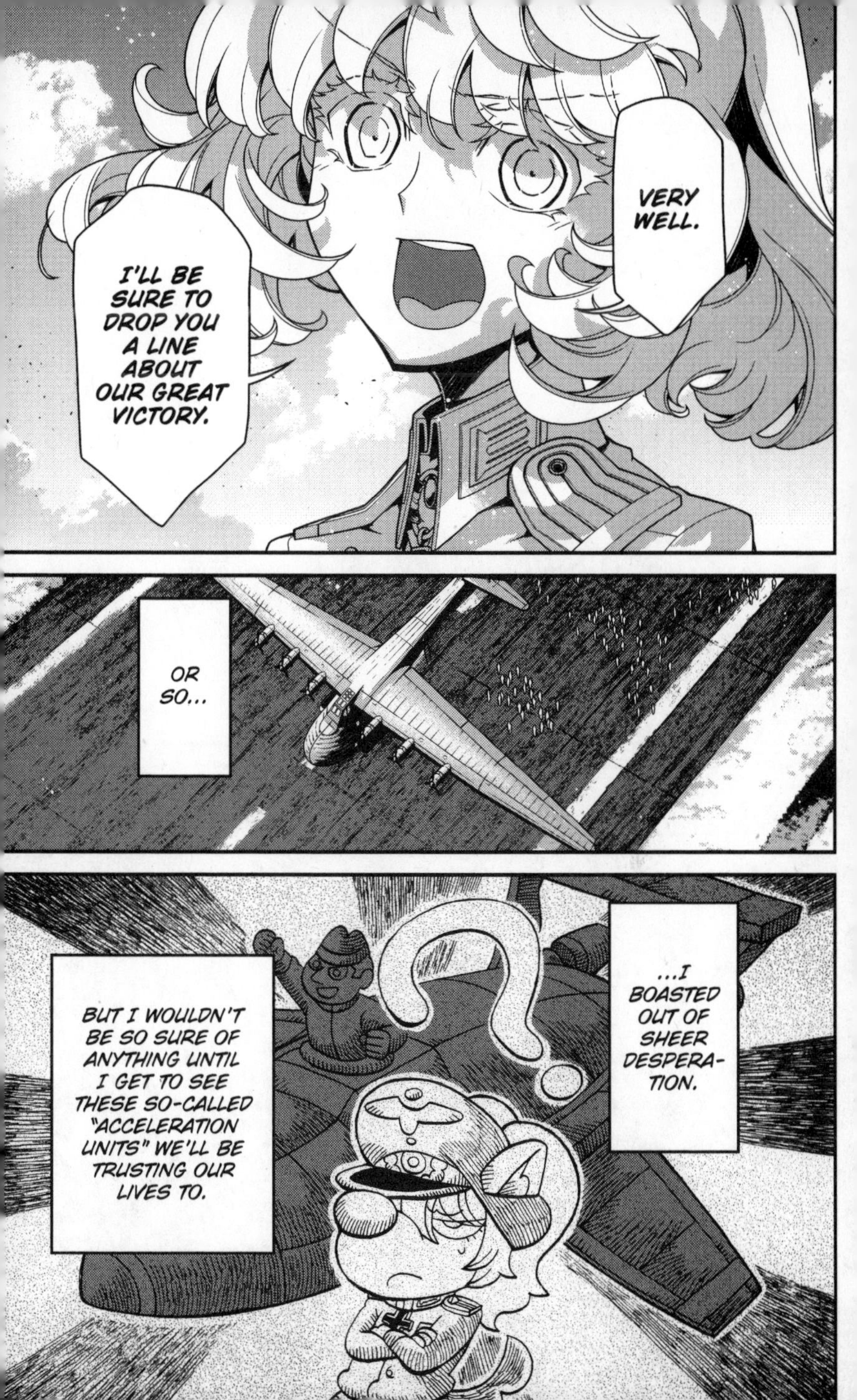
VERY WELL.
I'LL BE SURE TO DROP YOU A LINE ABOUT OUR GREAT VICTORY.
OR SO...
...I BOASTED OUT OF SHEER DESPERA-TION.
BUT I WOULDN'T BE SO SURE OF ANYTHING UNTIL I GET TO SEE THESE SO-CALLED "ACCELERATION UNITS" WE'LL BE TRUSTING OUR LIVES TO.

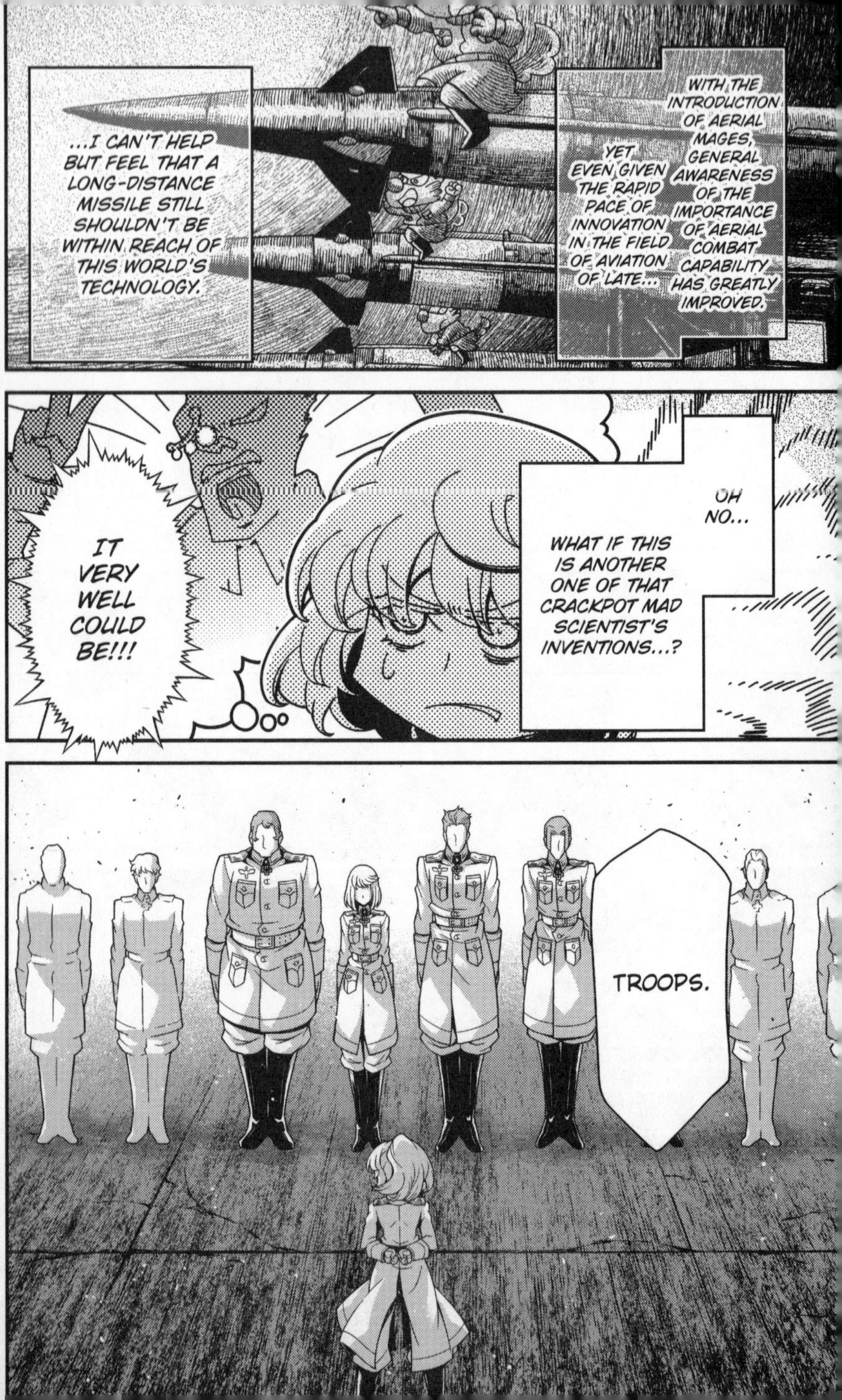
WITH THE INTRODUCTION OF AERIAL MAGES, GENERAL AWARENESS OF THE IMPORTANCE OF AERIAL COMBAT CAPABILITY HAS GREATLY IMPROVED.
YET EVEN GIVEN THE RAPID PACE OF INNOVATION IN THE FIELD OF AVIATION OF LATE...
...I CAN'T HELP BUT FEEL THAT A LONG-DISTANCE MISSILE STILL SHOULDN'T BE WITHIN REACH OF THIS WORLD'S TECHNOLOGY.
OH NO...
WHAT IF THIS IS ANOTHER ONE OF THAT CRACKPOT MAD SCIENTIST'S INVENTIONS...?
IT VERY WELL COULD BE!!!
TROOPS.

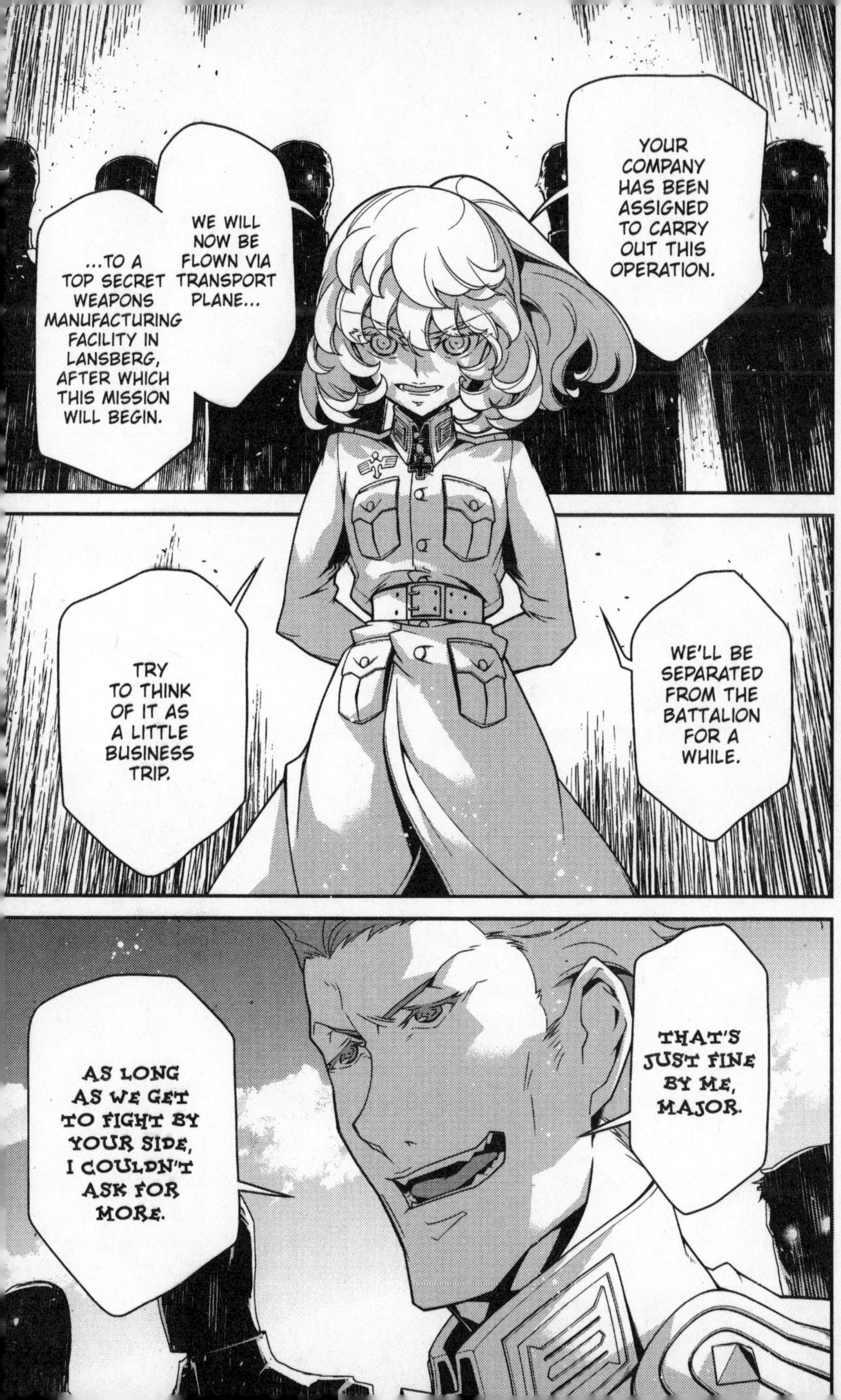
YOUR COMPANY HAS BEEN ASSIGNED TO CARRY OUT THIS OPERATION.
WE WILL NOW BE FLOWN VIA TRANSPORT PLANE...
...TO A TOP SECRET WEAPONS MANUFACTURING FACILITY IN LANSBERG, AFTER WHICH THIS MISSION WILL BEGIN.
WE'LL BE SEPARATED FROM THE BATTALION FOR A WHILE.
TRY TO THINK OF IT AS A LITTLE BUSINESS TRIP.
THAT'S JUST FINE BY ME, MAJOR.
AS LONG AS WE GET TO FIGHT BY YOUR SIDE, I COULDN'T ASK FOR MORE.

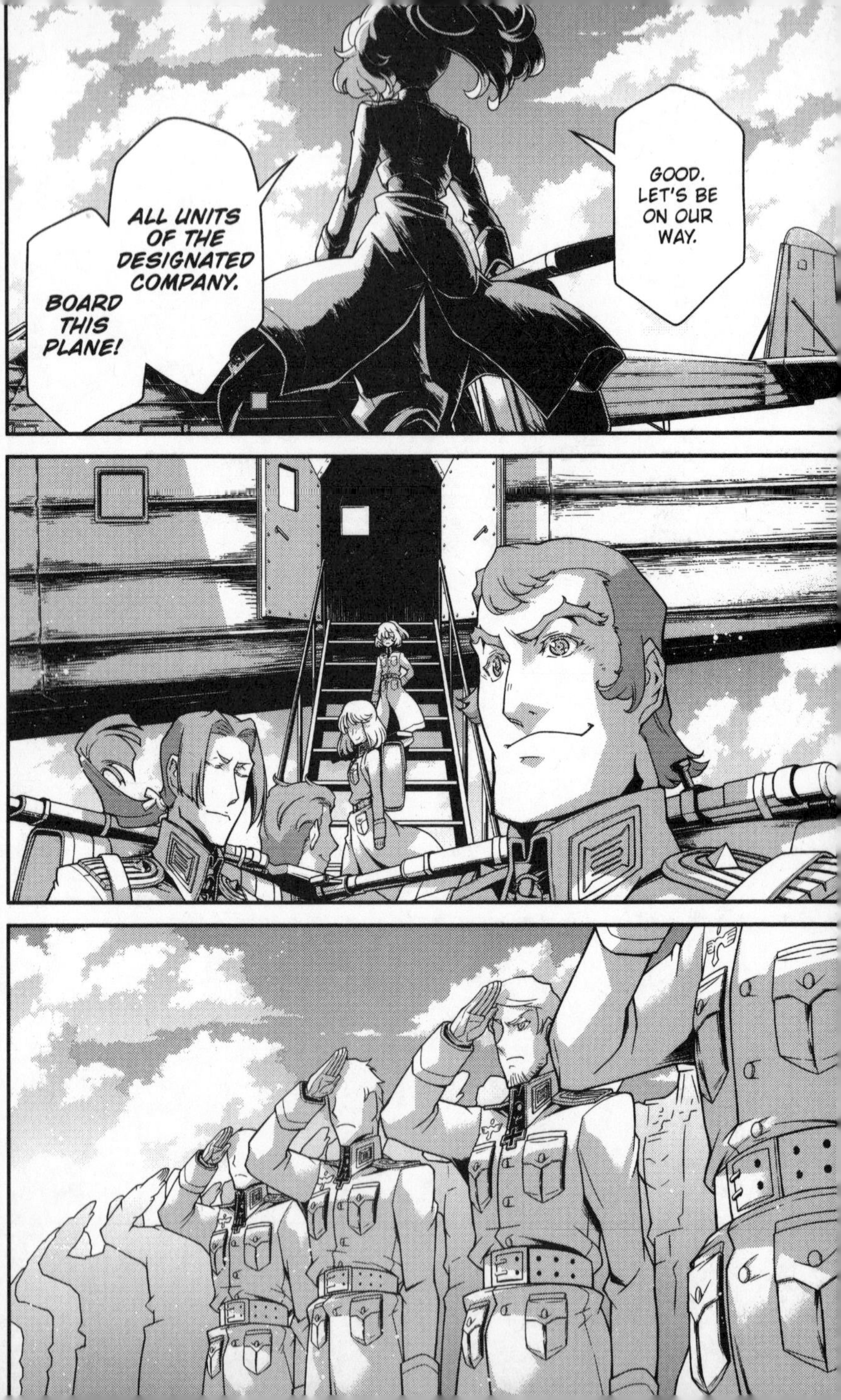
GOOD. LET'S BE ON OUR WAY.
ALL UNITS OF THE DESIGNATED COMPANY.
BOARD THIS PLANE!

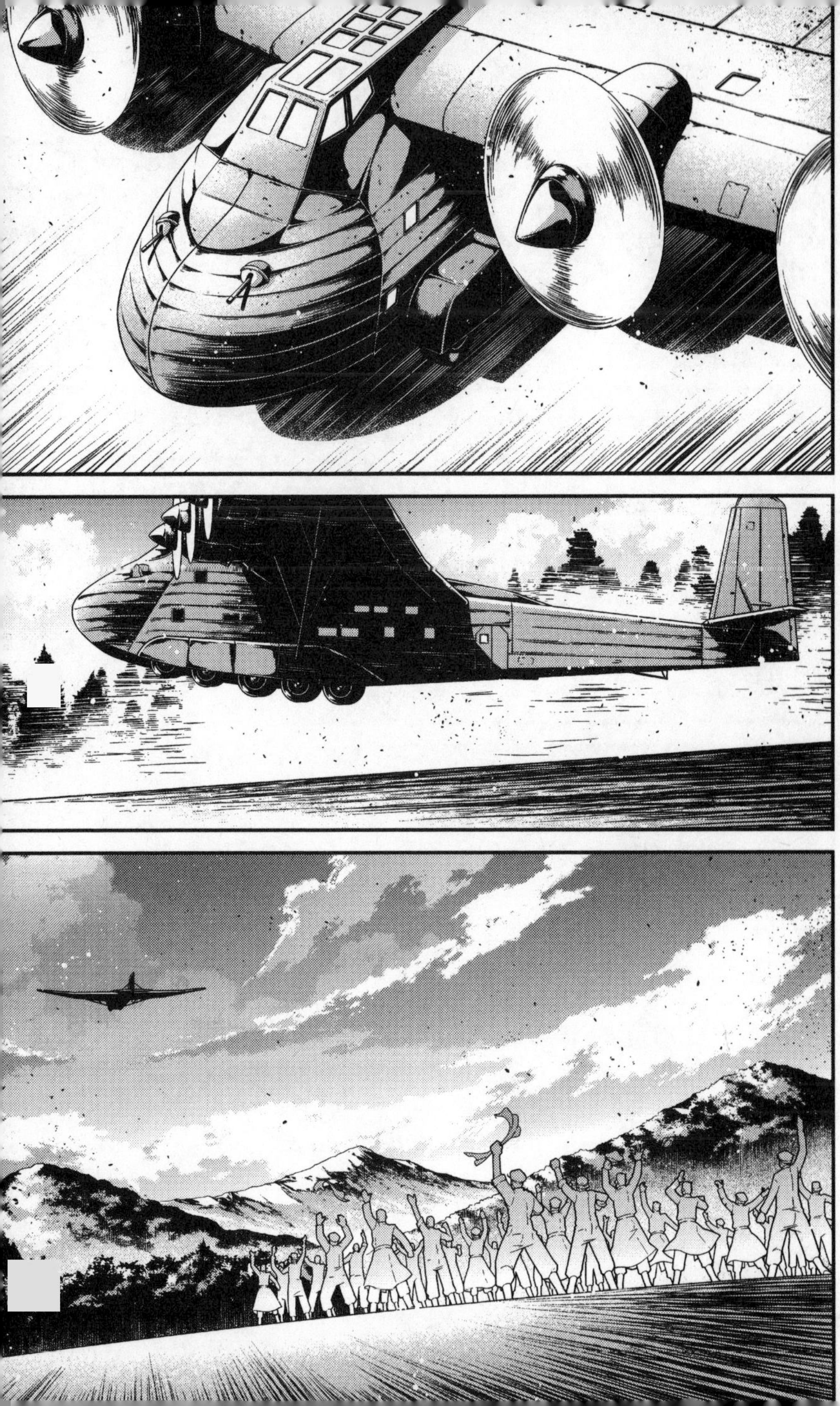

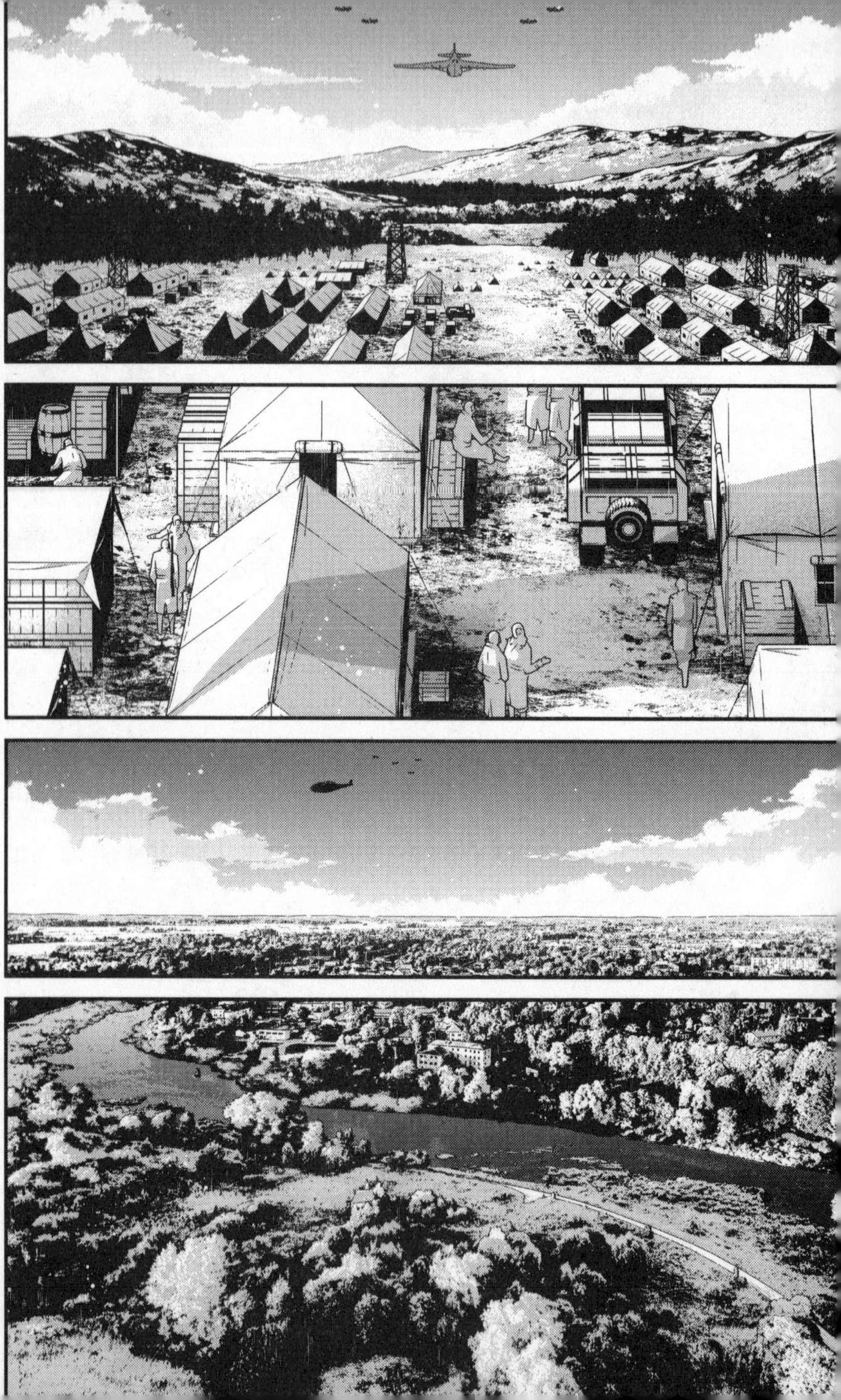

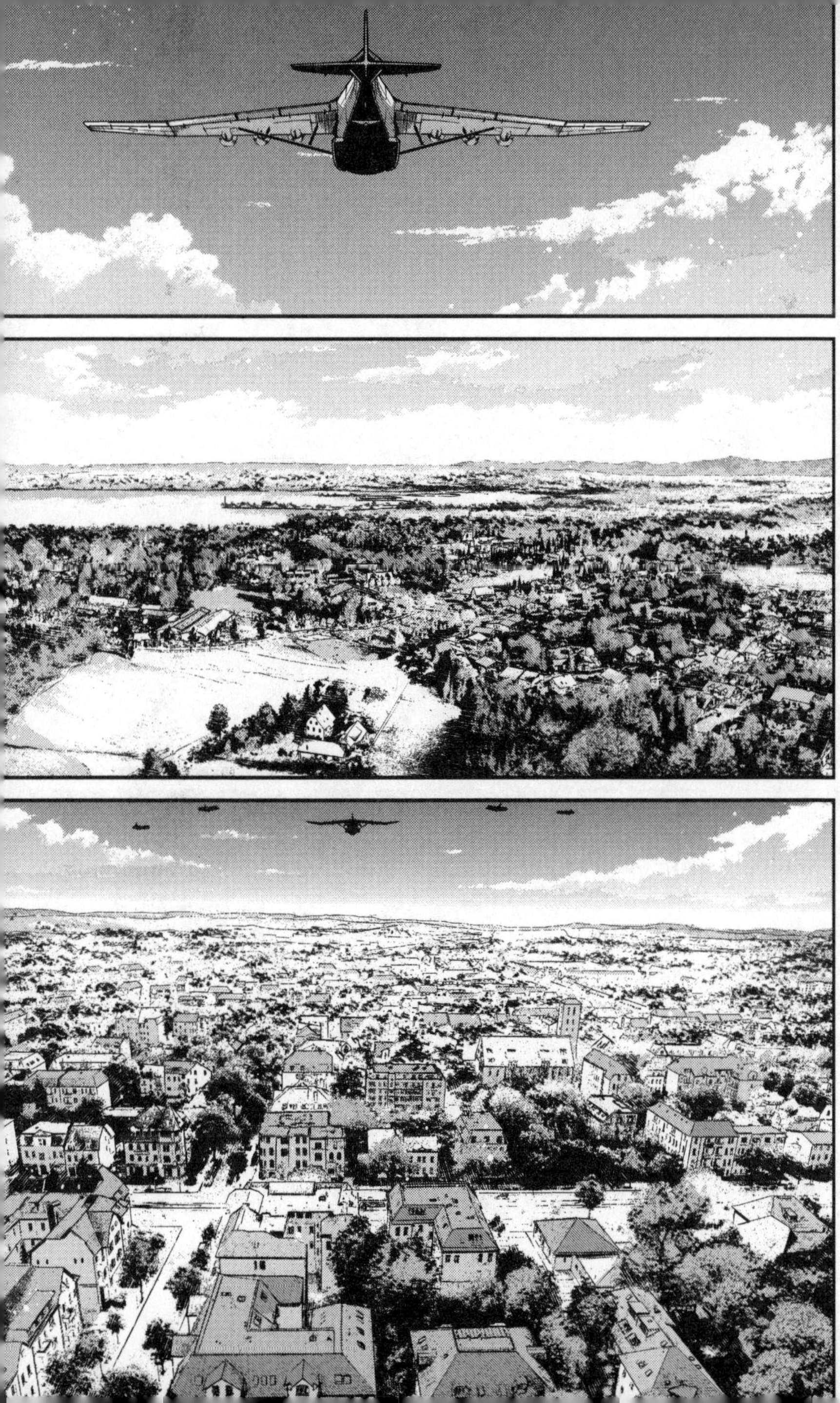

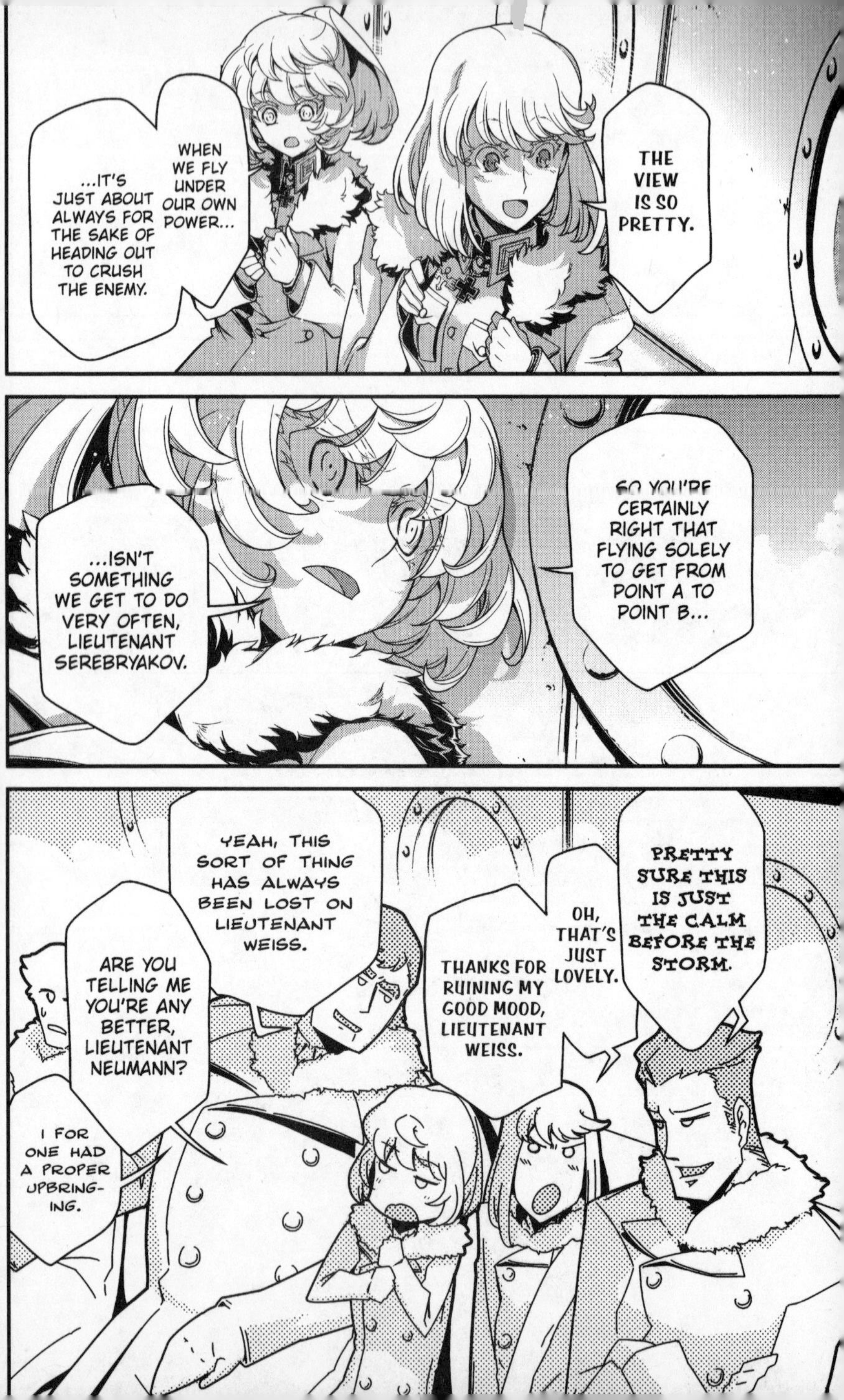
THE VIEW IS SO PRETTY.
WHEN WE FLY UNDER OUR OWN POWER...
...IT'S JUST ABOUT ALWAYS FOR THE SAKE OF HEADING OUT TO CRUSH THE ENEMY.
SO YOU'RE CERTAINLY RIGHT THAT FLYING SOLELY TO GET FROM POINT A TO POINT B...
...ISN'T SOMETHING WE GET TO DO VERY OFTEN, LIEUTENANT SEREBRYAKOV.
PRETTY SURE THIS IS JUST THE CALM BEFORE THE STORM.
OH, THAT'S JUST LOVELY.
THANKS FOR RUINING MY GOOD MOOD, LIEUTENANT WEISS.
YEAH, THIS SORT OF THING HAS ALWAYS BEEN LOST ON LIEUTENANT WEISS.
ARE YOU TELLING ME YOU'RE ANY BETTER, LIEUTENANT NEUMANN?
I FOR ONE HAD A PROPER UPBRINGING.

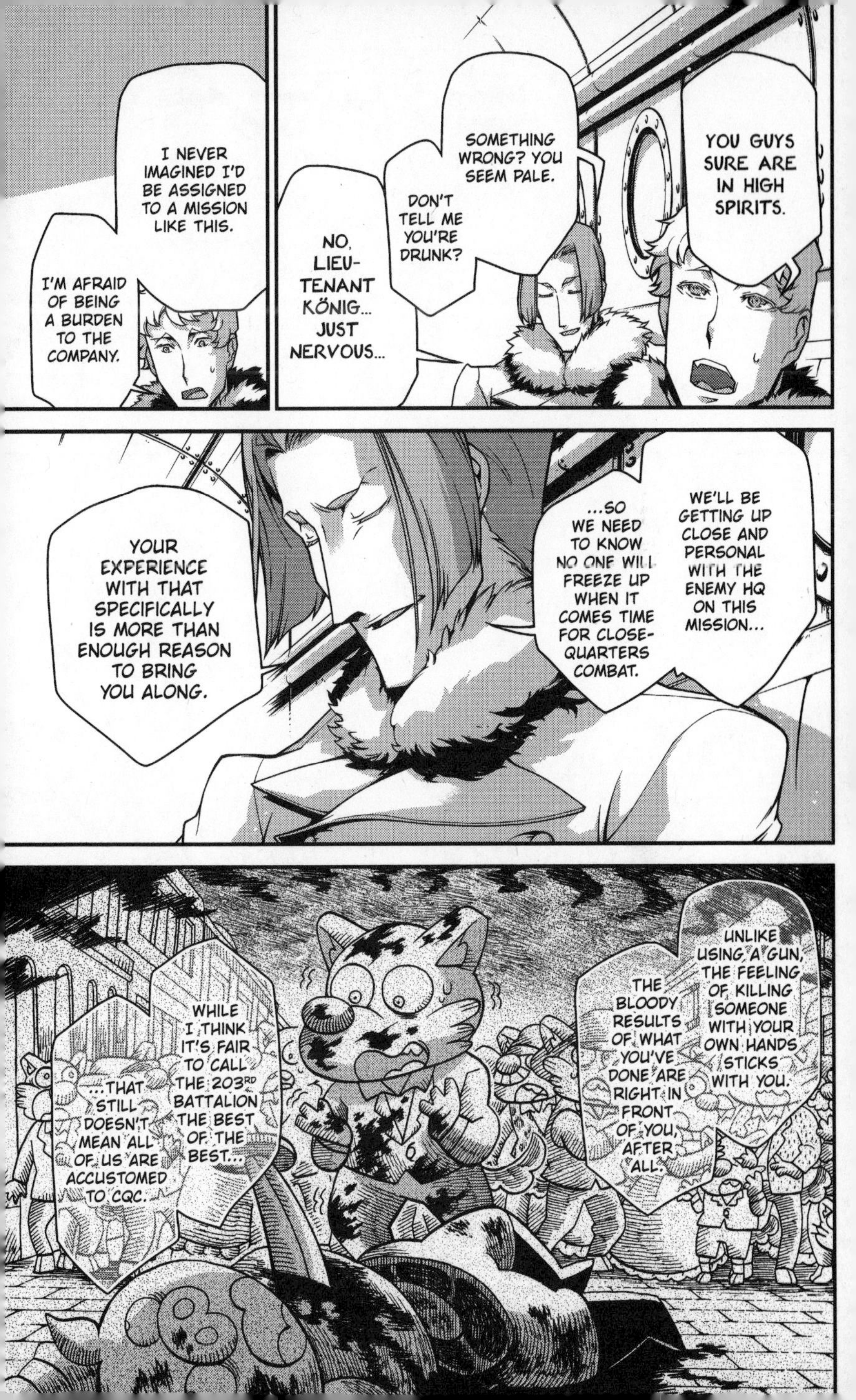
YOU GUYS SURE ARE IN HIGH SPIRITS.
SOMETHING WRONG? YOU SEEM PALE.
DON'T TELL ME YOU'RE DRUNK?
NO, LIEU-TENANT KÖNIG... JUST NERVOUS...
I NEVER IMAGINED I'D BE ASSIGNED TO A MISSION LIKE THIS.
I'M AFRAID OF BEING A BURDEN TO THE COMPANY.
WE'LL BE GETTING UP CLOSE AND PERSONAL WITH THE ENEMY HQ ON THIS MISSION...
...SO WE NEED TO KNOW NO ONE WILL FREEZE UP WHEN IT COMES TIME FOR CLOSE-QUARTERS COMBAT.
YOUR EXPERIENCE WITH THAT SPECIFICALLY IS MORE THAN ENOUGH REASON TO BRING YOU ALONG.
UNLIKE USING A GUN, THE FEELING OF KILLING SOMEONE WITH YOUR OWN HANDS STICKS WITH YOU.
THE BLOODY RESULTS OF WHAT YOU'VE DONE ARE RIGHT IN FRONT OF YOU, AFTER ALL.
WHILE I THINK IT'S FAIR TO CALL THE 203RD BATTALION THE BEST OF THE BEST...
...THAT STILL DOESN'T MEAN ALL OF US ARE ACCUSTOMED TO CQC.

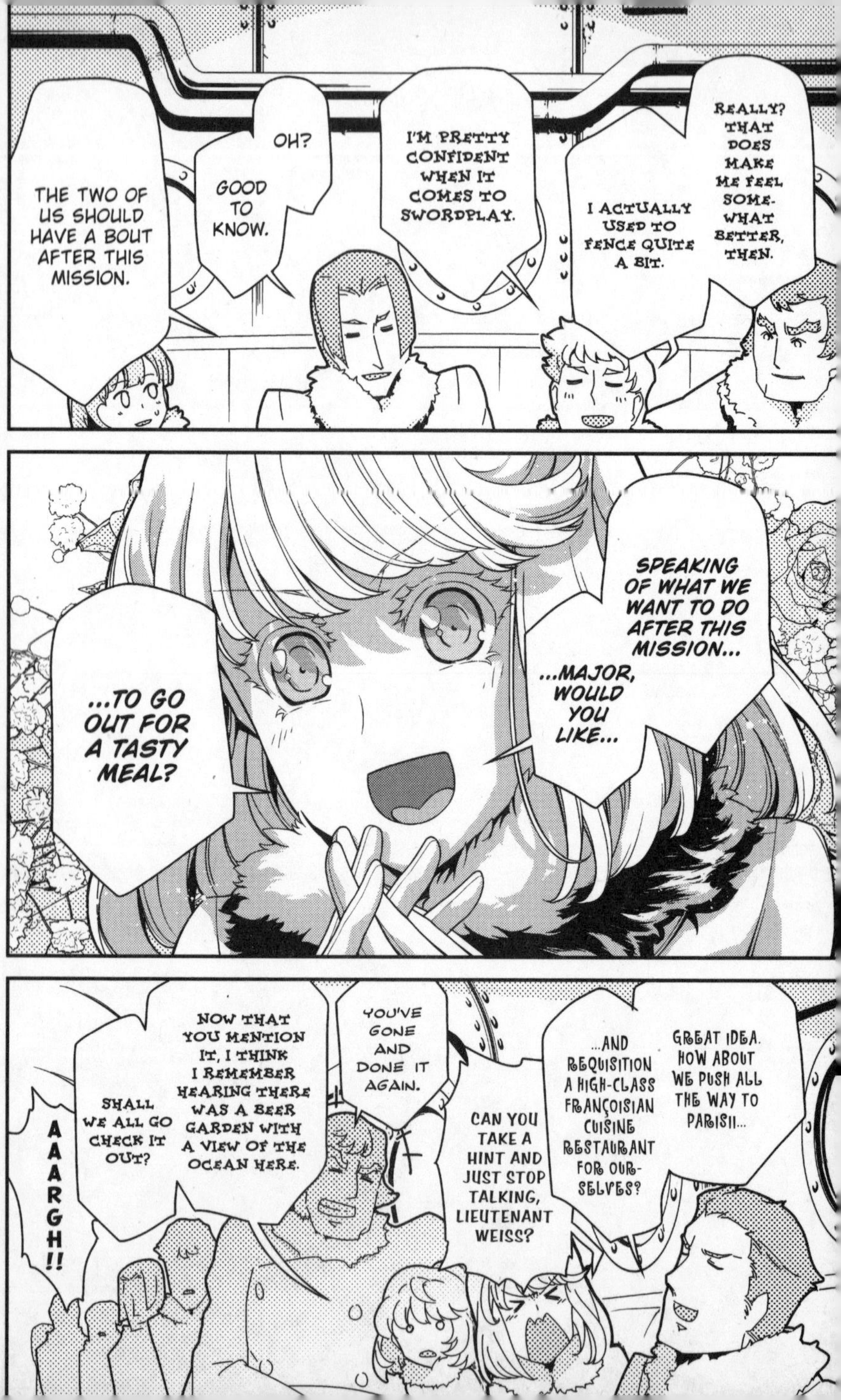
REALLY? THAT DOES MAKE ME FEEL SOME-WHAT BETTER, THEN.
I ACTUALLY USED TO FENCE QUITE A BIT.
I'M PRETTY CONFIDENT WHEN IT COMES TO SWORDPLAY.
OH?
GOOD TO KNOW.
THE TWO OF US SHOULD HAVE A BOUT AFTER THIS MISSION.
SPEAKING OF WHAT WE WANT TO DO AFTER THIS MISSION...
...MAJOR, WOULD YOU LIKE...
...TO GO OUT FOR A TASTY MEAL?
GREAT IDEA. HOW ABOUT WE PUSH ALL THE WAY TO PARISII...
...AND REQUISITION A HIGH-CLASS FRANÇOISIAN CUISINE RESTAURANT FOR OUR-SELVES?
CAN YOU TAKE A HINT AND JUST STOP TALKING, LIEUTENANT WEISS?
YOU'VE GONE AND DONE IT AGAIN.
NOW THAT YOU MENTION IT, I THINK I REMEMBER HEARING THERE WAS A BEER GARDEN WITH A VIEW OF THE OCEAN HERE.
SHALL WE ALL GO CHECK IT OUT?
AAAARGH!!

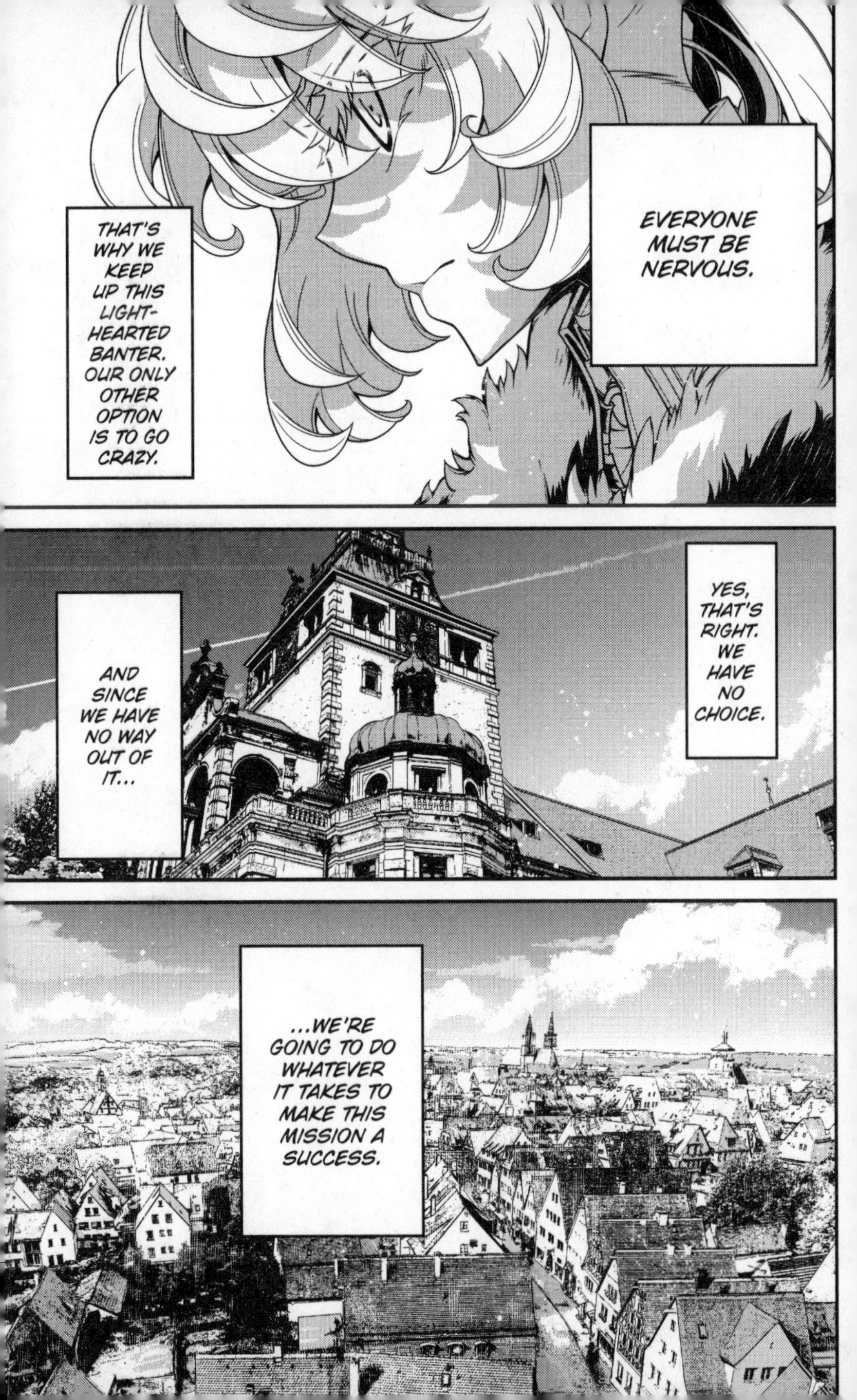
EVERYONE MUST BE NERVOUS.
THAT'S WHY WE KEEP UP THIS LIGHT-HEARTED BANTER. OUR ONLY OTHER OPTION IS TO GO CRAZY.
YES, THAT'S RIGHT. WE HAVE NO CHOICE.
AND SINCE WE HAVE NO WAY OUT OF IT...
...WE'RE GOING TO DO WHATEVER IT TAKES TO MAKE THIS MISSION A SUCCESS.

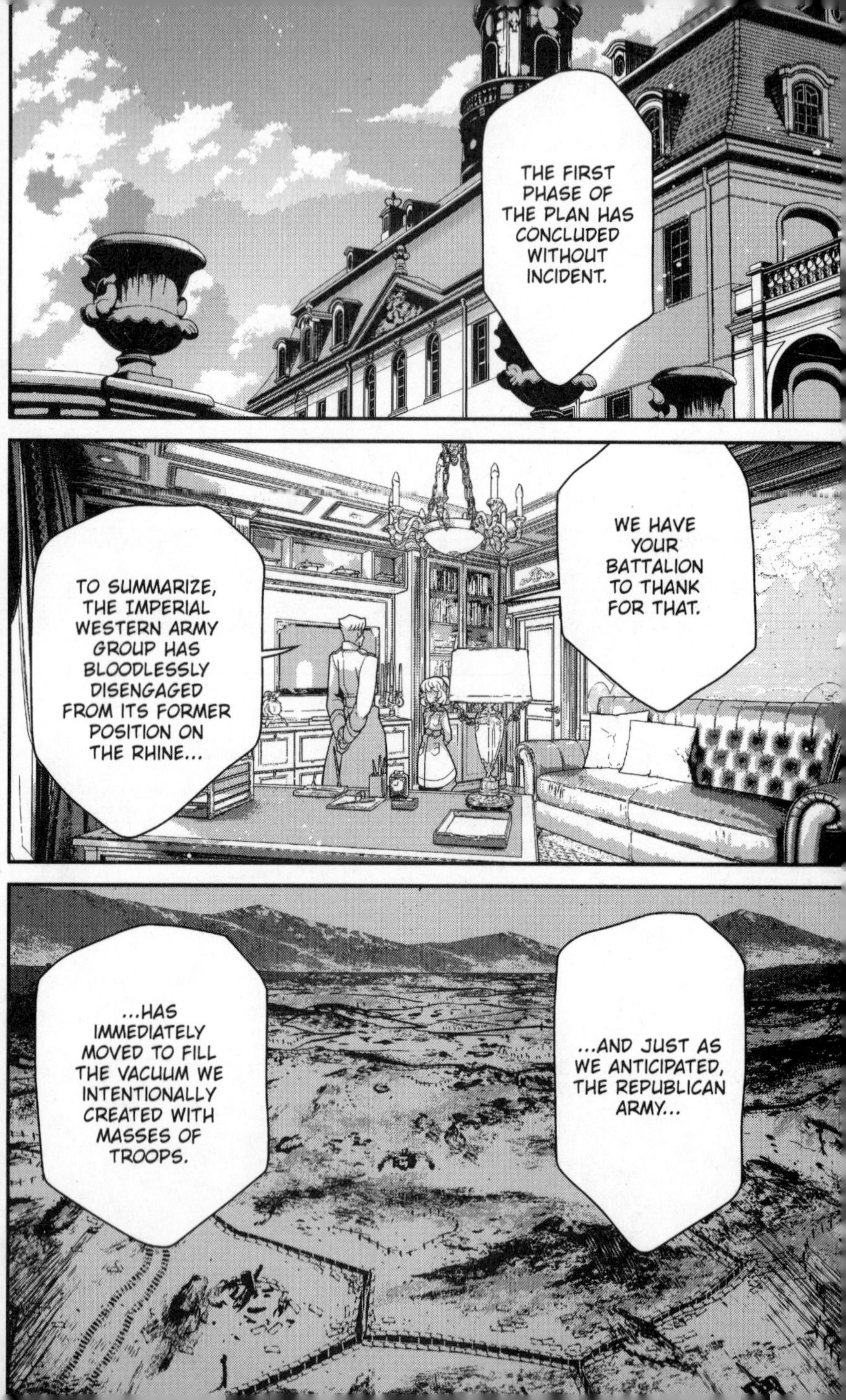
THE FIRST PHASE OF THE PLAN HAS CONCLUDED WITHOUT INCIDENT.
WE HAVE YOUR BATTALION TO THANK FOR THAT.
TO SUMMARIZE, THE IMPERIAL WESTERN ARMY GROUP HAS BLOODLESSLY DISENGAGED FROM ITS FORMER POSITION ON THE RHINE...
...AND JUST AS WE ANTICIPATED, THE REPUBLICAN ARMY...
...HAS IMMEDIATELY MOVED TO FILL THE VACUUM WE INTENTIONALLY CREATED WITH MASSES OF TROOPS.

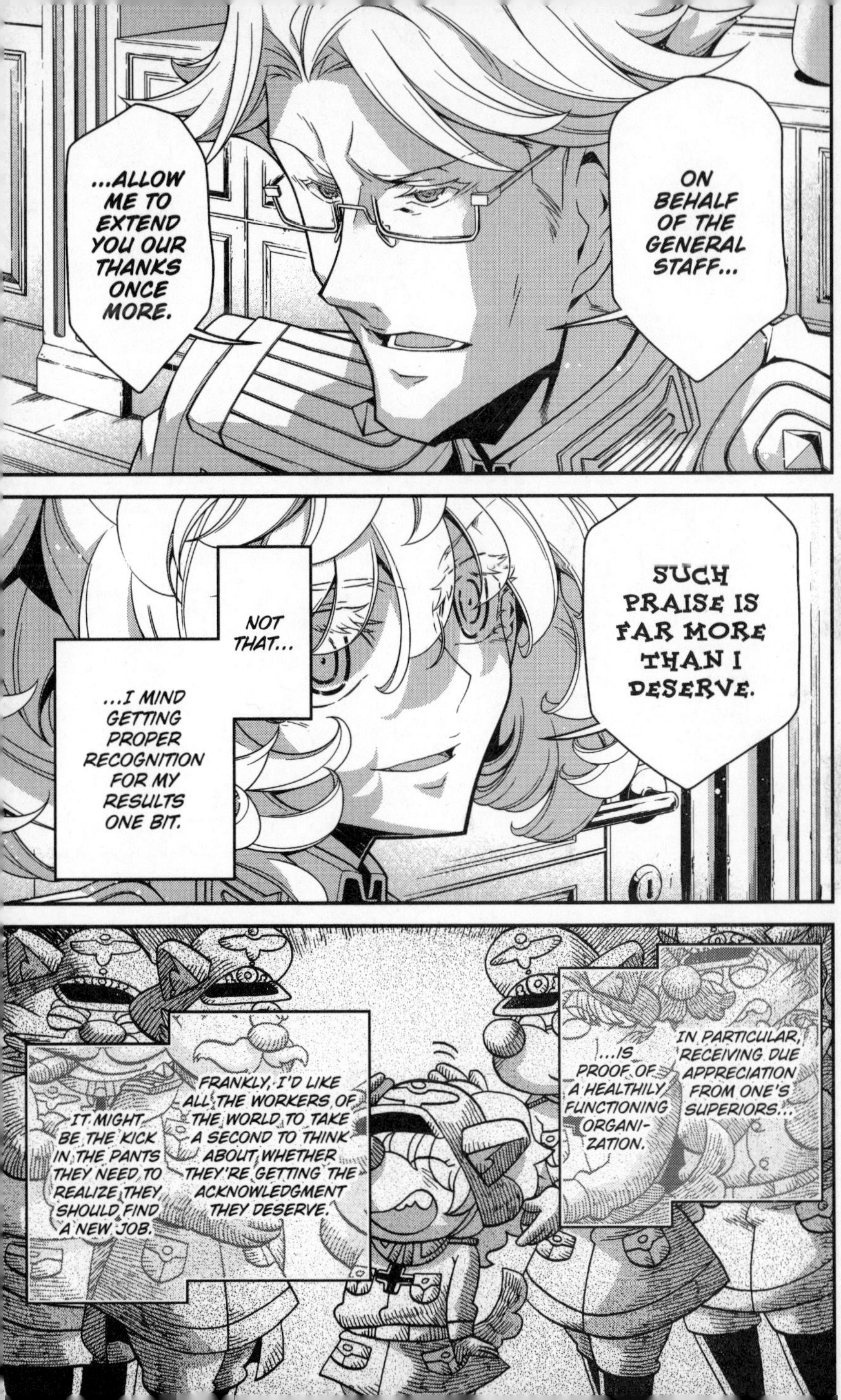
ON BEHALF OF THE GENERAL STAFF...
...ALLOW ME TO EXTEND YOU OUR THANKS ONCE MORE.
SUCH PRAISE IS FAR MORE THAN I DESERVE.
NOT THAT...
...I MIND GETTING PROPER RECOGNITION FOR MY RESULTS ONE BIT.
IN PARTICULAR, RECEIVING DUE APPRECIATION FROM ONE'S SUPERIORS...
...IS PROOF OF A HEALTHILY FUNCTIONING ORGANI-ZATION.
FRANKLY, I'D LIKE ALL THE WORKERS OF THE WORLD TO TAKE A SECOND TO THINK ABOUT WHETHER THEY'RE GETTING THE ACKNOWLEDGMENT THEY DESERVE.
IT MIGHT BE THE KICK IN THE PANTS THEY NEED TO REALIZE THEY SHOULD FIND A NEW JOB.

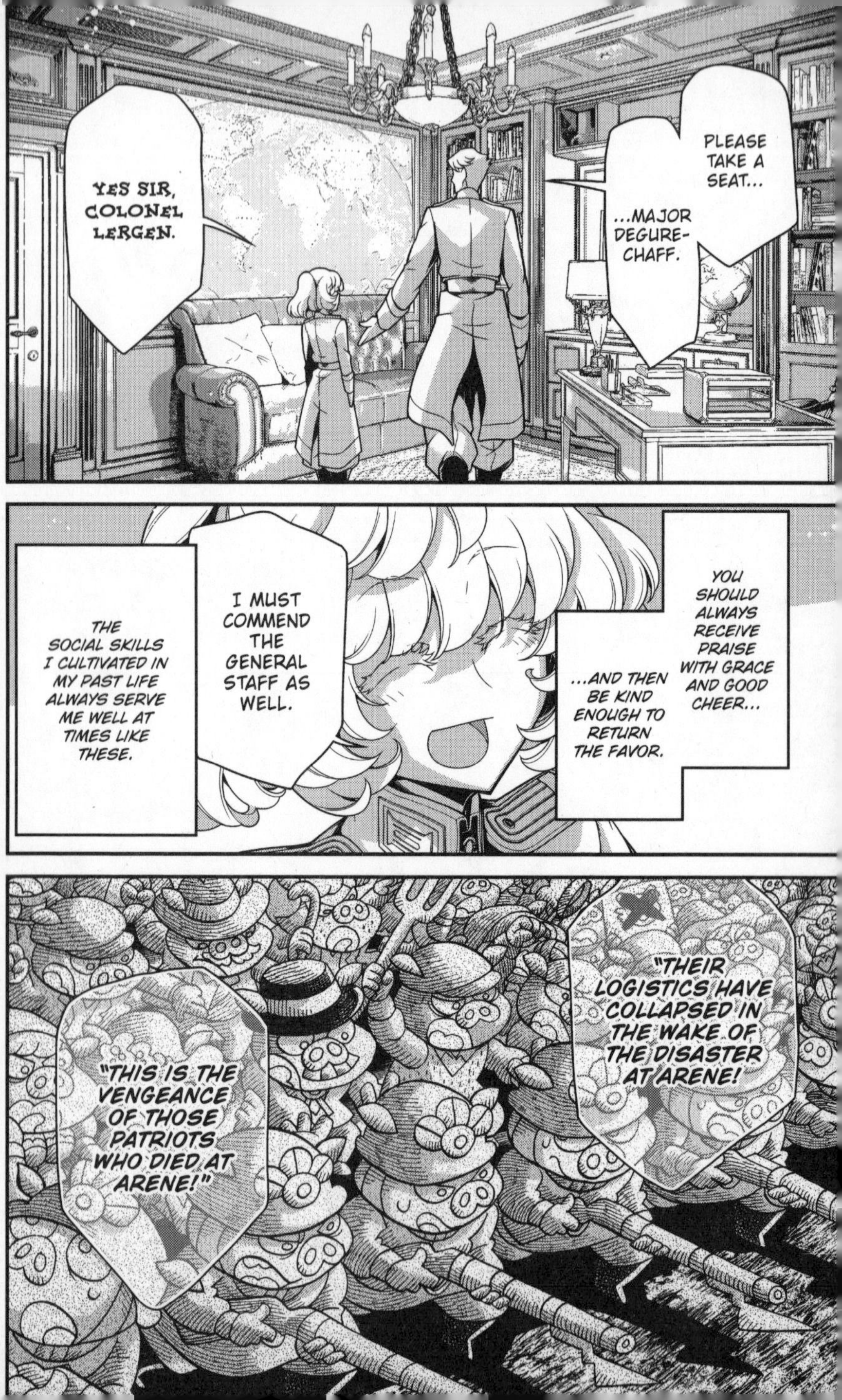
PLEASE TAKE A SEAT...
...MAJOR DEGURE-CHAFF.
YES SIR, COLONEL LERGEN.
YOU SHOULD ALWAYS RECEIVE PRAISE WITH GRACE AND GOOD CHEER...
...AND THEN BE KIND ENOUGH TO RETURN THE FAVOR.
I MUST COMMEND THE GENERAL STAFF AS WELL.
THE SOCIAL SKILLS I CULTIVATED IN MY PAST LIFE ALWAYS SERVE ME WELL AT TIMES LIKE THESE.
"THEIR LOGISTICS HAVE COLLAPSED IN THE WAKE OF THE DISASTER AT ARENE!
"THIS IS THE VENGEANCE OF THOSE PATRIOTS WHO DIED AT ARENE!"

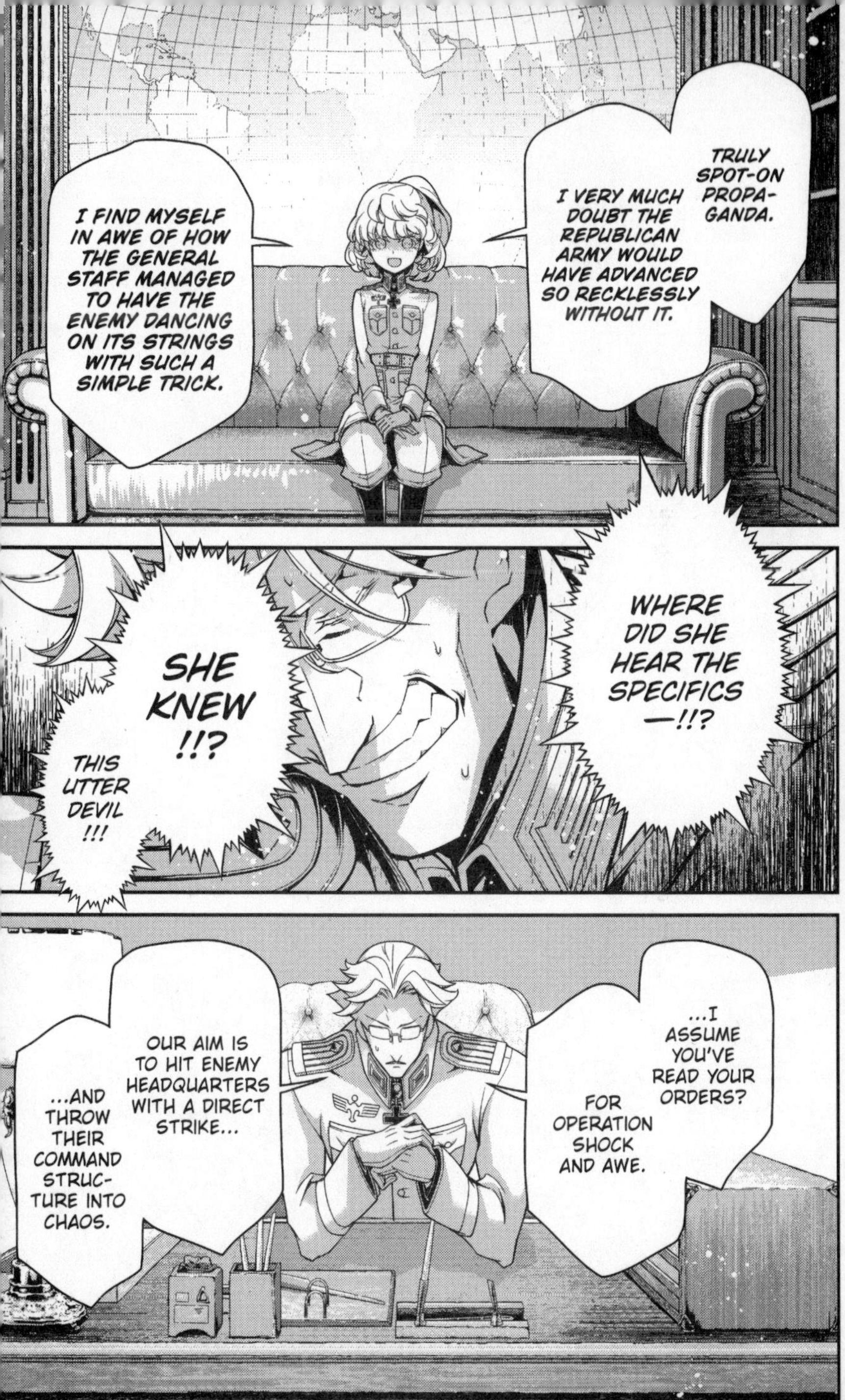
TRULY SPOT-ON PROPA-GANDA.
I VERY MUCH DOUBT THE REPUBLICAN ARMY WOULD HAVE ADVANCED SO RECKLESSLY WITHOUT IT.
I FIND MYSELF IN AWE OF HOW THE GENERAL STAFF MANAGED TO HAVE THE ENEMY DANCING ON ITS STRINGS WITH SUCH A SIMPLE TRICK.
WHERE DID SHE HEAR THE SPECIFICS—!!?
SHE KNEW!!?
THIS UTTER DEVIL!!!
...I ASSUME YOU'VE READ YOUR ORDERS?
FOR OPERATION SHOCK AND AWE.
OUR AIM IS TO HIT ENEMY HEADQUARTERS WITH A DIRECT STRIKE...
...AND THROW THEIR COMMAND STRUC-TURE INTO CHAOS.

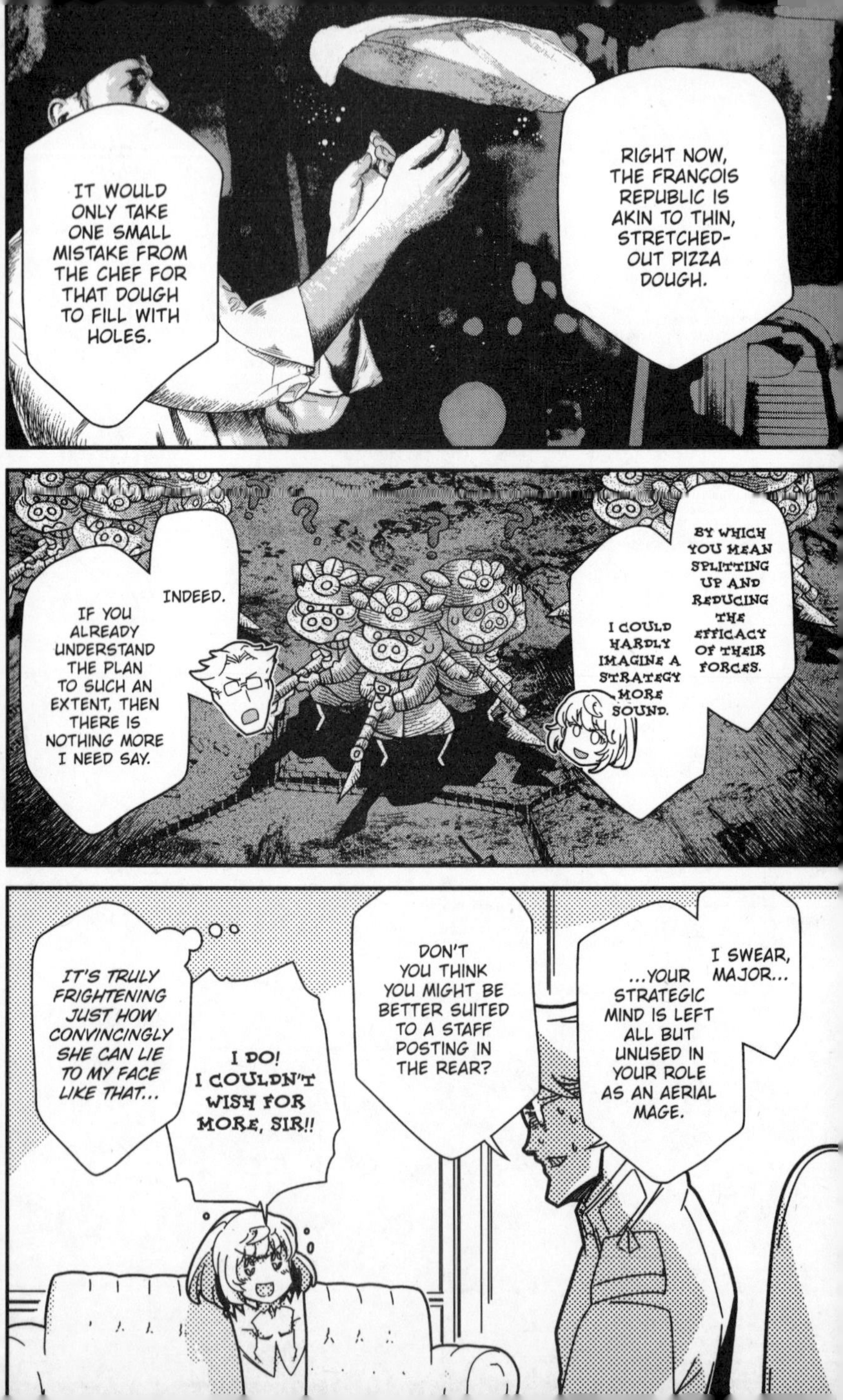
RIGHT NOW, THE FRANÇOIS REPUBLIC IS AKIN TO THIN, STRETCHED-OUT PIZZA DOUGH.
IT WOULD ONLY TAKE ONE SMALL MISTAKE FROM THE CHEF FOR THAT DOUGH TO FILL WITH HOLES.
BY WHICH YOU MEAN SPLITTING UP AND REDUCING THE EFFICACY OF THEIR FORCES.
I COULD HARDLY IMAGINE A STRATEGY MORE SOUND.
INDEED.
IF YOU ALREADY UNDERSTAND THE PLAN TO SUCH AN EXTENT, THEN THERE IS NOTHING MORE I NEED SAY.
I SWEAR, MAJOR...
...YOUR STRATEGIC MIND IS LEFT ALL BUT UNUSED IN YOUR ROLE AS AN AERIAL MAGE.
DON'T YOU THINK YOU MIGHT BE BETTER SUITED TO A STAFF POSTING IN THE REAR?
I DO! I COULDN'T WISH FOR MORE, SIR!!
IT'S TRULY FRIGHTENING JUST HOW CONVINCINGLY SHE CAN LIE TO MY FACE LIKE THAT...

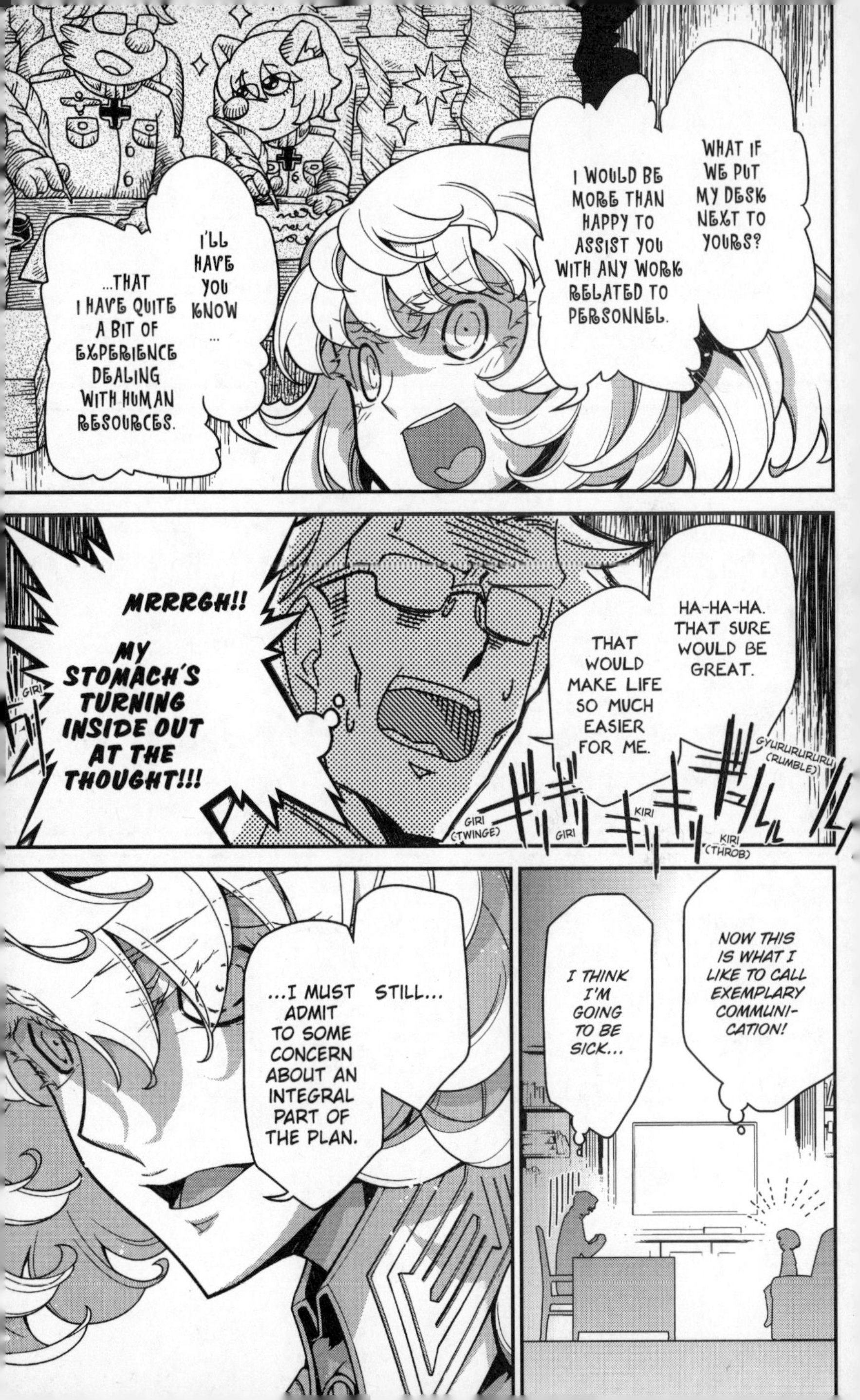
WHAT IF WE PUT MY DESK NEXT TO YOURS?
I WOULD BE MORE THAN HAPPY TO ASSIST YOU WITH ANY WORK RELATED TO PERSONNEL.
I'LL HAVE YOU KNOW...
...THAT I HAVE QUITE A BIT OF EXPERIENCE DEALING WITH HUMAN RESOURCES.
HA-HA-HA. THAT SURE WOULD BE GREAT.
THAT WOULD MAKE LIFE SO MUCH EASIER FOR ME.
GYURURURURU (RUMBLE)
KIRI (THROB)
KIRI
GIRI
GIRI (TWINGE)
MRRRGH!!
MY STOMACH'S TURNING INSIDE OUT AT THE THOUGHT!!!
GIRI
NOW THIS IS WHAT I LIKE TO CALL EXEMPLARY COMMUNI-CATION!
I THINK I'M GOING TO BE SICK...
STILL...
...I MUST ADMIT TO SOME CONCERN ABOUT AN INTEGRAL PART OF THE PLAN.

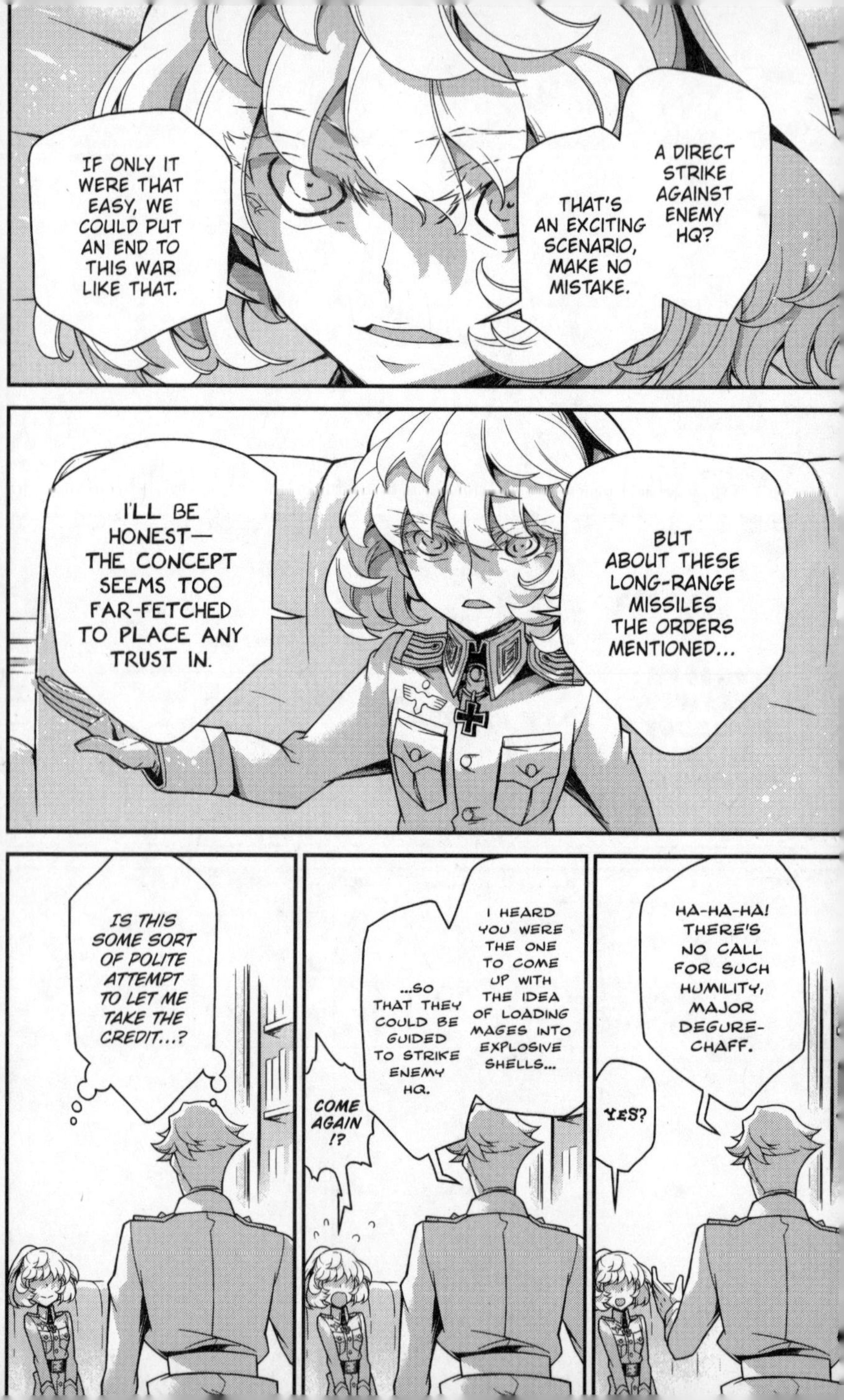
A DIRECT STRIKE AGAINST ENEMY HQ?
THAT'S AN EXCITING SCENARIO, MAKE NO MISTAKE.
IF ONLY IT WERE THAT EASY, WE COULD PUT AN END TO THIS WAR LIKE THAT.
BUT ABOUT THESE LONG-RANGE MISSILES THE ORDERS MENTIONED...
I'LL BE HONEST—THE CONCEPT SEEMS TOO FAR-FETCHED TO PLACE ANY TRUST IN.
HA-HA-HA! THERE'S NO CALL FOR SUCH HUMILITY, MAJOR DEGURE-CHAFF.
YES?
I HEARD YOU WERE THE ONE TO COME UP WITH THE IDEA OF LOADING MAGES INTO EXPLOSIVE SHELLS...
...SO THAT THEY COULD BE GUIDED TO STRIKE ENEMY HQ.
COME AGAIN!?
IS THIS SOME SORT OF POLITE ATTEMPT TO LET ME TAKE THE CREDIT...?

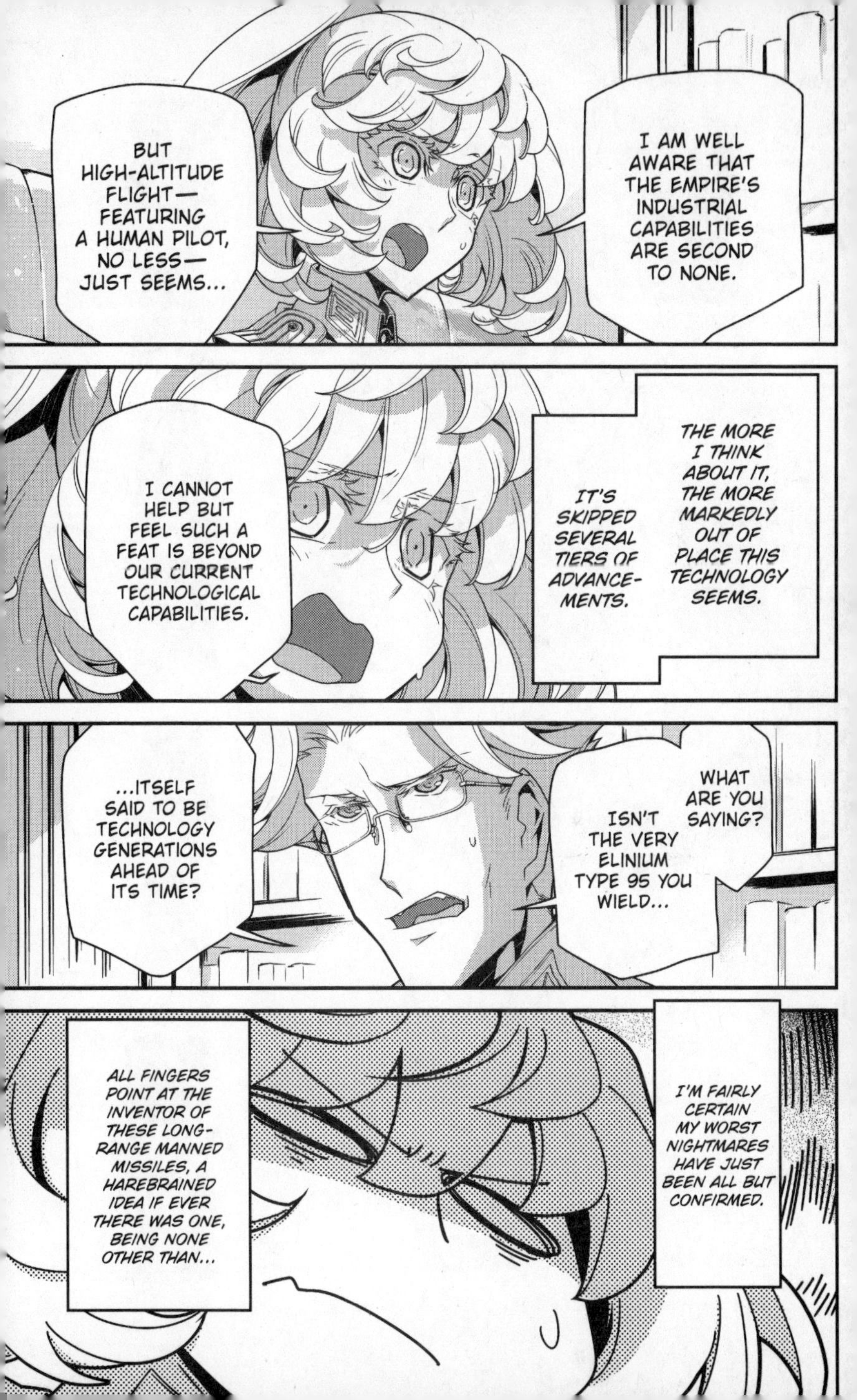
I AM WELL AWARE THAT THE EMPIRE'S INDUSTRIAL CAPABILITIES ARE SECOND TO NONE.
BUT HIGH-ALTITUDE FLIGHT—FEATURING A HUMAN PILOT, NO LESS—JUST SEEMS...
THE MORE I THINK ABOUT IT, THE MORE MARKEDLY OUT OF PLACE THIS TECHNOLOGY SEEMS.
IT'S SKIPPED SEVERAL TIERS OF ADVANCE-MENTS.
I CANNOT HELP BUT FEEL SUCH A FEAT IS BEYOND OUR CURRENT TECHNOLOGICAL CAPABILITIES.
WHAT ARE YOU SAYING?
ISN'T THE VERY ELINIUM TYPE 95 YOU WIELD...
...ITSELF SAID TO BE TECHNOLOGY GENERATIONS AHEAD OF ITS TIME?
I'M FAIRLY CERTAIN MY WORST NIGHTMARES HAVE JUST BEEN ALL BUT CONFIRMED.
ALL FINGERS POINT AT THE INVENTOR OF THESE LONG-RANGE MANNED MISSILES, A HAREBRAINED IDEA IF EVER THERE WAS ONE, BEING NONE OTHER THAN...

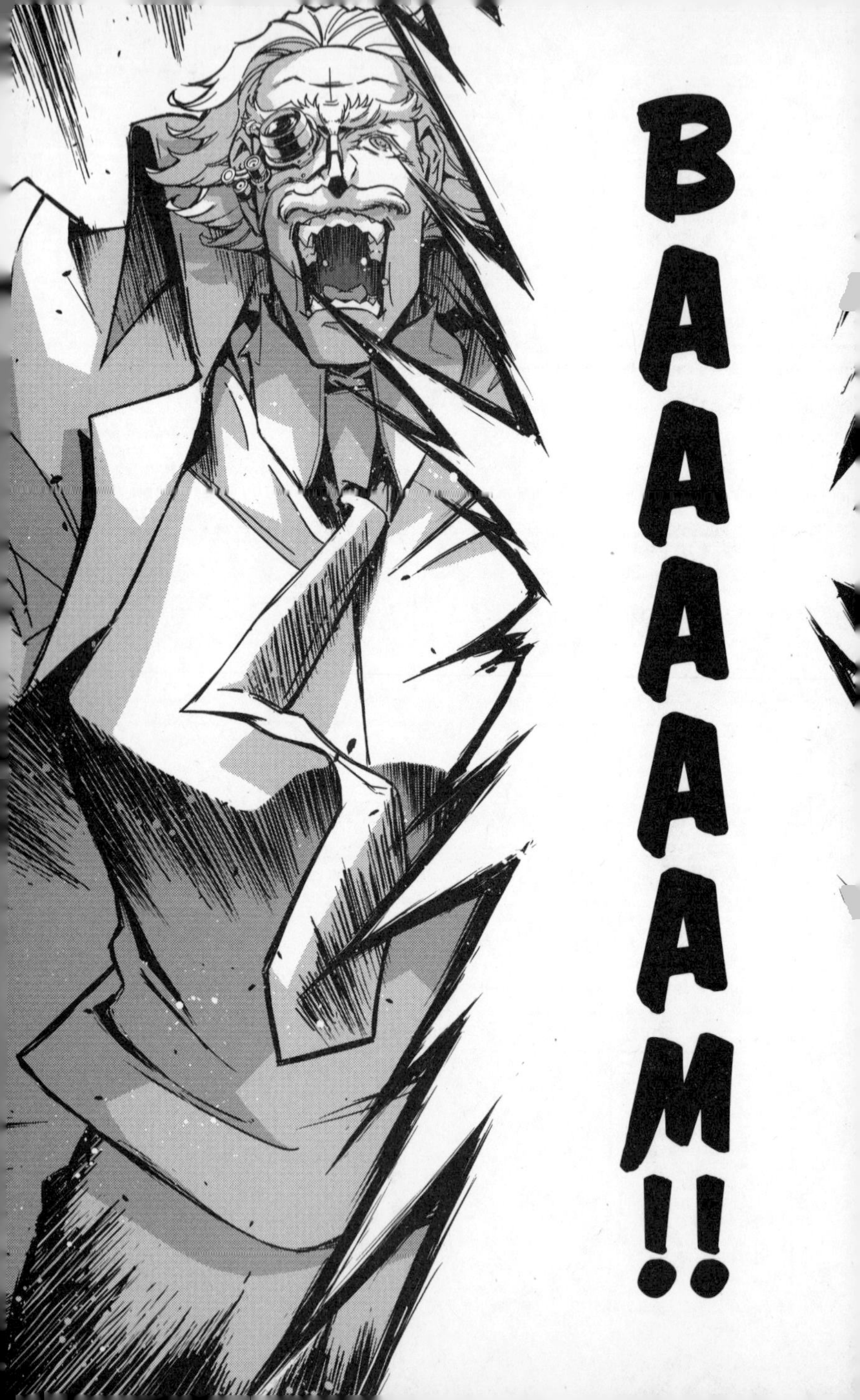
BAAAAAM!!

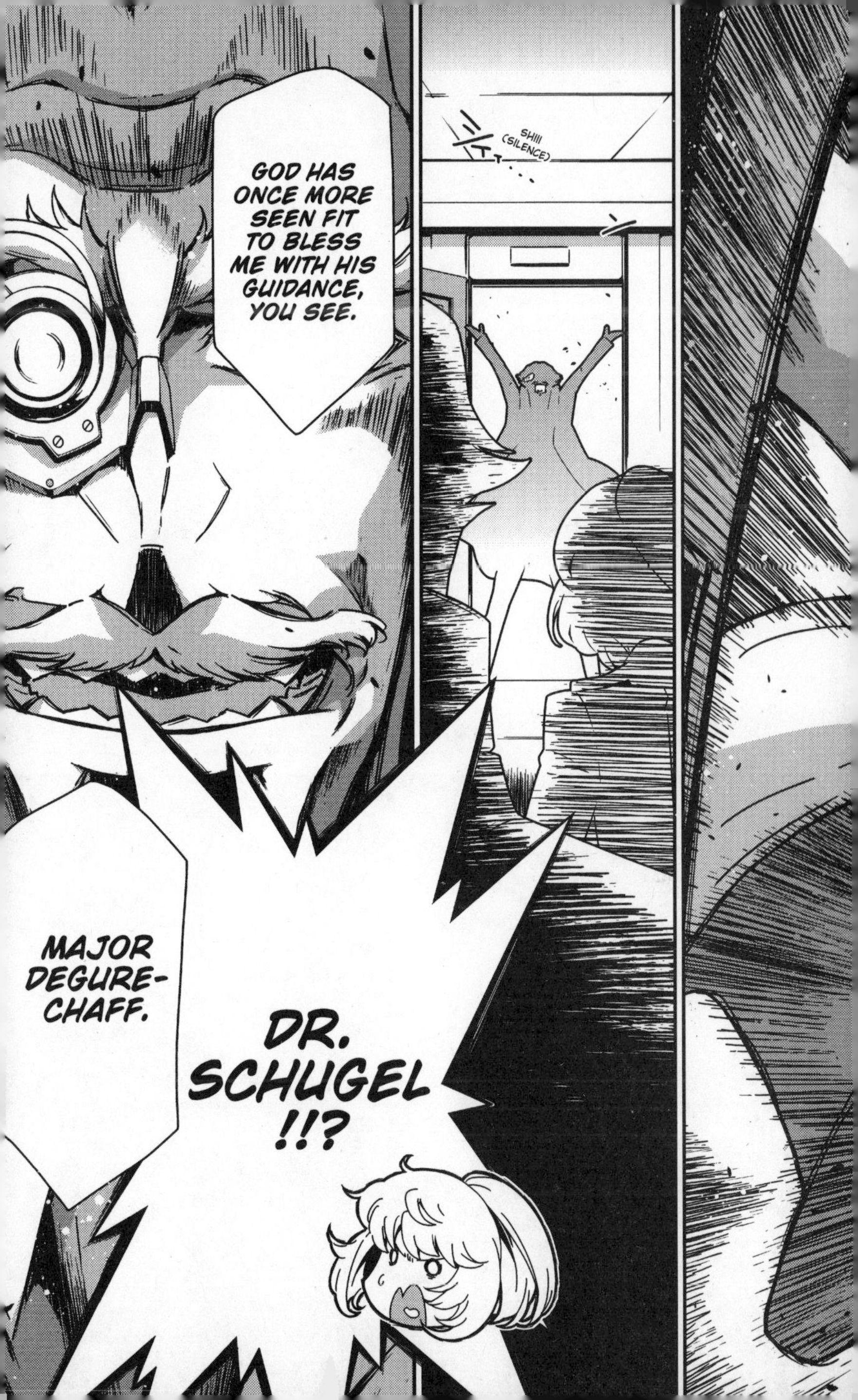
SHIII (SILENCE)
GOD HAS ONCE MORE SEEN FIT TO BLESS ME WITH HIS GUIDANCE, YOU SEE.
DR. SCHUGEL!!?
MAJOR DEGURE-CHAFF.

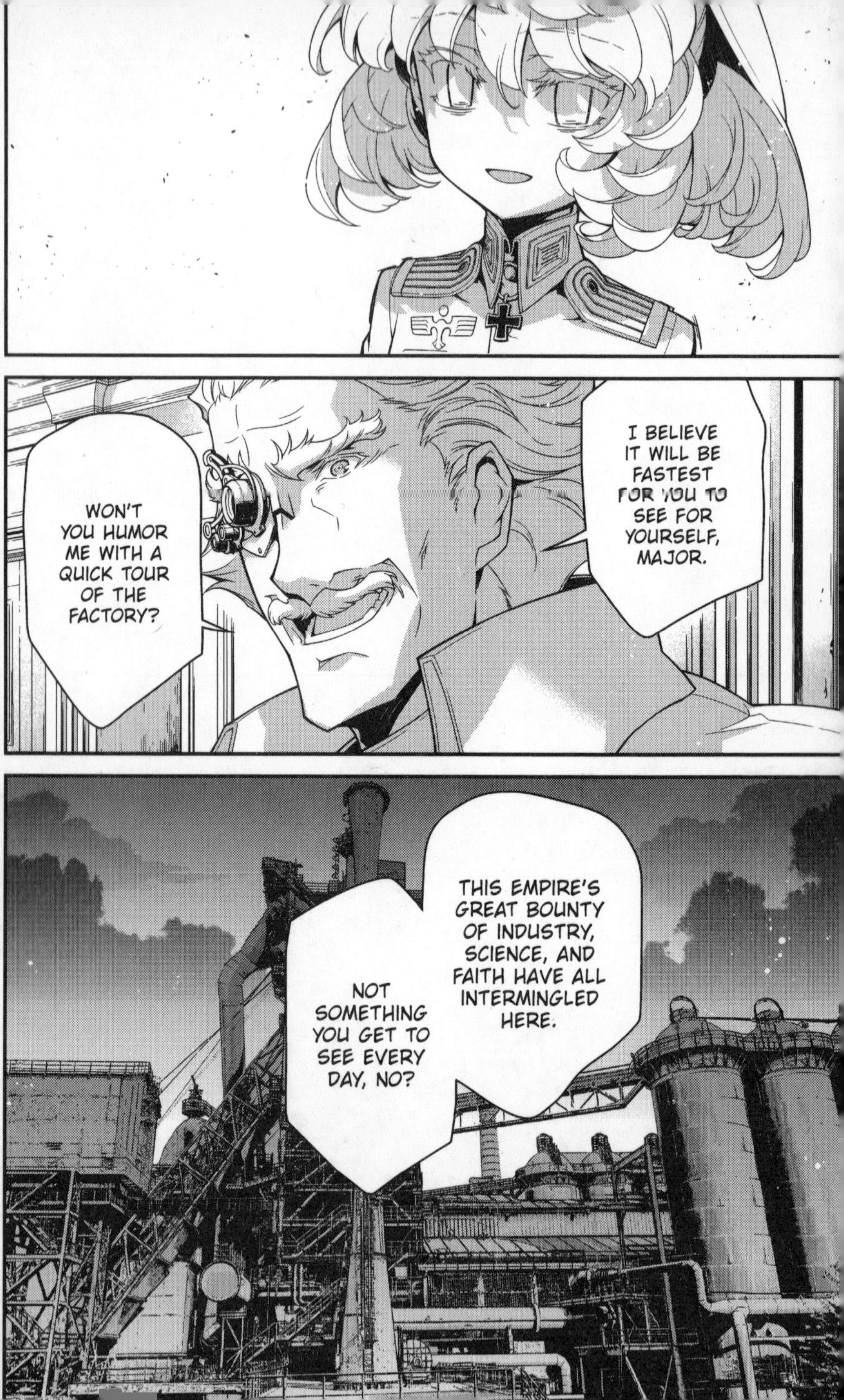
I BELIEVE IT WILL BE FASTEST FOR YOU TO SEE FOR YOURSELF, MAJOR.
WON'T YOU HUMOR ME WITH A QUICK TOUR OF THE FACTORY?
THIS EMPIRE'S GREAT BOUNTY OF INDUSTRY, SCIENCE, AND FAITH HAVE ALL INTERMINGLED HERE.
NOT SOMETHING YOU GET TO SEE EVERY DAY, NO?

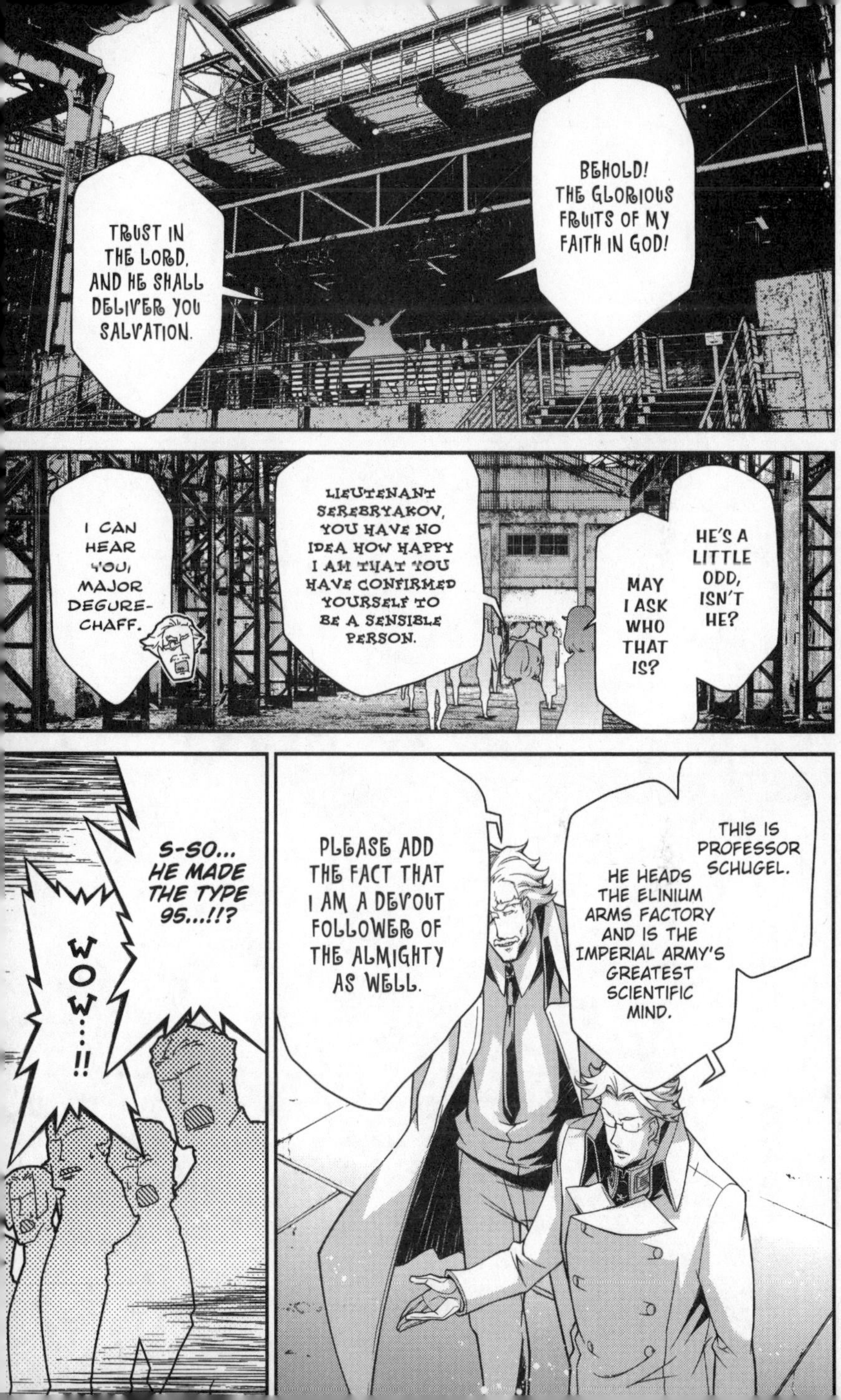
BEHOLD! THE GLORIOUS FRUITS OF MY FAITH IN GOD!
TRUST IN THE LORD, AND HE SHALL DELIVER YOU SALVATION.
HE'S A LITTLE ODD, ISN'T HE?
MAY I ASK WHO THAT IS?
LIEUTENANT SEREBRYAKOV, YOU HAVE NO IDEA HOW HAPPY I AM THAT YOU HAVE CONFIRMED YOURSELF TO BE A SENSIBLE PERSON.
I CAN HEAR YOU, MAJOR DEGURECHAFF.
THIS IS PROFESSOR SCHUGEL.
HE HEADS THE ELINIUM ARMS FACTORY AND IS THE IMPERIAL ARMY'S GREATEST SCIENTIFIC MIND.
PLEASE ADD THE FACT THAT I AM A DEVOUT FOLLOWER OF THE ALMIGHTY AS WELL.
S-SO... HE MADE THE TYPE 95...!!?
WOW...!!

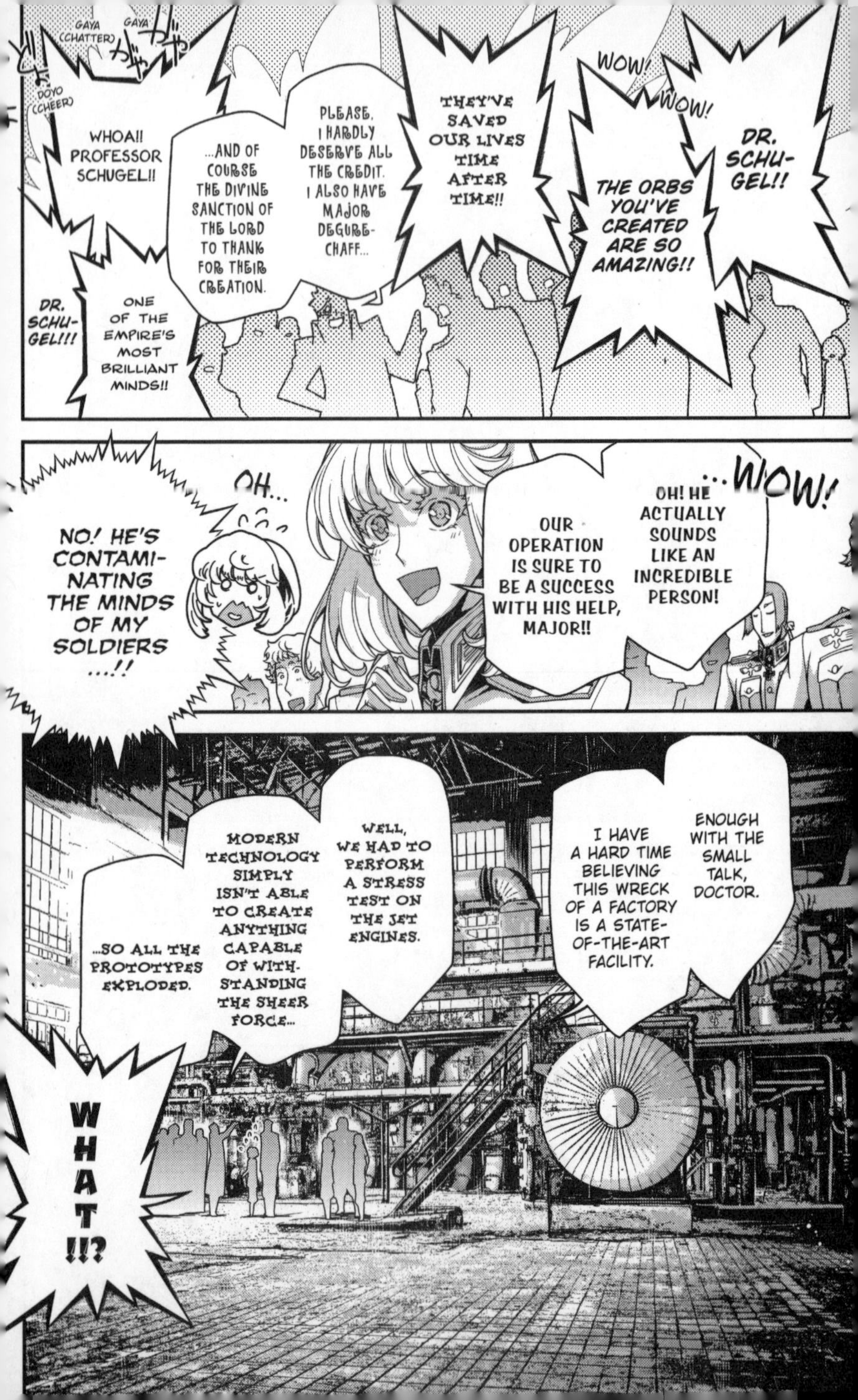
DR. SCHU-GEL!!
WOW!
WOW!
THE ORBS YOU'VE CREATED ARE SO AMAZING!!
THEY'VE SAVED OUR LIVES TIME AFTER TIME!!
PLEASE. I HARDLY DESERVE ALL THE CREDIT. I ALSO HAVE MAJOR DEGURE-CHAFF...
...AND OF COURSE THE DIVINE SANCTION OF THE LORD TO THANK FOR THEIR CREATION.
GAYA GAYA (CHATTER)
DOYO (CHEER)
WHOA!! PROFESSOR SCHUGEL!!
ONE OF THE EMPIRE'S MOST BRILLIANT MINDS!!
DR. SCHU-GEL!!!
...WOW!
OH! HE ACTUALLY SOUNDS LIKE AN INCREDIBLE PERSON!
OUR OPERATION IS SURE TO BE A SUCCESS WITH HIS HELP, MAJOR!!
OH...
NO! HE'S CONTAMI-NATING THE MINDS OF MY SOLDIERS ...!!
ENOUGH WITH THE SMALL TALK, DOCTOR.
I HAVE A HARD TIME BELIEVING THIS WRECK OF A FACTORY IS A STATE-OF-THE-ART FACILITY.
WELL, WE HAD TO PERFORM A STRESS TEST ON THE JET ENGINES.
MODERN TECHNOLOGY SIMPLY ISN'T ABLE TO CREATE ANYTHING CAPABLE OF WITH-STANDING THE SHEER FORCE...
...SO ALL THE PROTOTYPES EXPLODED.
WHAT!!?

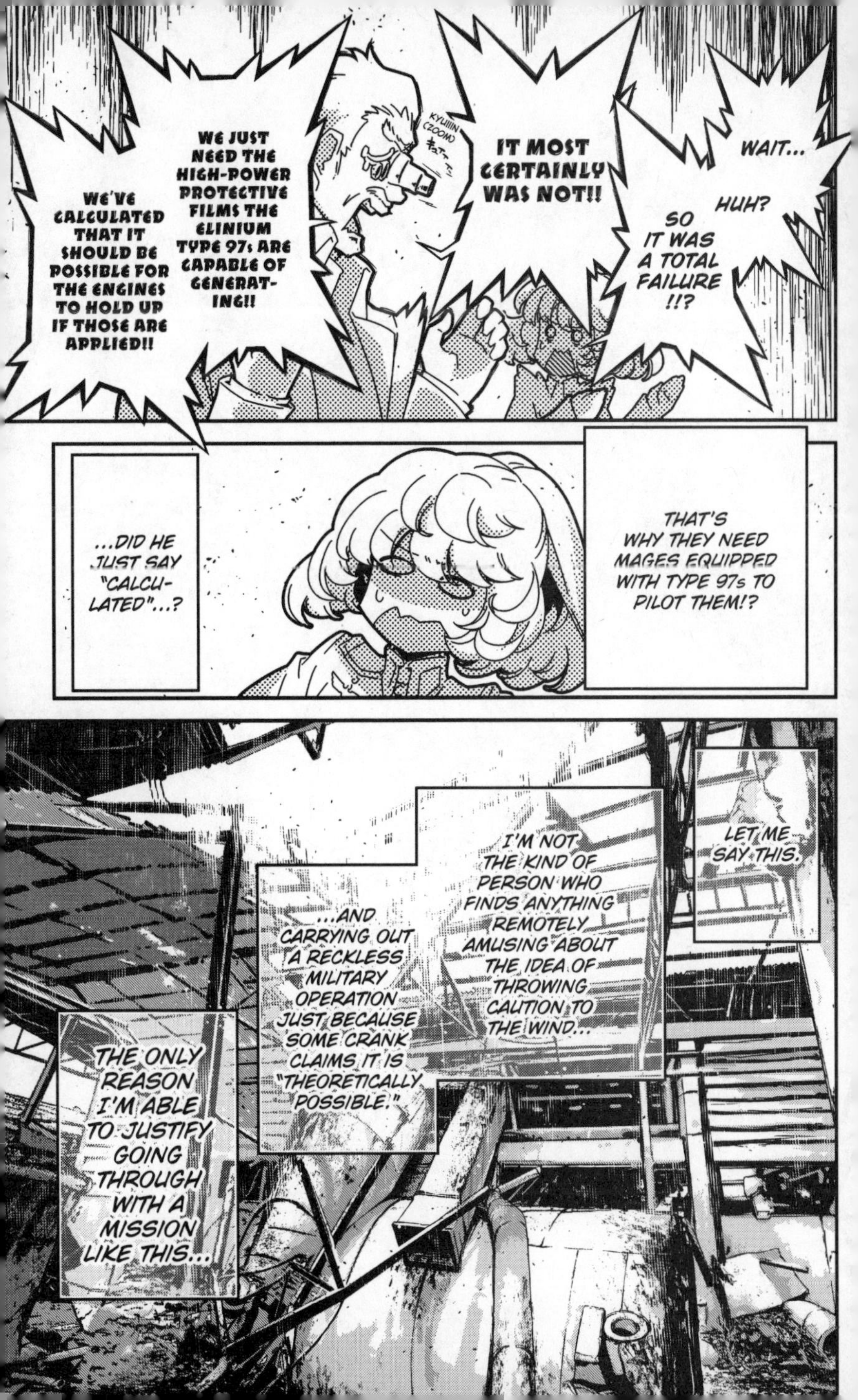
WAIT...
HUH?
SO IT WAS A TOTAL FAILURE!!?
IT MOST CERTAINLY WAS NOT!!
KYUIIIN (ZOOM)
WE JUST NEED THE HIGH-POWER PROTECTIVE FILMS THE ELINIUM TYPE 97s ARE CAPABLE OF GENERAT-ING!!
WE'VE CALCULATED THAT IT SHOULD BE POSSIBLE FOR THE ENGINES TO HOLD UP IF THOSE ARE APPLIED!!
THAT'S WHY THEY NEED MAGES EQUIPPED WITH TYPE 97s TO PILOT THEM!?
...DID HE JUST SAY "CALCU-LATED"...?
LET ME SAY THIS.
I'M NOT THE KIND OF PERSON WHO FINDS ANYTHING REMOTELY AMUSING ABOUT THE IDEA OF THROWING CAUTION TO THE WIND...
...AND CARRYING OUT A RECKLESS MILITARY OPERATION JUST BECAUSE SOME CRANK CLAIMS IT IS "THEORETICALLY POSSIBLE."
THE ONLY REASON I'M ABLE TO JUSTIFY GOING THROUGH WITH A MISSION LIKE THIS...

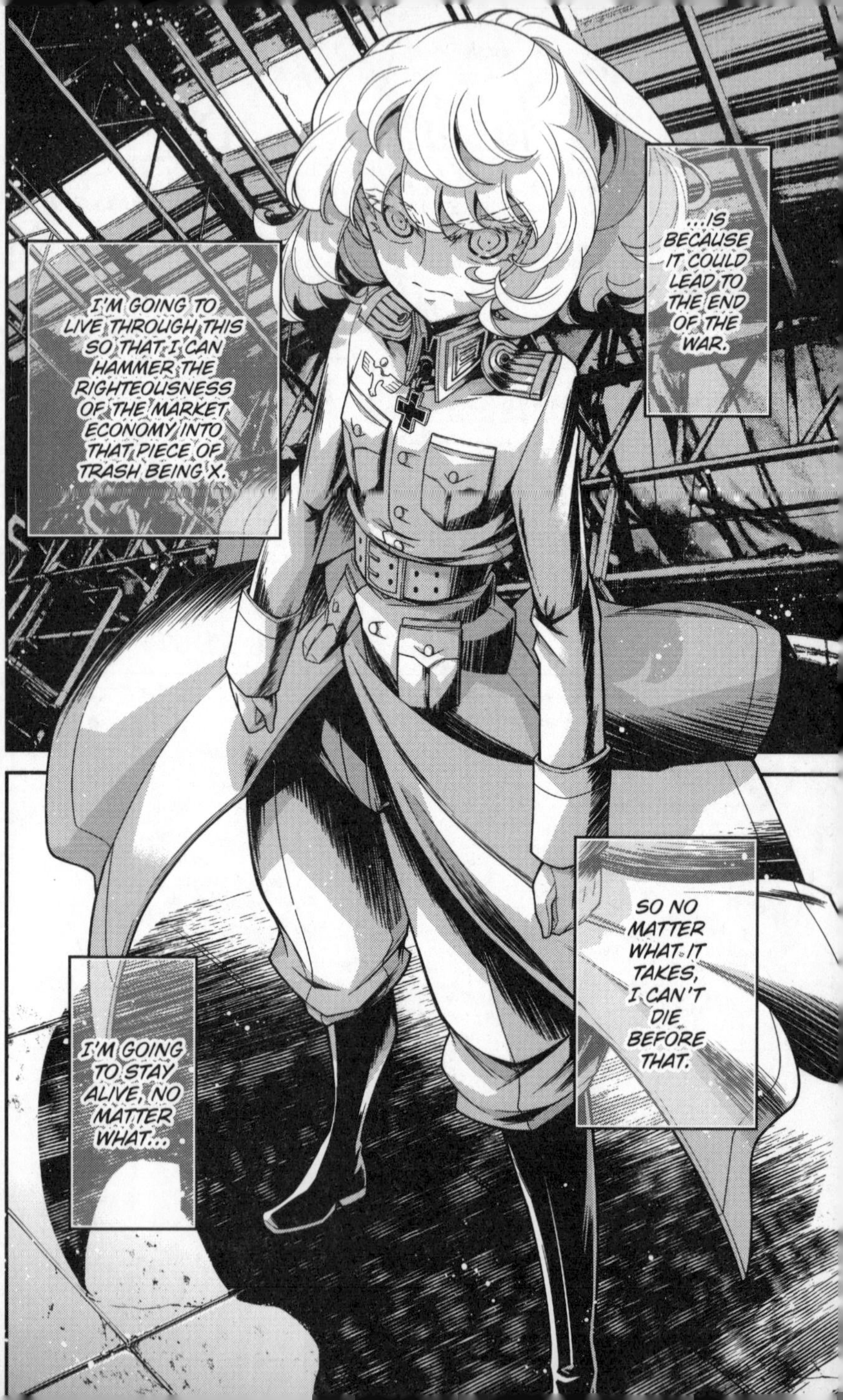
...IS BECAUSE IT COULD LEAD TO THE END OF THE WAR.
I'M GOING TO LIVE THROUGH THIS SO THAT I CAN HAMMER THE RIGHTEOUSNESS OF THE MARKET ECONOMY INTO THAT PIECE OF TRASH BEING X.
SO NO MATTER WHAT IT TAKES, I CAN'T DIE BEFORE THAT.
I'M GOING TO STAY ALIVE, NO MATTER WHAT...

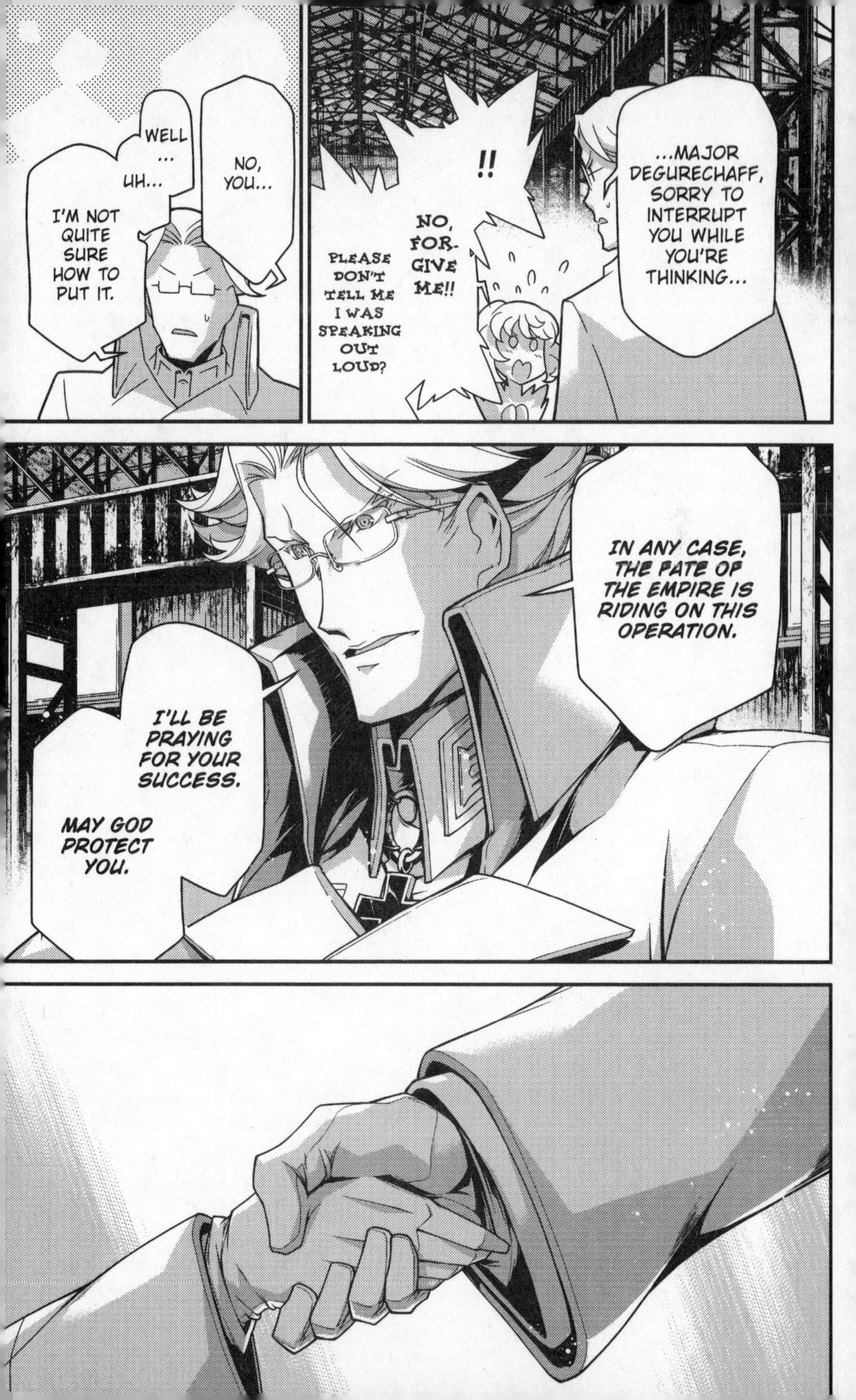
...MAJOR DEGURECHAFF, SORRY TO INTERRUPT YOU WHILE YOU'RE THINKING...
!!
NO, FOR-GIVE ME!!
PLEASE DON'T TELL ME I WAS SPEAKING OUT LOUD?
NO, YOU...
WELL ... UH...
I'M NOT QUITE SURE HOW TO PUT IT.
IN ANY CASE, THE FATE OF THE EMPIRE IS RIDING ON THIS OPERATION.
I'LL BE PRAYING FOR YOUR SUCCESS.
MAY GOD PROTECT YOU.

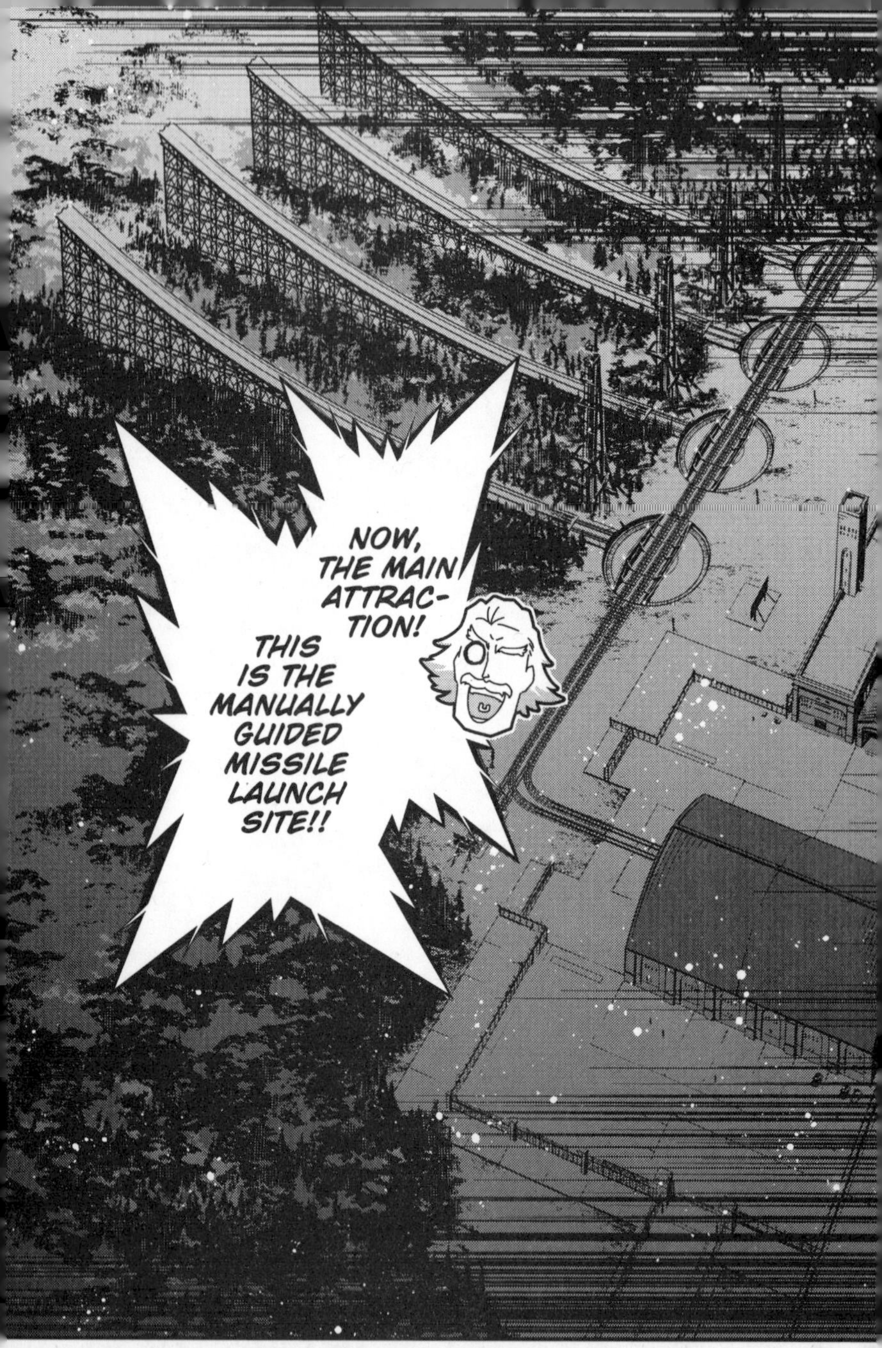
NOW, THE MAIN ATTRAC-TION!
THIS IS THE MANUALLY GUIDED MISSILE LAUNCH SITE!!

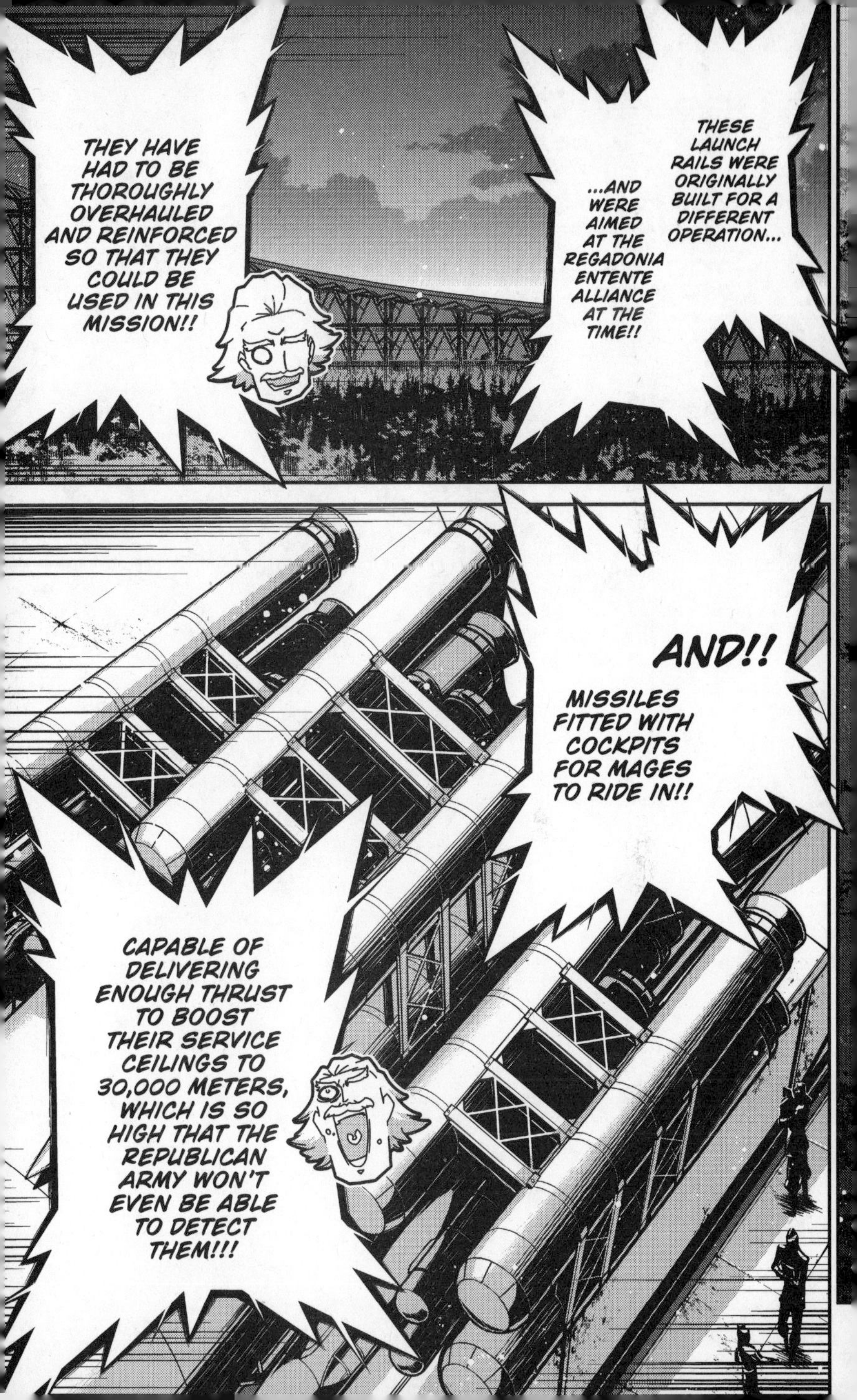
THESE LAUNCH RAILS WERE ORIGINALLY BUILT FOR A DIFFERENT OPERATION...
...AND WERE AIMED AT THE REGADONIA ENTENTE ALLIANCE AT THE TIME!!
THEY HAVE HAD TO BE THOROUGHLY OVERHAULED AND REINFORCED SO THAT THEY COULD BE USED IN THIS MISSION!!
AND!!
MISSILES FITTED WITH COCKPITS FOR MAGES TO RIDE IN!!
CAPABLE OF DELIVERING ENOUGH THRUST TO BOOST THEIR SERVICE CEILINGS TO 30,000 METERS, WHICH IS SO HIGH THAT THE REPUBLICAN ARMY WON'T EVEN BE ABLE TO DETECT THEM!!!

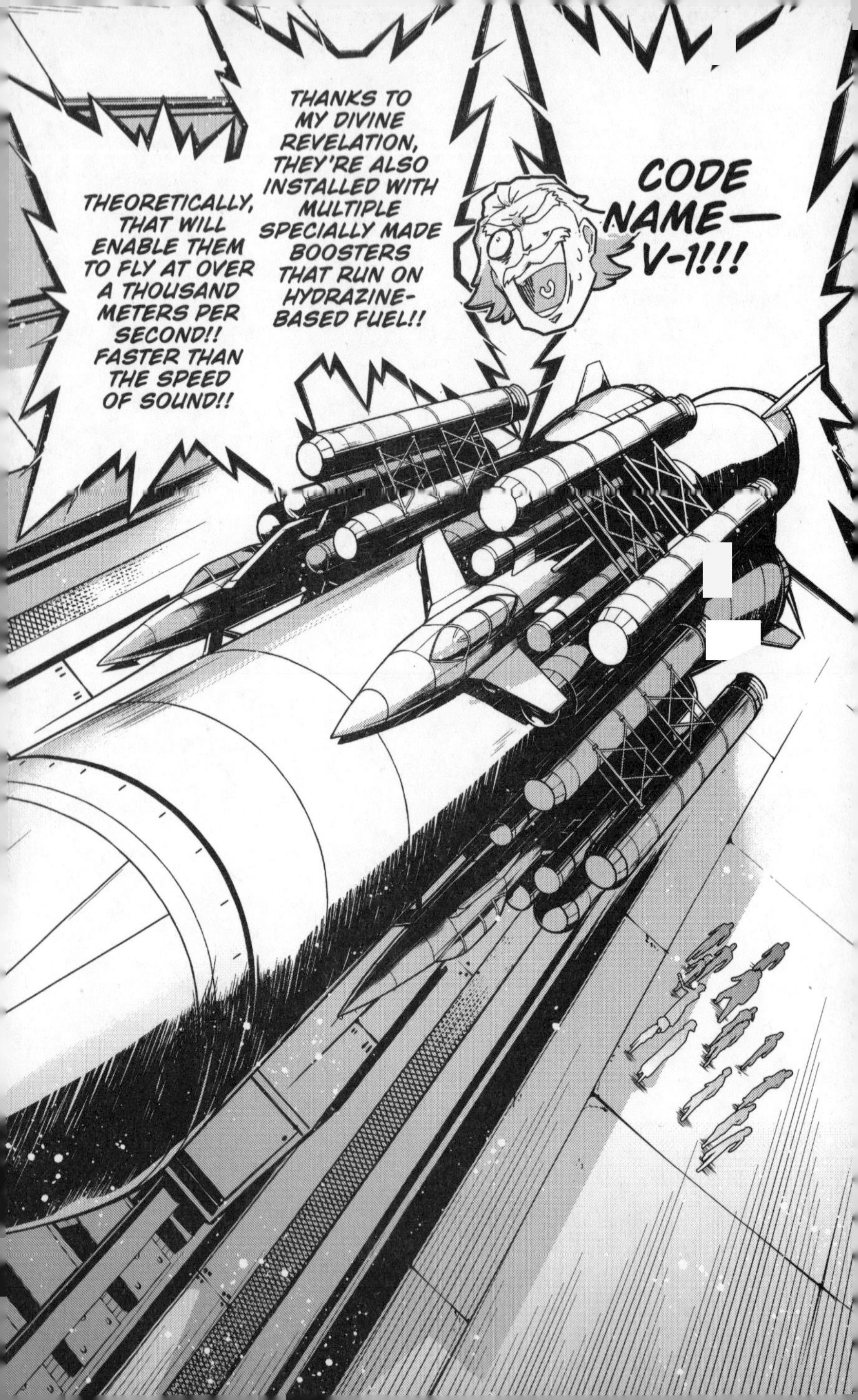
CODE NAME—V-1!!!
THANKS TO MY DIVINE REVELATION, THEY'RE ALSO INSTALLED WITH MULTIPLE SPECIALLY MADE BOOSTERS THAT RUN ON HYDRAZINE-BASED FUEL!!
THEORETICALLY, THAT WILL ENABLE THEM TO FLY AT OVER A THOUSAND METERS PER SECOND!! FASTER THAN THE SPEED OF SOUND!!

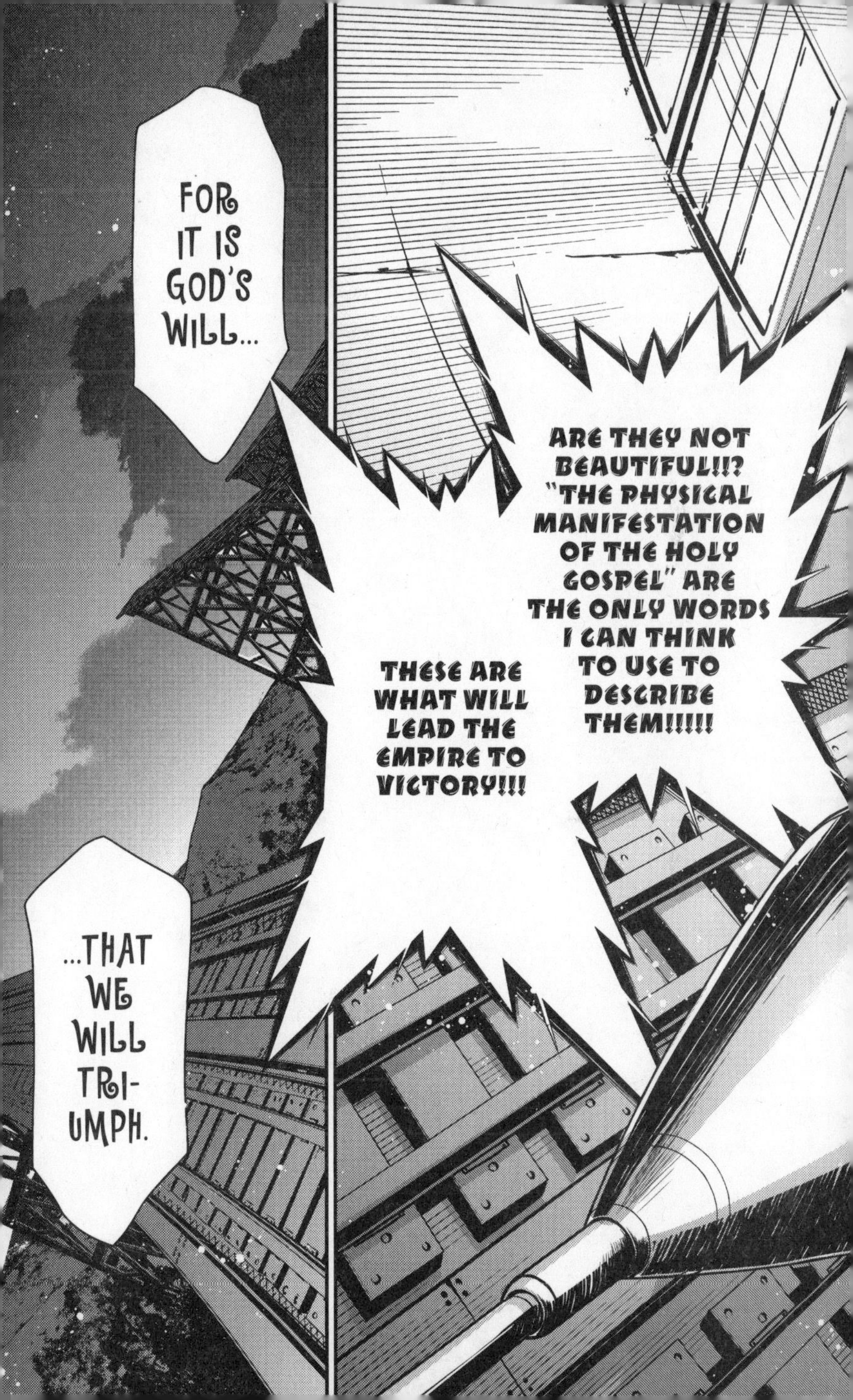
ARE THEY NOT BEAUTIFUL!!? "THE PHYSICAL MANIFESTATION OF THE HOLY GOSPEL" ARE THE ONLY WORDS I CAN THINK TO USE TO DESCRIBE THEM!!!!!
THESE ARE WHAT WILL LEAD THE EMPIRE TO VICTORY!!!
FOR IT IS GOD'S WILL...
...THAT WE WILL TRI-UMPH.

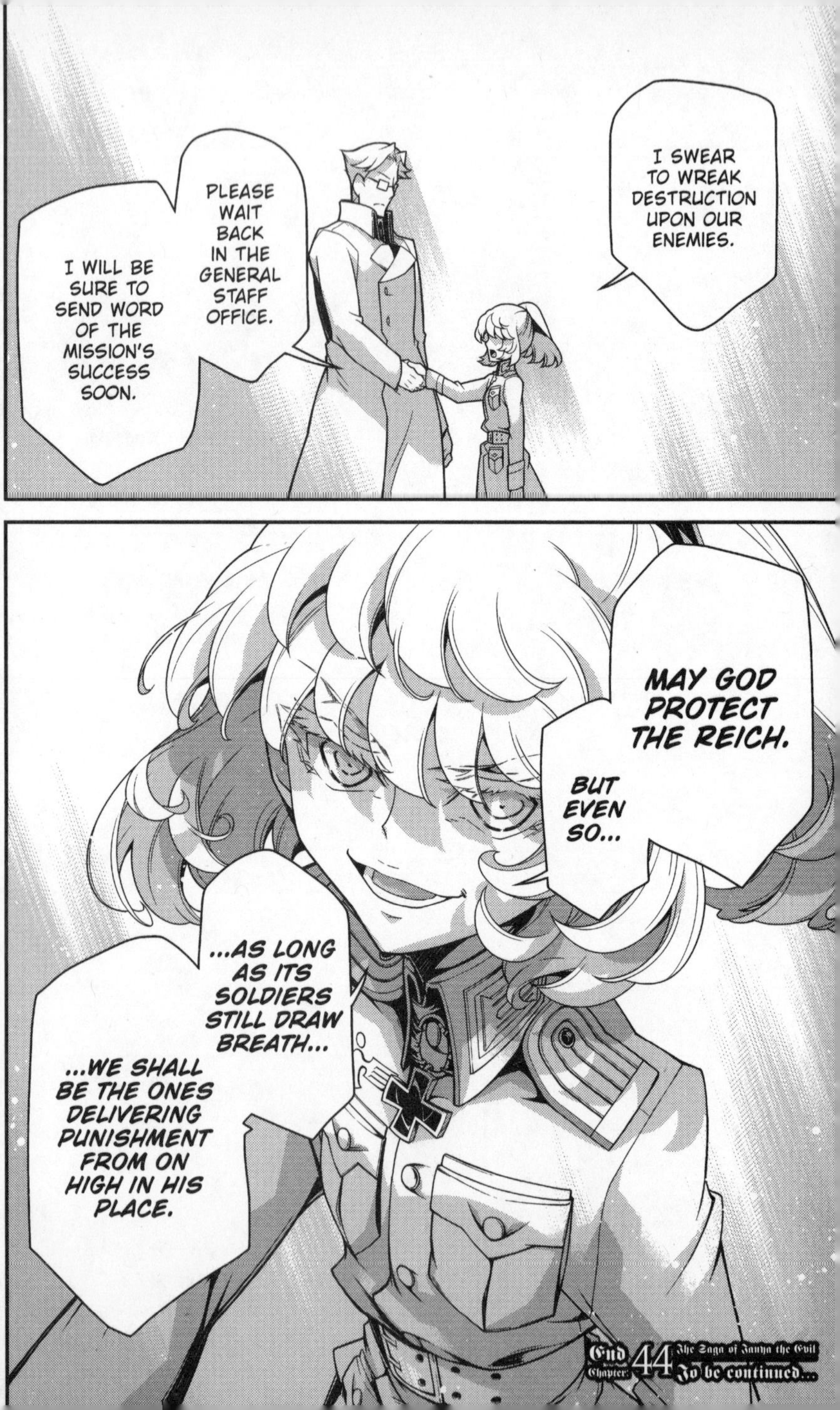
I SWEAR TO WREAK DESTRUCTION UPON OUR ENEMIES.
PLEASE WAIT BACK IN THE GENERAL STAFF OFFICE.
I WILL BE SURE TO SEND WORD OF THE MISSION'S SUCCESS SOON.
MAY GOD PROTECT THE REICH.
BUT EVEN SO...
...AS LONG AS ITS SOLDIERS STILL DRAW BREATH...
...WE SHALL BE THE ONES DELIVERING PUNISHMENT FROM ON HIGH IN HIS PLACE.
End Chapter 44 The Saga of Tanya the Evil
To be continued...

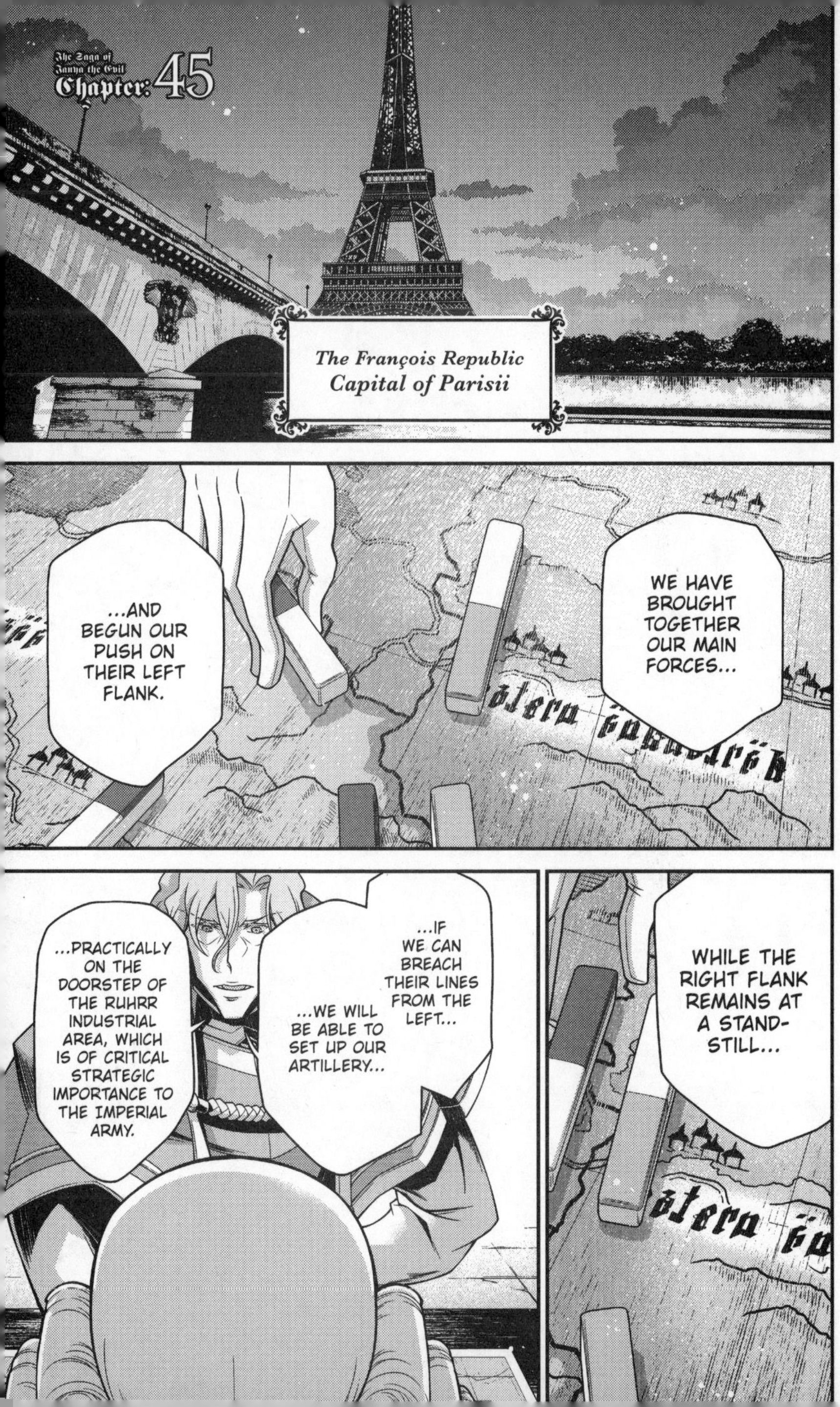
The Saga of Tanya the Evil Chapter: 45
The François Republic Capital of Parisii
WE HAVE BROUGHT TOGETHER OUR MAIN FORCES...
...AND BEGUN OUR PUSH ON THEIR LEFT FLANK.
WHILE THE RIGHT FLANK REMAINS AT A STAND-STILL...
...IF WE CAN BREACH THEIR LINES FROM THE LEFT...
...WE WILL BE ABLE TO SET UP OUR ARTILLERY...
...PRACTICALLY ON THE DOORSTEP OF THE RUHRR INDUSTRIAL AREA, WHICH IS OF CRITICAL STRATEGIC IMPORTANCE TO THE IMPERIAL ARMY.

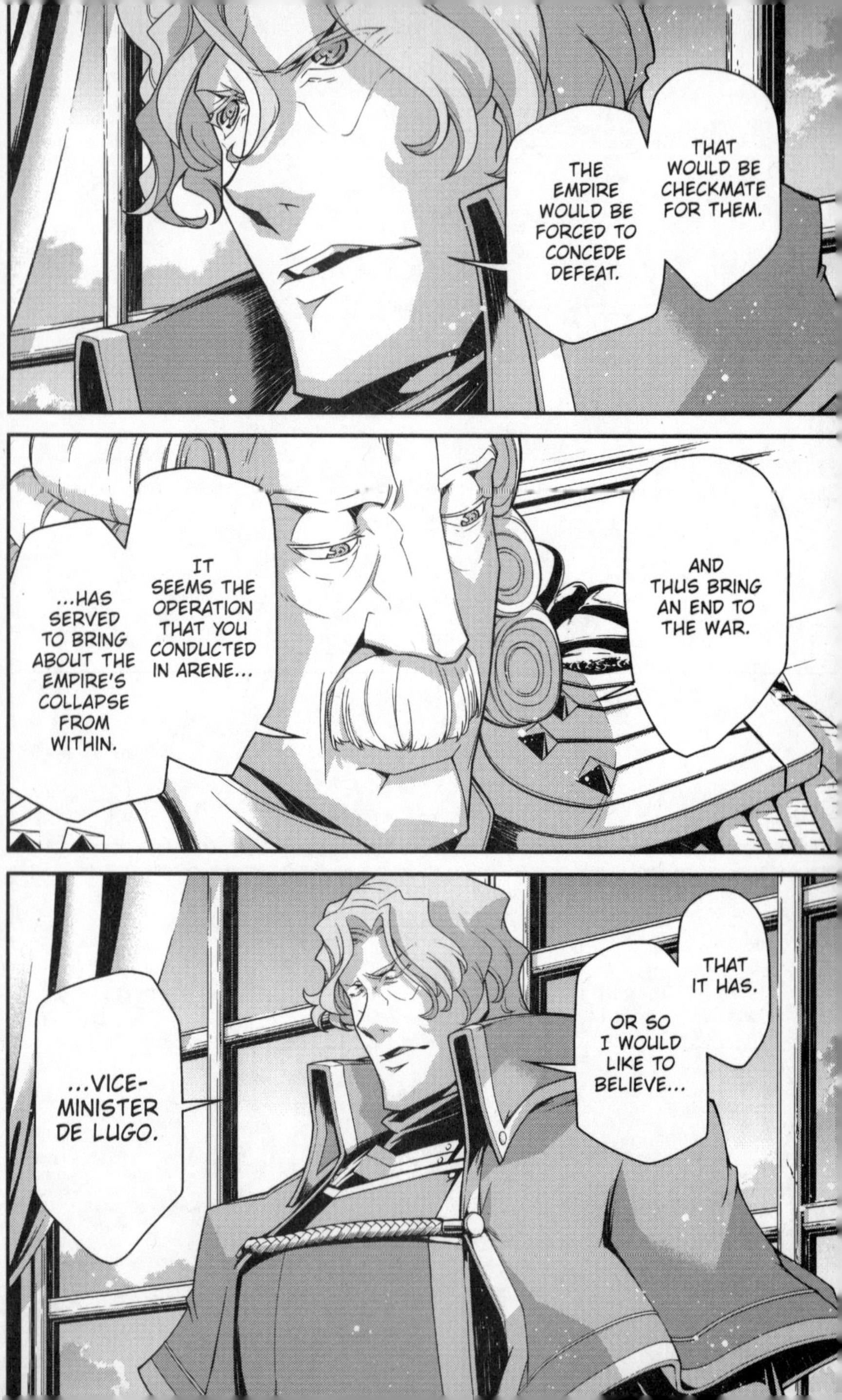
THAT WOULD BE CHECKMATE FOR THEM.
THE EMPIRE WOULD BE FORCED TO CONCEDE DEFEAT.
AND THUS BRING AN END TO THE WAR.
IT SEEMS THE OPERATION THAT YOU CONDUCTED IN ARENE...
...HAS SERVED TO BRING ABOUT THE EMPIRE'S COLLAPSE FROM WITHIN.
THAT IT HAS.
OR SO I WOULD LIKE TO BELIEVE...
...VICE-MINISTER DE LUGO.

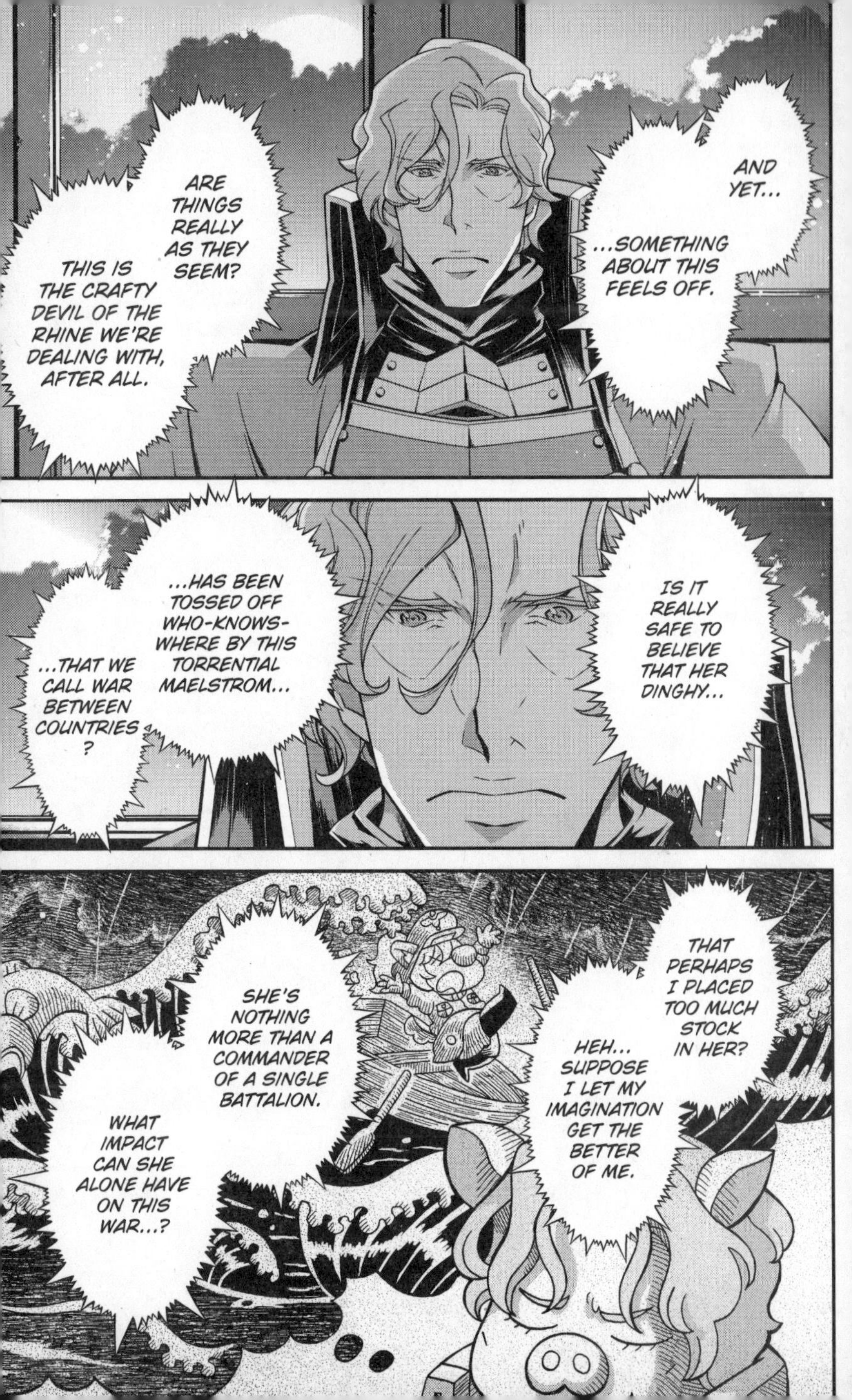
AND YET...
...SOMETHING ABOUT THIS FEELS OFF.
ARE THINGS REALLY AS THEY SEEM?
THIS IS THE CRAFTY DEVIL OF THE RHINE WE'RE DEALING WITH, AFTER ALL.
IS IT REALLY SAFE TO BELIEVE THAT HER DINGHY...
...HAS BEEN TOSSED OFF WHO-KNOWS-WHERE BY THIS TORRENTIAL MAELSTROM...
...THAT WE CALL WAR BETWEEN COUNTRIES?
THAT PERHAPS I PLACED TOO MUCH STOCK IN HER?
HEH... SUPPOSE I LET MY IMAGINATION GET THE BETTER OF ME.
SHE'S NOTHING MORE THAN A COMMANDER OF A SINGLE BATTALION.
WHAT IMPACT CAN SHE ALONE HAVE ON THIS WAR...?

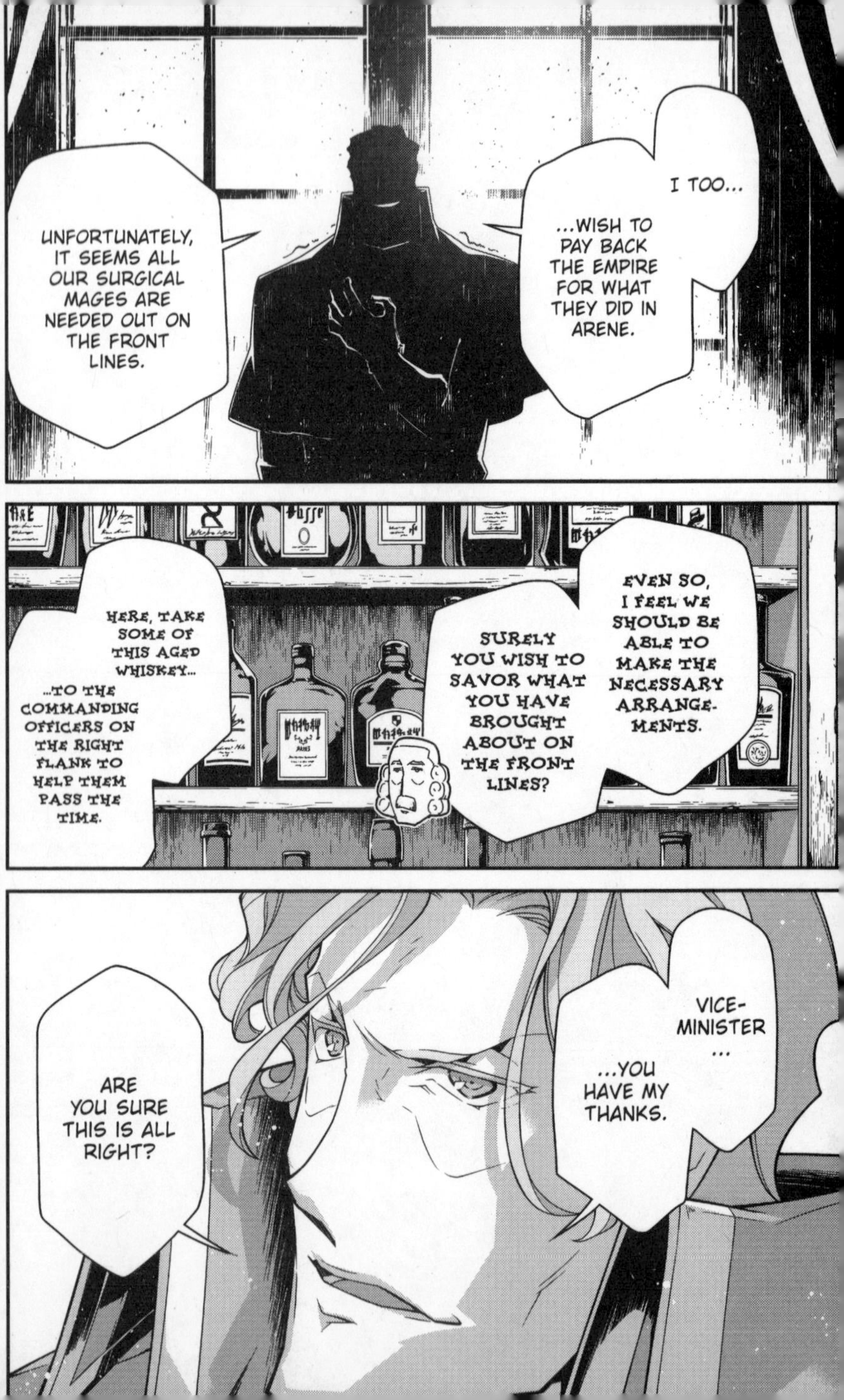
I TOO...
...WISH TO PAY BACK THE EMPIRE FOR WHAT THEY DID IN ARENE.
UNFORTUNATELY, IT SEEMS ALL OUR SURGICAL MAGES ARE NEEDED OUT ON THE FRONT LINES.
EVEN SO, I FEEL WE SHOULD BE ABLE TO MAKE THE NECESSARY ARRANGEMENTS.
SURELY YOU WISH TO SAVOR WHAT YOU HAVE BROUGHT ABOUT ON THE FRONT LINES?
HERE, TAKE SOME OF THIS AGED WHISKEY...
...TO THE COMMANDING OFFICERS ON THE RIGHT FLANK TO HELP THEM PASS THE TIME.
VICE-MINISTER...
...YOU HAVE MY THANKS.
ARE YOU SURE THIS IS ALL RIGHT?

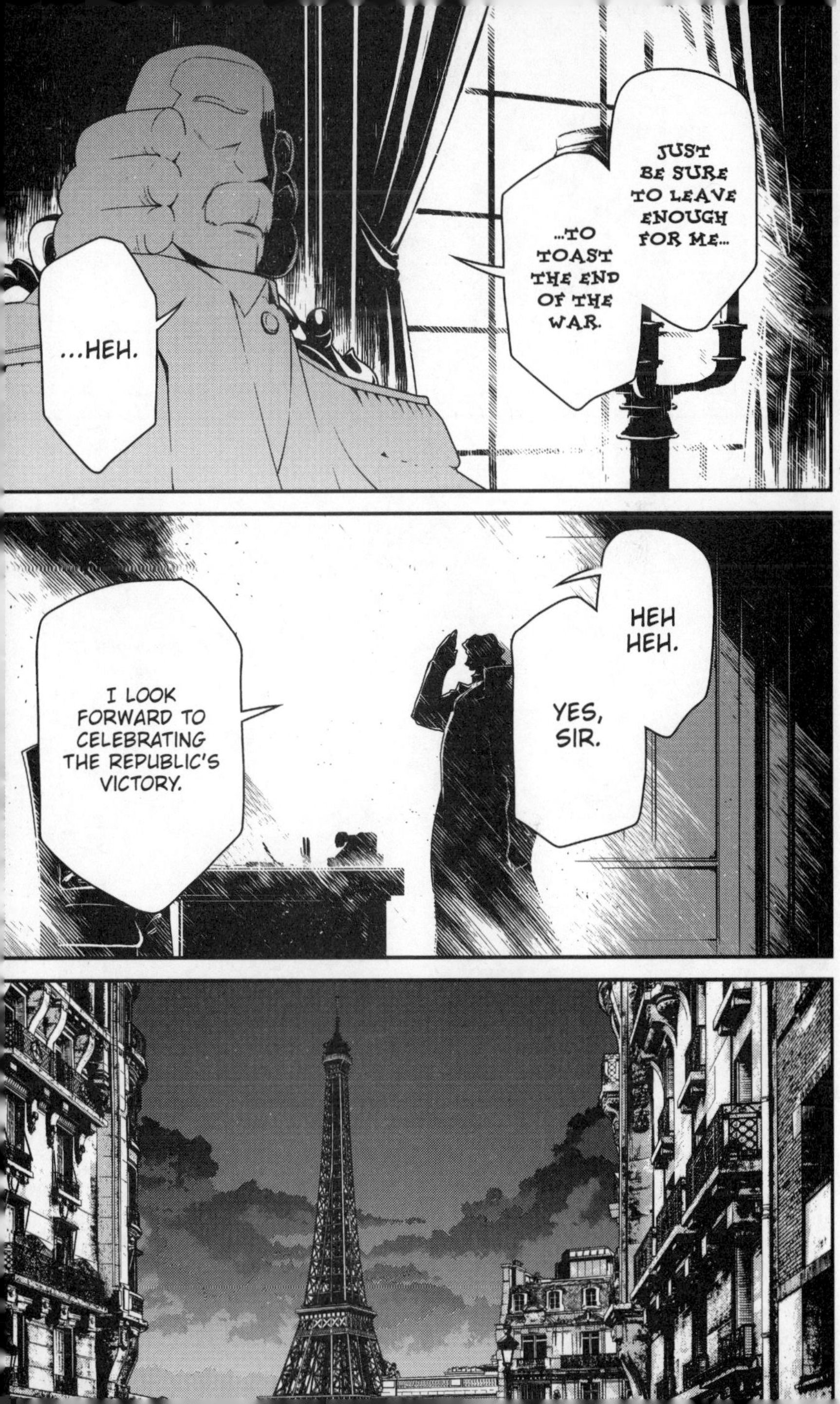
JUST BE SURE TO LEAVE ENOUGH FOR ME...
...TO TOAST THE END OF THE WAR.
...HEH.
HEH HEH.
YES, SIR.
I LOOK FORWARD TO CELEBRATING THE REPUBLIC'S VICTORY.

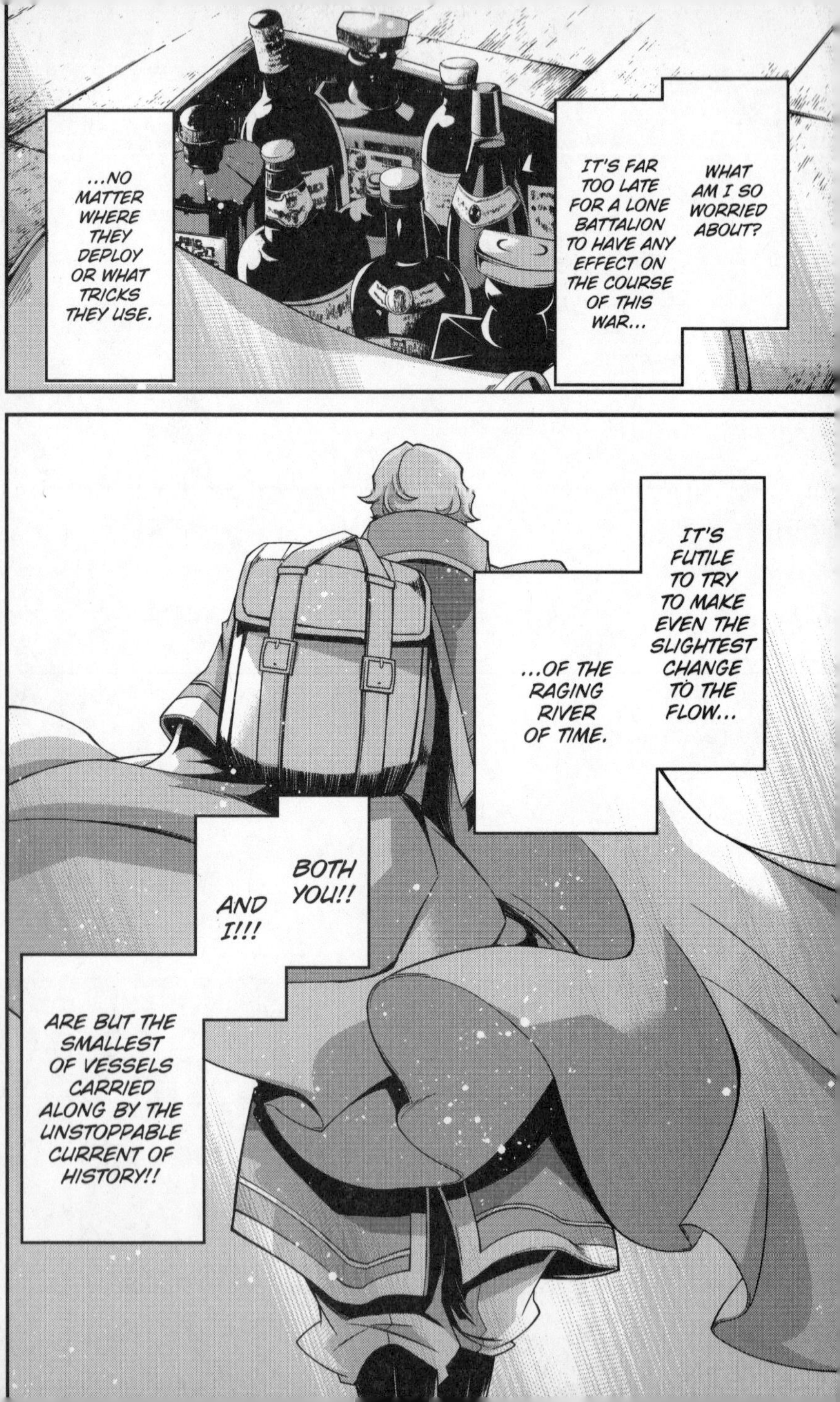
WHAT AM I SO WORRIED ABOUT?
IT'S FAR TOO LATE FOR A LONE BATTALION TO HAVE ANY EFFECT ON THE COURSE OF THIS WAR...
...NO MATTER WHERE THEY DEPLOY OR WHAT TRICKS THEY USE.
IT'S FUTILE TO TRY TO MAKE EVEN THE SLIGHTEST CHANGE TO THE FLOW...
...OF THE RAGING RIVER OF TIME.
BOTH YOU!!
AND I!!!
ARE BUT THE SMALLEST OF VESSELS CARRIED ALONG BY THE UNSTOPPABLE CURRENT OF HISTORY!!

The Saga of
Tanya the Evil
Chapter: 45

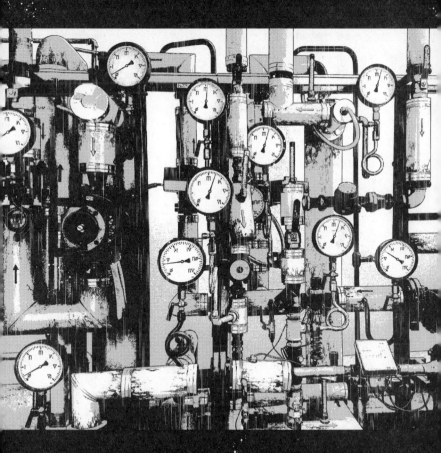

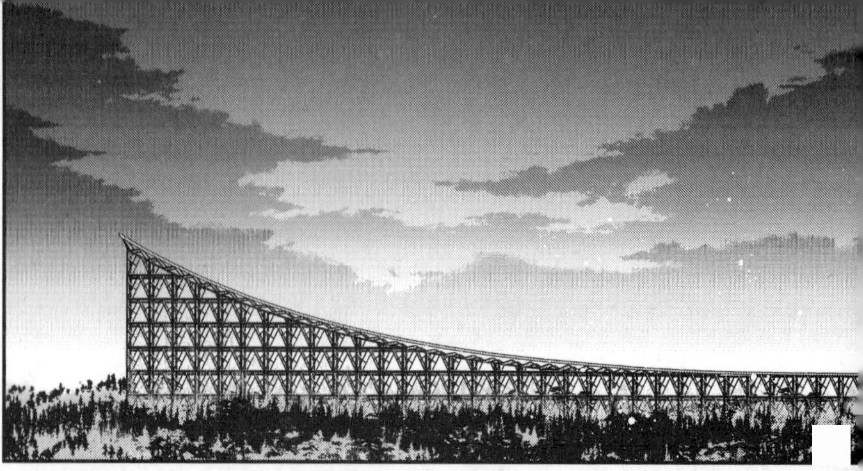
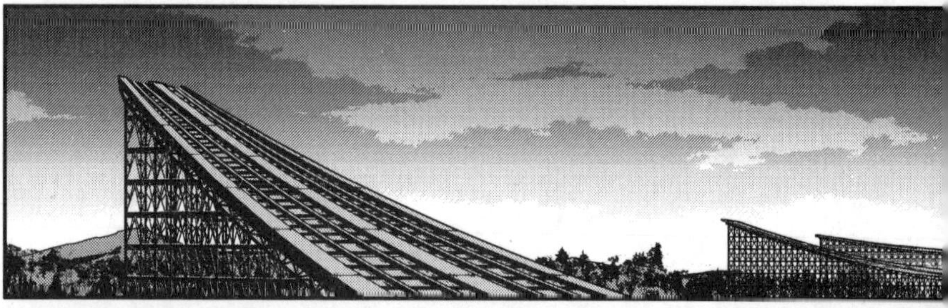
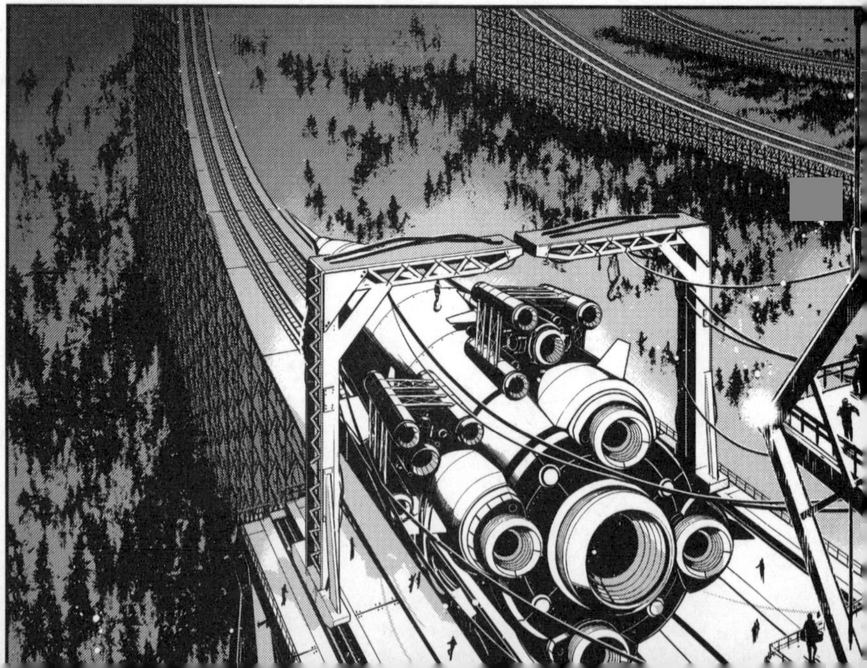

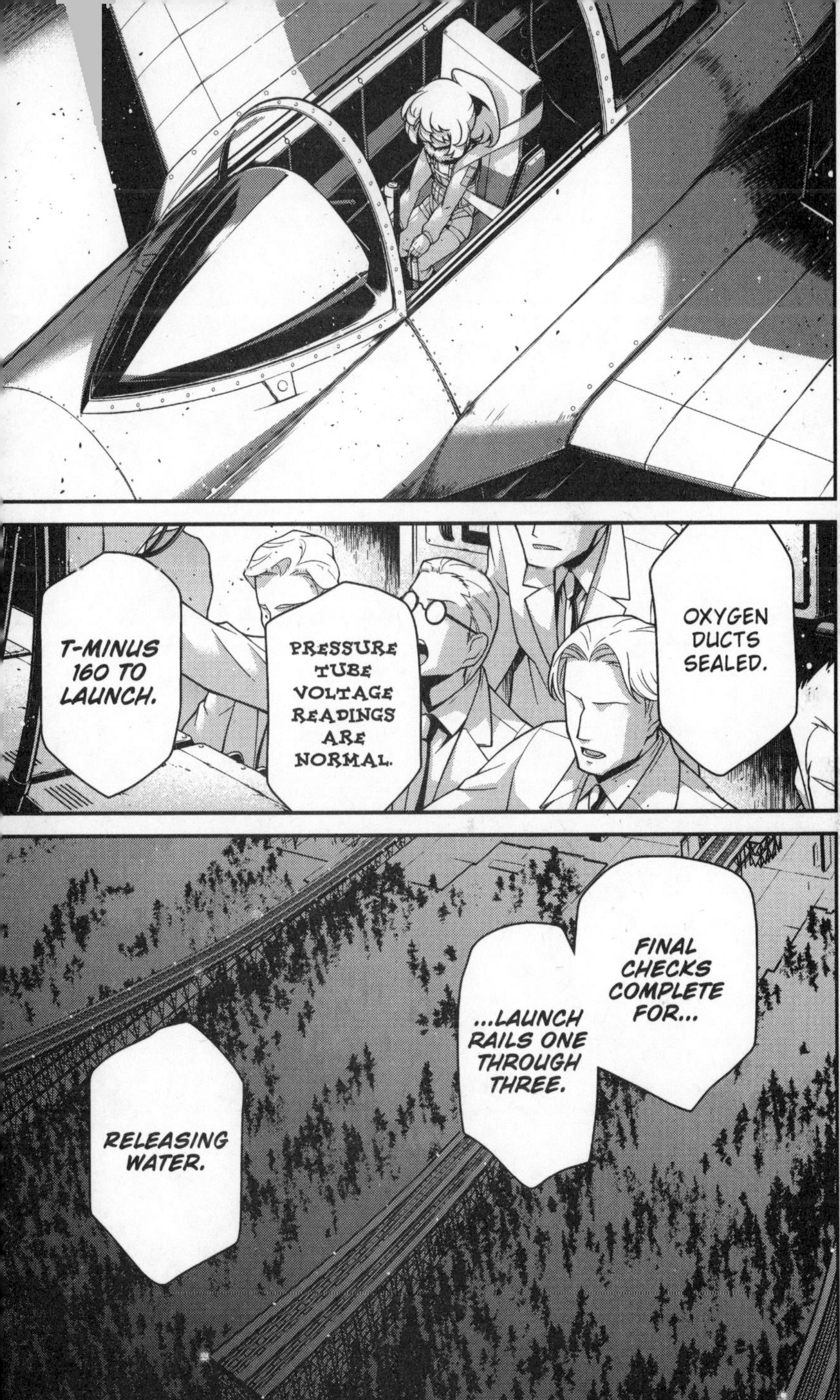
OXYGEN DUCTS SEALED.
PRESSURE TUBE VOLTAGE READINGS ARE NORMAL.
T-MINUS 160 TO LAUNCH.
FINAL CHECKS COMPLETE FOR...
...LAUNCH RAILS ONE THROUGH THREE.
RELEASING WATER.

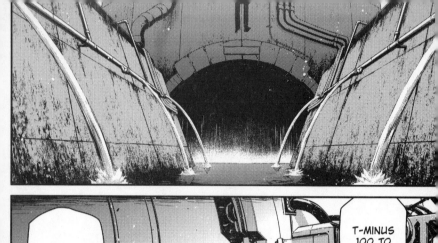

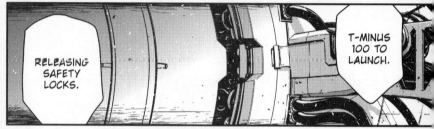

T-MINUS 100 TO LAUNCH.

RELEASING SAFETY LOCKS.

MESSAGE TO ALL MAGE PILOTS.

ACTIVATE YOUR ELINIUM TYPE 97 ASSAULT COMPUTATION ORBS...

...AND DEPLOY PHYSICAL PROTECTIVE FILMS.

MAINTAIN MAXIMUM OUTPUT TO GENERATE A FIELD STRONG ENOUGH TO BLOCK THE THERMAL PRESSURE.

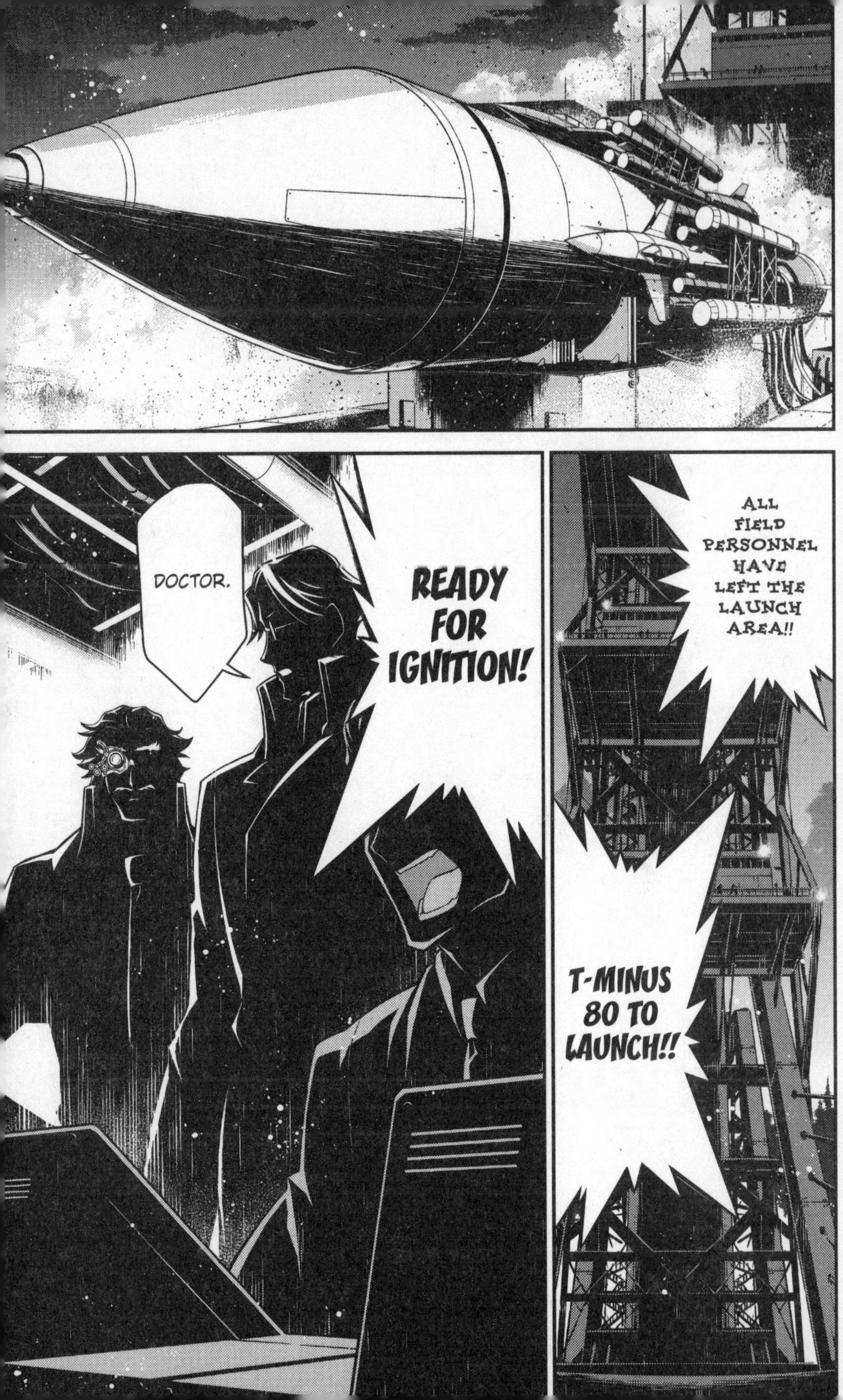
ALL FIELD PERSONNEL HAVE LEFT THE LAUNCH AREA!!
T-MINUS 80 TO LAUNCH!!
READY FOR IGNITION!
DOCTOR.

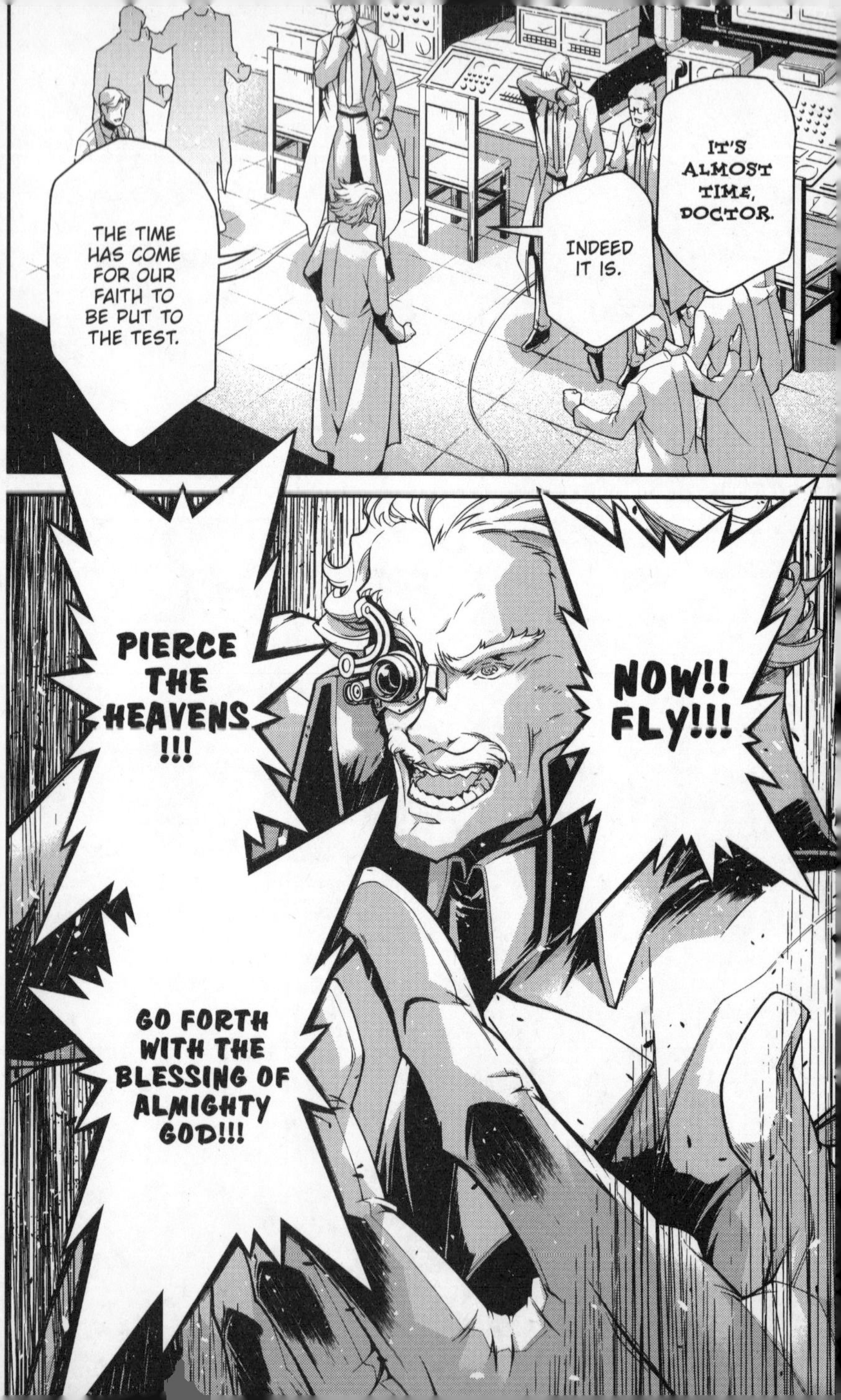
IT'S ALMOST TIME, DOCTOR.
INDEED IT IS.
THE TIME HAS COME FOR OUR FAITH TO BE PUT TO THE TEST.
NOW!! FLY!!!
PIERCE THE HEAVENS!!!
GO FORTH WITH THE BLESSING OF ALMIGHTY GOD!!!

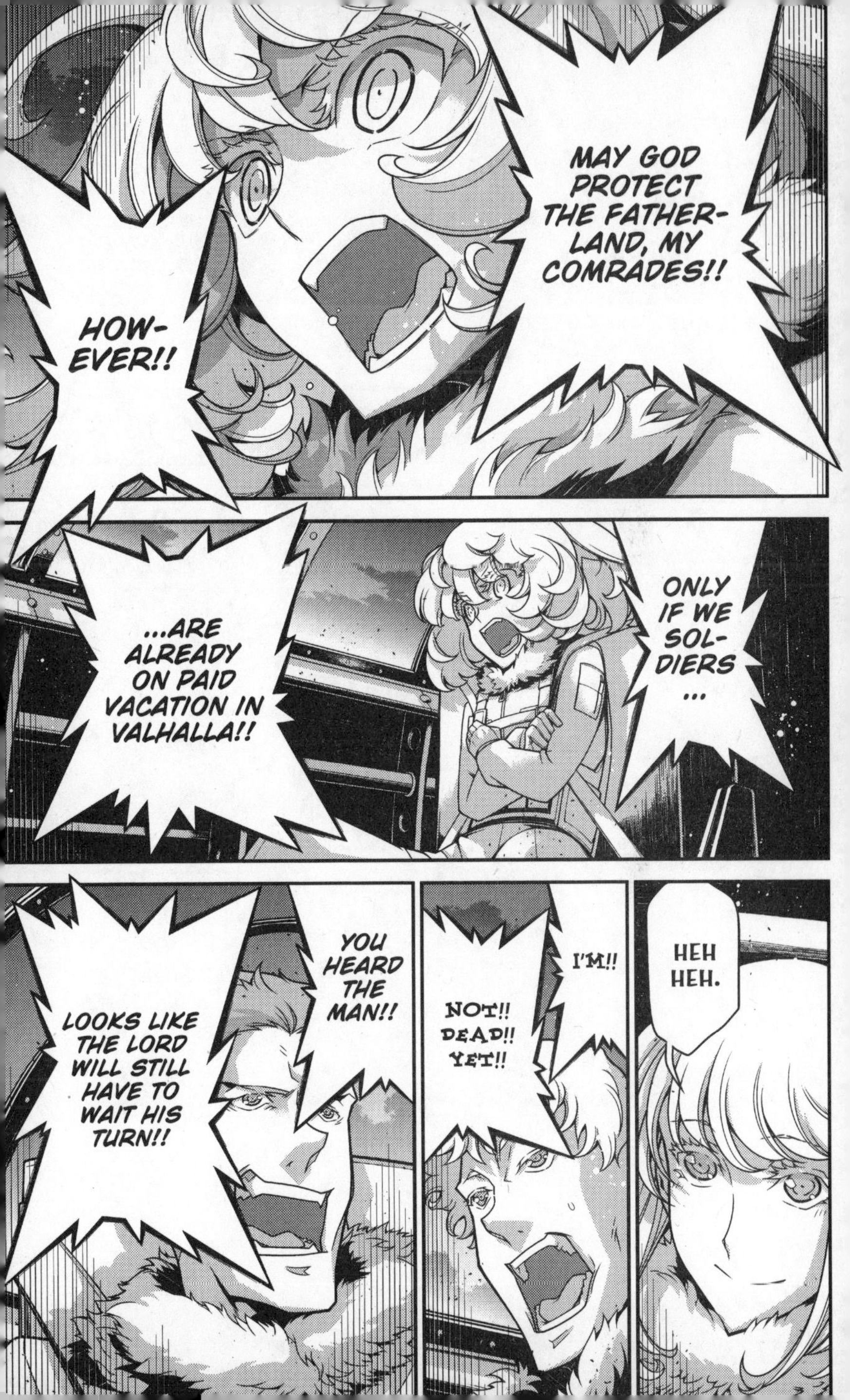
MAY GOD PROTECT THE FATHER-LAND, MY COMRADES!!
HOW-EVER!!
ONLY IF WE SOL-DIERS ...
...ARE ALREADY ON PAID VACATION IN VALHALLA!!
HEH HEH.
I'M!!
NOT!! DEAD!! YET!!
YOU HEARD THE MAN!!
LOOKS LIKE THE LORD WILL STILL HAVE TO WAIT HIS TURN!!

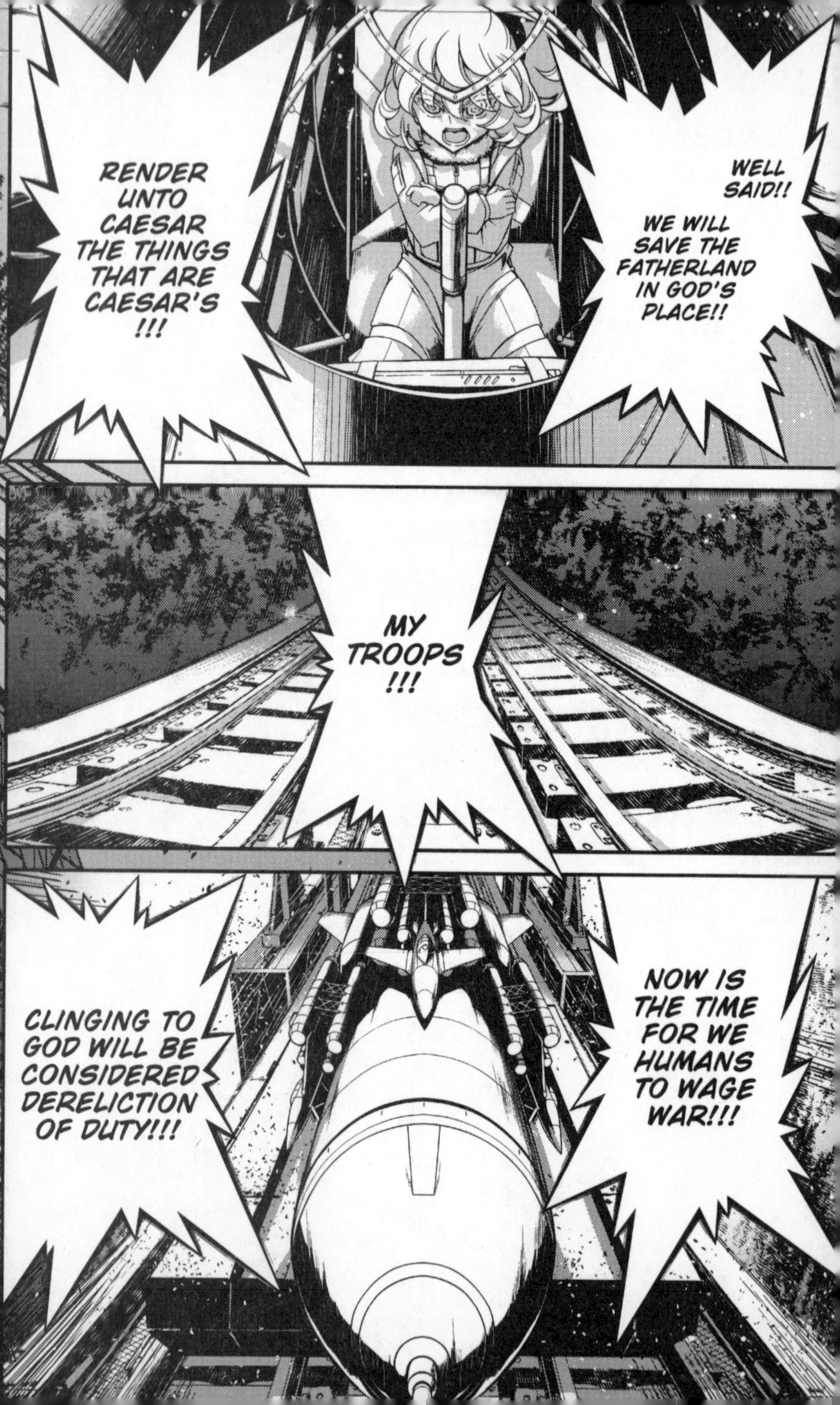
WELL SAID!!
WE WILL SAVE THE FATHERLAND IN GOD'S PLACE!!
RENDER UNTO CAESAR THE THINGS THAT ARE CAESAR'S!!!
MY TROOPS!!!
NOW IS THE TIME FOR WE HUMANS TO WAGE WAR!!!
CLINGING TO GOD WILL BE CONSIDERED DERELICTION OF DUTY!!!

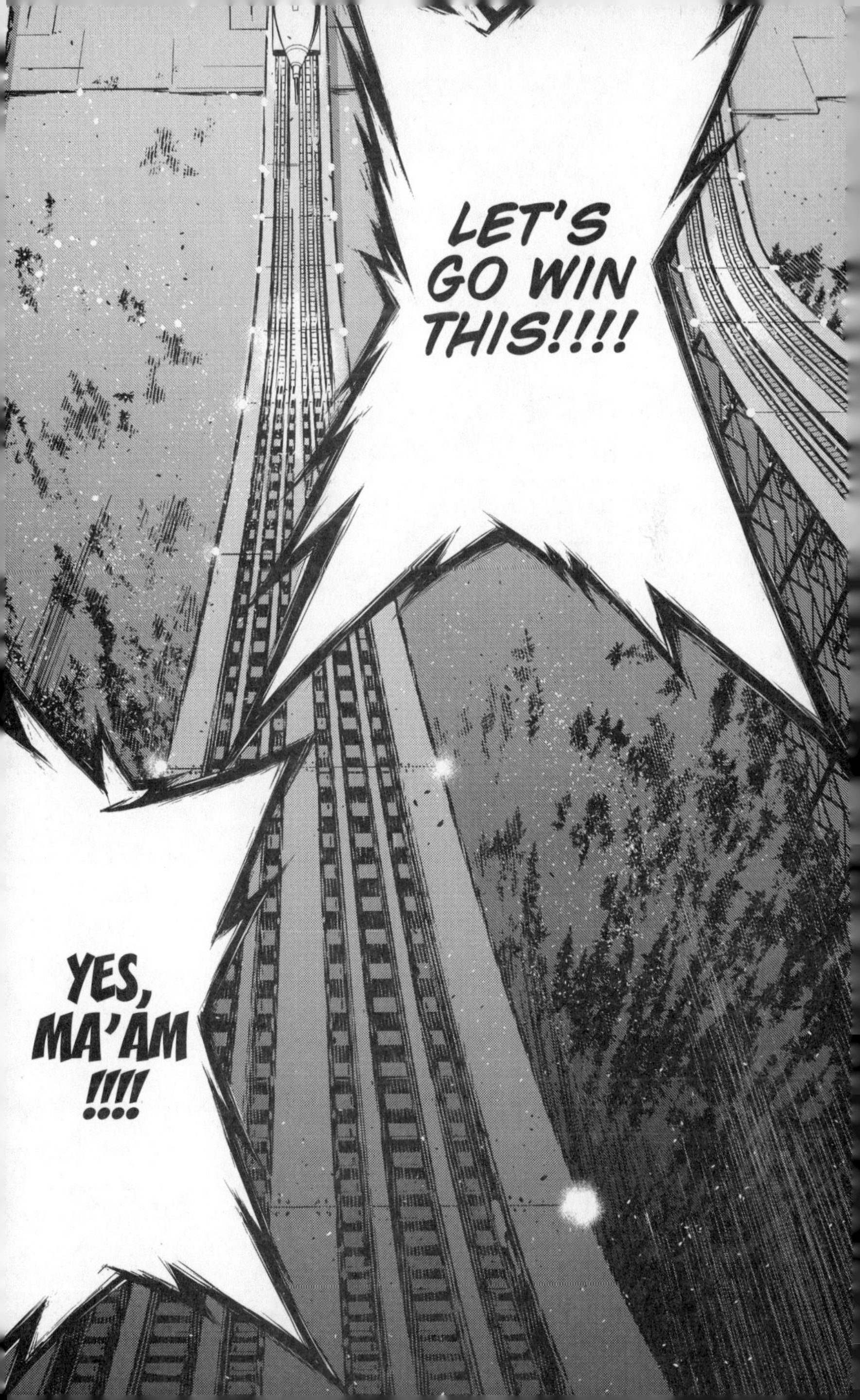
LET'S GO WIN THIS!!!!
YES, MA'AM !!!!

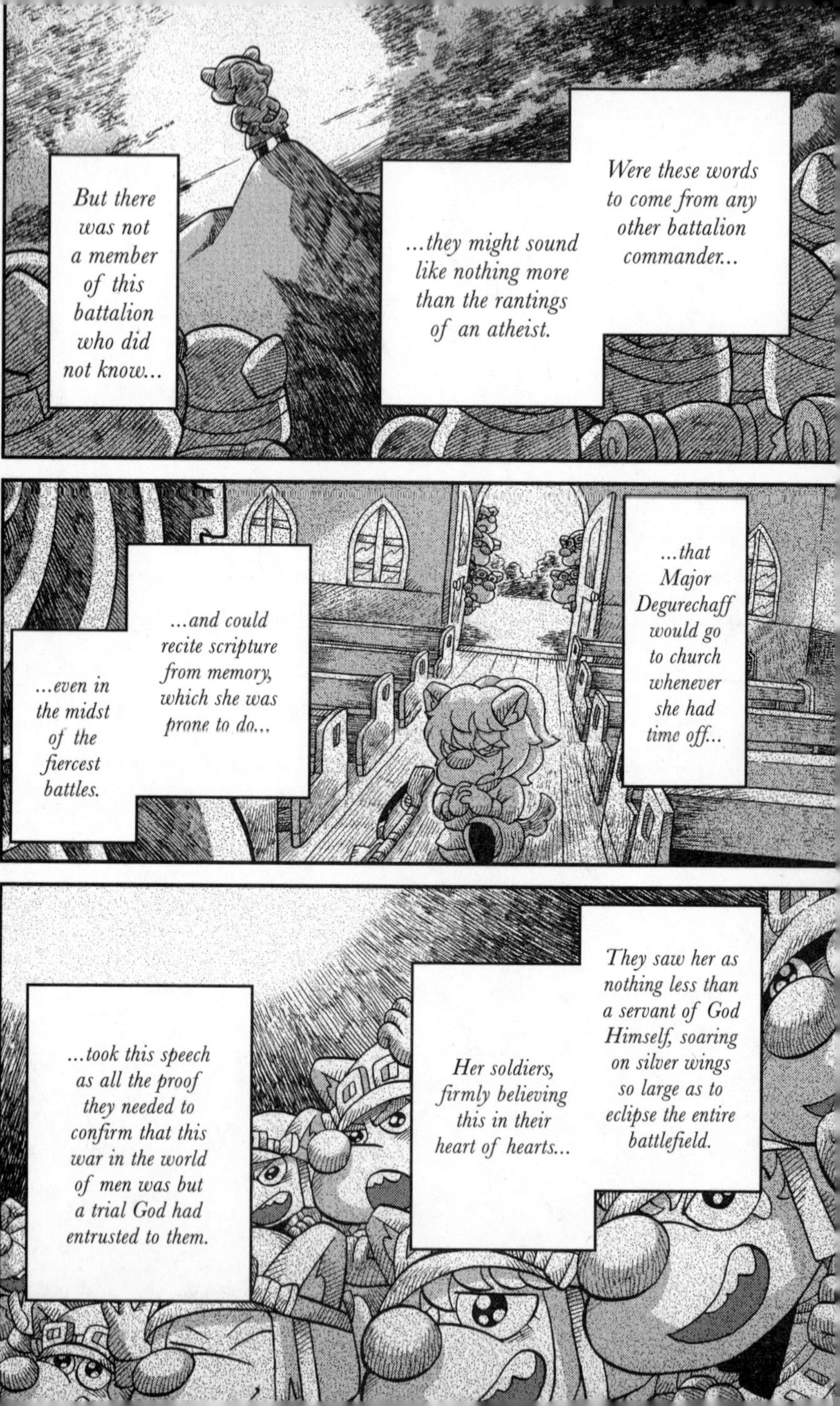
Were these words to come from any other battalion commander...
...they might sound like nothing more than the rantings of an atheist.
But there was not a member of this battalion who did not know...
...that Major Degurechaff would go to church whenever she had time off...
...and could recite scripture from memory, which she was prone to do...
...even in the midst of the fiercest battles.
They saw her as nothing less than a servant of God Himself, soaring on silver wings so large as to eclipse the entire battlefield.
Her soldiers, firmly believing this in their heart of hearts...
...took this speech as all the proof they needed to confirm that this war in the world of men was but a trial God had entrusted to them.

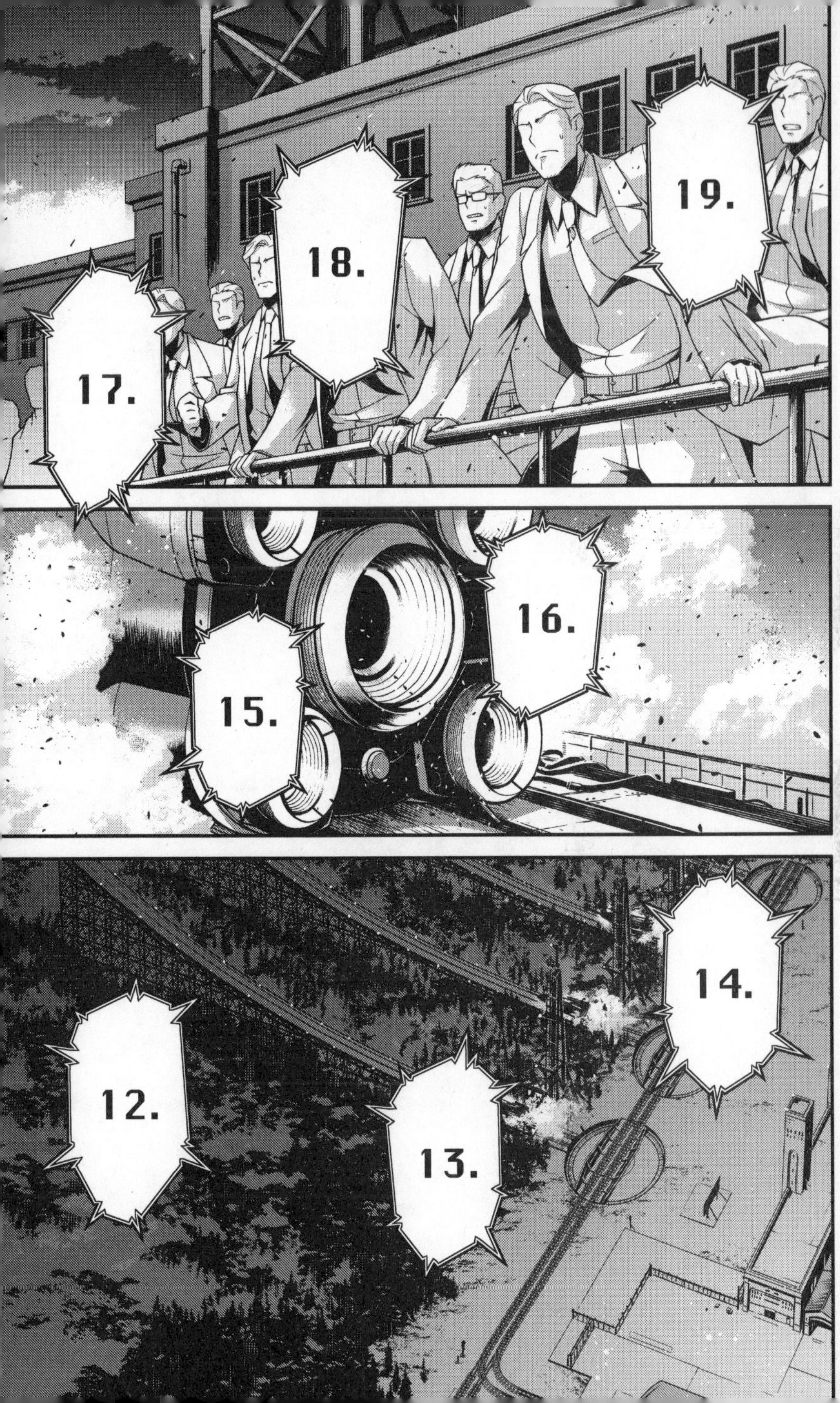
19.
18.
17.
16.
15.
14.
13.
12.

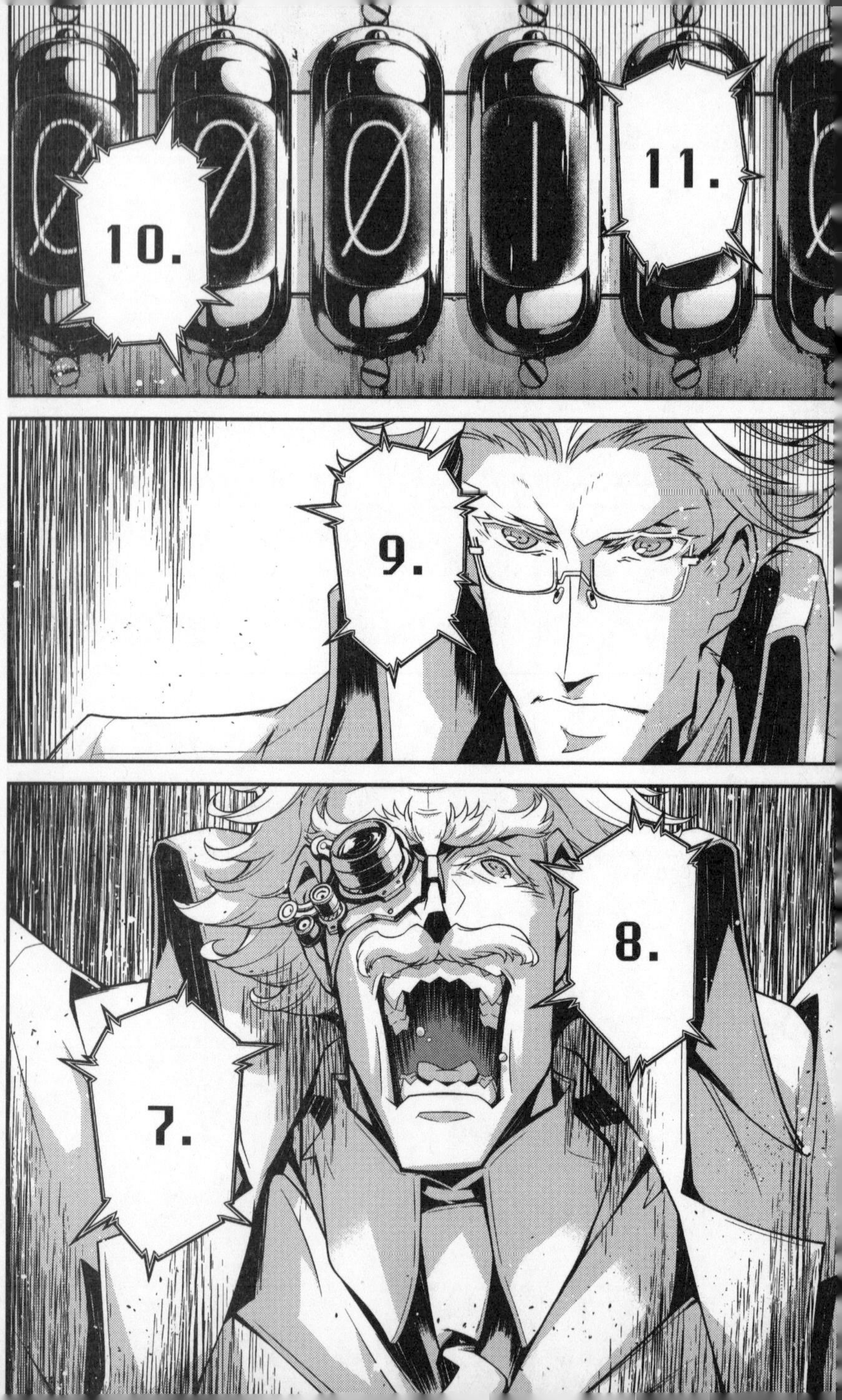
11.
10.
9.
8.
7.

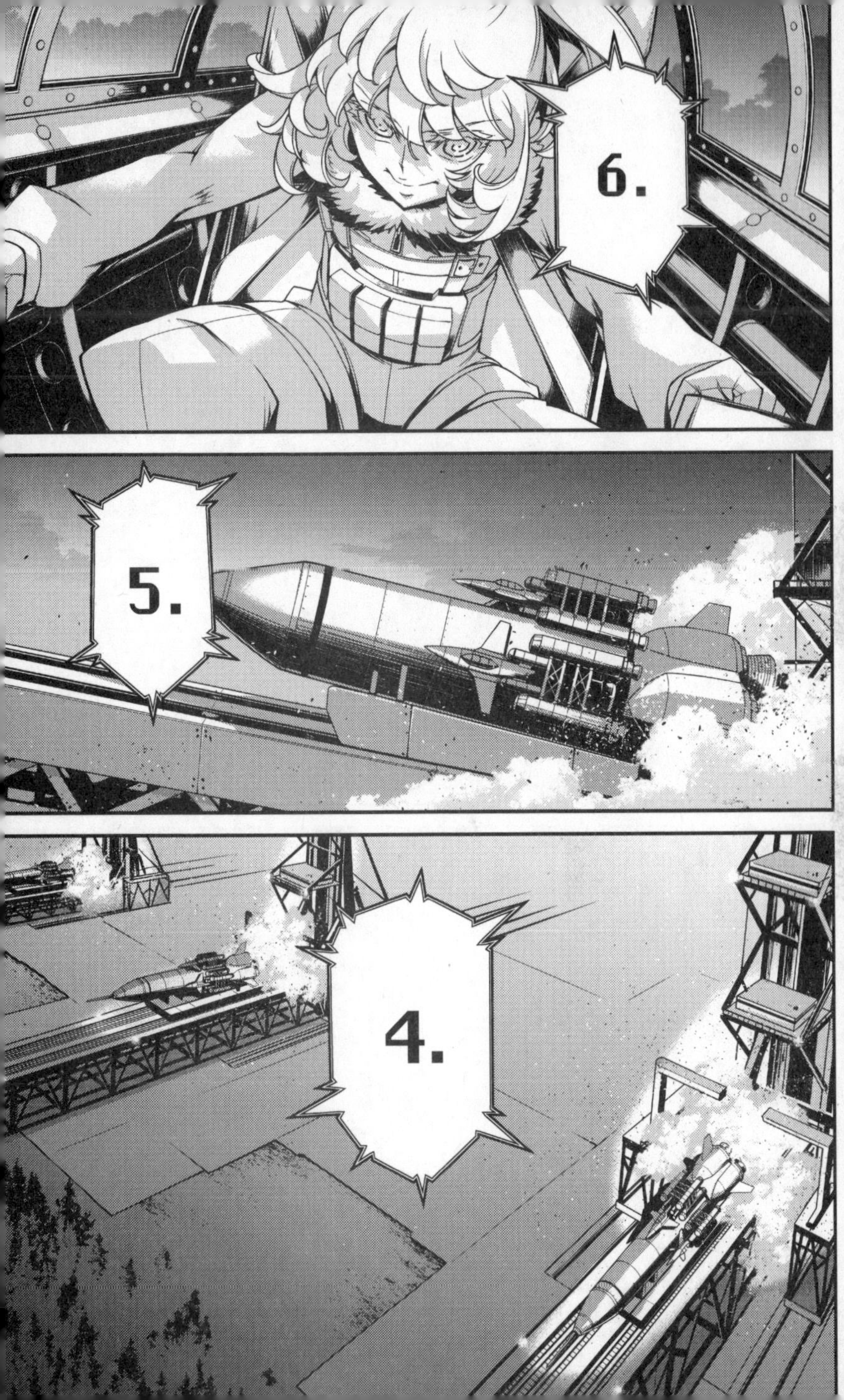
6.
5.
4.

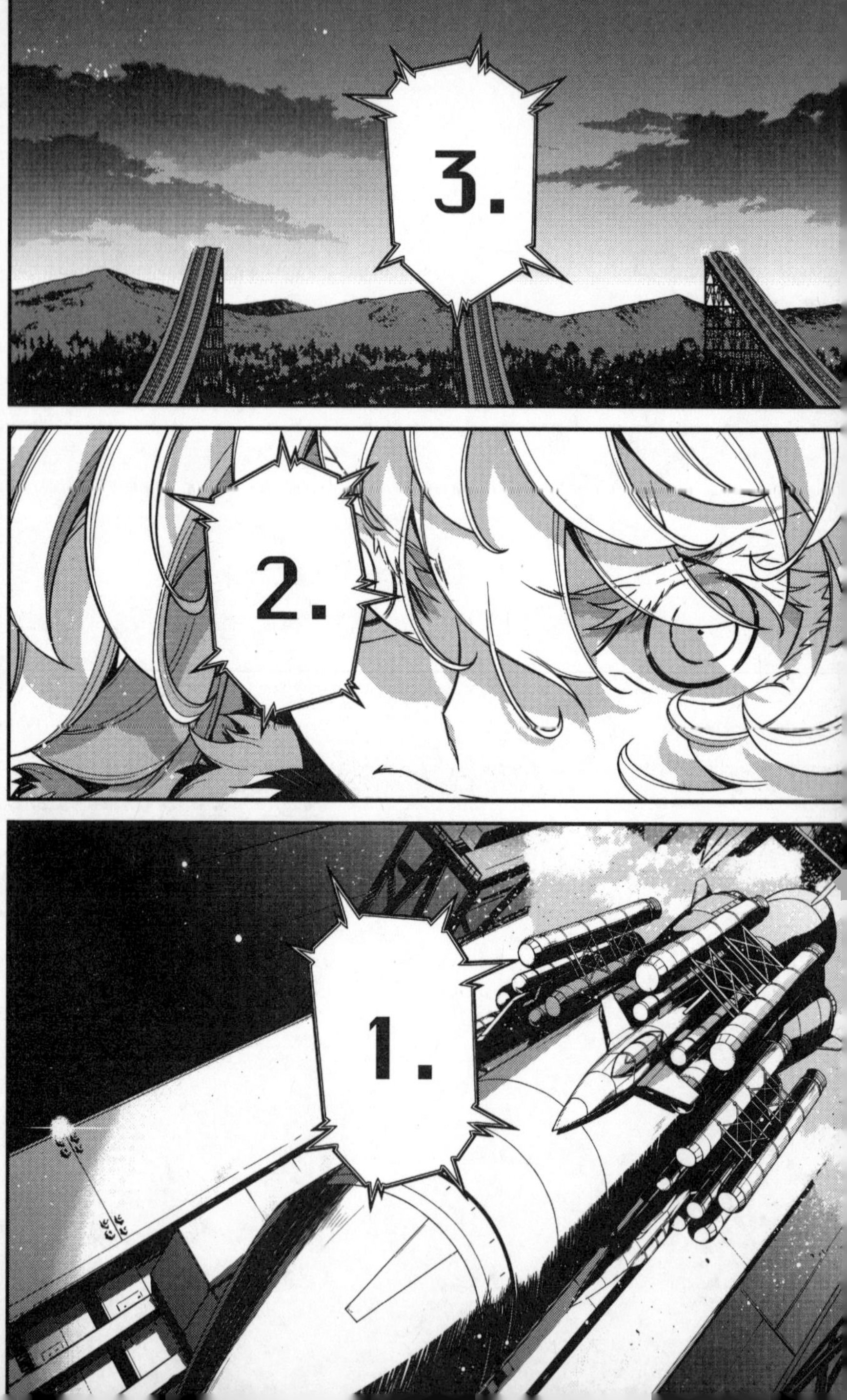
3.
2.
1.

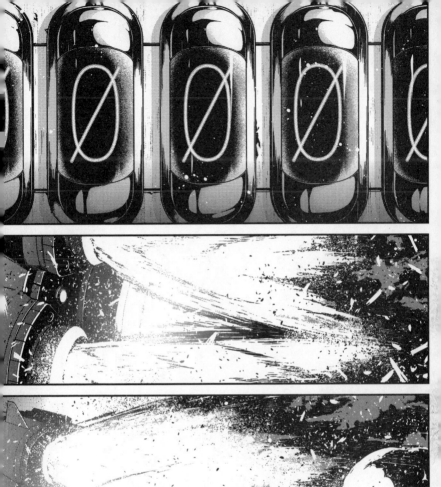

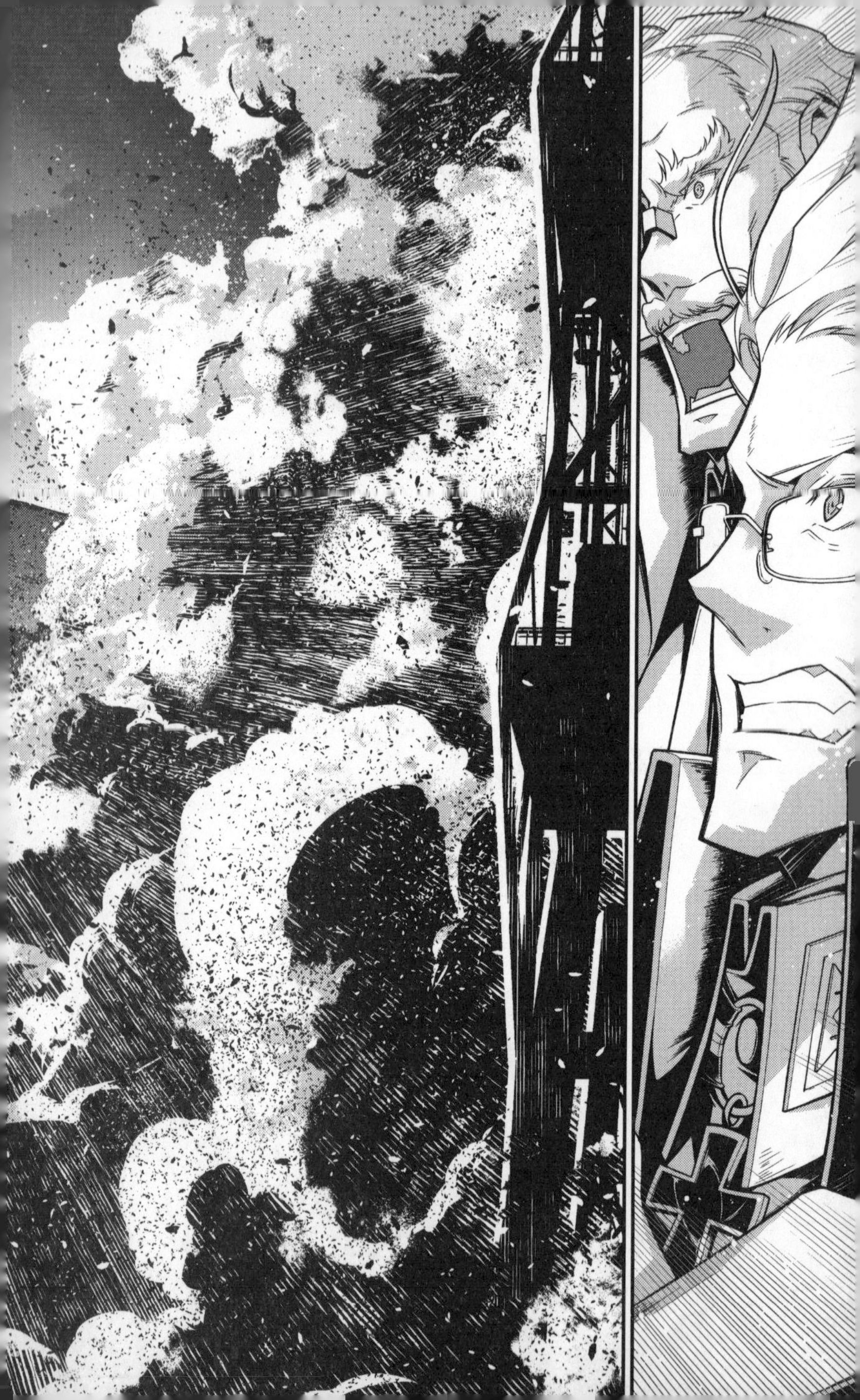

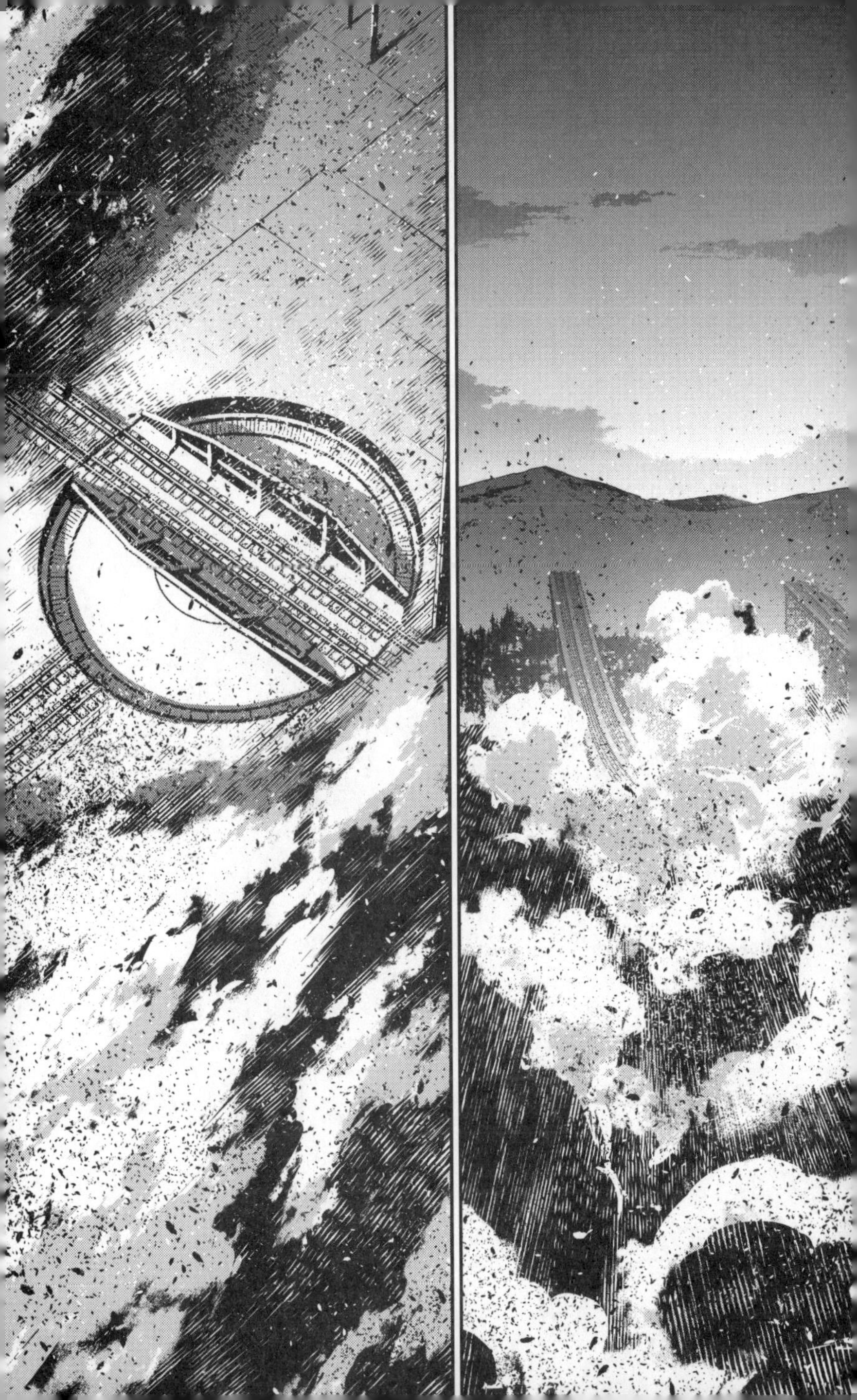

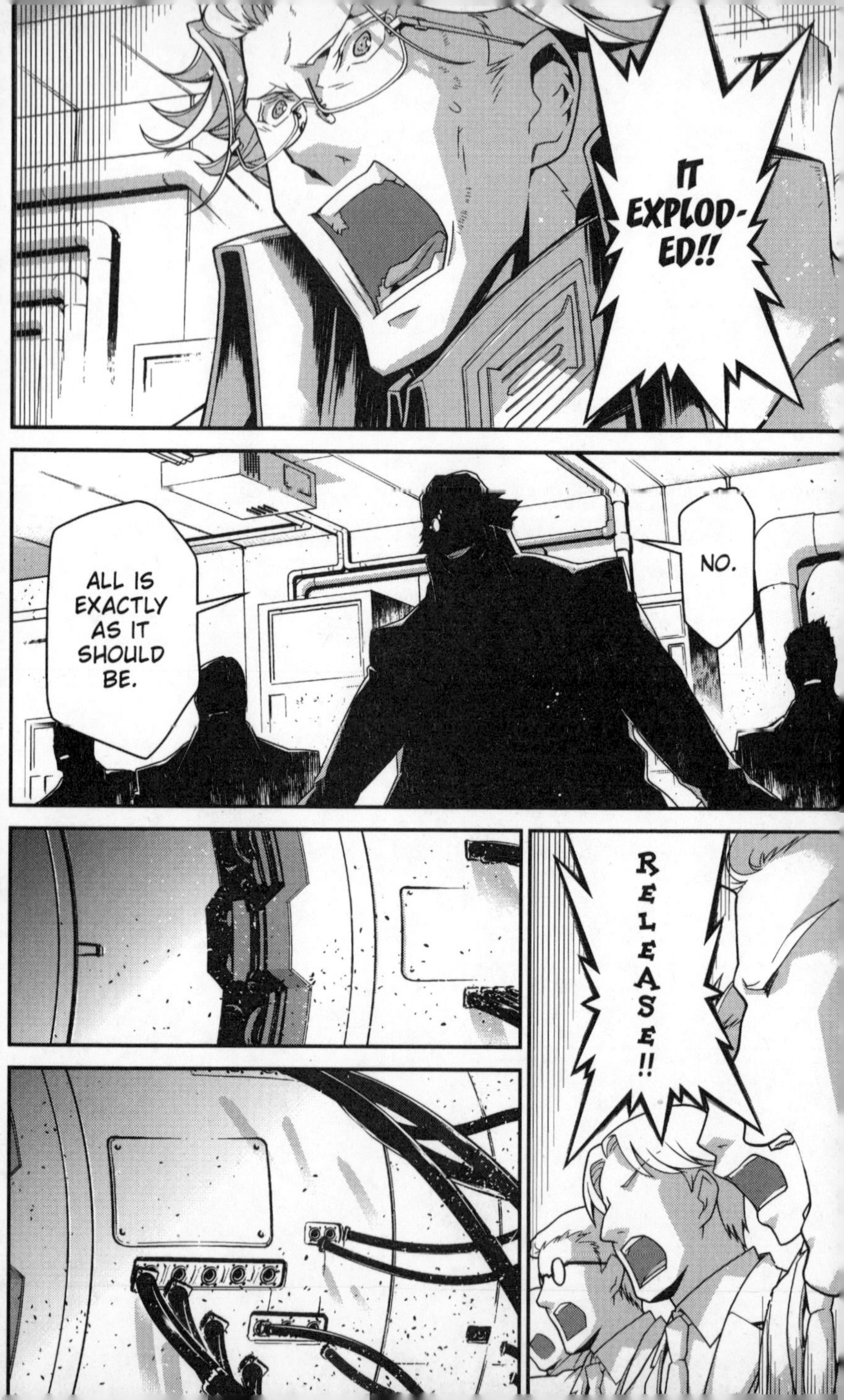
IT EXPLOD-ED!!
NO.
ALL IS EXACTLY AS IT SHOULD BE.
RELEASE!!

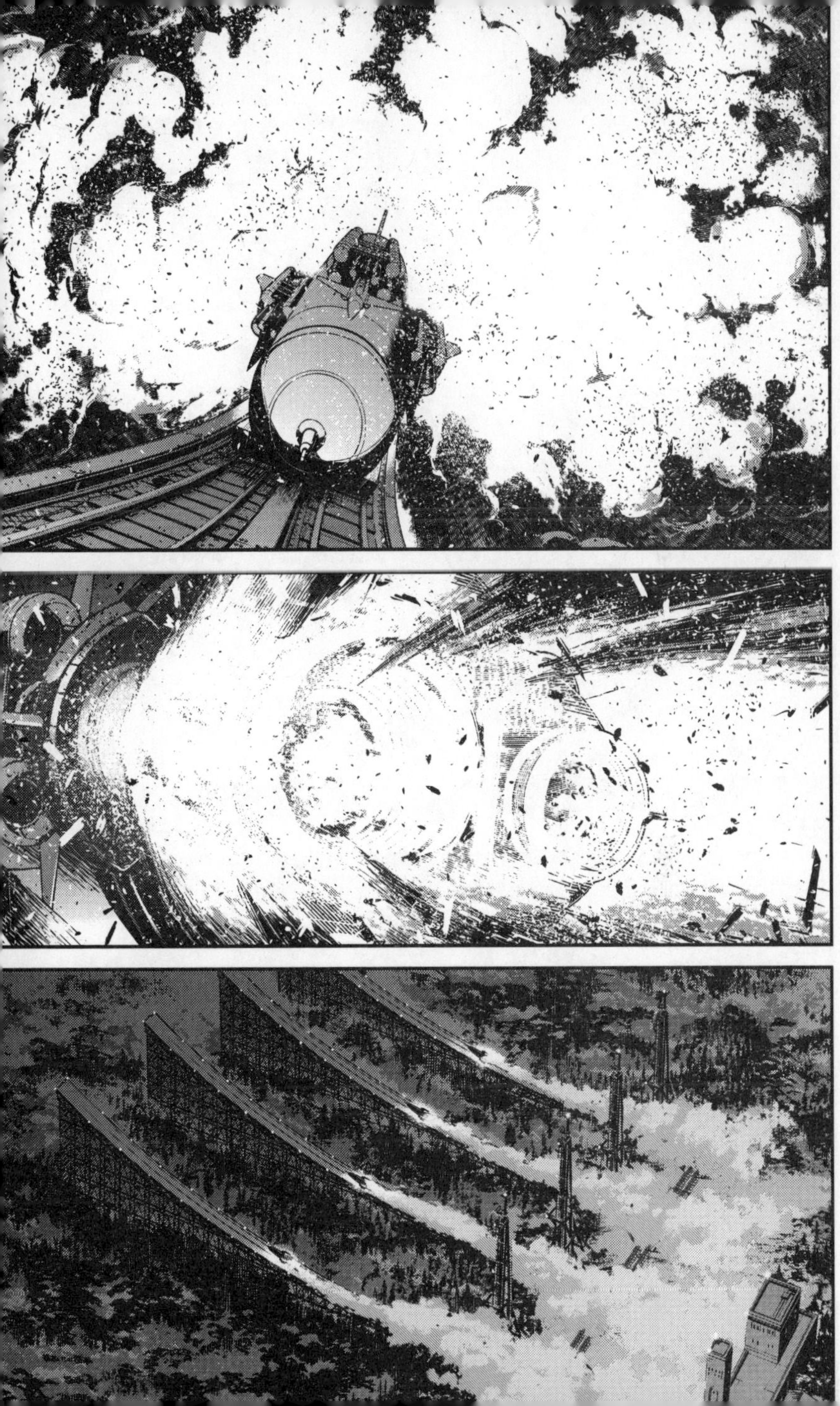

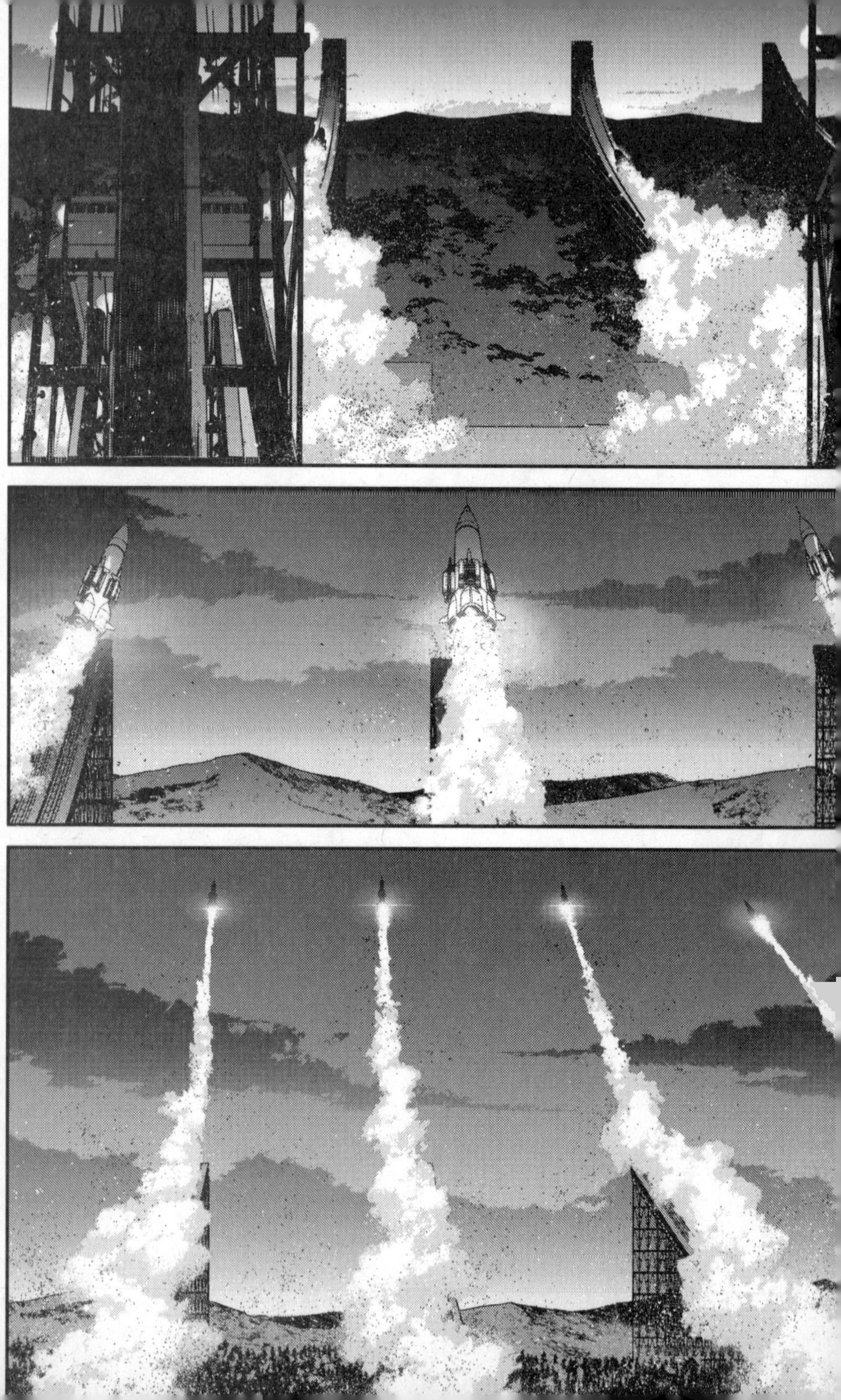

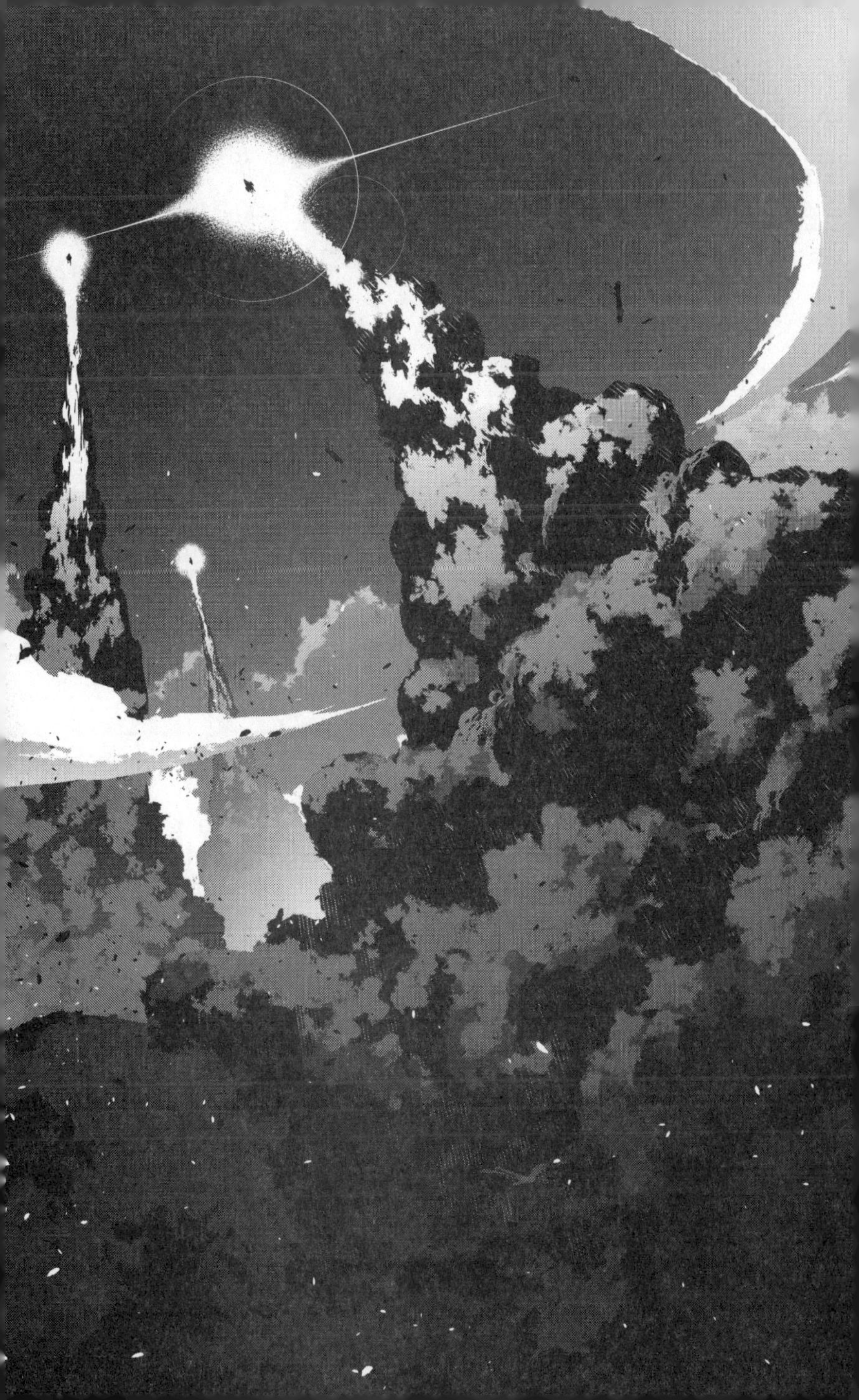

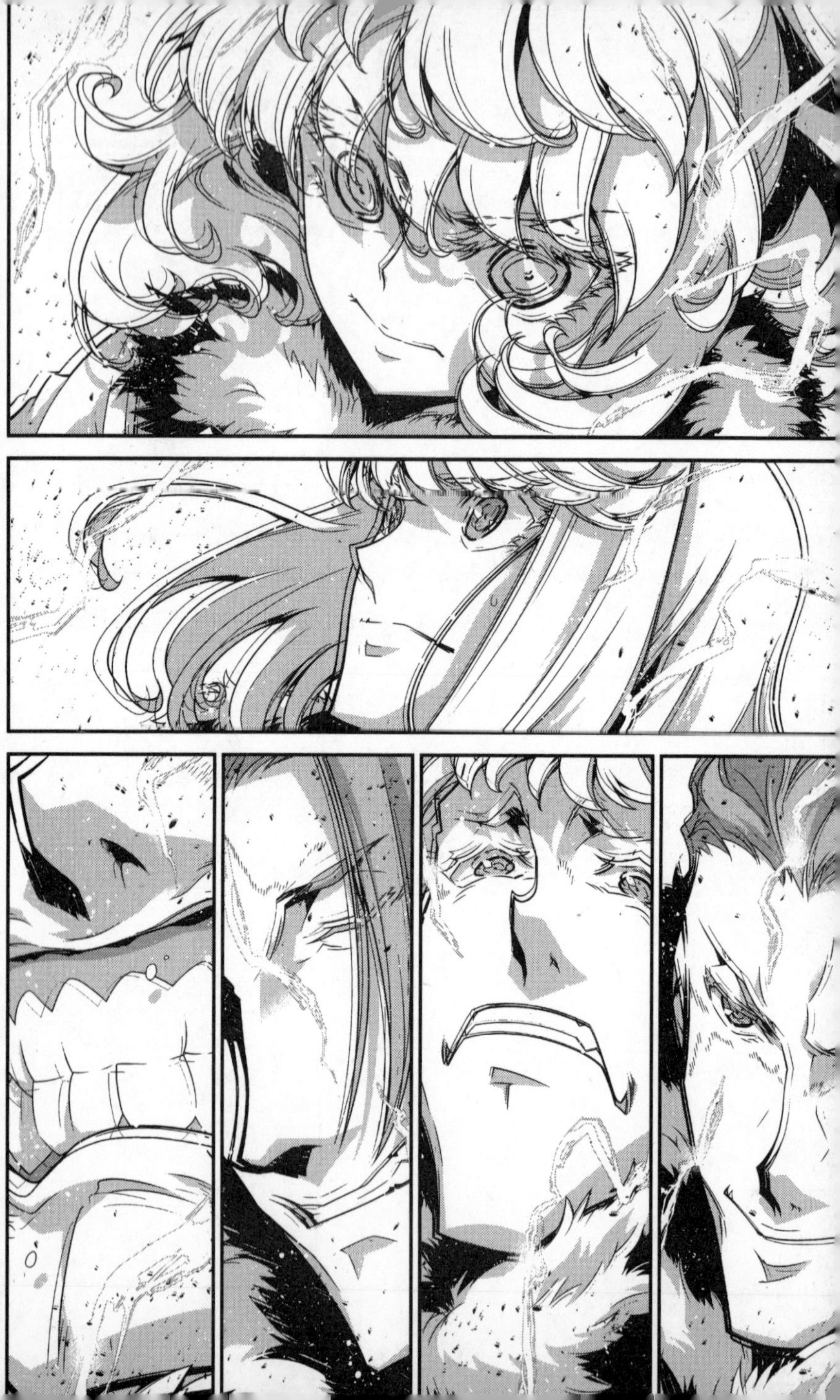

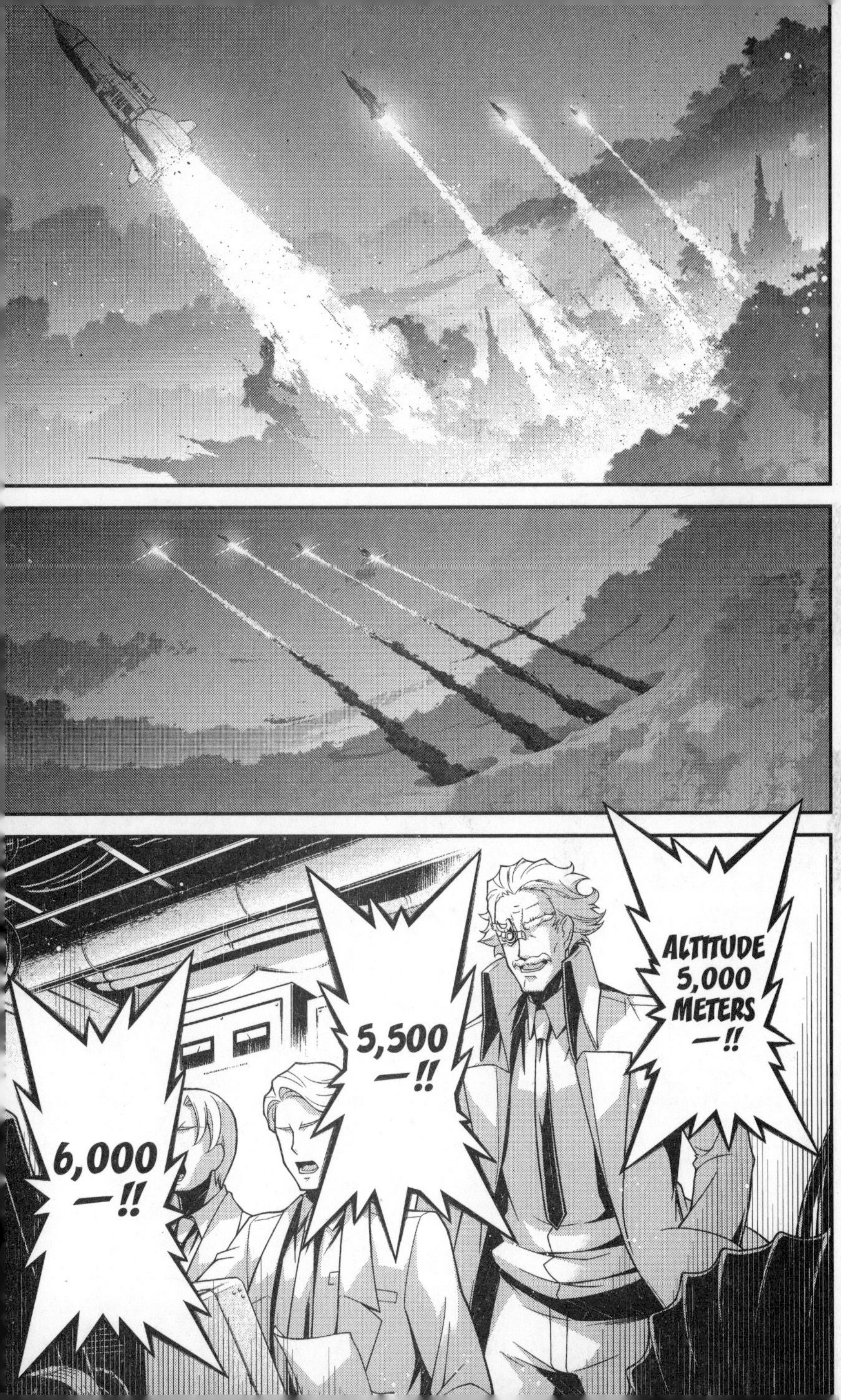
ALTITUDE 5,000 METERS —!!
5,500 —!!
6,000 —!!

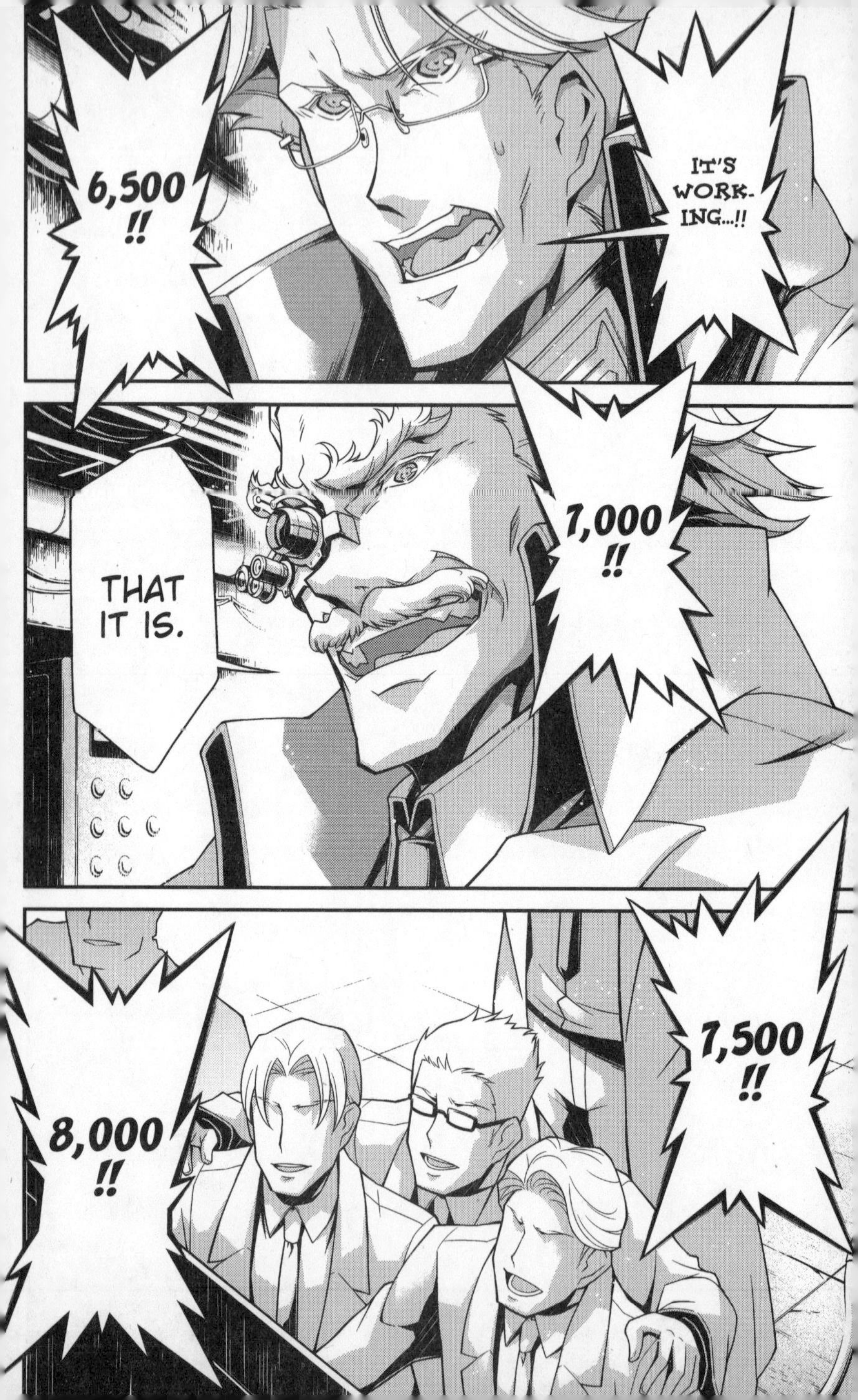
IT'S WORKING...!!
6,500 !!
7,000 !!
THAT IT IS.
7,500 !!
8,000 !!

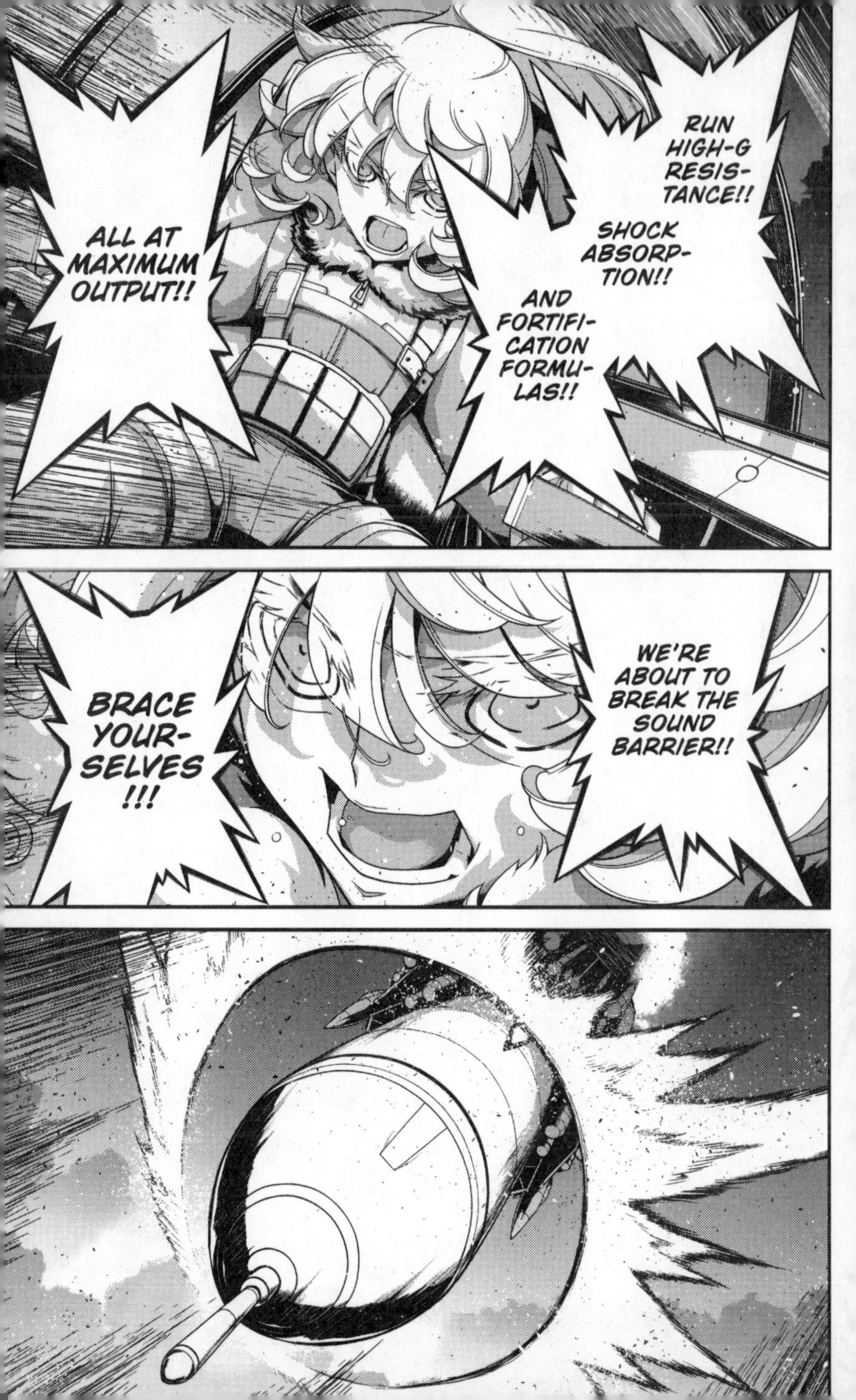
RUN HIGH-G RESISTANCE!!
SHOCK ABSORPTION!!
AND FORTIFICATION FORMULAS!!
ALL AT MAXIMUM OUTPUT!!
WE'RE ABOUT TO BREAK THE SOUND BARRIER!!
BRACE YOURSELVES!!!

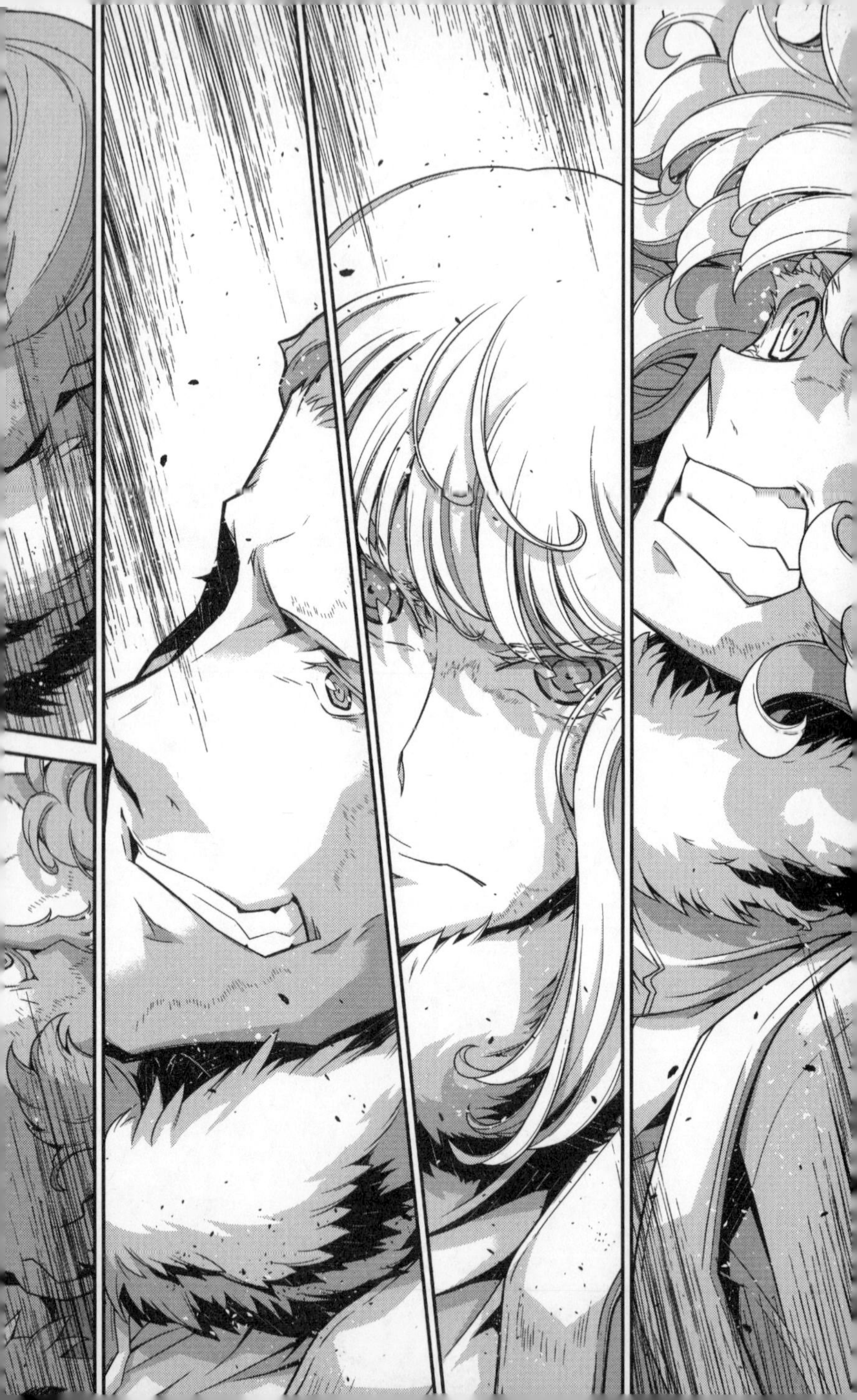

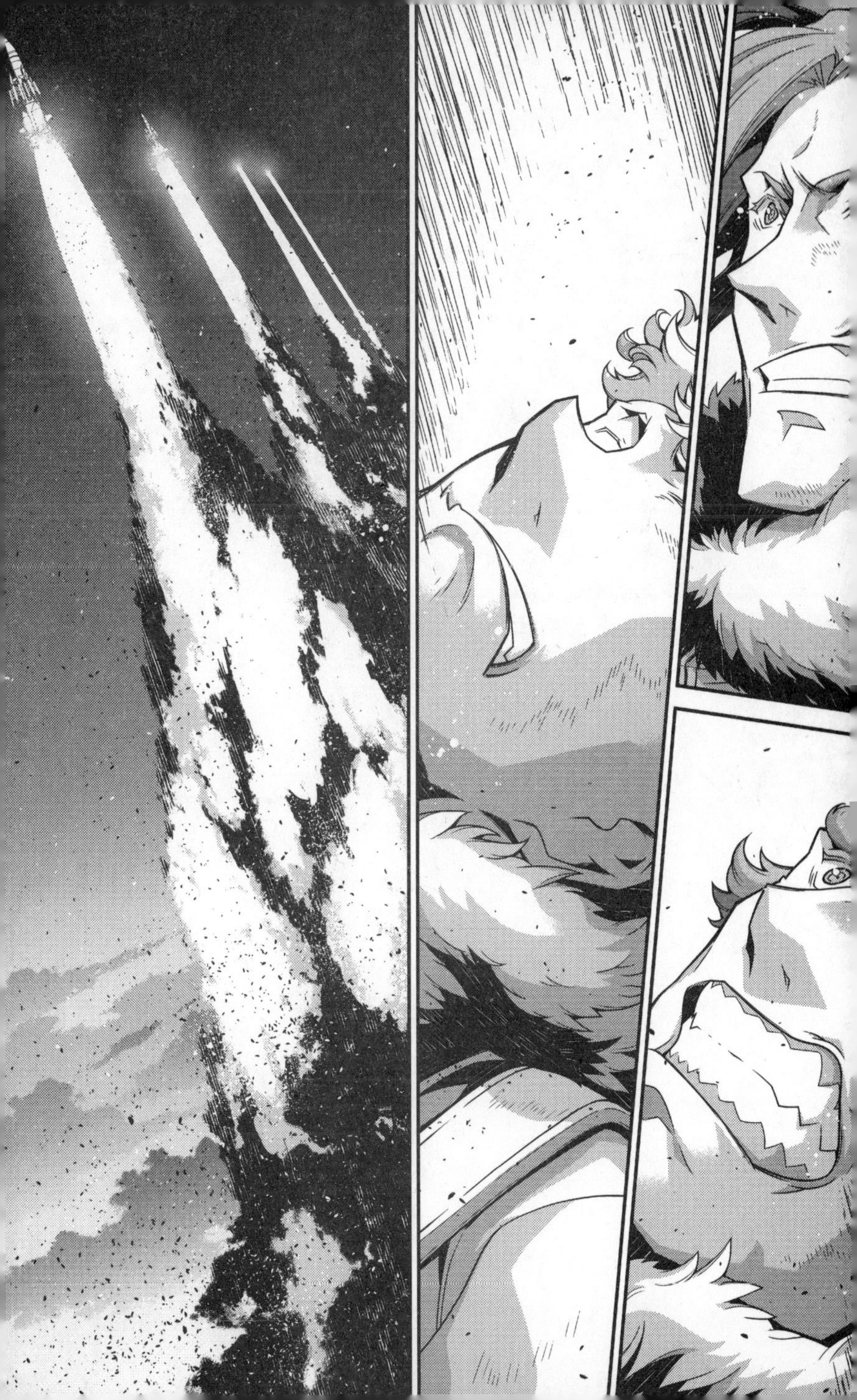

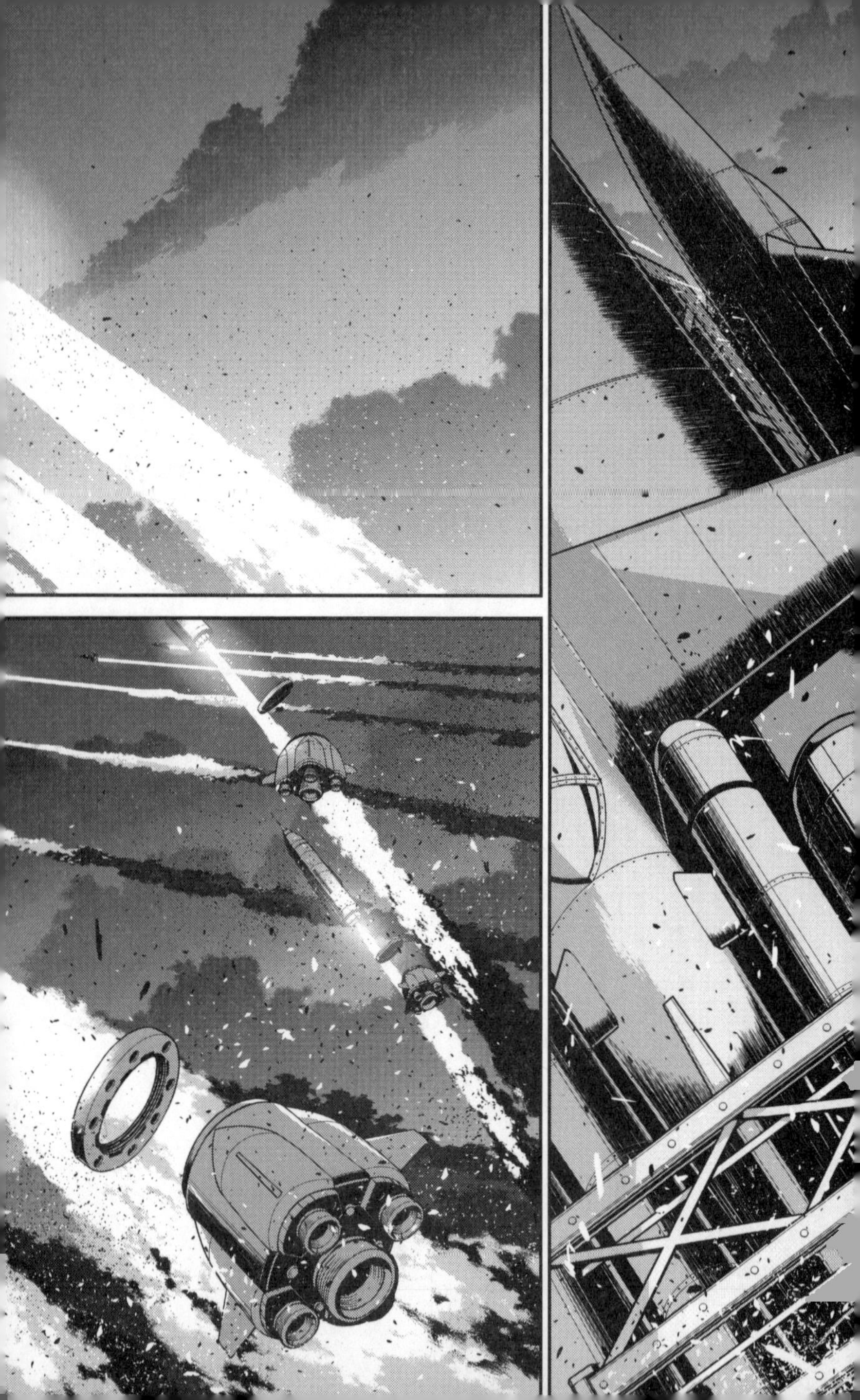

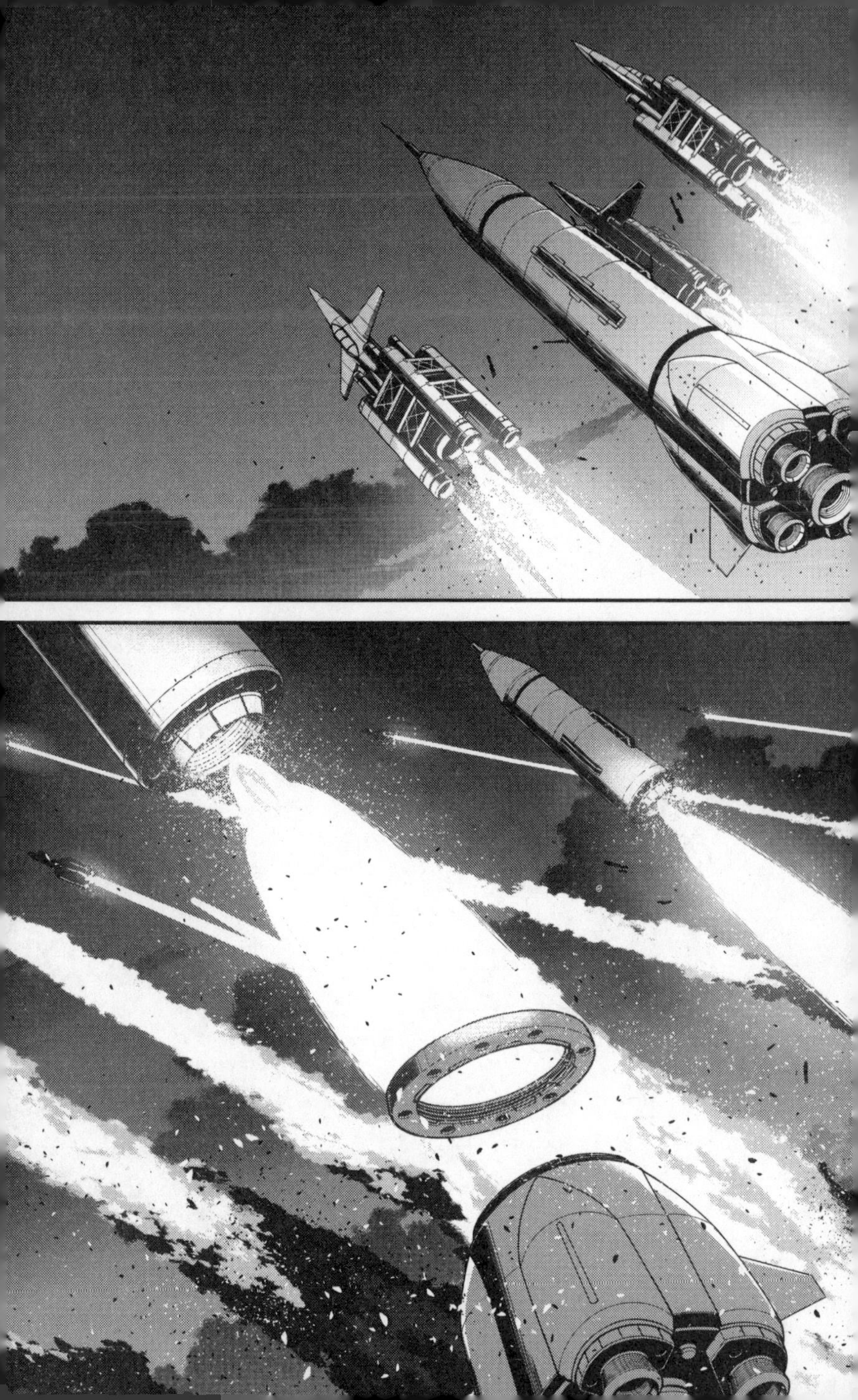

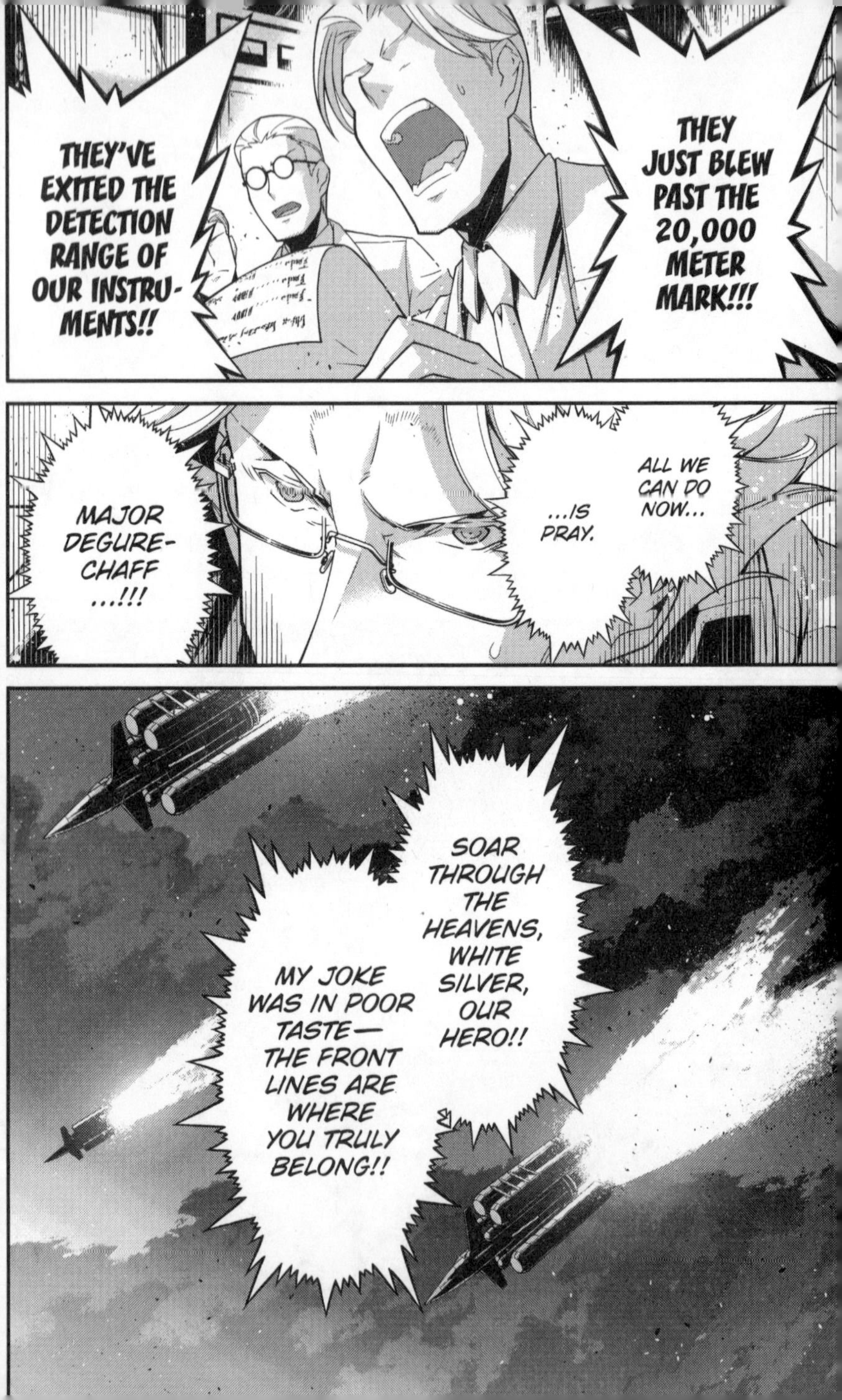
THEY JUST BLEW PAST THE 20,000 METER MARK!!!
THEY'VE EXITED THE DETECTION RANGE OF OUR INSTRU-MENTS!!
ALL WE CAN DO NOW...
...IS PRAY.
MAJOR DEGURE-CHAFF ...!!!
SOAR THROUGH THE HEAVENS, WHITE SILVER, OUR HERO!!
MY JOKE WAS IN POOR TASTE—THE FRONT LINES ARE WHERE YOU TRULY BELONG!!

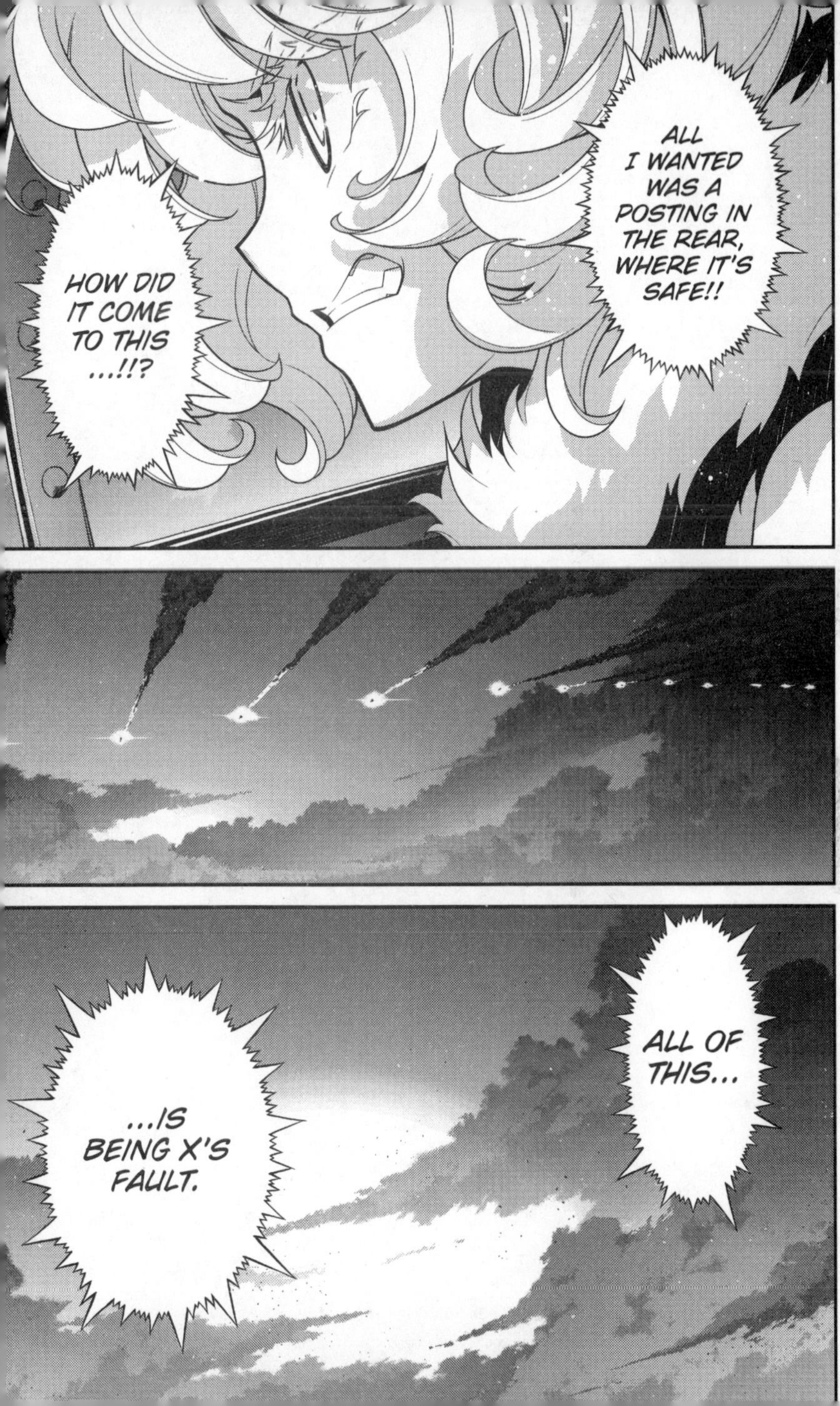
ALL I WANTED WAS A POSTING IN THE REAR, WHERE IT'S SAFE!!
HOW DID IT COME TO THIS ...!!?
ALL OF THIS...
...IS BEING X'S FAULT.

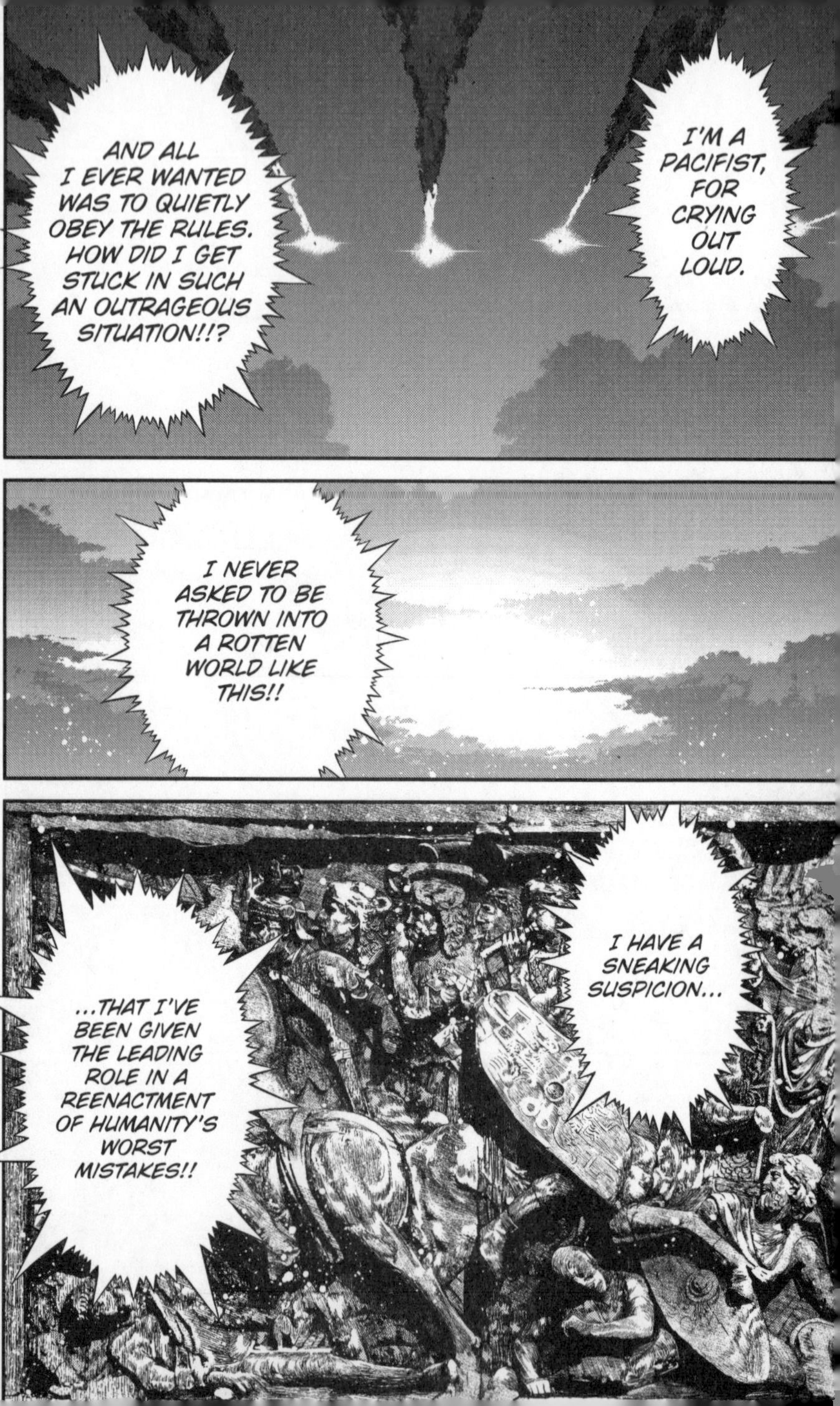
I'M A PACIFIST, FOR CRYING OUT LOUD.
AND ALL I EVER WANTED WAS TO QUIETLY OBEY THE RULES. HOW DID I GET STUCK IN SUCH AN OUTRAGEOUS SITUATION!!?
I NEVER ASKED TO BE THROWN INTO A ROTTEN WORLD LIKE THIS!!
I HAVE A SNEAKING SUSPICION...
...THAT I'VE BEEN GIVEN THE LEADING ROLE IN A REENACTMENT OF HUMANITY'S WORST MISTAKES!!

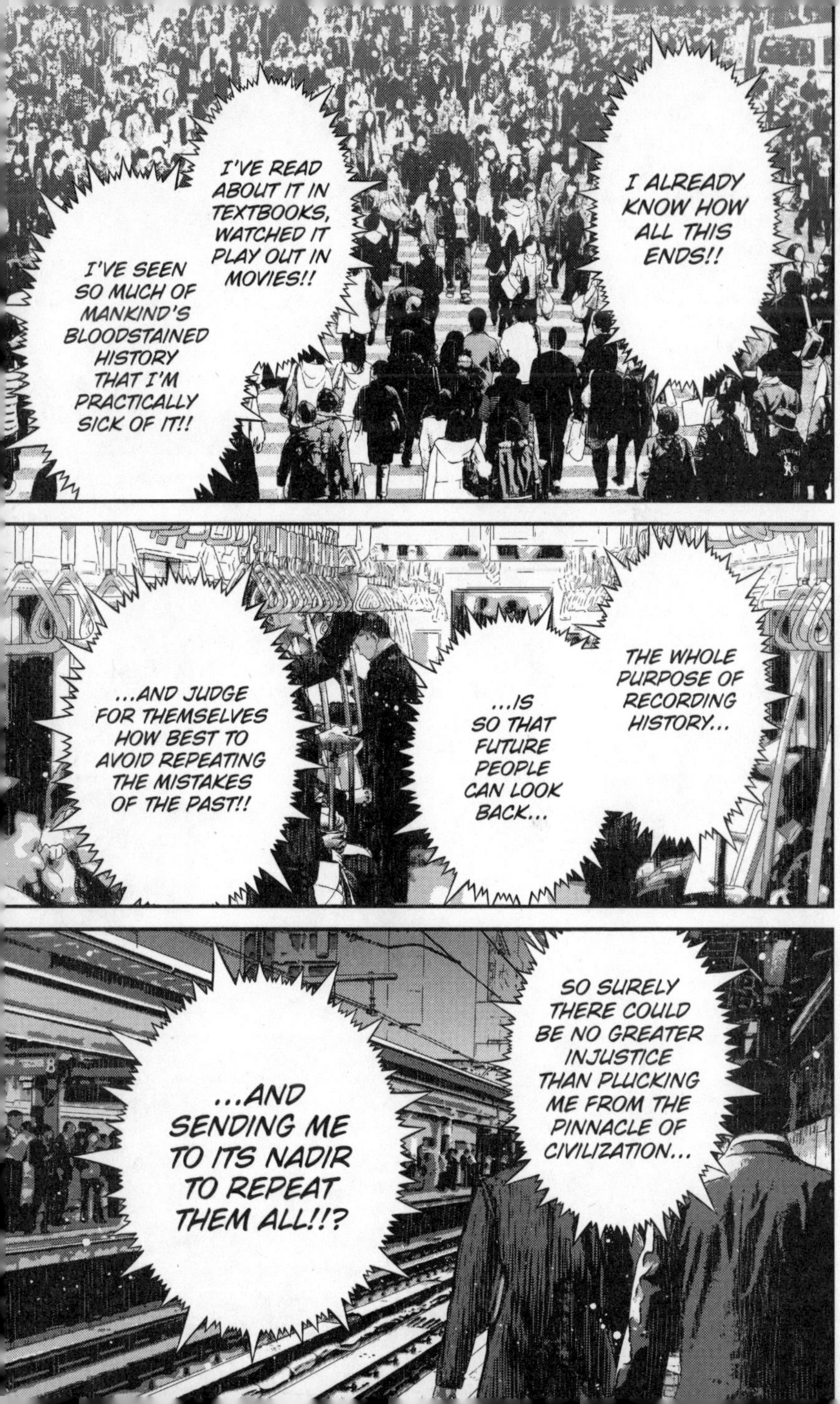
I ALREADY KNOW HOW ALL THIS ENDS!!
I'VE READ ABOUT IT IN TEXTBOOKS, WATCHED IT PLAY OUT IN MOVIES!!
I'VE SEEN SO MUCH OF MANKIND'S BLOODSTAINED HISTORY THAT I'M PRACTICALLY SICK OF IT!!
THE WHOLE PURPOSE OF RECORDING HISTORY...
...IS SO THAT FUTURE PEOPLE CAN LOOK BACK...
...AND JUDGE FOR THEMSELVES HOW BEST TO AVOID REPEATING THE MISTAKES OF THE PAST!!
SO SURELY THERE COULD BE NO GREATER INJUSTICE THAN PLUCKING ME FROM THE PINNACLE OF CIVILIZATION...
...AND SENDING ME TO ITS NADIR TO REPEAT THEM ALL!!?

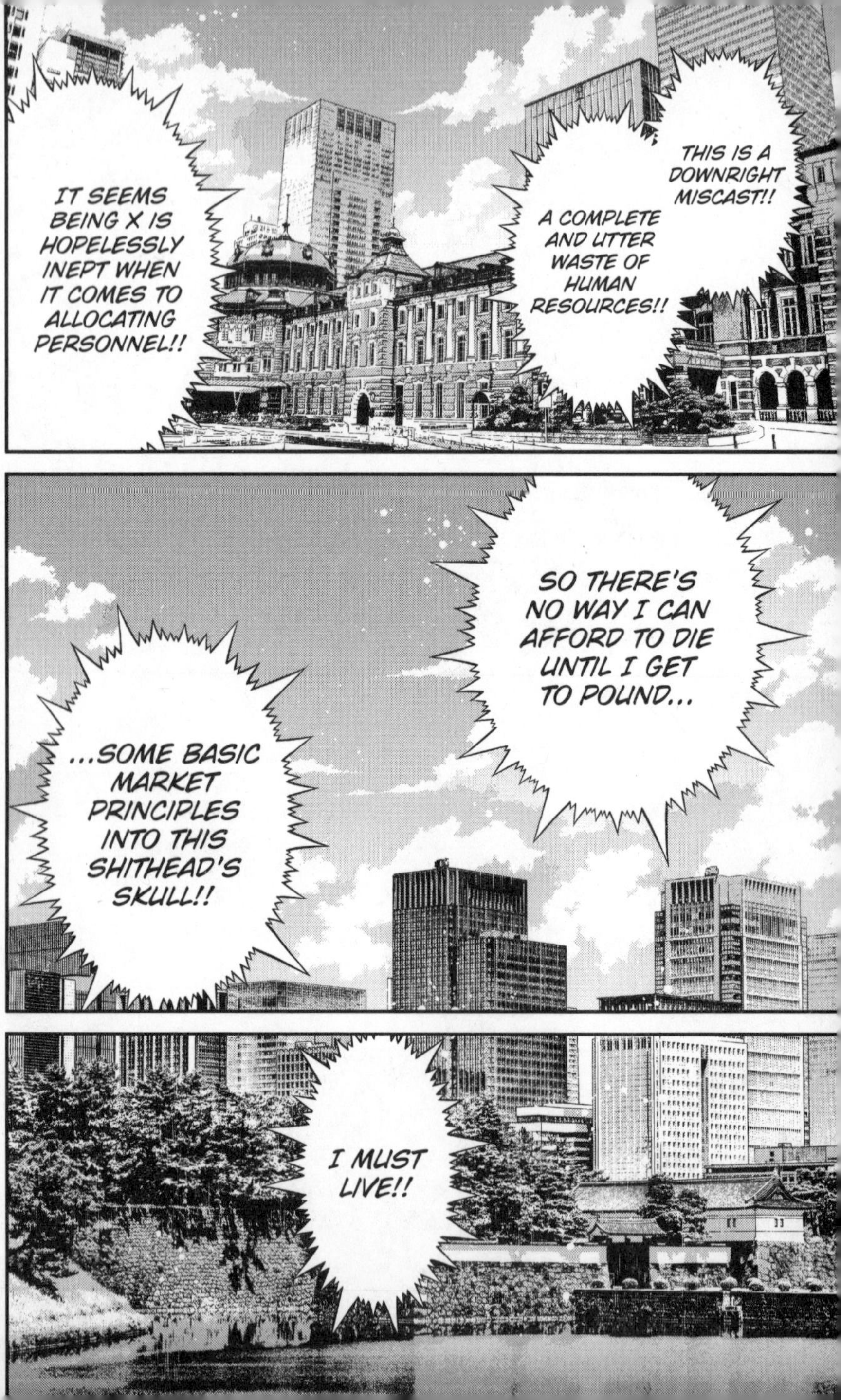
THIS IS A DOWNRIGHT MISCAST!!
A COMPLETE AND UTTER WASTE OF HUMAN RESOURCES!!
IT SEEMS BEING X IS HOPELESSLY INEPT WHEN IT COMES TO ALLOCATING PERSONNEL!!
SO THERE'S NO WAY I CAN AFFORD TO DIE UNTIL I GET TO POUND...
...SOME BASIC MARKET PRINCIPLES INTO THIS SHITHEAD'S SKULL!!
I MUST LIVE!!

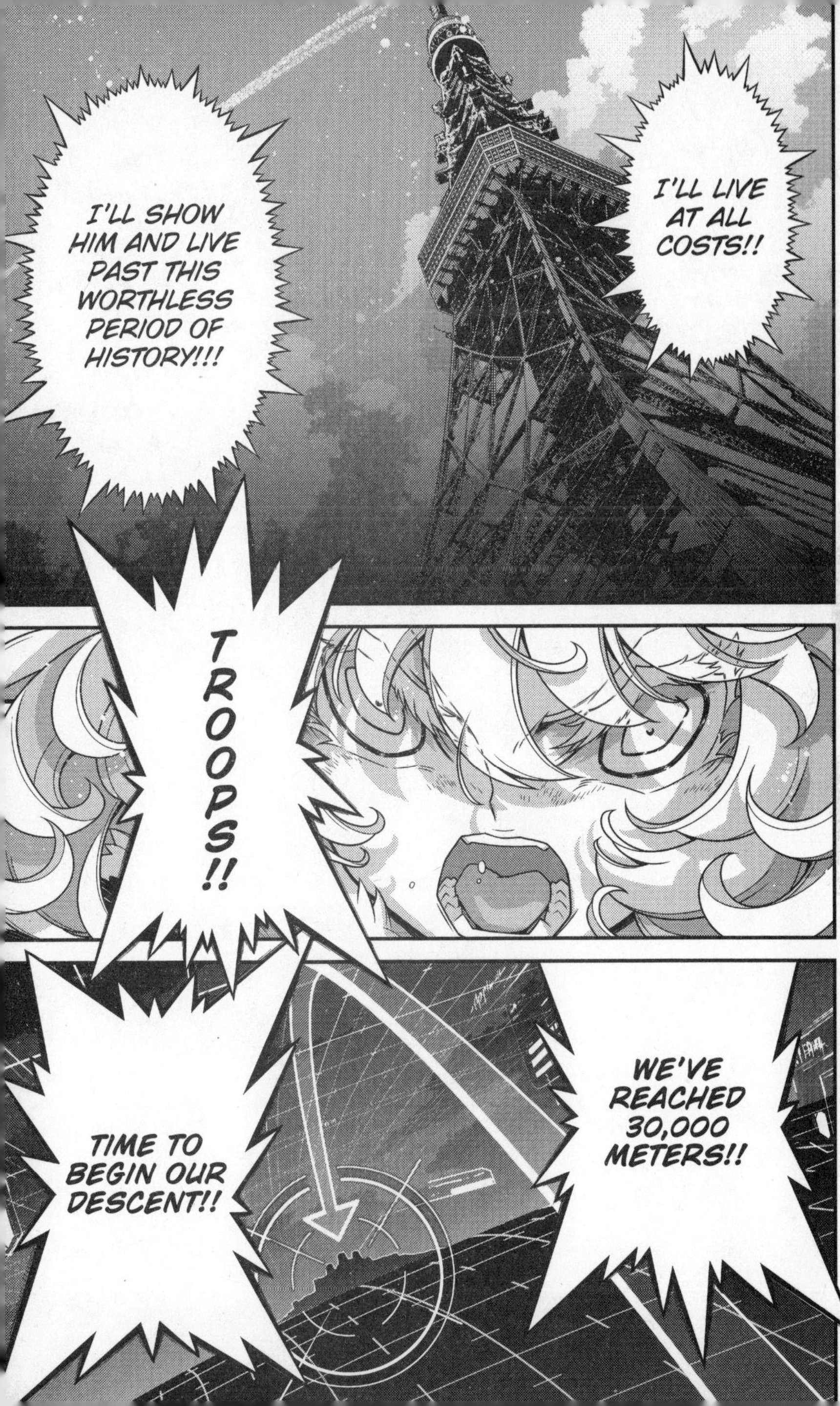
I'LL LIVE AT ALL COSTS!!
I'LL SHOW HIM AND LIVE PAST THIS WORTHLESS PERIOD OF HISTORY!!!
TROOPS!!
WE'VE REACHED 30,000 METERS!!
TIME TO BEGIN OUR DESCENT!!

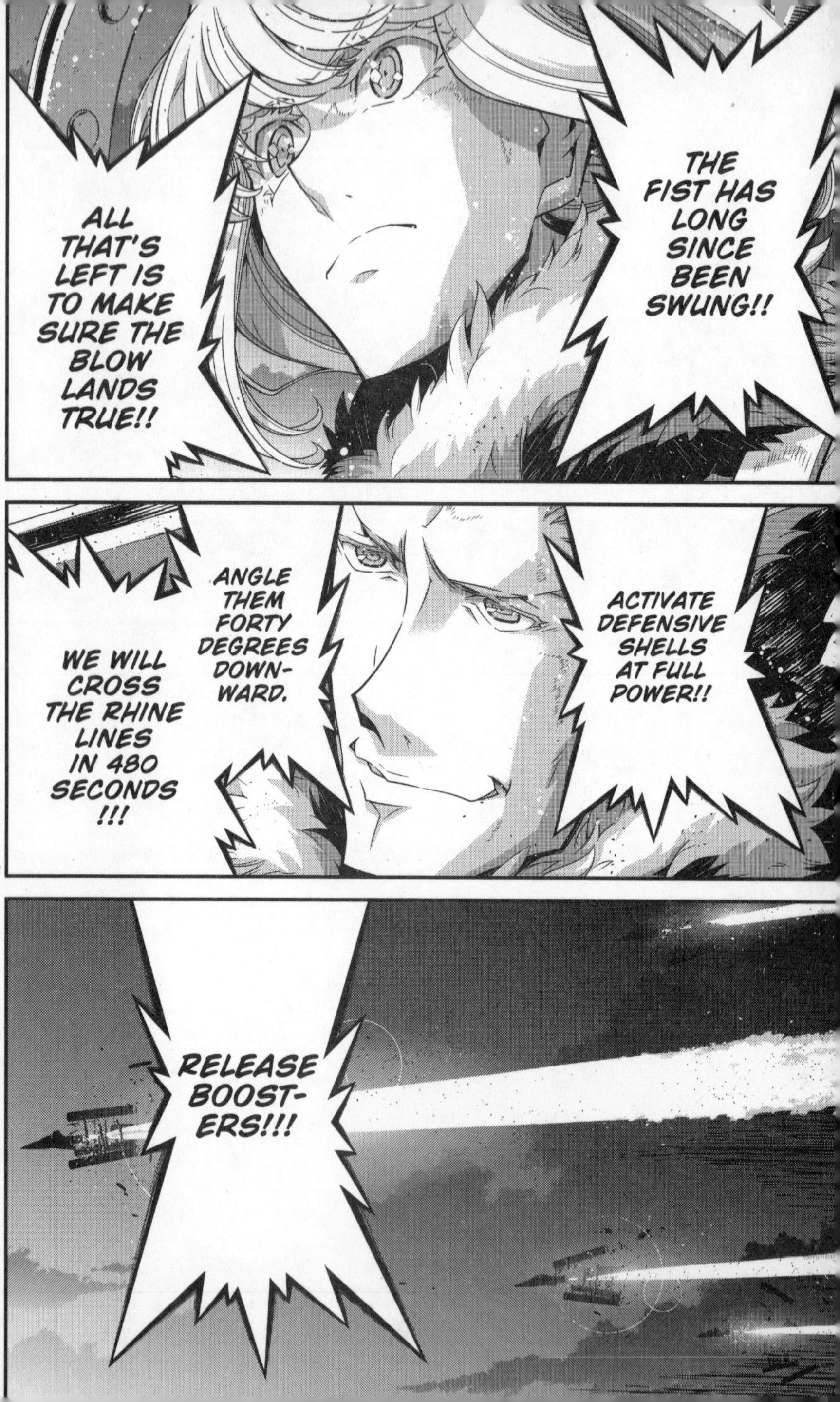
THE FIST HAS LONG SINCE BEEN SWUNG!!
ALL THAT'S LEFT IS TO MAKE SURE THE BLOW LANDS TRUE!!
ACTIVATE DEFENSIVE SHELLS AT FULL POWER!!
ANGLE THEM FORTY DEGREES DOWN-WARD.
WE WILL CROSS THE RHINE LINES IN 480 SECONDS!!!
RELEASE BOOST-ERS!!!

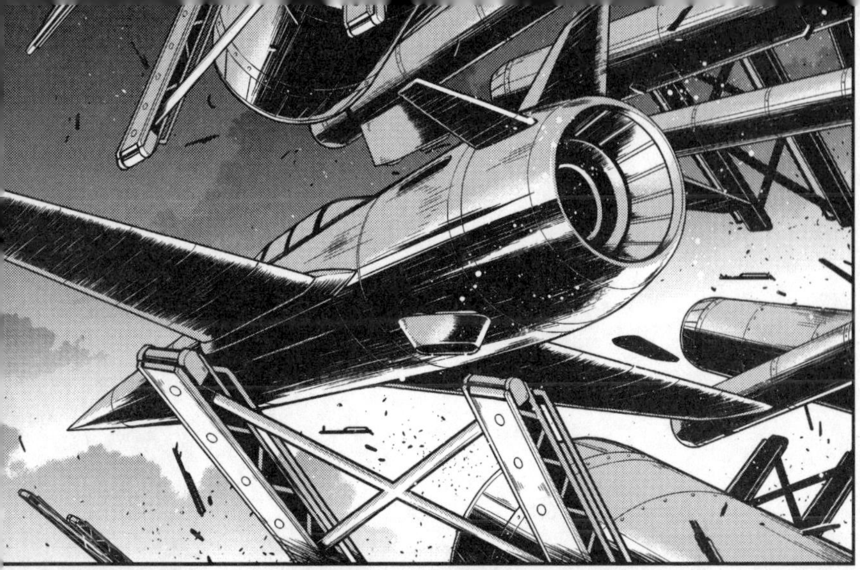
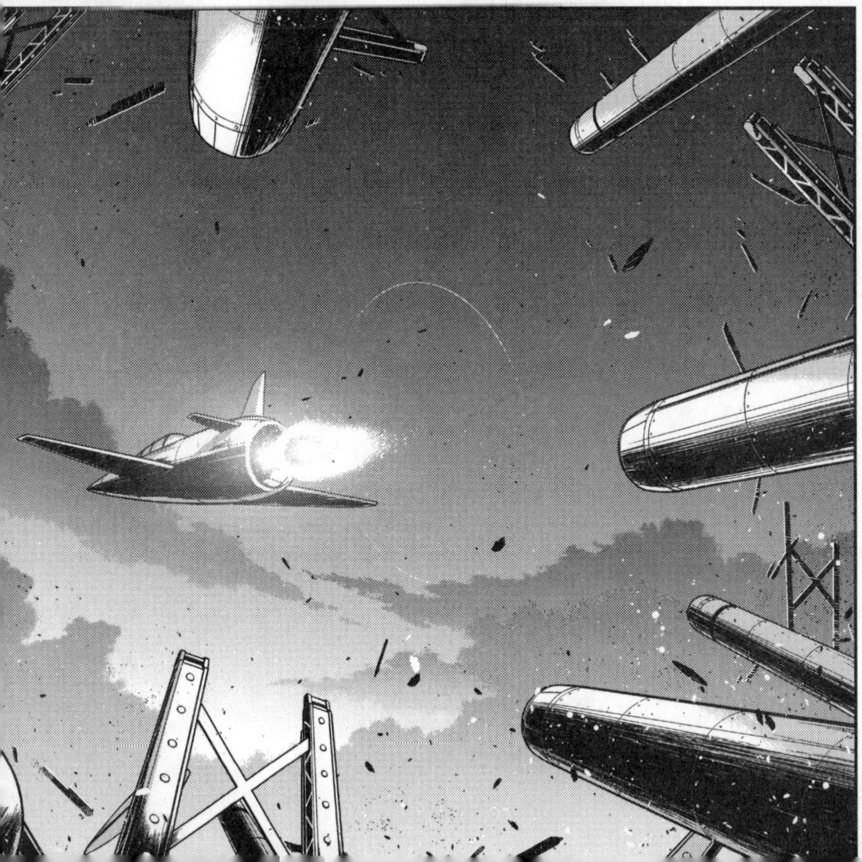

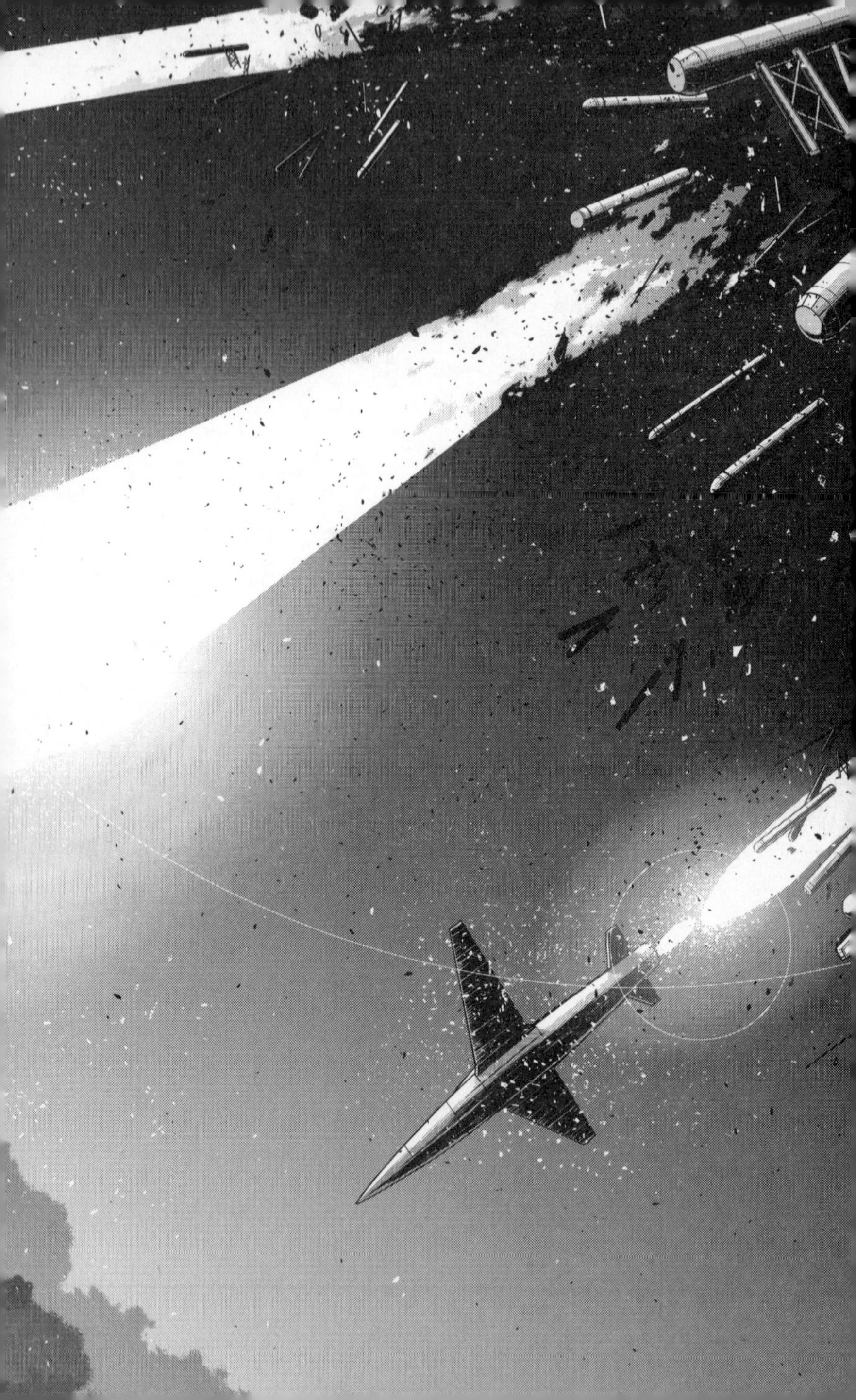

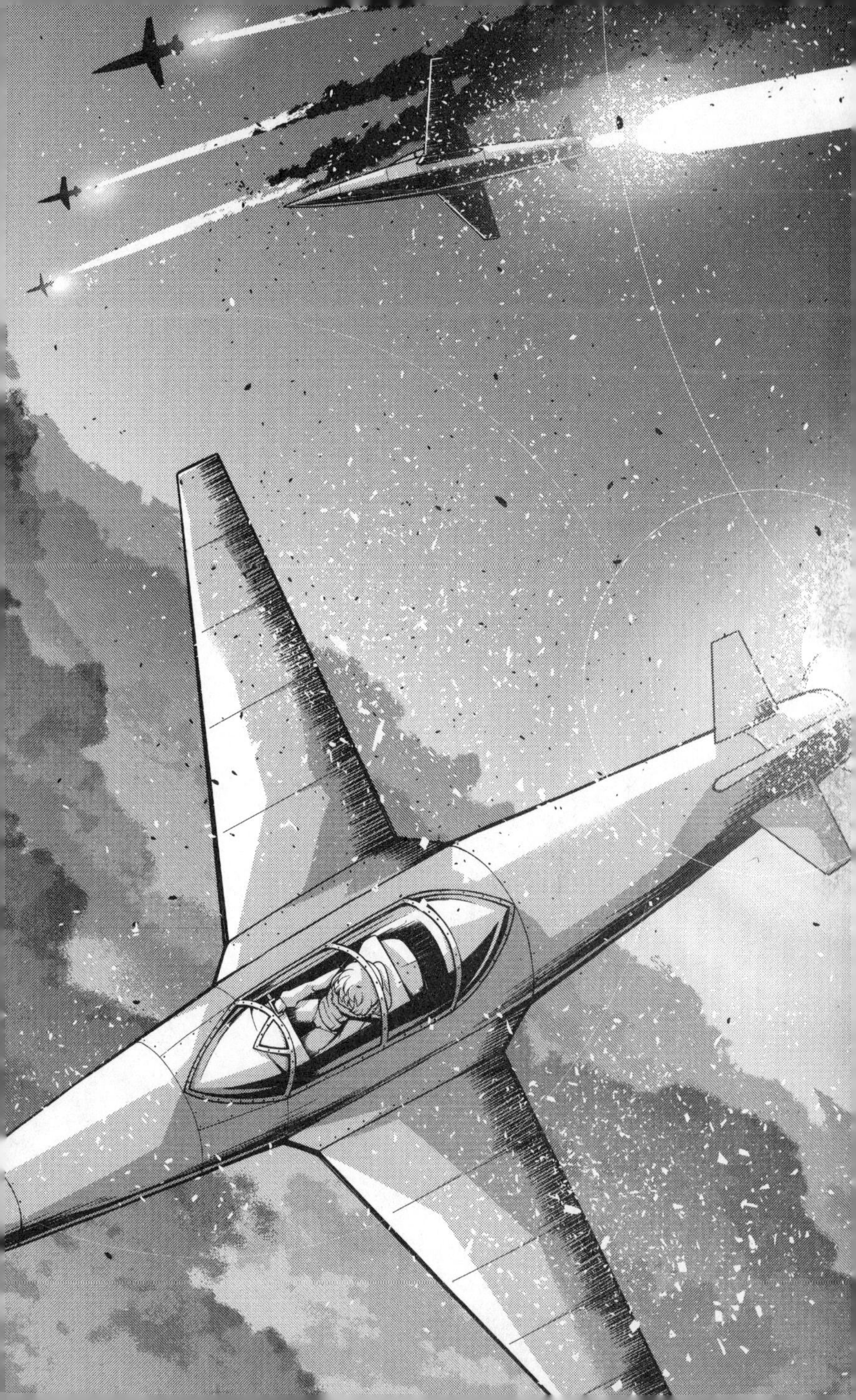

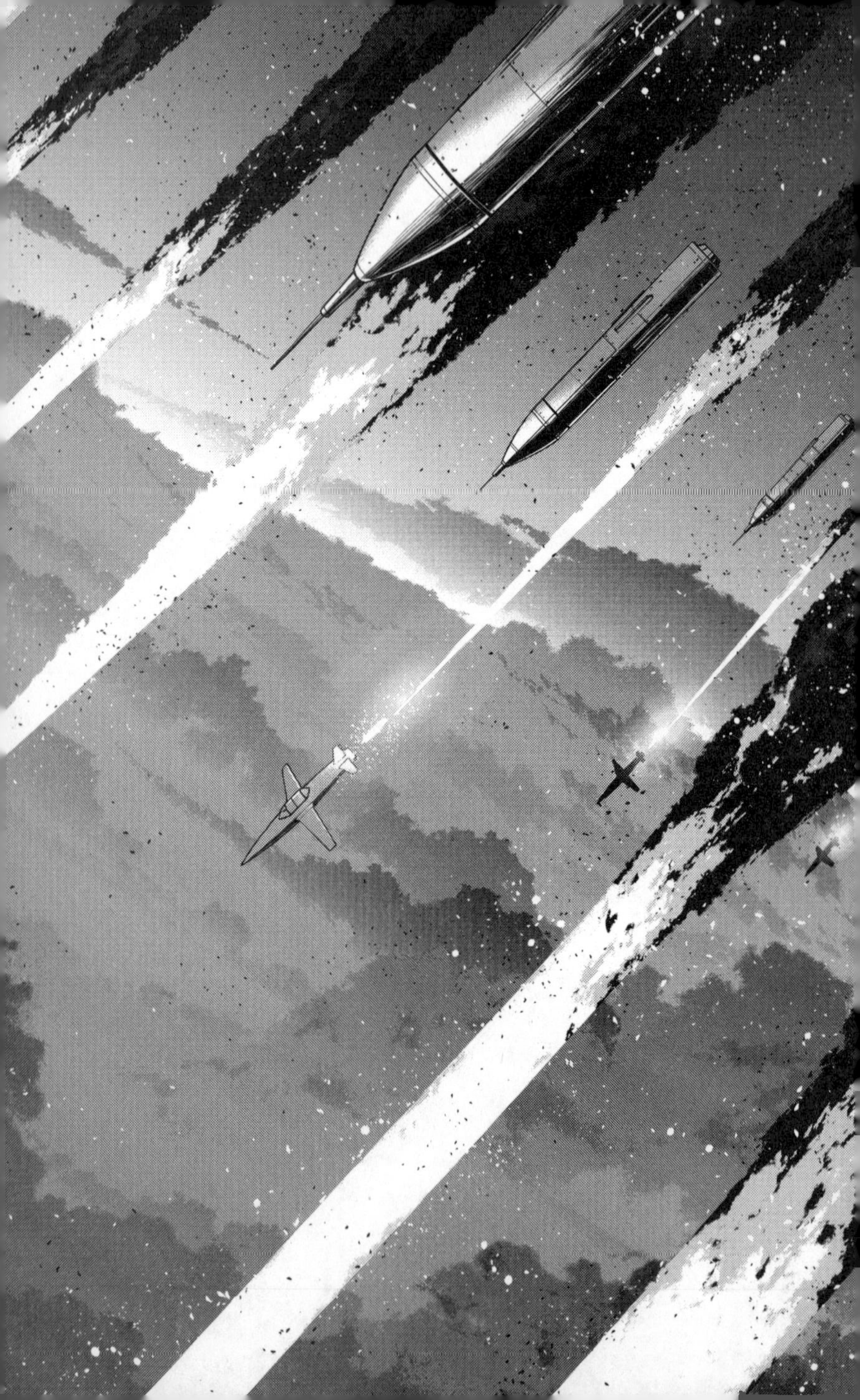

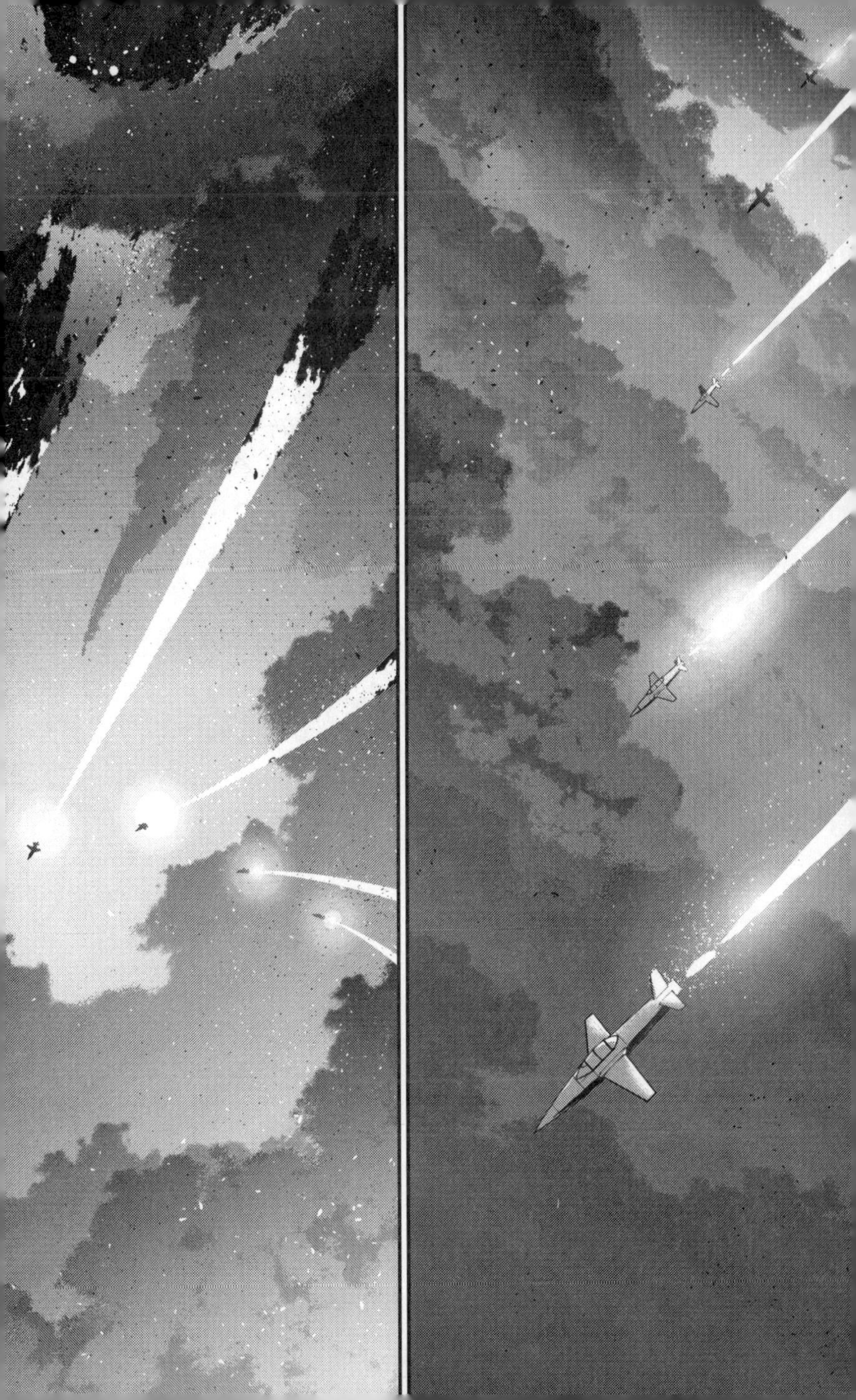

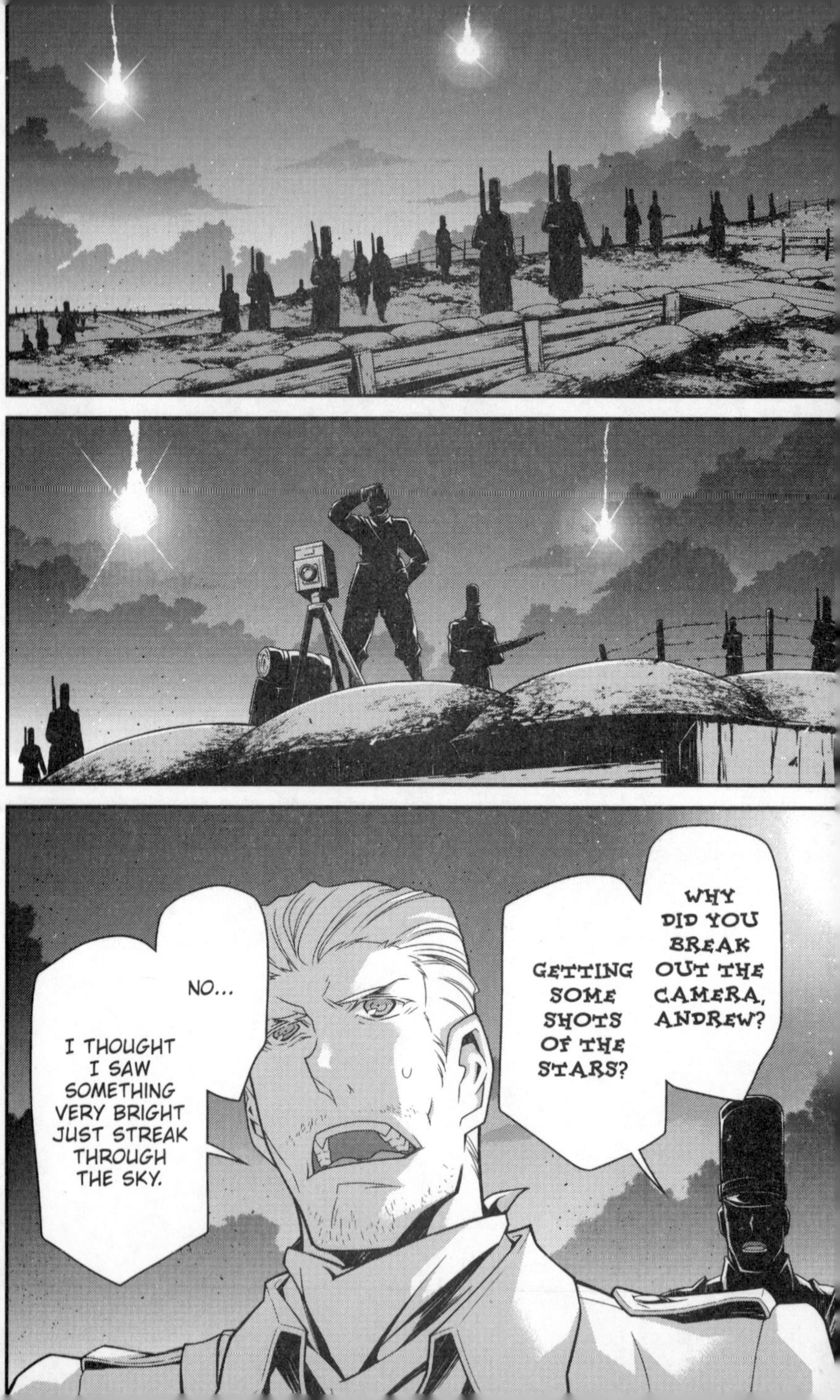
WHY DID YOU BREAK OUT THE CAMERA, ANDREW?
GETTING SOME SHOTS OF THE STARS?
NO...
I THOUGHT I SAW SOMETHING VERY BRIGHT JUST STREAK THROUGH THE SKY.

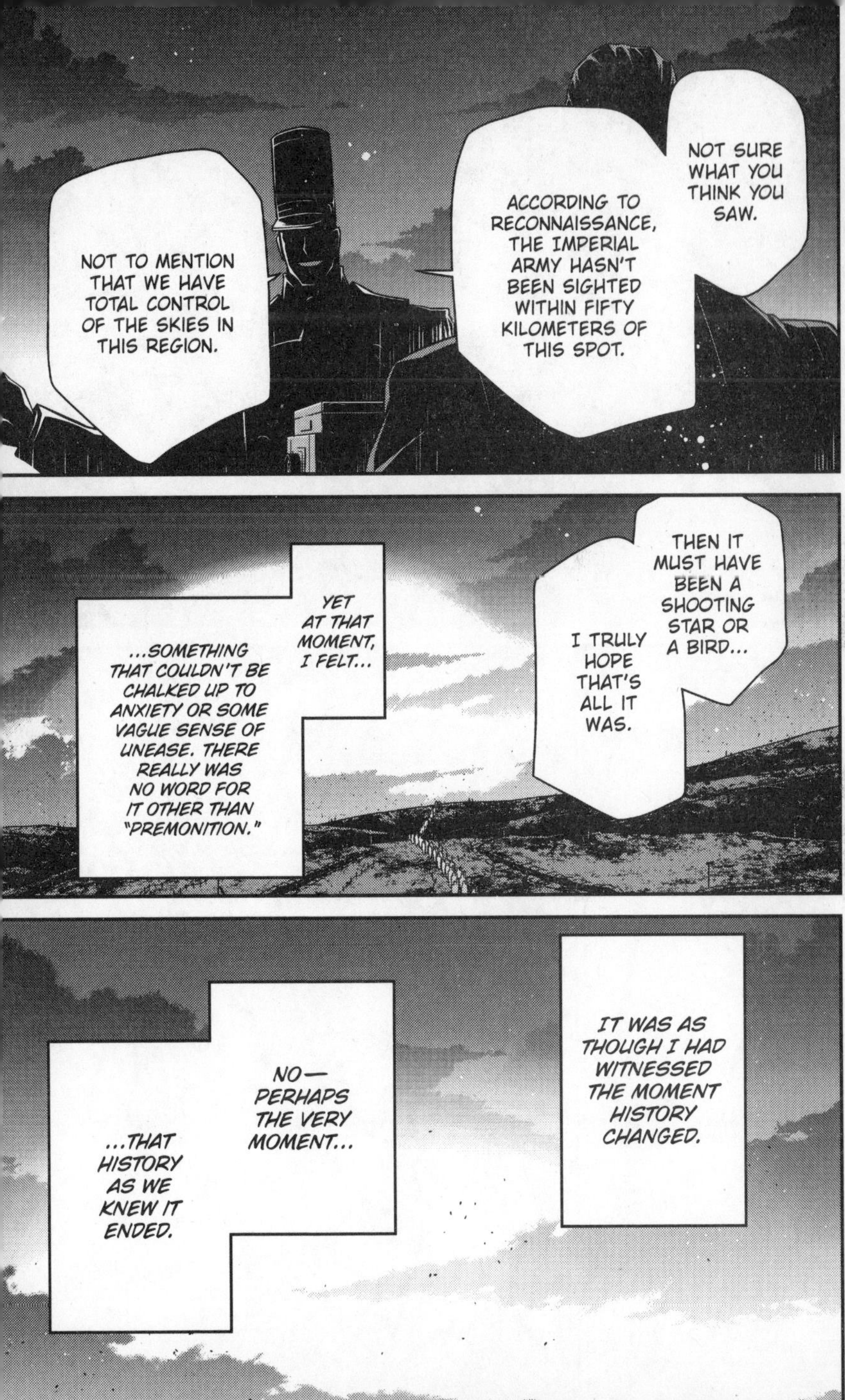
NOT SURE WHAT YOU THINK YOU SAW.
ACCORDING TO RECONNAISSANCE, THE IMPERIAL ARMY HASN'T BEEN SIGHTED WITHIN FIFTY KILOMETERS OF THIS SPOT.
NOT TO MENTION THAT WE HAVE TOTAL CONTROL OF THE SKIES IN THIS REGION.
THEN IT MUST HAVE BEEN A SHOOTING STAR OR A BIRD...
I TRULY HOPE THAT'S ALL IT WAS.
YET AT THAT MOMENT, I FELT...
...SOMETHING THAT COULDN'T BE CHALKED UP TO ANXIETY OR SOME VAGUE SENSE OF UNEASE. THERE REALLY WAS NO WORD FOR IT OTHER THAN "PREMONITION."
IT WAS AS THOUGH I HAD WITNESSED THE MOMENT HISTORY CHANGED.
NO— PERHAPS THE VERY MOMENT...
...THAT HISTORY AS WE KNEW IT ENDED.

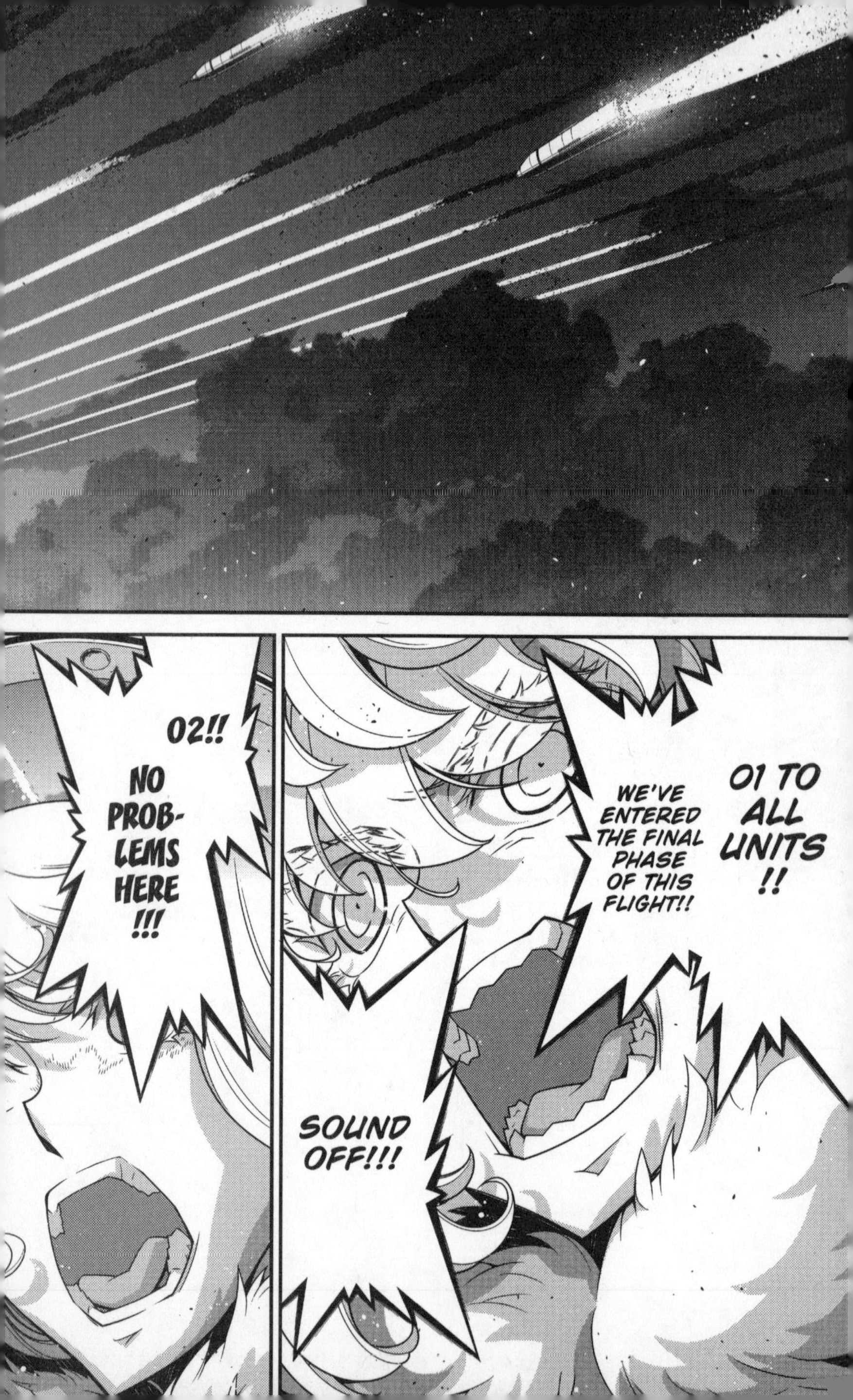
01 TO ALL UNITS!!
WE'VE ENTERED THE FINAL PHASE OF THIS FLIGHT!!
SOUND OFF!!!
02!!
NO PROBLEMS HERE!!!

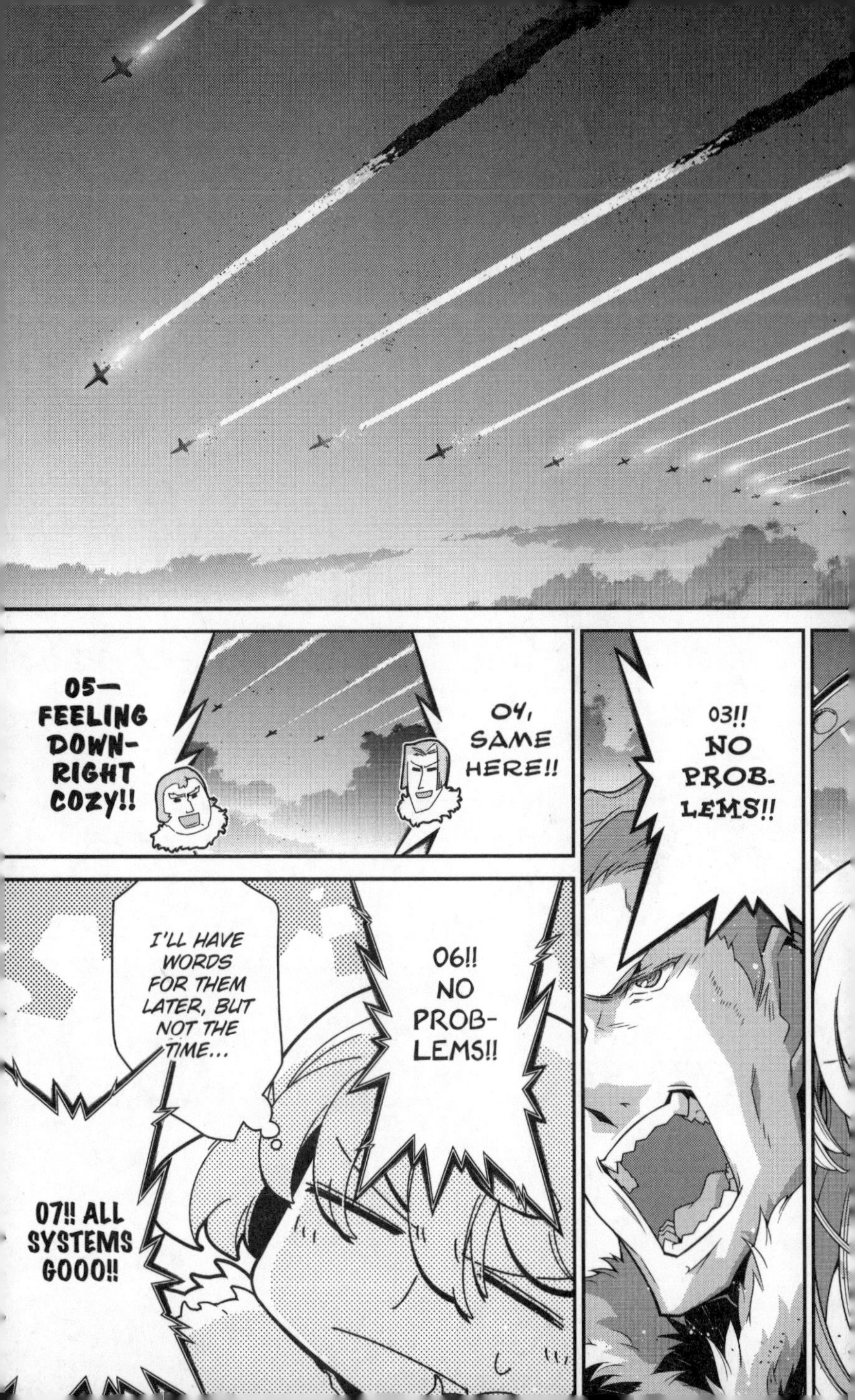
03!! NO PROBLEMS!!
04, SAME HERE!!
05—FEELING DOWNRIGHT COZY!!
06!! NO PROBLEMS!!
I'LL HAVE WORDS FOR THEM LATER, BUT NOT THE TIME...
07!! ALL SYSTEMS GOOO!!

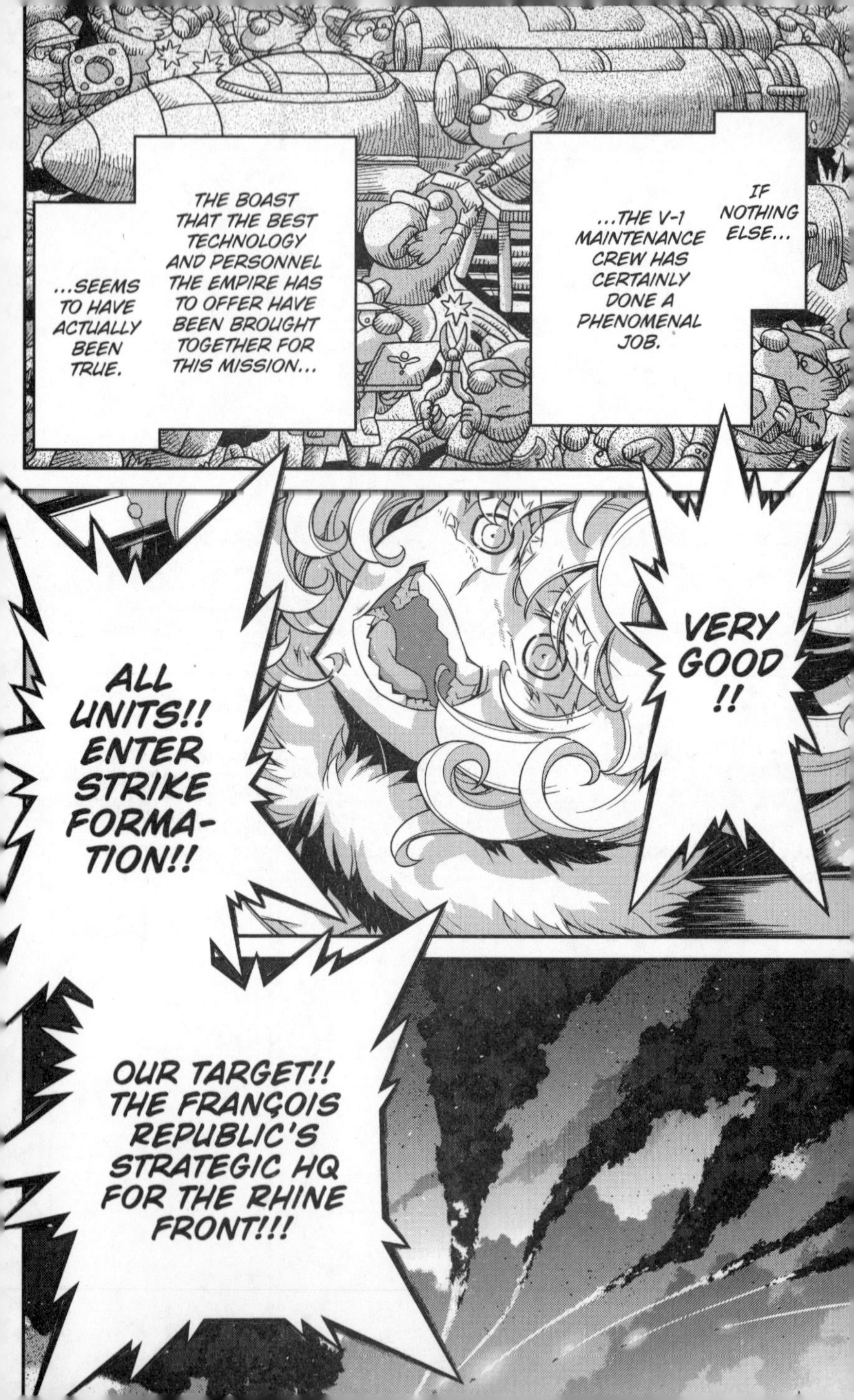

IF NOTHING ELSE...
...THE V-1 MAINTENANCE CREW HAS CERTAINLY DONE A PHENOMENAL JOB.
THE BOAST THAT THE BEST TECHNOLOGY AND PERSONNEL THE EMPIRE HAS TO OFFER HAVE BEEN BROUGHT TOGETHER FOR THIS MISSION...
...SEEMS TO HAVE ACTUALLY BEEN TRUE.
VERY GOOD!!
ALL UNITS!! ENTER STRIKE FORMATION!!
OUR TARGET!! THE FRANÇOIS REPUBLIC'S STRATEGIC HQ FOR THE RHINE FRONT!!!

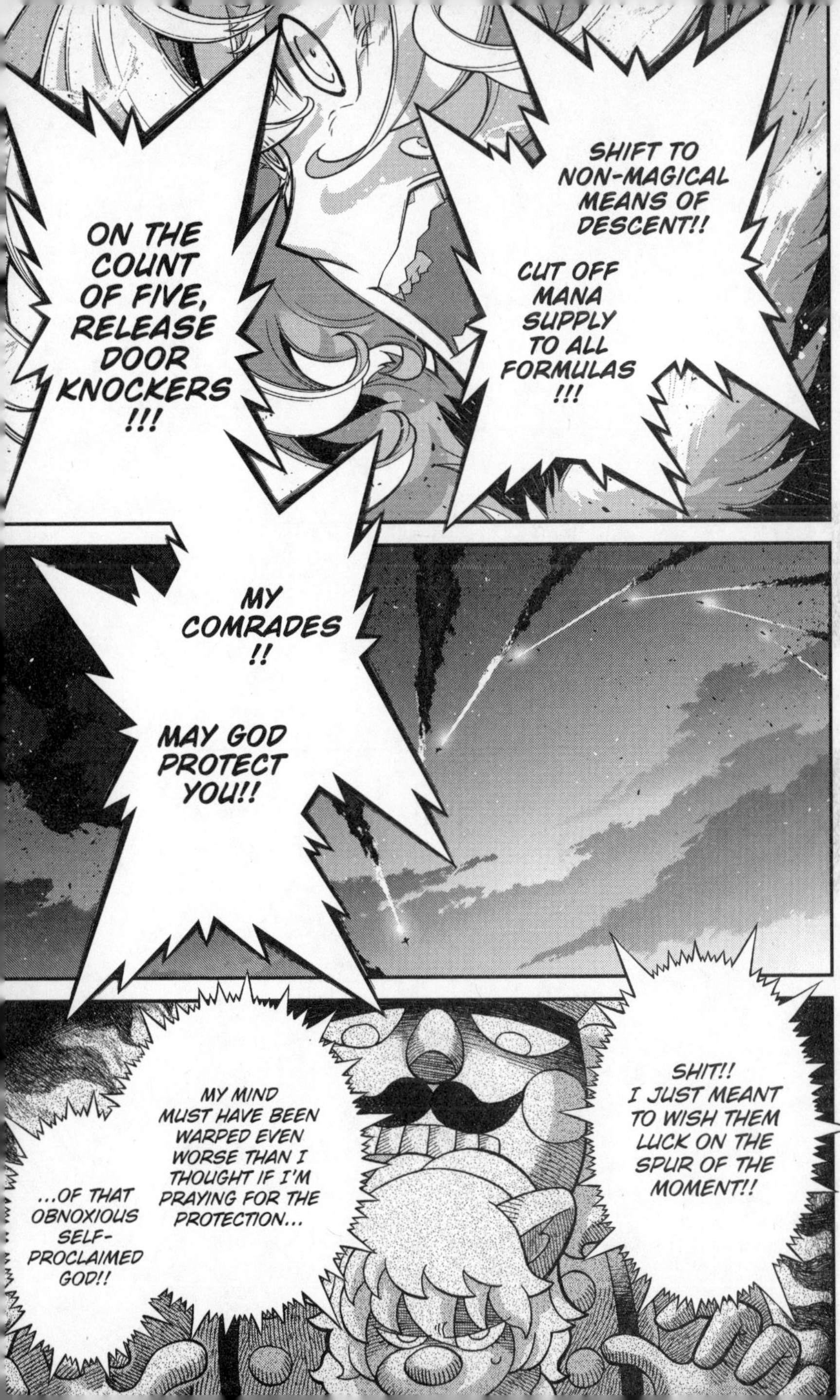
SHIFT TO NON-MAGICAL MEANS OF DESCENT!!
CUT OFF MANA SUPPLY TO ALL FORMULAS !!!
ON THE COUNT OF FIVE, RELEASE DOOR KNOCKERS !!!
MY COMRADES !!
MAY GOD PROTECT YOU!!
SHIT!! I JUST MEANT TO WISH THEM LUCK ON THE SPUR OF THE MOMENT!!
MY MIND MUST HAVE BEEN WARPED EVEN WORSE THAN I THOUGHT IF I'M PRAYING FOR THE PROTECTION...
...OF THAT OBNOXIOUS SELF-PROCLAIMED GOD!!

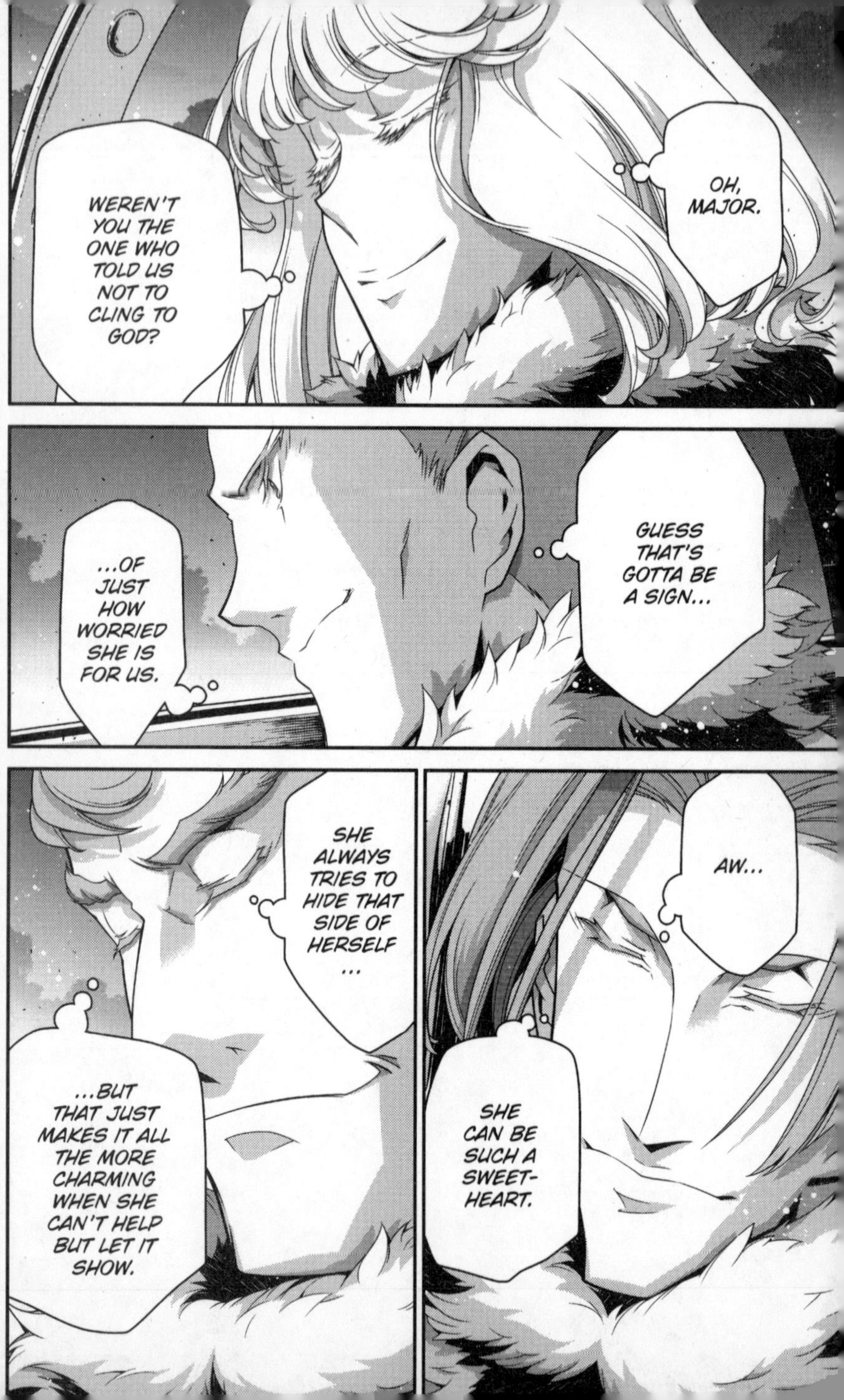
OH, MAJOR.
WEREN'T YOU THE ONE WHO TOLD US NOT TO CLING TO GOD?
GUESS THAT'S GOTTA BE A SIGN...
...OF JUST HOW WORRIED SHE IS FOR US.
AW...
SHE CAN BE SUCH A SWEET-HEART.
SHE ALWAYS TRIES TO HIDE THAT SIDE OF HERSELF...
...BUT THAT JUST MAKES IT ALL THE MORE CHARMING WHEN SHE CAN'T HELP BUT LET IT SHOW.

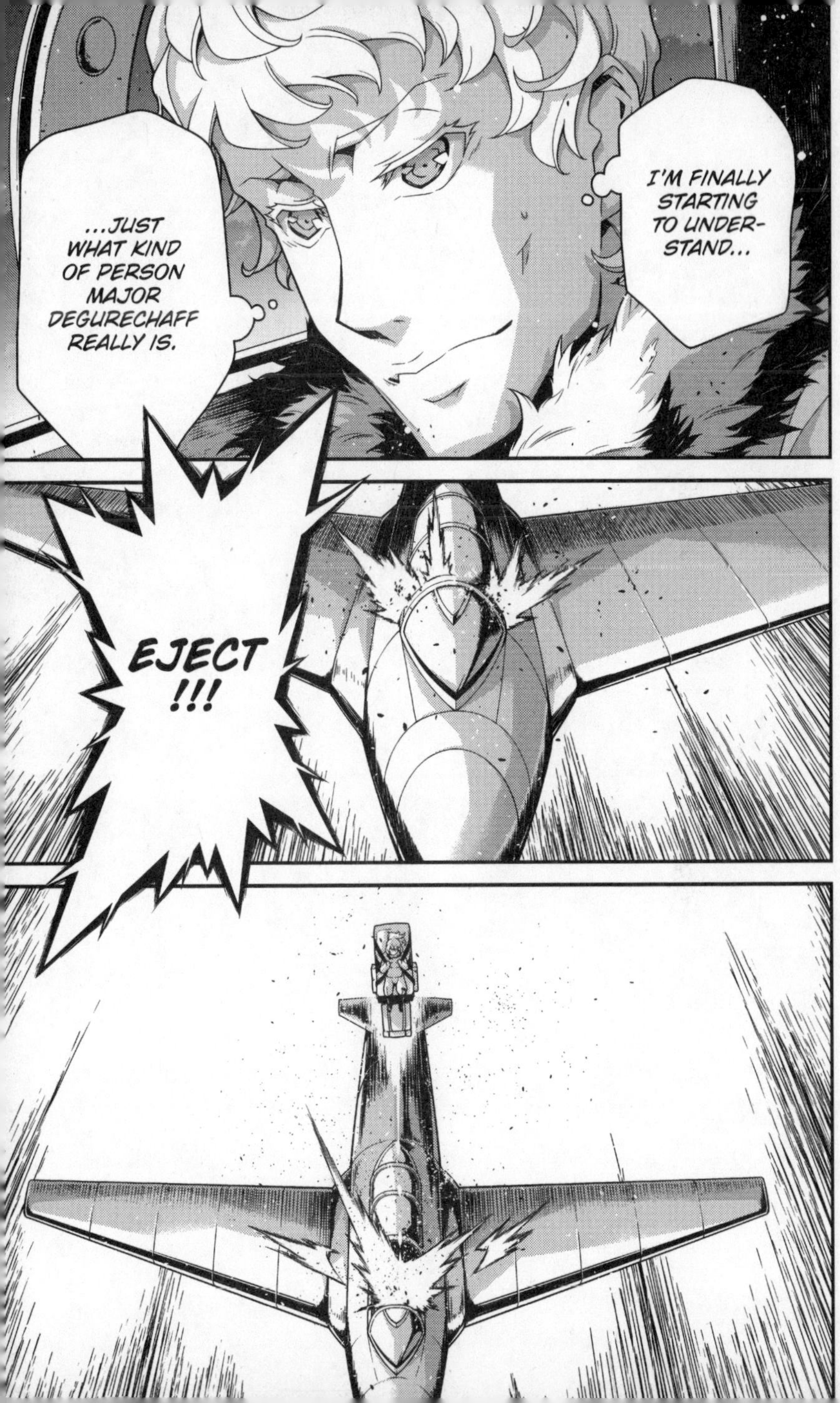
I'M FINALLY STARTING TO UNDER-STAND...
...JUST WHAT KIND OF PERSON MAJOR DEGURECHAFF REALLY IS.
EJECT !!!

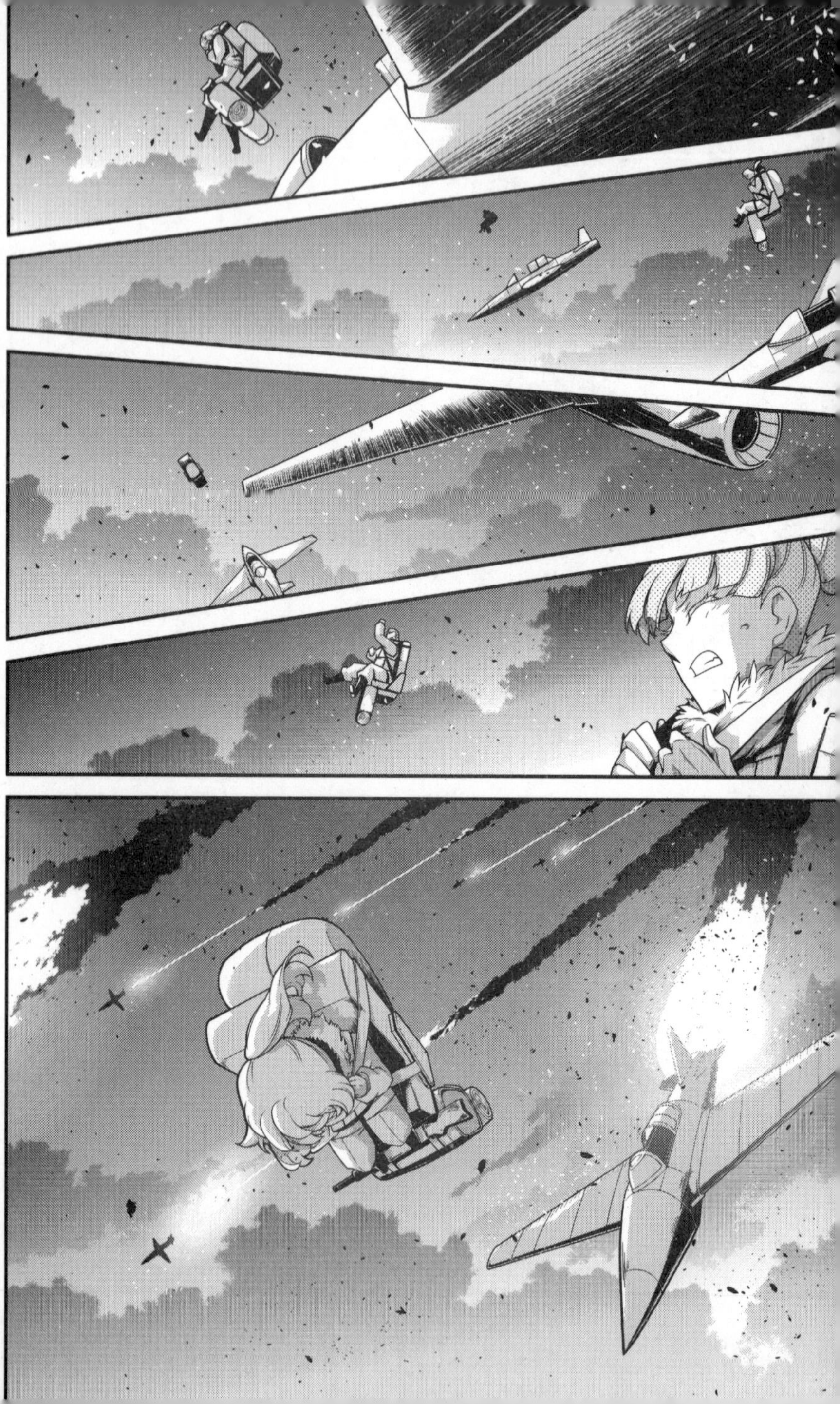

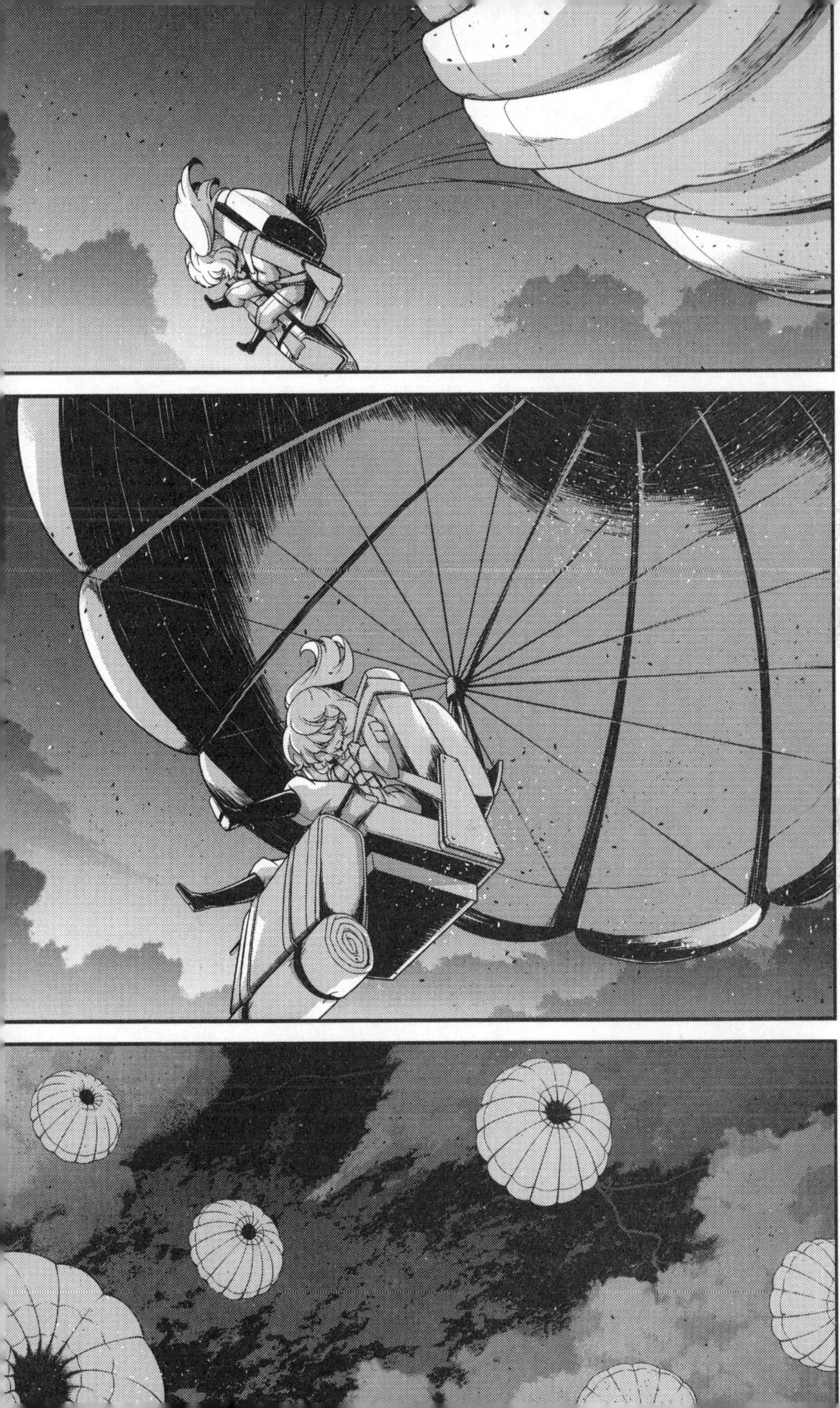

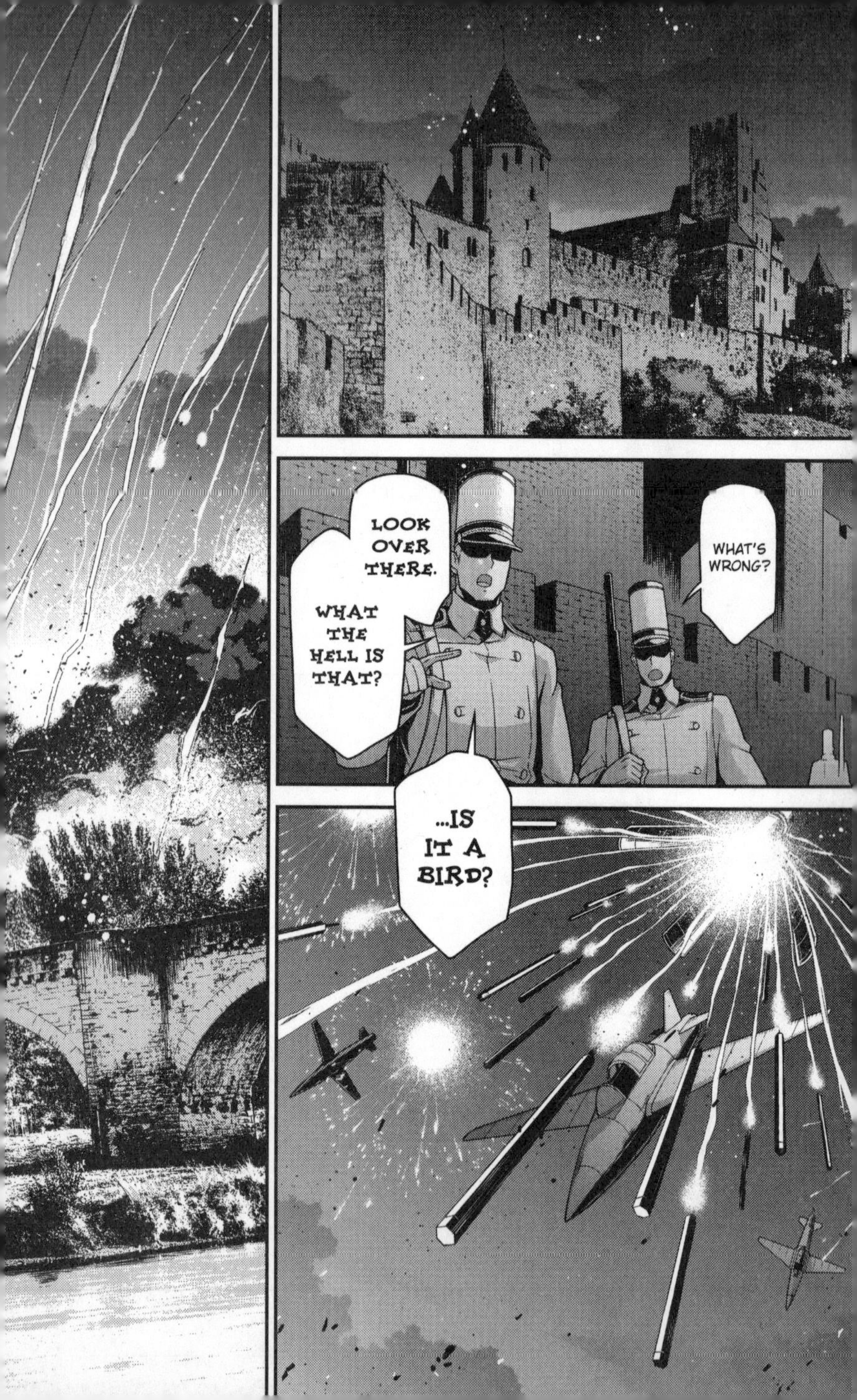
WHAT'S WRONG?
LOOK OVER THERE.
WHAT THE HELL IS THAT?
...IS IT A BIRD?

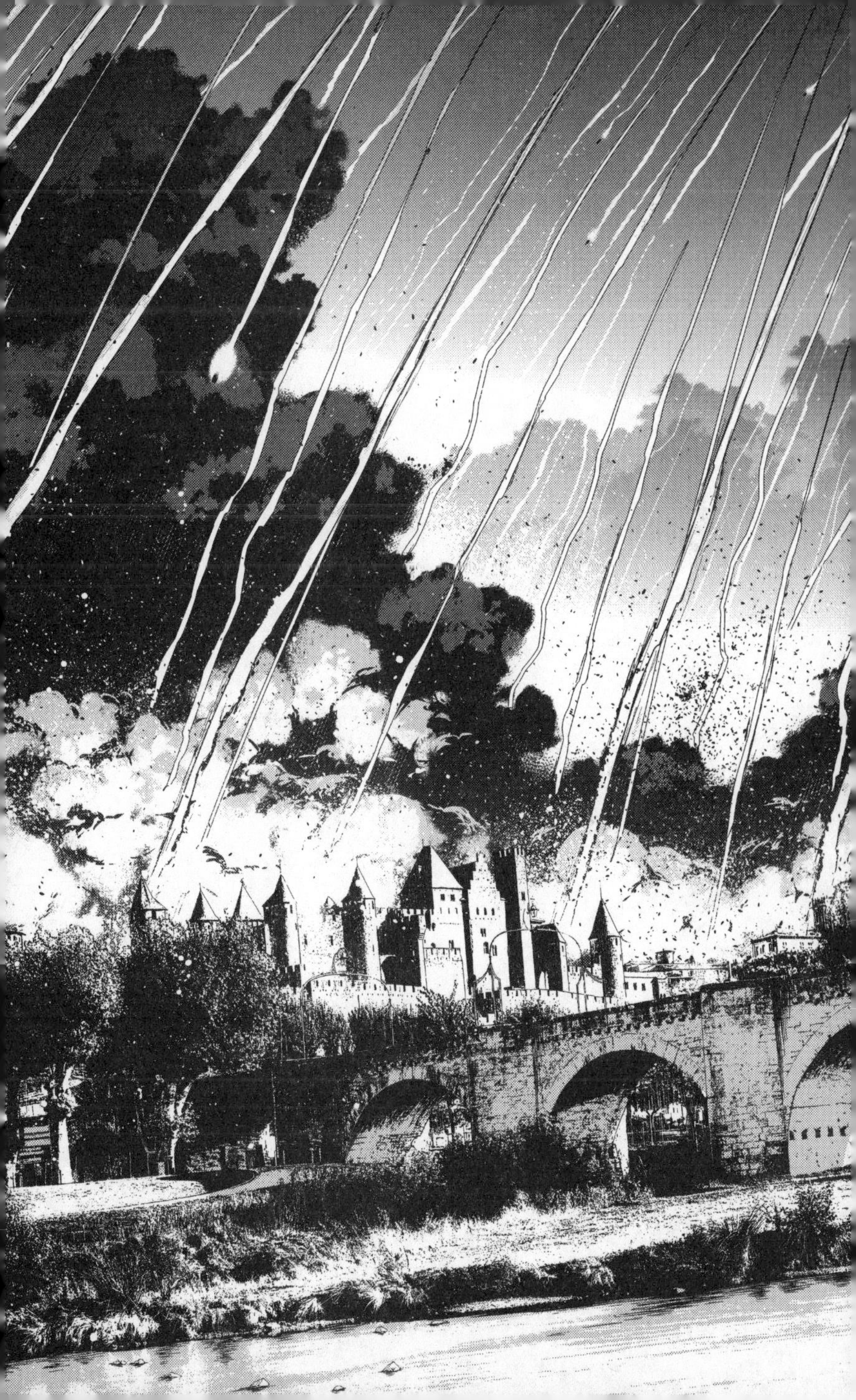

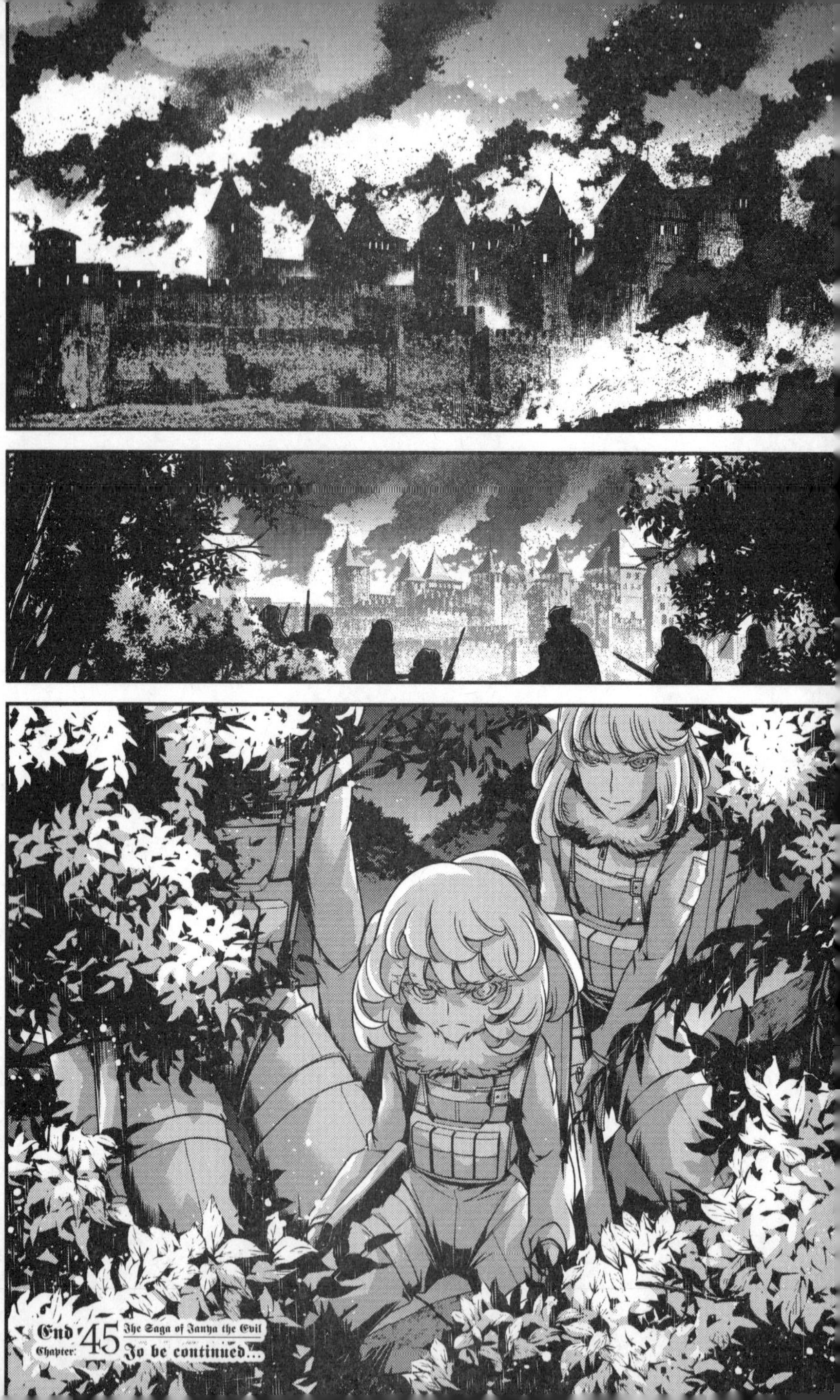
End Chapter: 45
The Saga of Tanya the Evil
To be continued...

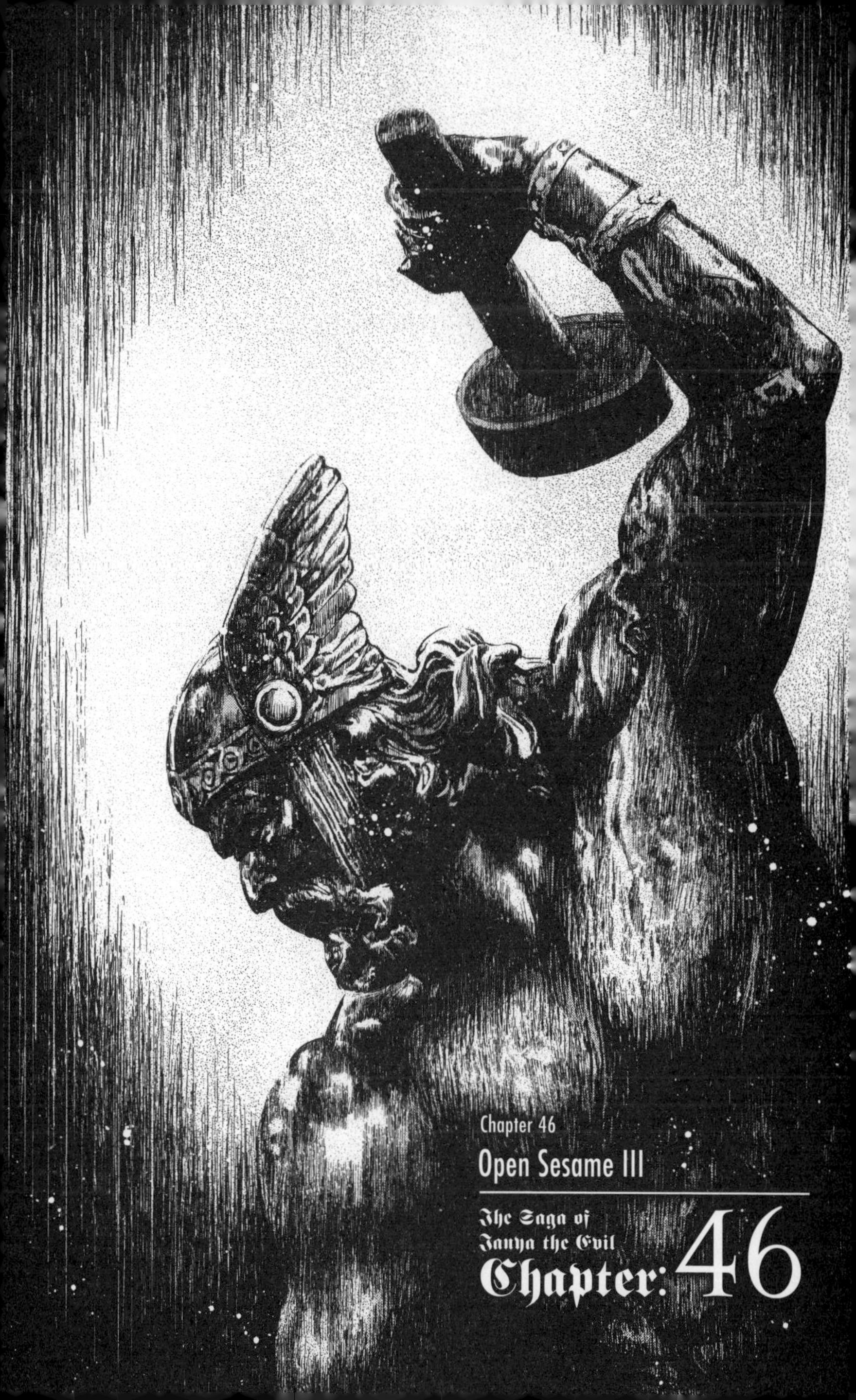
Chapter 46
Open Sesame III
The Saga of Tanya the Evil
Chapter: 46

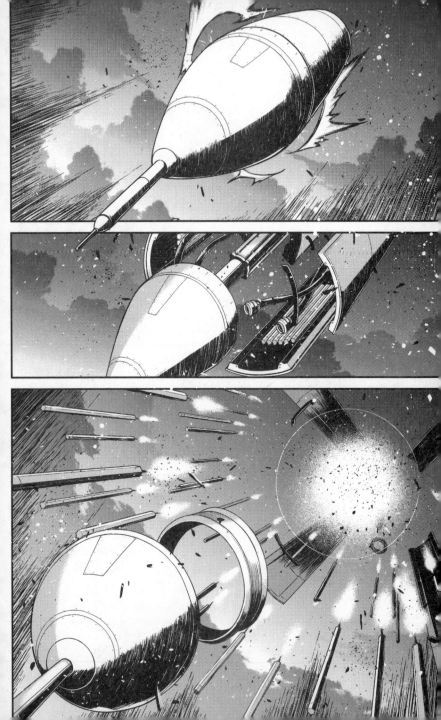

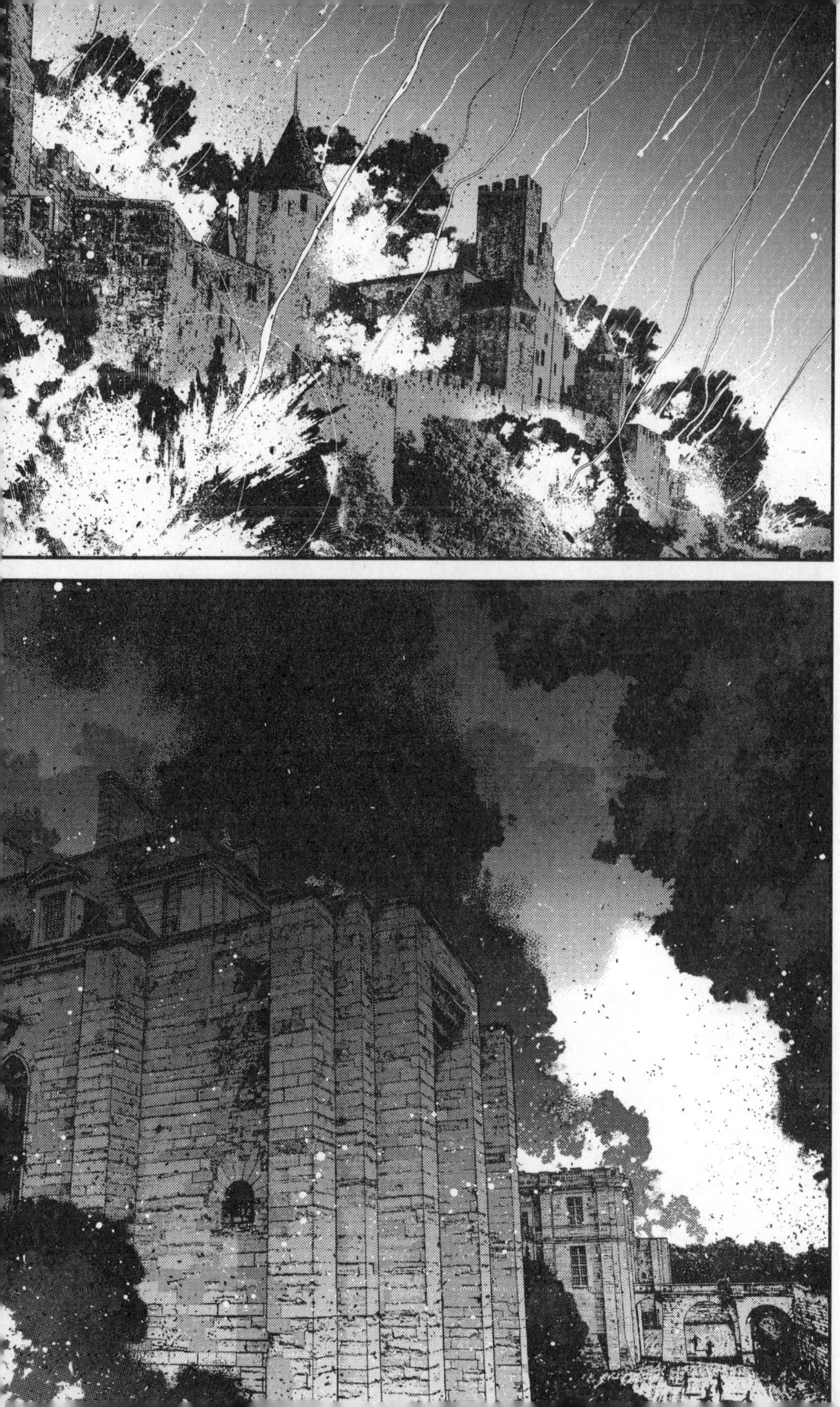

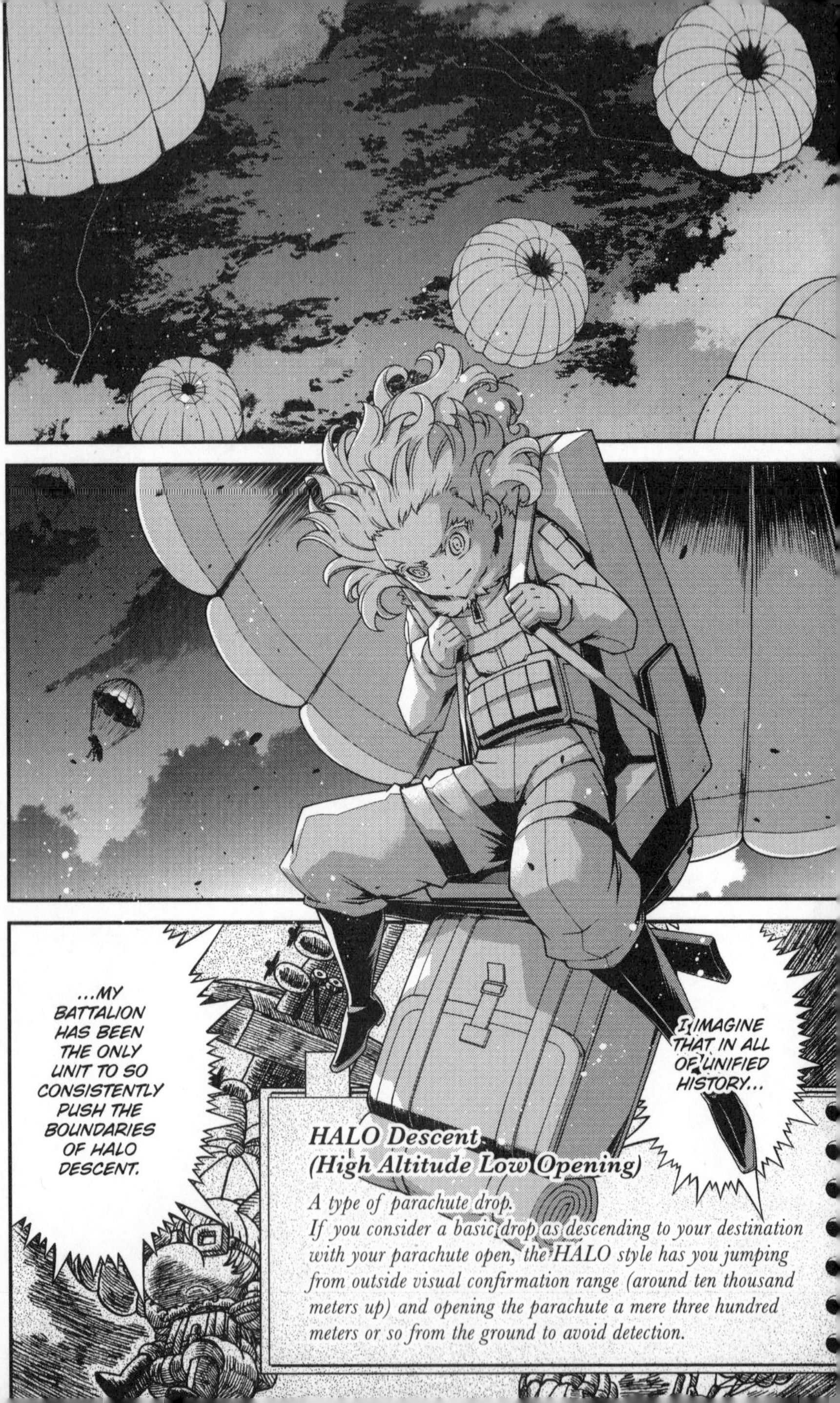
I IMAGINE THAT IN ALL OF UNIFIED HISTORY...
...MY BATTALION HAS BEEN THE ONLY UNIT TO SO CONSISTENTLY PUSH THE BOUNDARIES OF HALO DESCENT.
HALO Descent
(High Altitude Low Opening)
A type of parachute drop.
If you consider a basic drop as descending to your destination with your parachute open, the HALO style has you jumping from outside visual confirmation range (around ten thousand meters up) and opening the parachute a mere three hundred meters or so from the ground to avoid detection.

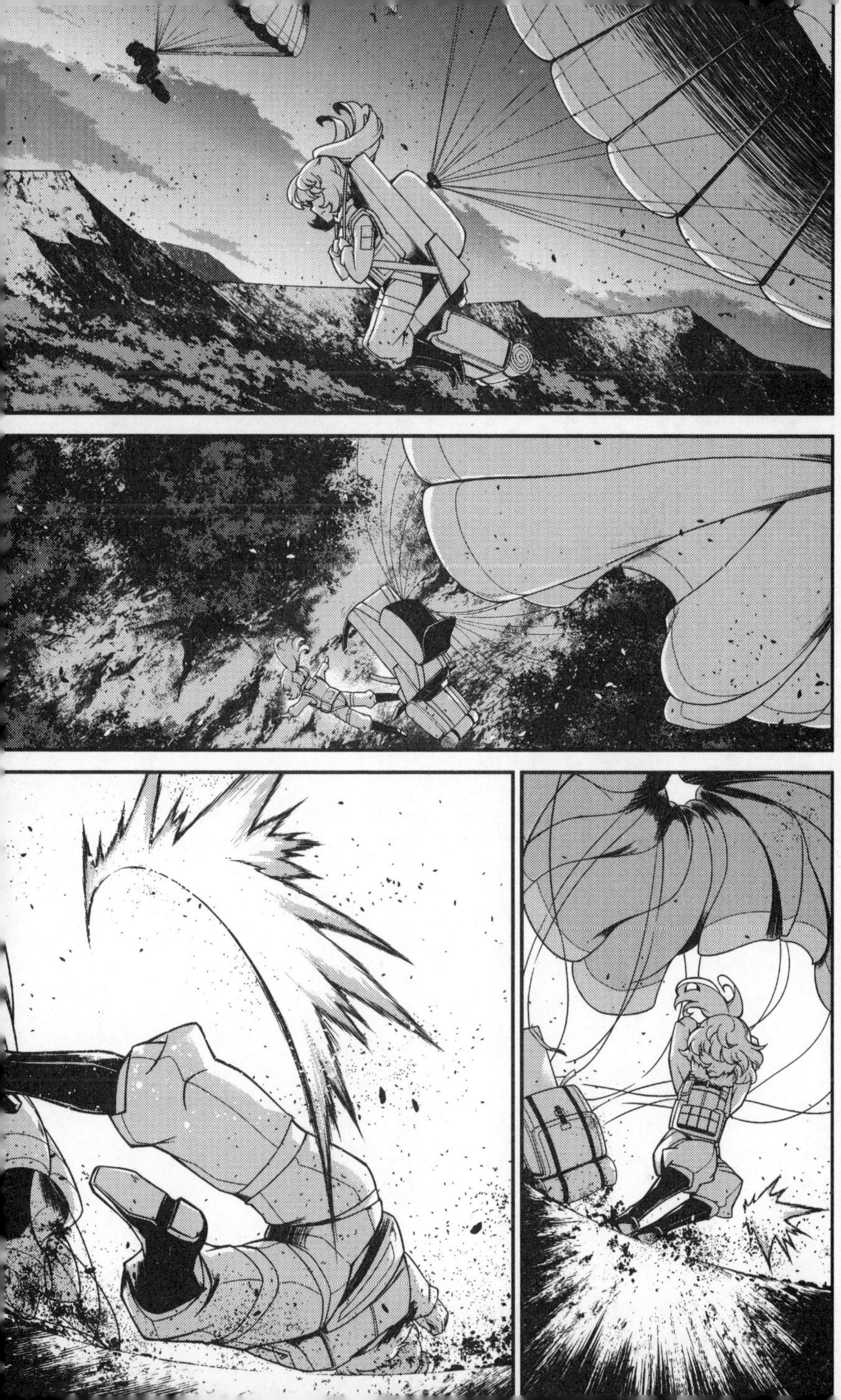

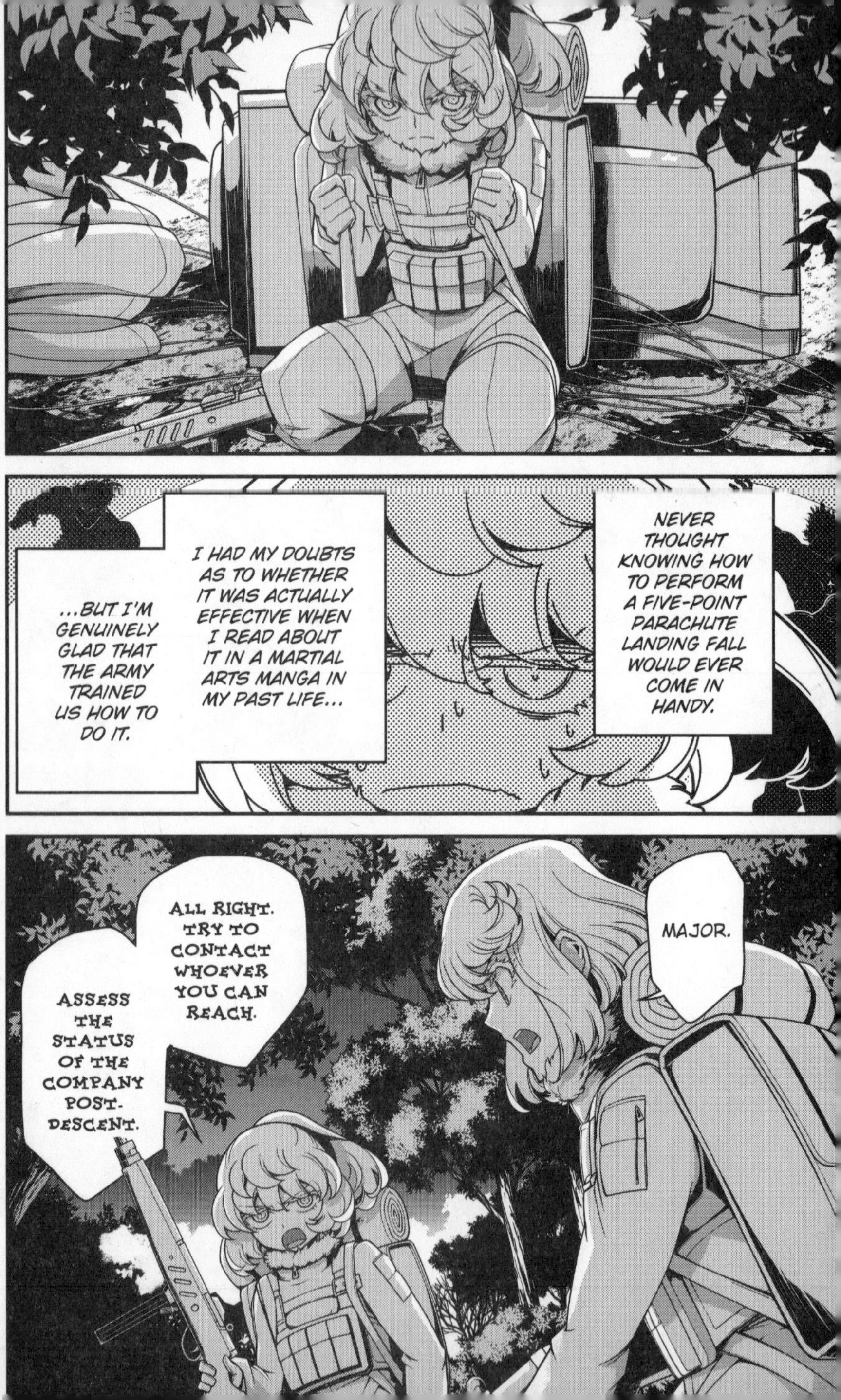
NEVER THOUGHT KNOWING HOW TO PERFORM A FIVE-POINT PARACHUTE LANDING FALL WOULD EVER COME IN HANDY.
I HAD MY DOUBTS AS TO WHETHER IT WAS ACTUALLY EFFECTIVE WHEN I READ ABOUT IT IN A MARTIAL ARTS MANGA IN MY PAST LIFE...
...BUT I'M GENUINELY GLAD THAT THE ARMY TRAINED US HOW TO DO IT.
MAJOR.
ALL RIGHT. TRY TO CONTACT WHOEVER YOU CAN REACH.
ASSESS THE STATUS OF THE COMPANY POST-DESCENT.

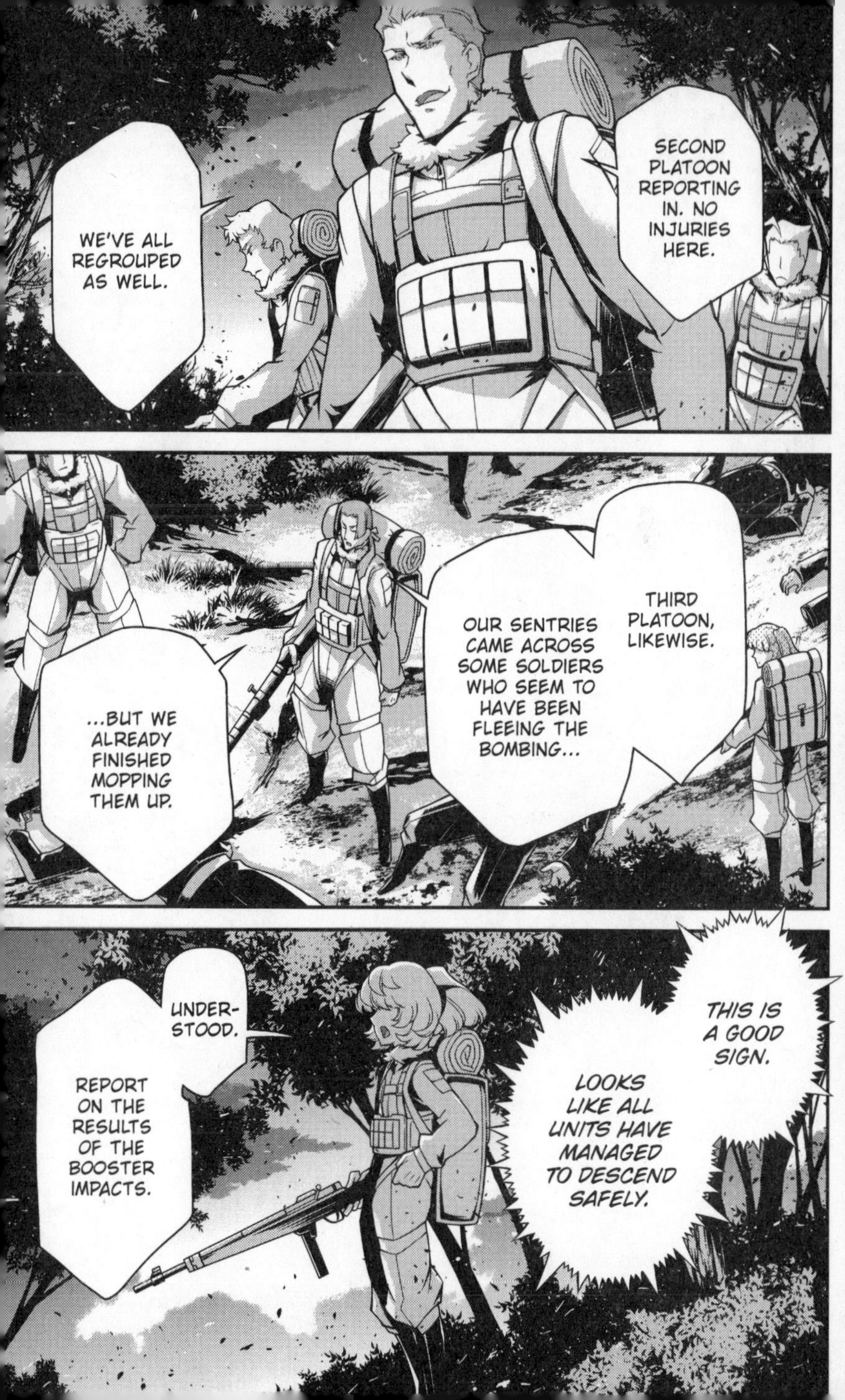
SECOND PLATOON REPORTING IN. NO INJURIES HERE.
WE'VE ALL REGROUPED AS WELL.
THIRD PLATOON, LIKEWISE.
OUR SENTRIES CAME ACROSS SOME SOLDIERS WHO SEEM TO HAVE BEEN FLEEING THE BOMBING...
...BUT WE ALREADY FINISHED MOPPING THEM UP.
THIS IS A GOOD SIGN.
LOOKS LIKE ALL UNITS HAVE MANAGED TO DESCEND SAFELY.
UNDER-STOOD.
REPORT ON THE RESULTS OF THE BOOSTER IMPACTS.

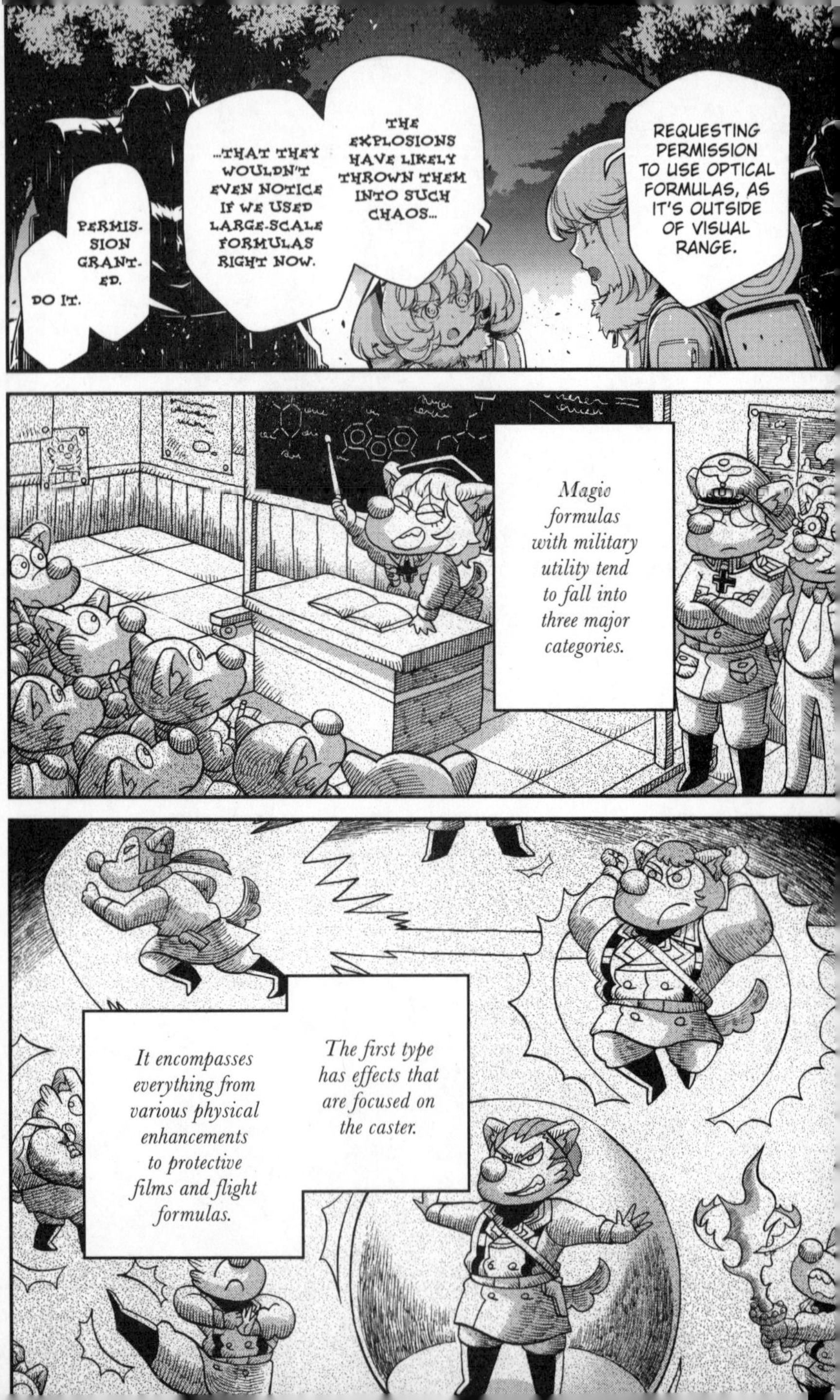
REQUESTING PERMISSION TO USE OPTICAL FORMULAS, AS IT'S OUTSIDE OF VISUAL RANGE.
THE EXPLOSIONS HAVE LIKELY THROWN THEM INTO SUCH CHAOS...
...THAT THEY WOULDN'T EVEN NOTICE IF WE USED LARGE-SCALE FORMULAS RIGHT NOW.
PERMISSION GRANTED.
DO IT.
Magic formulas with military utility tend to fall into three major categories.
The first type has effects that are focused on the caster.
It encompasses everything from various physical enhancements to protective films and flight formulas.

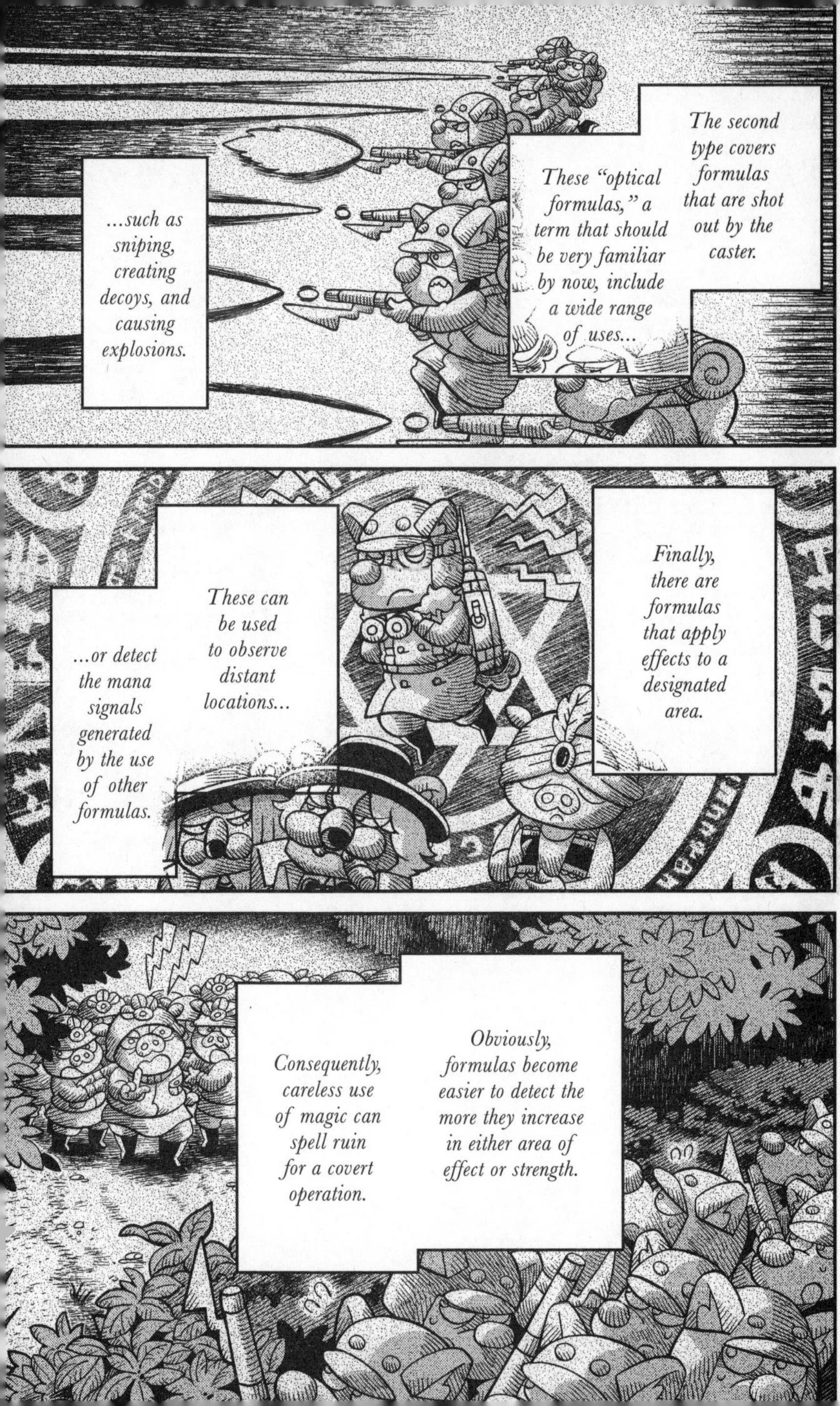
The second type covers formulas that are shot out by the caster.
These "optical formulas," a term that should be very familiar by now, include a wide range of uses...
...such as sniping, creating decoys, and causing explosions.
Finally, there are formulas that apply effects to a designated area.
These can be used to observe distant locations...
...or detect the mana signals generated by the use of other formulas.
Obviously, formulas become easier to detect the more they increase in either area of effect or strength.
Consequently, careless use of magic can spell ruin for a covert operation.

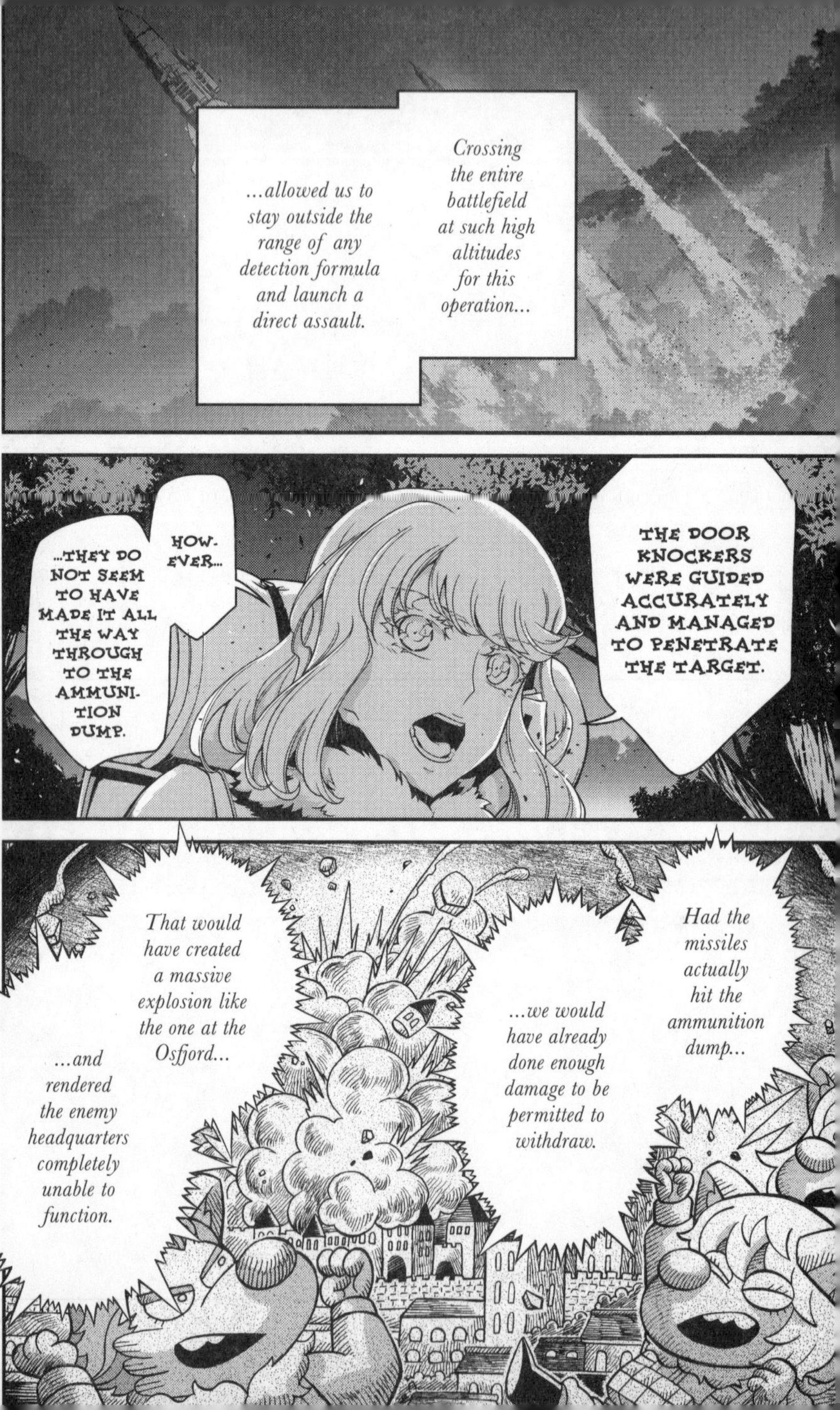
Crossing the entire battlefield at such high altitudes for this operation...
...allowed us to stay outside the range of any detection formula and launch a direct assault.
THE DOOR KNOCKERS WERE GUIDED ACCURATELY AND MANAGED TO PENETRATE THE TARGET.
HOWEVER...
...THEY DO NOT SEEM TO HAVE MADE IT ALL THE WAY THROUGH TO THE AMMUNITION DUMP.
Had the missiles actually hit the ammunition dump...
...we would have already done enough damage to be permitted to withdraw.
That would have created a massive explosion like the one at the Osfjord...
...and rendered the enemy headquarters completely unable to function.

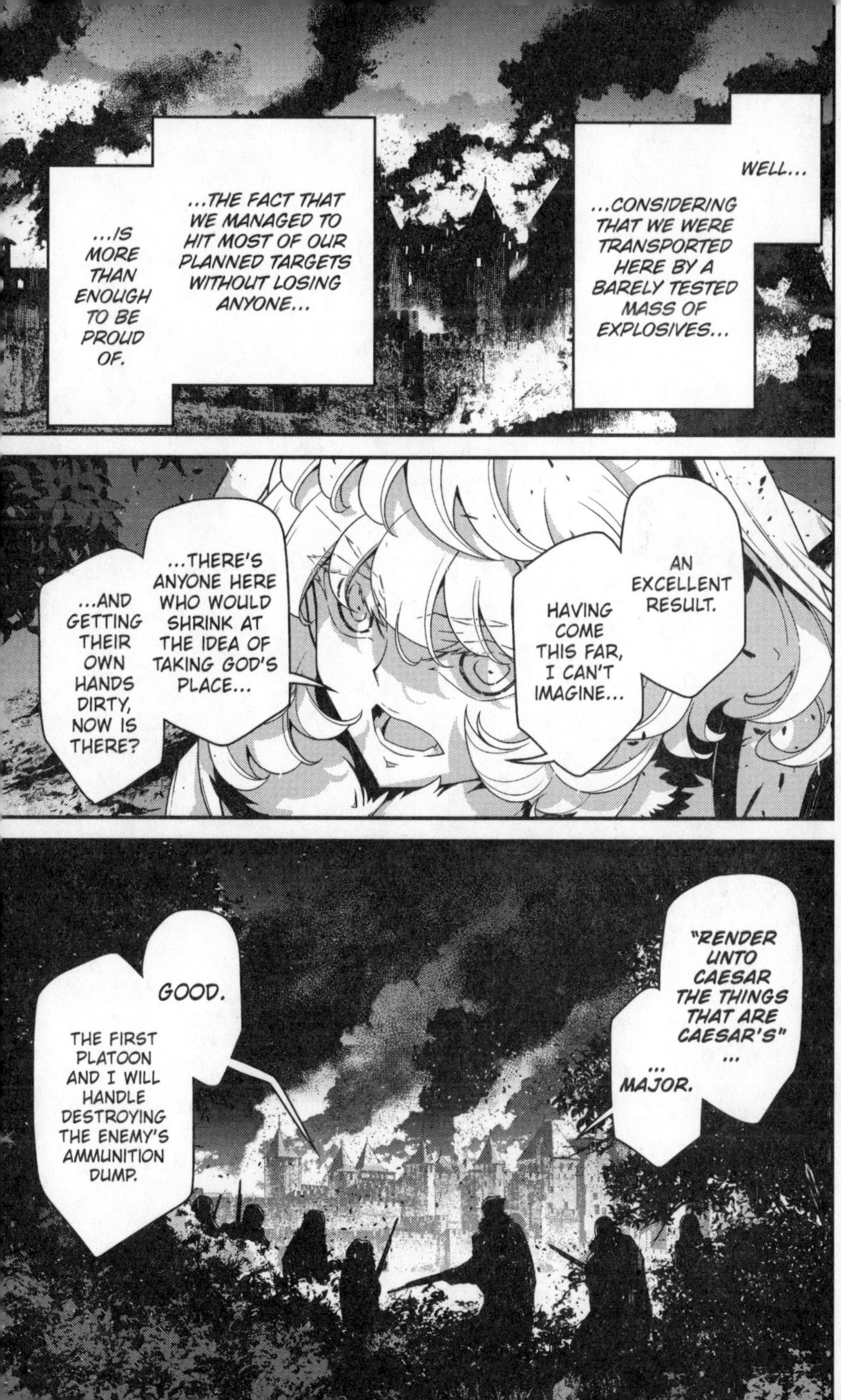
WELL...
...CONSIDERING THAT WE WERE TRANSPORTED HERE BY A BARELY TESTED MASS OF EXPLOSIVES...
...THE FACT THAT WE MANAGED TO HIT MOST OF OUR PLANNED TARGETS WITHOUT LOSING ANYONE...
...IS MORE THAN ENOUGH TO BE PROUD OF.
AN EXCELLENT RESULT.
HAVING COME THIS FAR, I CAN'T IMAGINE...
...THERE'S ANYONE HERE WHO WOULD SHRINK AT THE IDEA OF TAKING GOD'S PLACE...
...AND GETTING THEIR OWN HANDS DIRTY, NOW IS THERE?
"RENDER UNTO CAESAR THE THINGS THAT ARE CAESAR'S"... ...MAJOR.
GOOD.
THE FIRST PLATOON AND I WILL HANDLE DESTROYING THE ENEMY'S AMMUNITION DUMP.

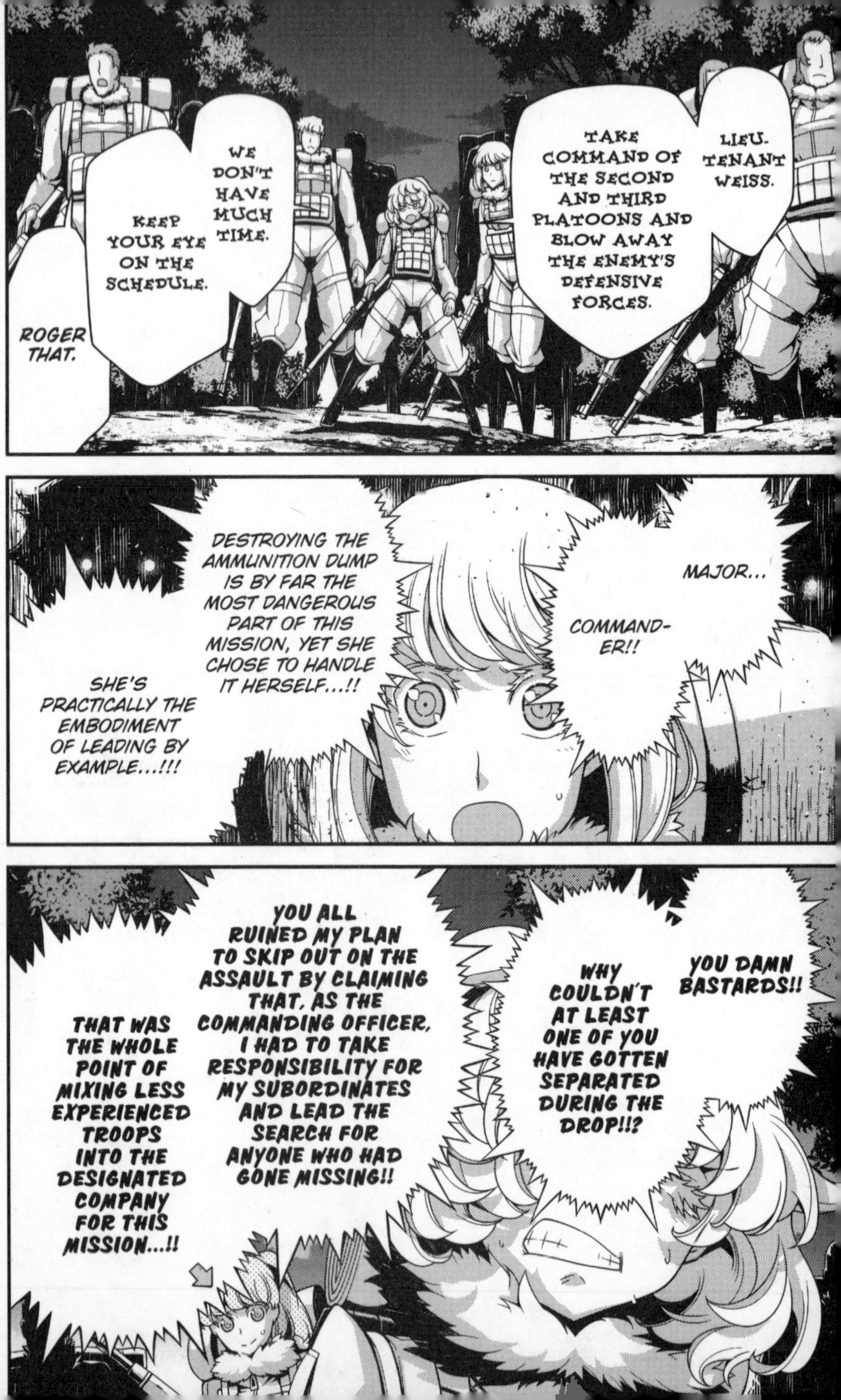
LIEU-TENANT WEISS.
TAKE COMMAND OF THE SECOND AND THIRD PLATOONS AND BLOW AWAY THE ENEMY'S DEFENSIVE FORCES.
WE DON'T HAVE MUCH TIME.
KEEP YOUR EYE ON THE SCHEDULE.
ROGER THAT.
MAJOR...
COMMAND-ER!!
DESTROYING THE AMMUNITION DUMP IS BY FAR THE MOST DANGEROUS PART OF THIS MISSION, YET SHE CHOSE TO HANDLE IT HERSELF...!!
SHE'S PRACTICALLY THE EMBODIMENT OF LEADING BY EXAMPLE...!!!
YOU DAMN BASTARDS!!
WHY COULDN'T AT LEAST ONE OF YOU HAVE GOTTEN SEPARATED DURING THE DROP!!?
YOU ALL RUINED MY PLAN TO SKIP OUT ON THE ASSAULT BY CLAIMING THAT, AS THE COMMANDING OFFICER, I HAD TO TAKE RESPONSIBILITY FOR MY SUBORDINATES AND LEAD THE SEARCH FOR ANYONE WHO HAD GONE MISSING!!
THAT WAS THE WHOLE POINT OF MIXING LESS EXPERIENCED TROOPS INTO THE DESIGNATED COMPANY FOR THIS MISSION...!!

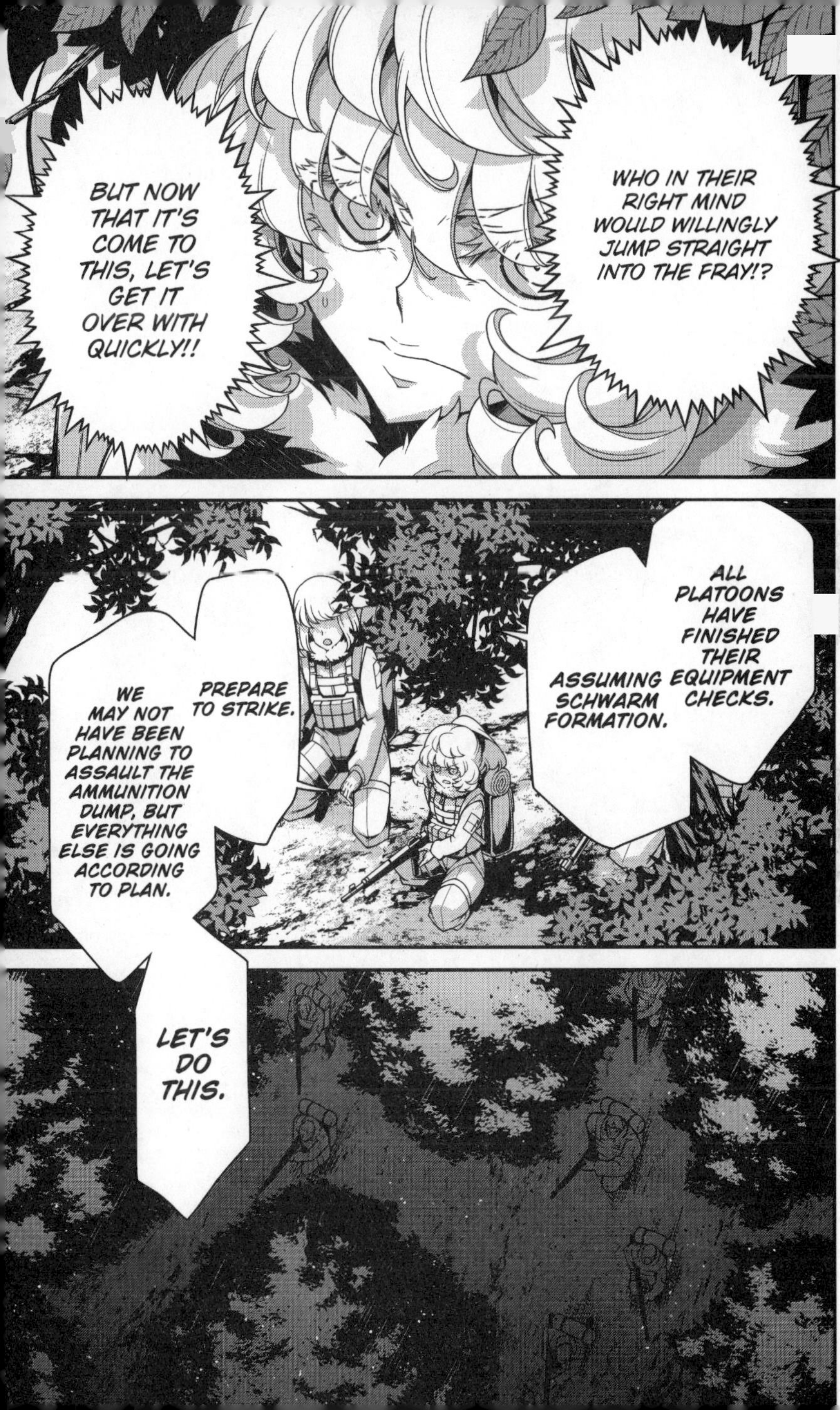
WHO IN THEIR RIGHT MIND WOULD WILLINGLY JUMP STRAIGHT INTO THE FRAY!?
BUT NOW THAT IT'S COME TO THIS, LET'S GET IT OVER WITH QUICKLY!!
ALL PLATOONS HAVE FINISHED THEIR EQUIPMENT CHECKS.
ASSUMING SCHWARM FORMATION.
PREPARE TO STRIKE.
WE MAY NOT HAVE BEEN PLANNING TO ASSAULT THE AMMUNITION DUMP, BUT EVERYTHING ELSE IS GOING ACCORDING TO PLAN.
LET'S DO THIS.

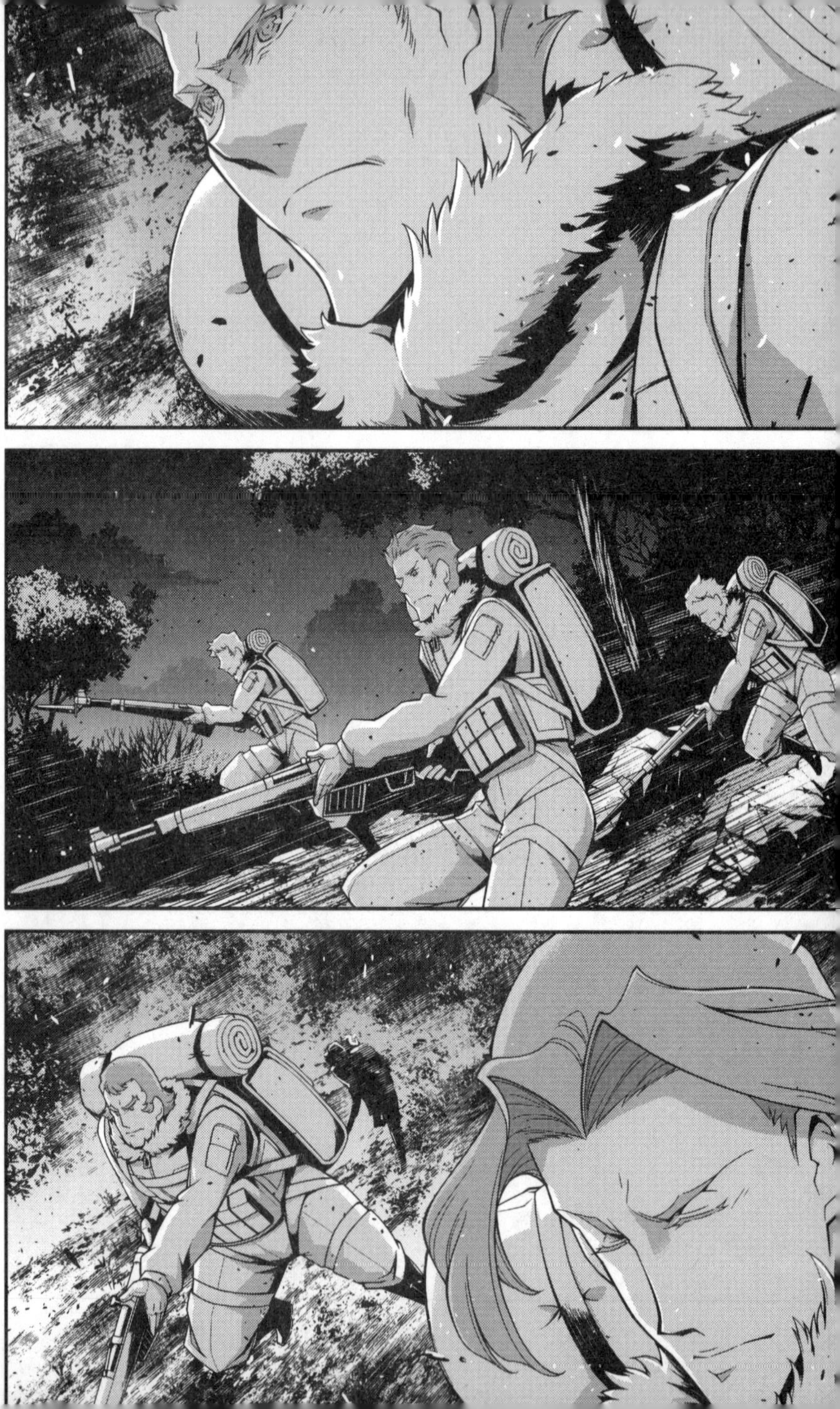

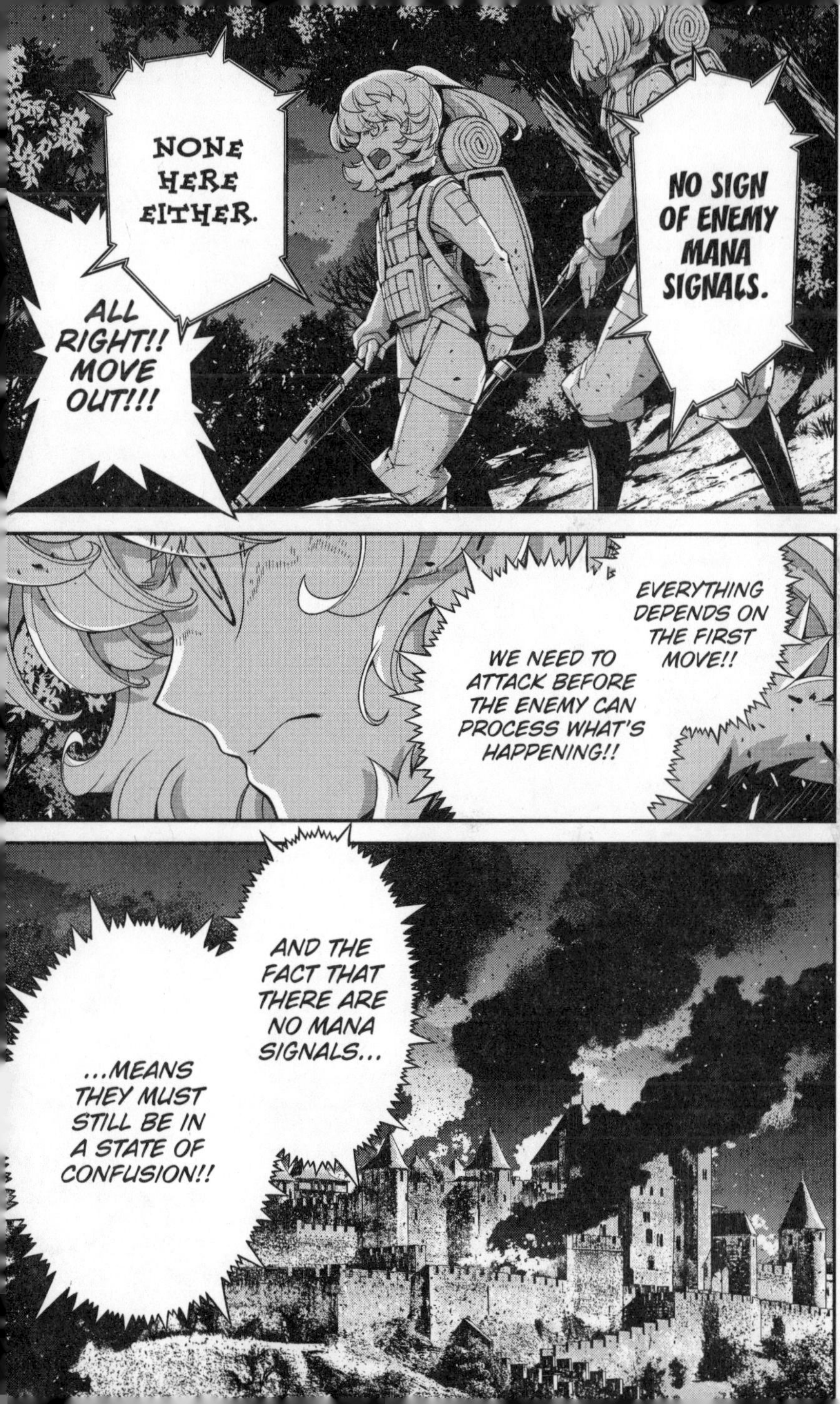
NO SIGN OF ENEMY MANA SIGNALS.
NONE HERE EITHER.
ALL RIGHT!! MOVE OUT!!!
EVERYTHING DEPENDS ON THE FIRST MOVE!!
WE NEED TO ATTACK BEFORE THE ENEMY CAN PROCESS WHAT'S HAPPENING!!
AND THE FACT THAT THERE ARE NO MANA SIGNALS...
...MEANS THEY MUST STILL BE IN A STATE OF CONFUSION!!

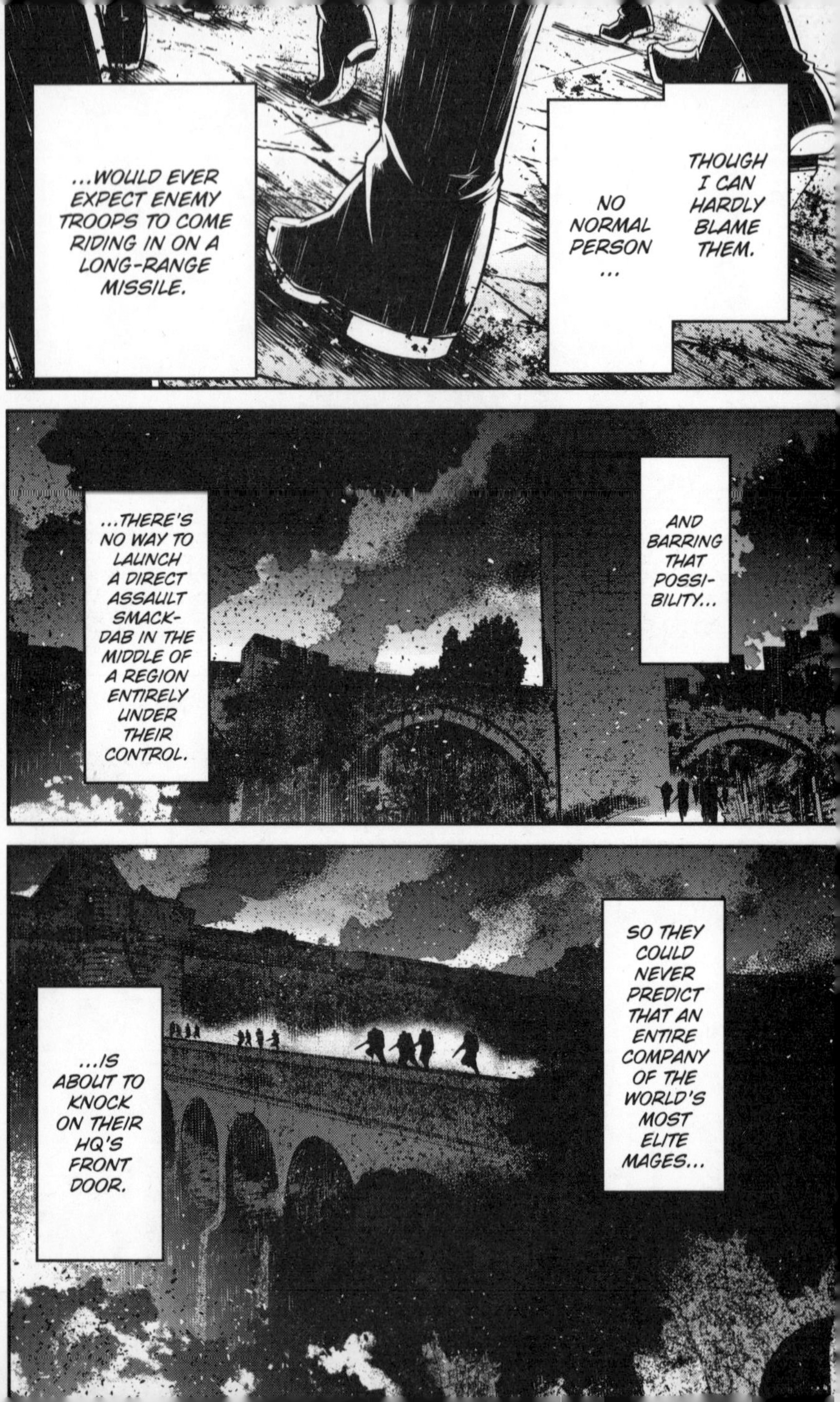
THOUGH I CAN HARDLY BLAME THEM.
NO NORMAL PERSON...
...WOULD EVER EXPECT ENEMY TROOPS TO COME RIDING IN ON A LONG-RANGE MISSILE.
AND BARRING THAT POSSIBILITY...
...THERE'S NO WAY TO LAUNCH A DIRECT ASSAULT SMACK-DAB IN THE MIDDLE OF A REGION ENTIRELY UNDER THEIR CONTROL.
SO THEY COULD NEVER PREDICT THAT AN ENTIRE COMPANY OF THE WORLD'S MOST ELITE MAGES...
...IS ABOUT TO KNOCK ON THEIR HQ'S FRONT DOOR.

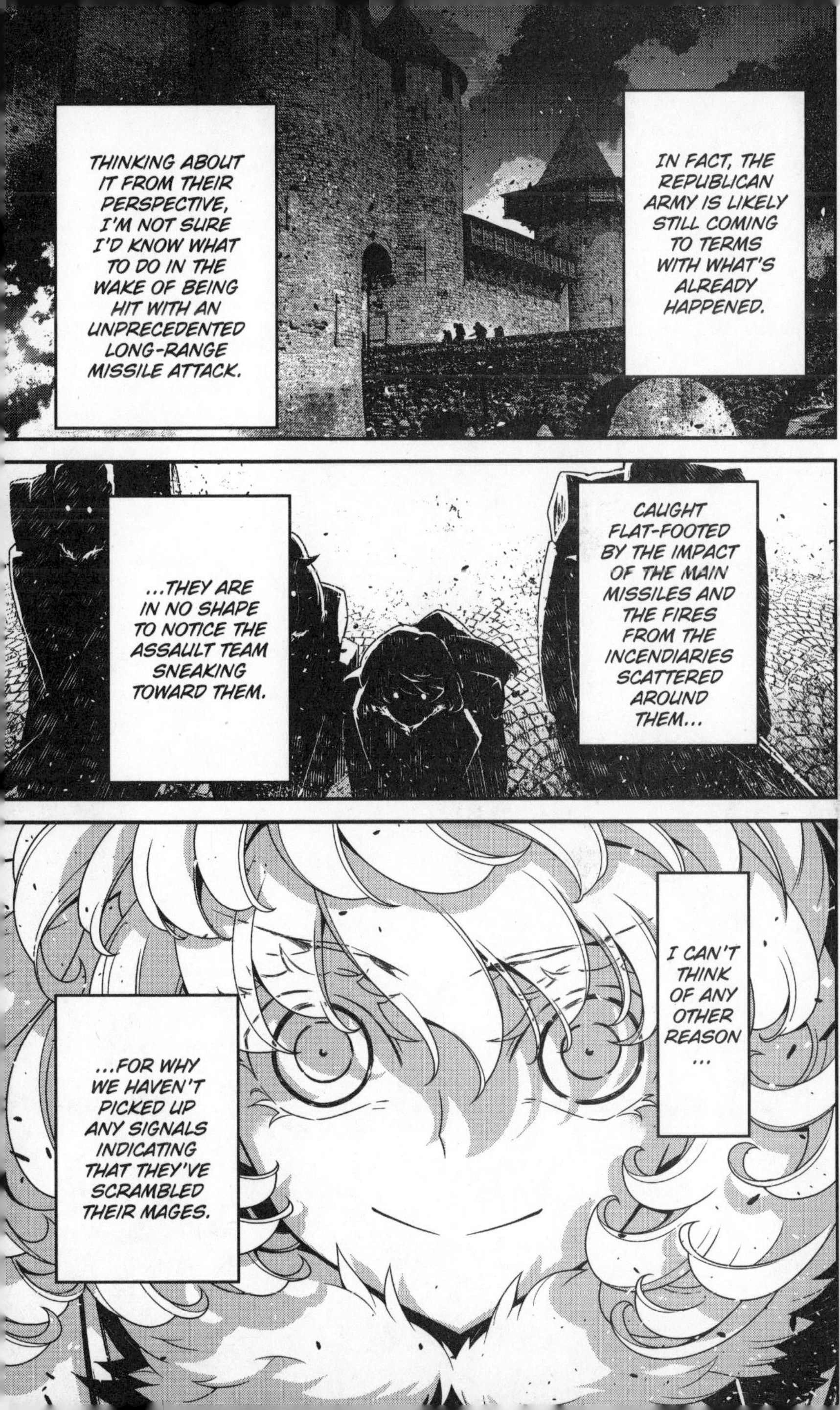
IN FACT, THE REPUBLICAN ARMY IS LIKELY STILL COMING TO TERMS WITH WHAT'S ALREADY HAPPENED.
THINKING ABOUT IT FROM THEIR PERSPECTIVE, I'M NOT SURE I'D KNOW WHAT TO DO IN THE WAKE OF BEING HIT WITH AN UNPRECEDENTED LONG-RANGE MISSILE ATTACK.
CAUGHT FLAT-FOOTED BY THE IMPACT OF THE MAIN MISSILES AND THE FIRES FROM THE INCENDIARIES SCATTERED AROUND THEM...
...THEY ARE IN NO SHAPE TO NOTICE THE ASSAULT TEAM SNEAKING TOWARD THEM.
I CAN'T THINK OF ANY OTHER REASON ...
...FOR WHY WE HAVEN'T PICKED UP ANY SIGNALS INDICATING THAT THEY'VE SCRAMBLED THEIR MAGES.

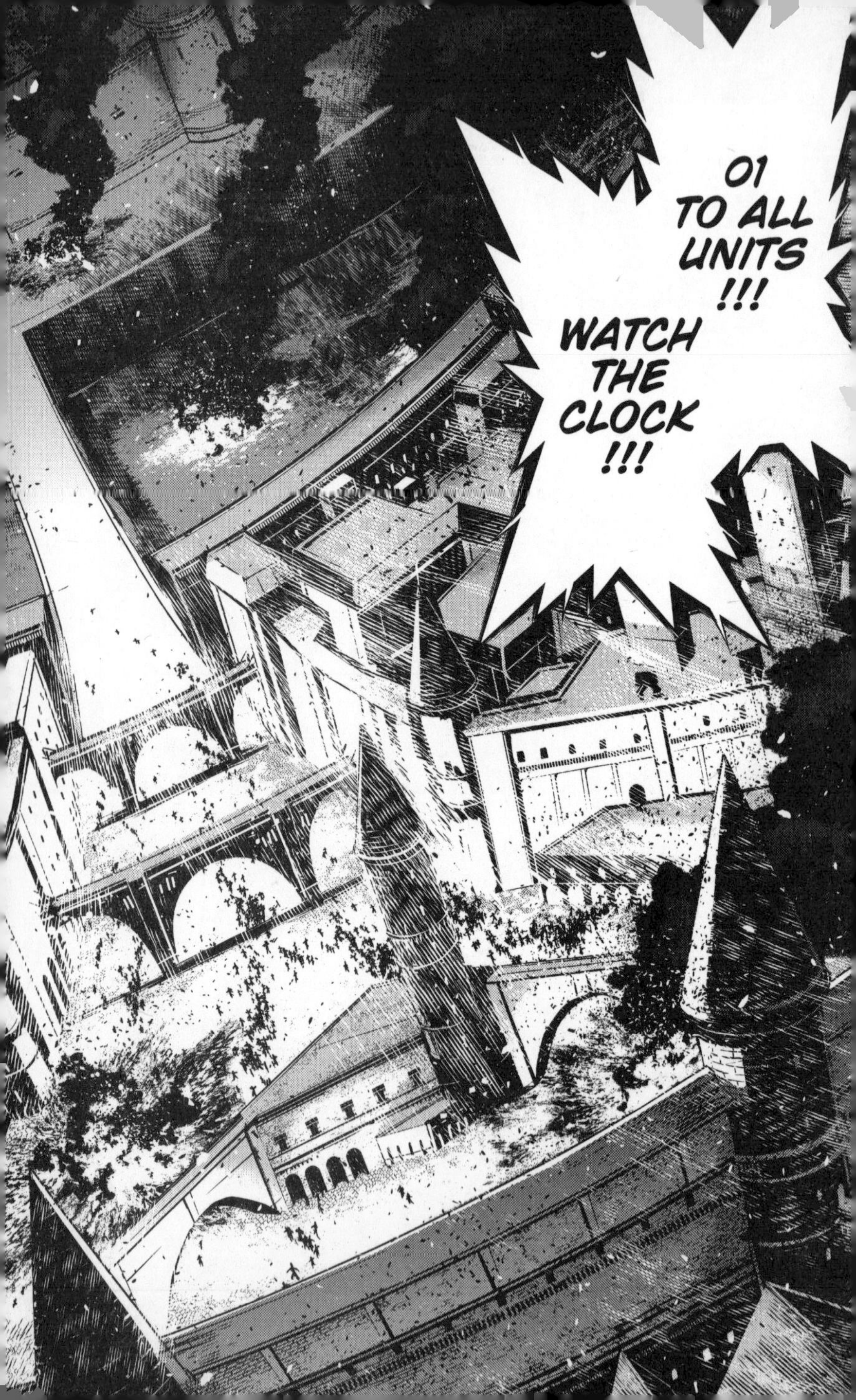
01 TO ALL UNITS!!!
WATCH THE CLOCK!!!

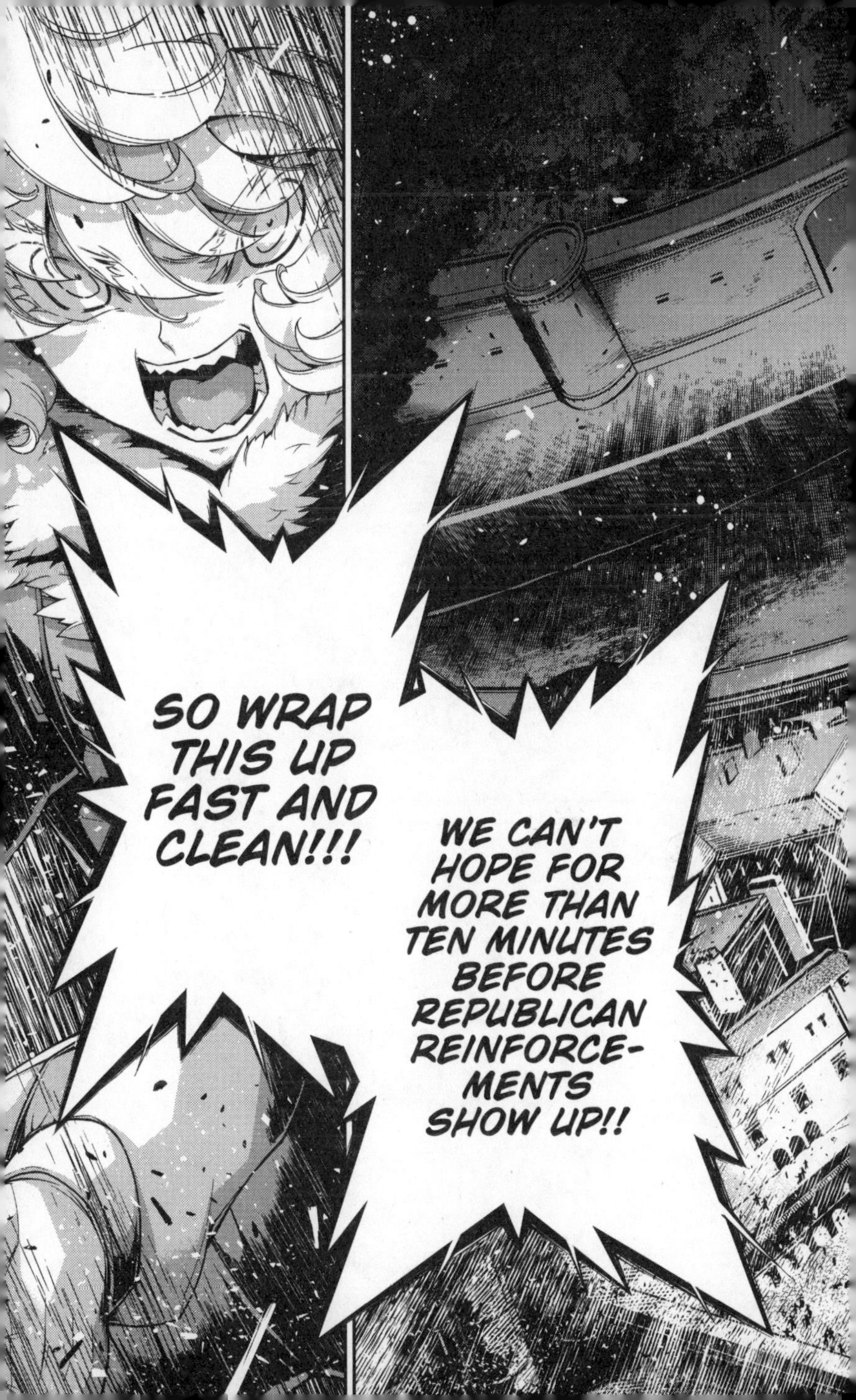
WE CAN'T HOPE FOR MORE THAN TEN MINUTES BEFORE REPUBLICAN REINFORCE-MENTS SHOW UP!!
SO WRAP THIS UP FAST AND CLEAN!!!

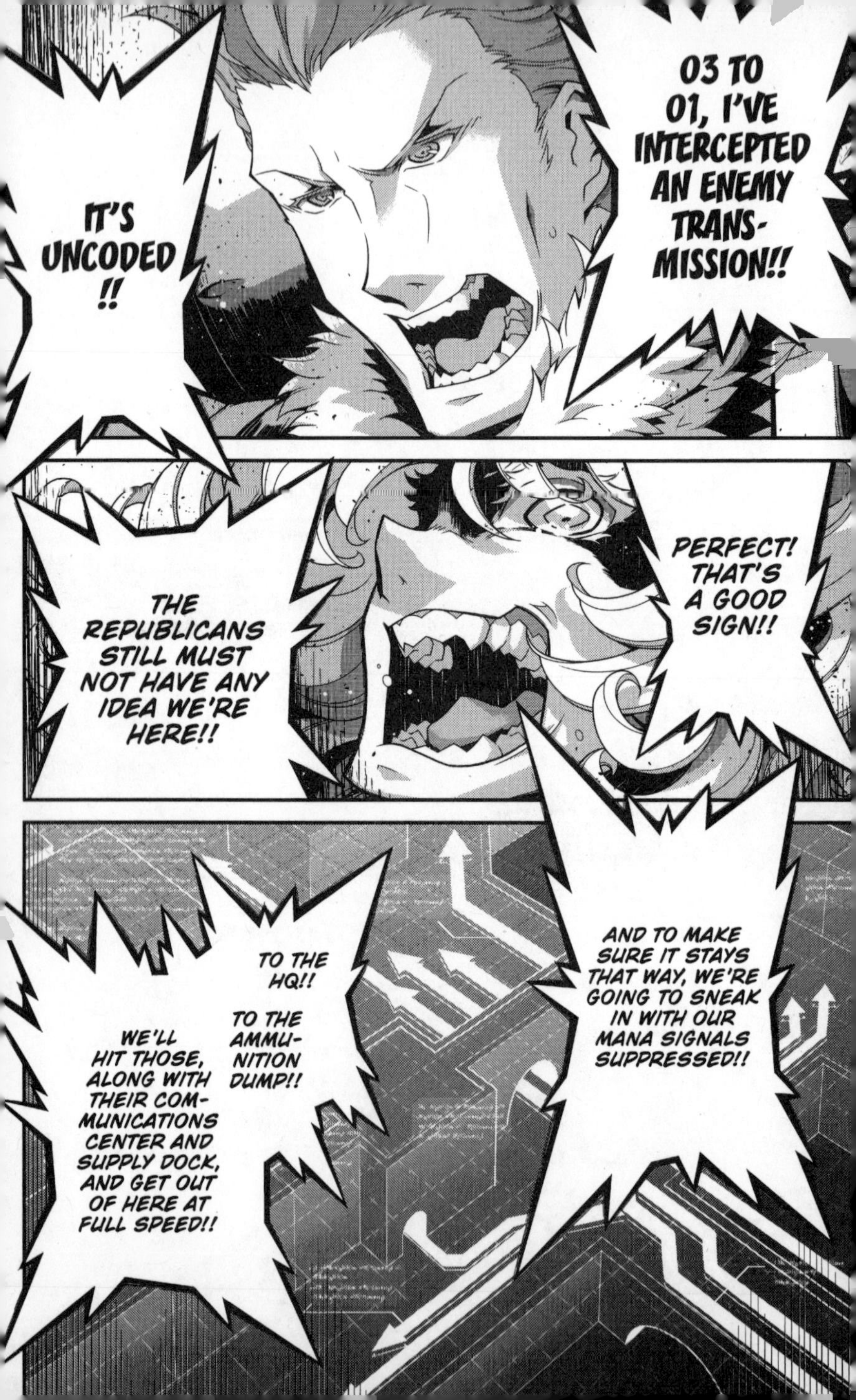
03 TO 01, I'VE INTERCEPTED AN ENEMY TRANS-MISSION!!
IT'S UNCODED!!
PERFECT! THAT'S A GOOD SIGN!!
THE REPUBLICANS STILL MUST NOT HAVE ANY IDEA WE'RE HERE!!
AND TO MAKE SURE IT STAYS THAT WAY, WE'RE GOING TO SNEAK IN WITH OUR MANA SIGNALS SUPPRESSED!!
TO THE HQ!!
TO THE AMMU-NITION DUMP!!
WE'LL HIT THOSE, ALONG WITH THEIR COM-MUNICATIONS CENTER AND SUPPLY DOCK, AND GET OUT OF HERE AT FULL SPEED!!

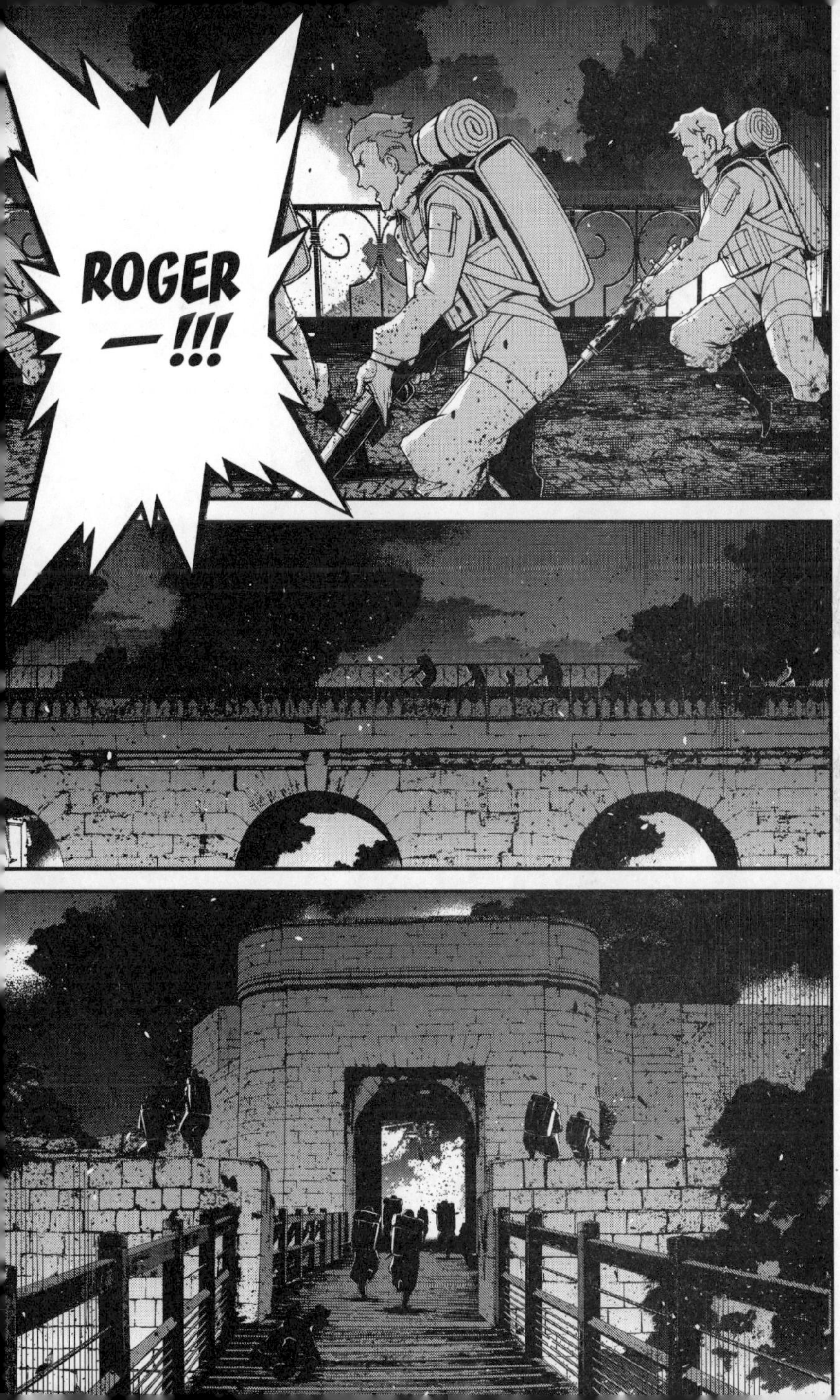
ROGER—!!!

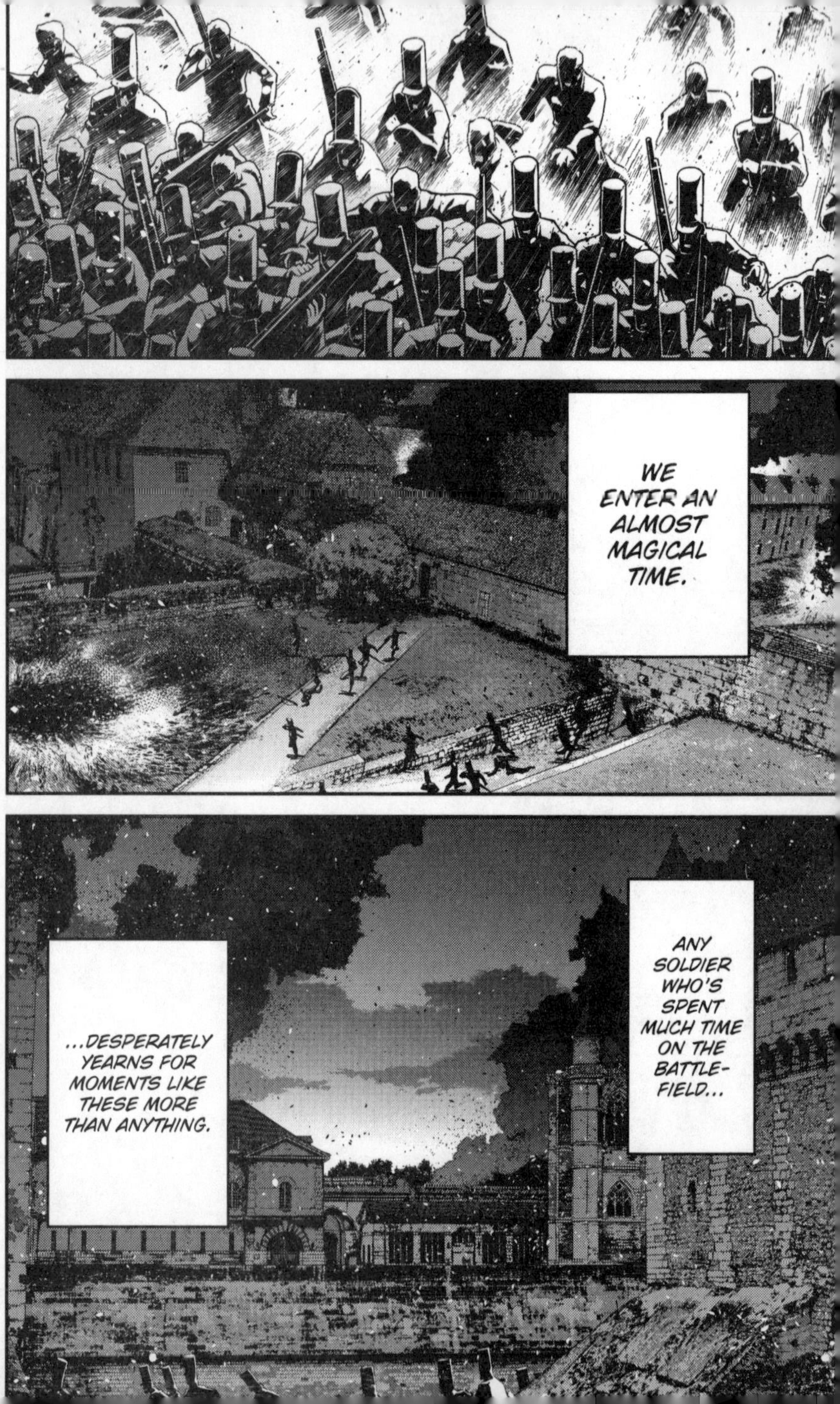
WE ENTER AN ALMOST MAGICAL TIME.
ANY SOLDIER WHO'S SPENT MUCH TIME ON THE BATTLE-FIELD...
...DESPERATELY YEARNS FOR MOMENTS LIKE THESE MORE THAN ANYTHING.

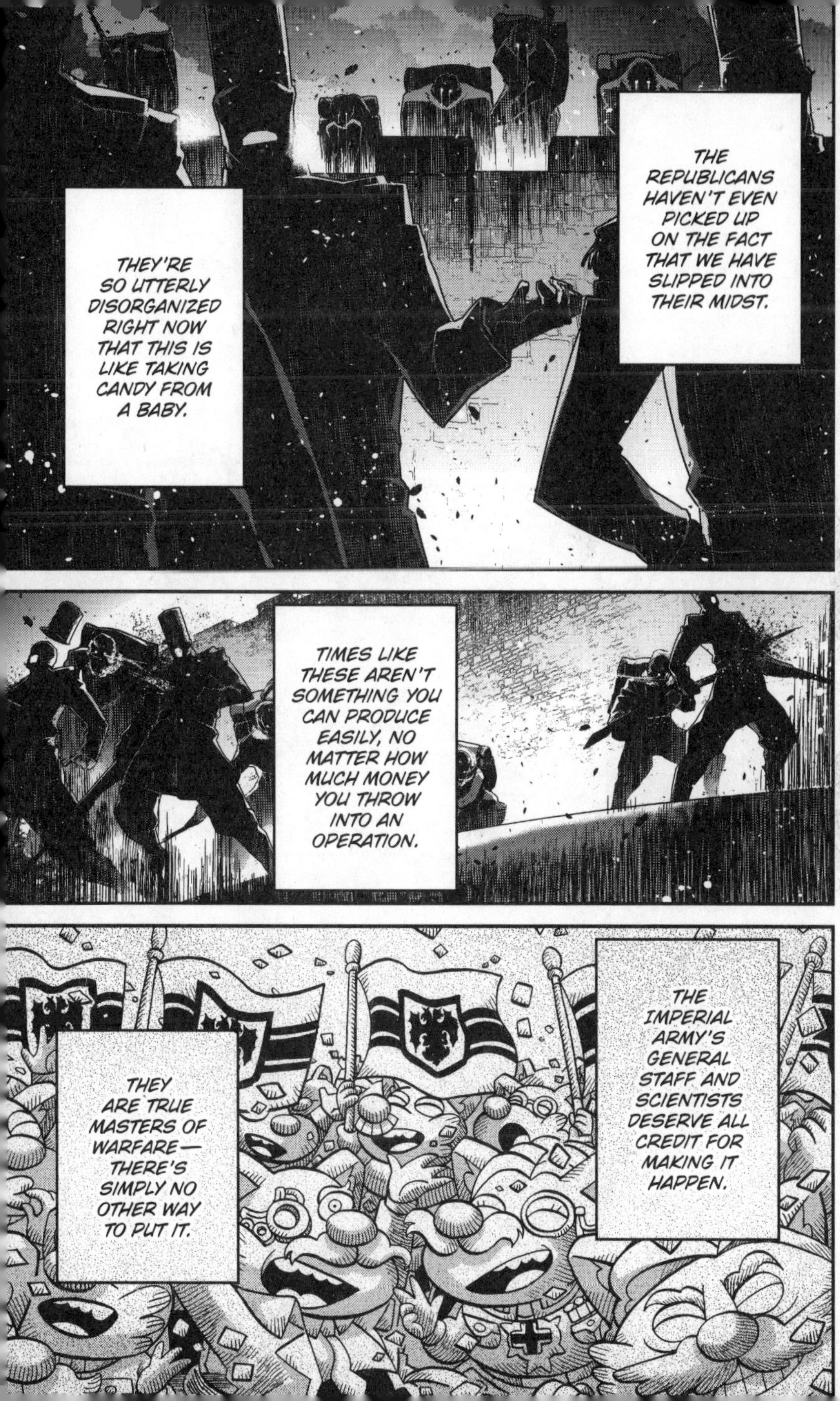
THE REPUBLICANS HAVEN'T EVEN PICKED UP ON THE FACT THAT WE HAVE SLIPPED INTO THEIR MIDST.
THEY'RE SO UTTERLY DISORGANIZED RIGHT NOW THAT THIS IS LIKE TAKING CANDY FROM A BABY.
TIMES LIKE THESE AREN'T SOMETHING YOU CAN PRODUCE EASILY, NO MATTER HOW MUCH MONEY YOU THROW INTO AN OPERATION.
THE IMPERIAL ARMY'S GENERAL STAFF AND SCIENTISTS DESERVE ALL CREDIT FOR MAKING IT HAPPEN.
THEY ARE TRUE MASTERS OF WARFARE—THERE'S SIMPLY NO OTHER WAY TO PUT IT.

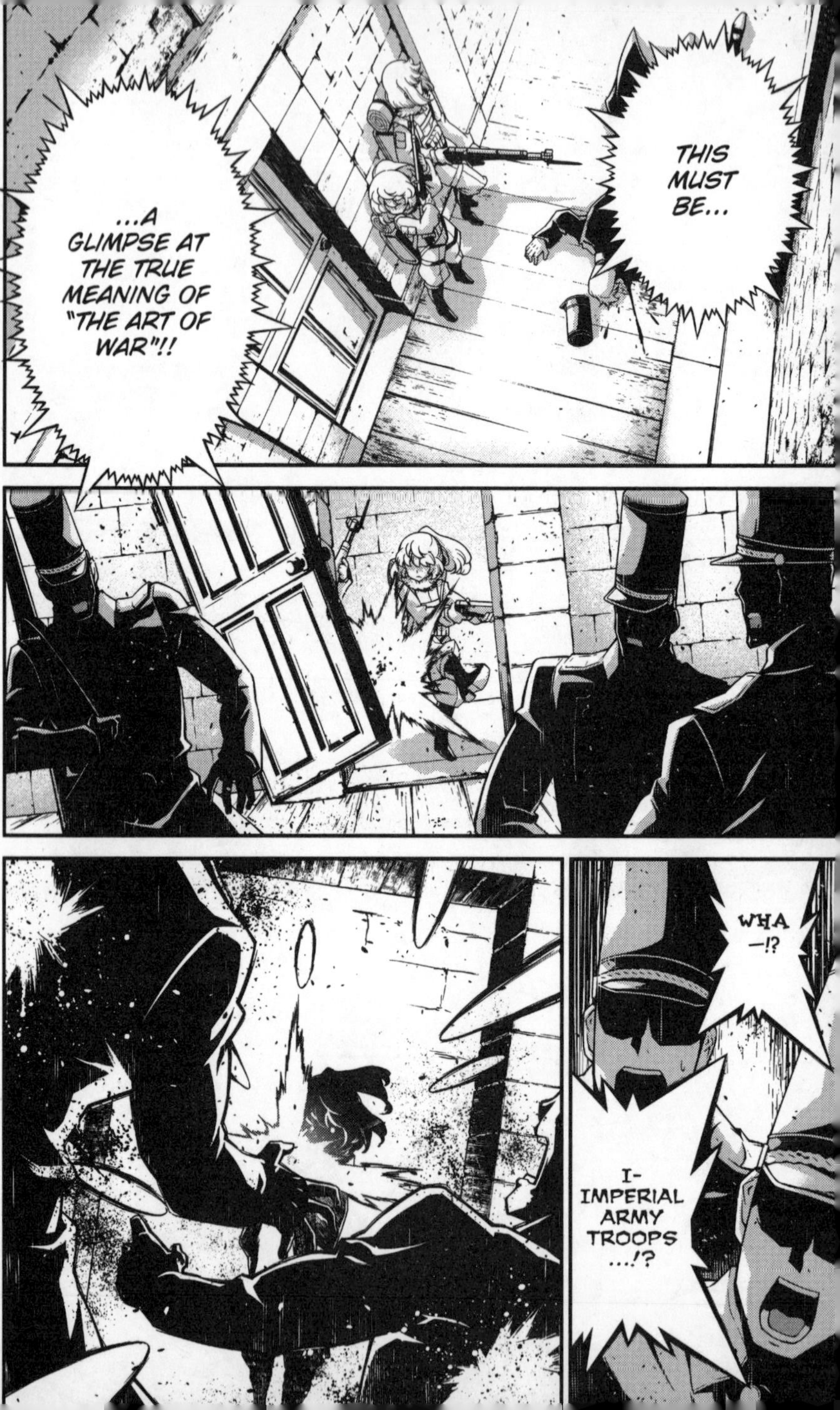
THIS MUST BE...
...A GLIMPSE AT THE TRUE MEANING OF "THE ART OF WAR"!!
WHA—!?
I- IMPERIAL ARMY TROOPS...!?
!?

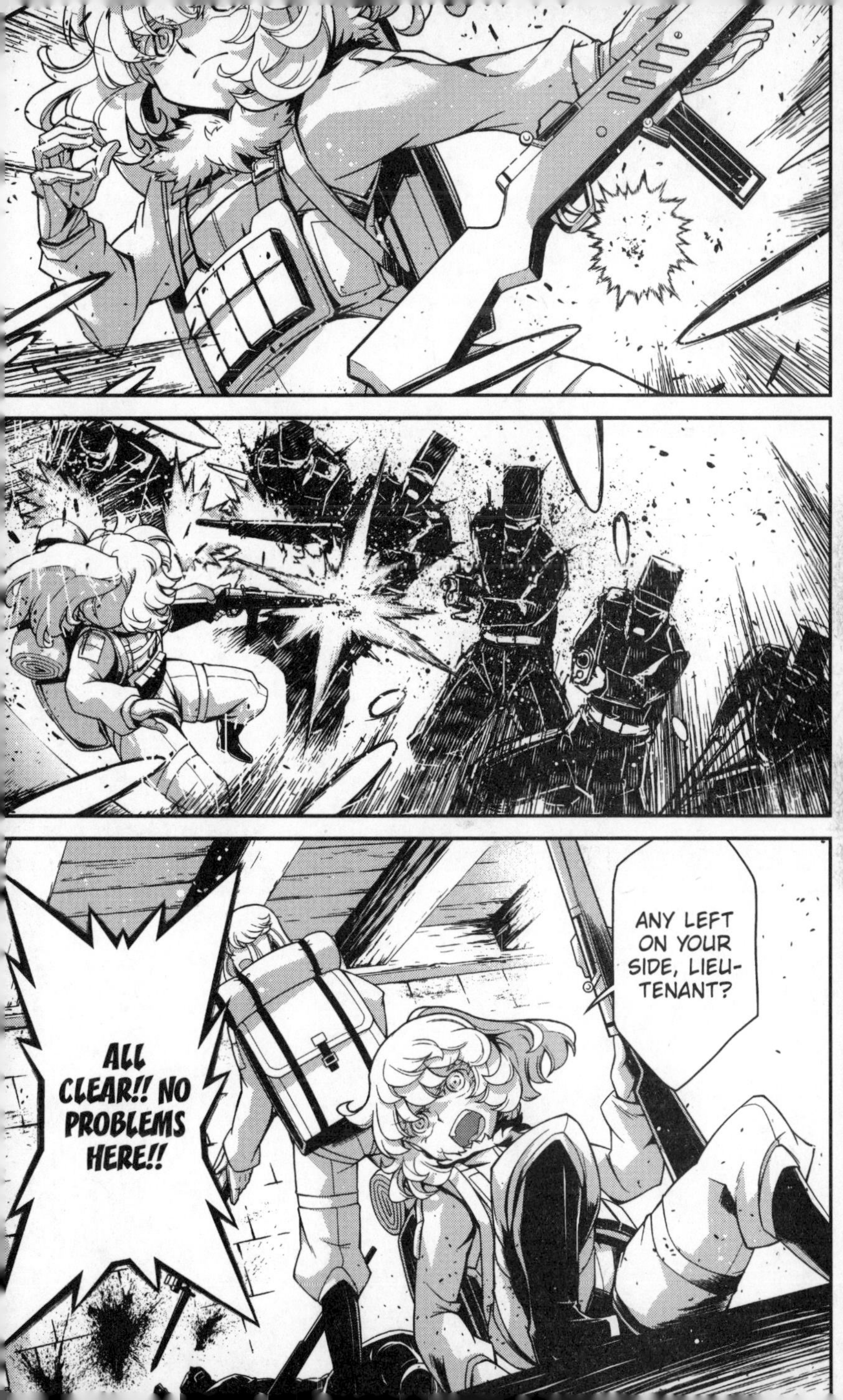
ANY LEFT ON YOUR SIDE, LIEU-TENANT?
ALL CLEAR!! NO PROBLEMS HERE!!

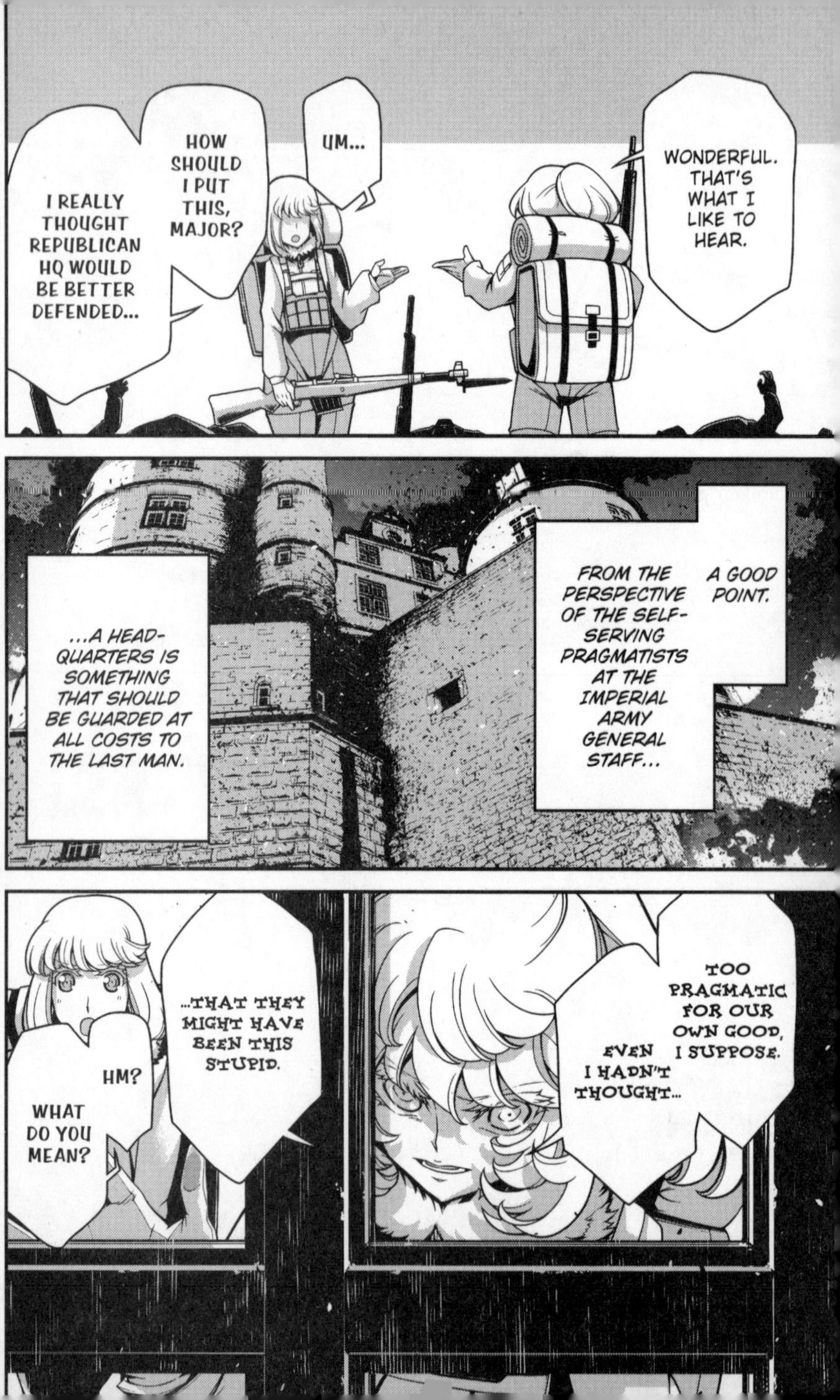
WONDERFUL. THAT'S WHAT I LIKE TO HEAR.
UM...
HOW SHOULD I PUT THIS, MAJOR?
I REALLY THOUGHT REPUBLICAN HQ WOULD BE BETTER DEFENDED...
A GOOD POINT.
FROM THE PERSPECTIVE OF THE SELF-SERVING PRAGMATISTS AT THE IMPERIAL ARMY GENERAL STAFF...
...A HEAD-QUARTERS IS SOMETHING THAT SHOULD BE GUARDED AT ALL COSTS TO THE LAST MAN.
TOO PRAGMATIC FOR OUR OWN GOOD, I SUPPOSE.
EVEN I HADN'T THOUGHT...
...THAT THEY MIGHT HAVE BEEN THIS STUPID.
HM? WHAT DO YOU MEAN?

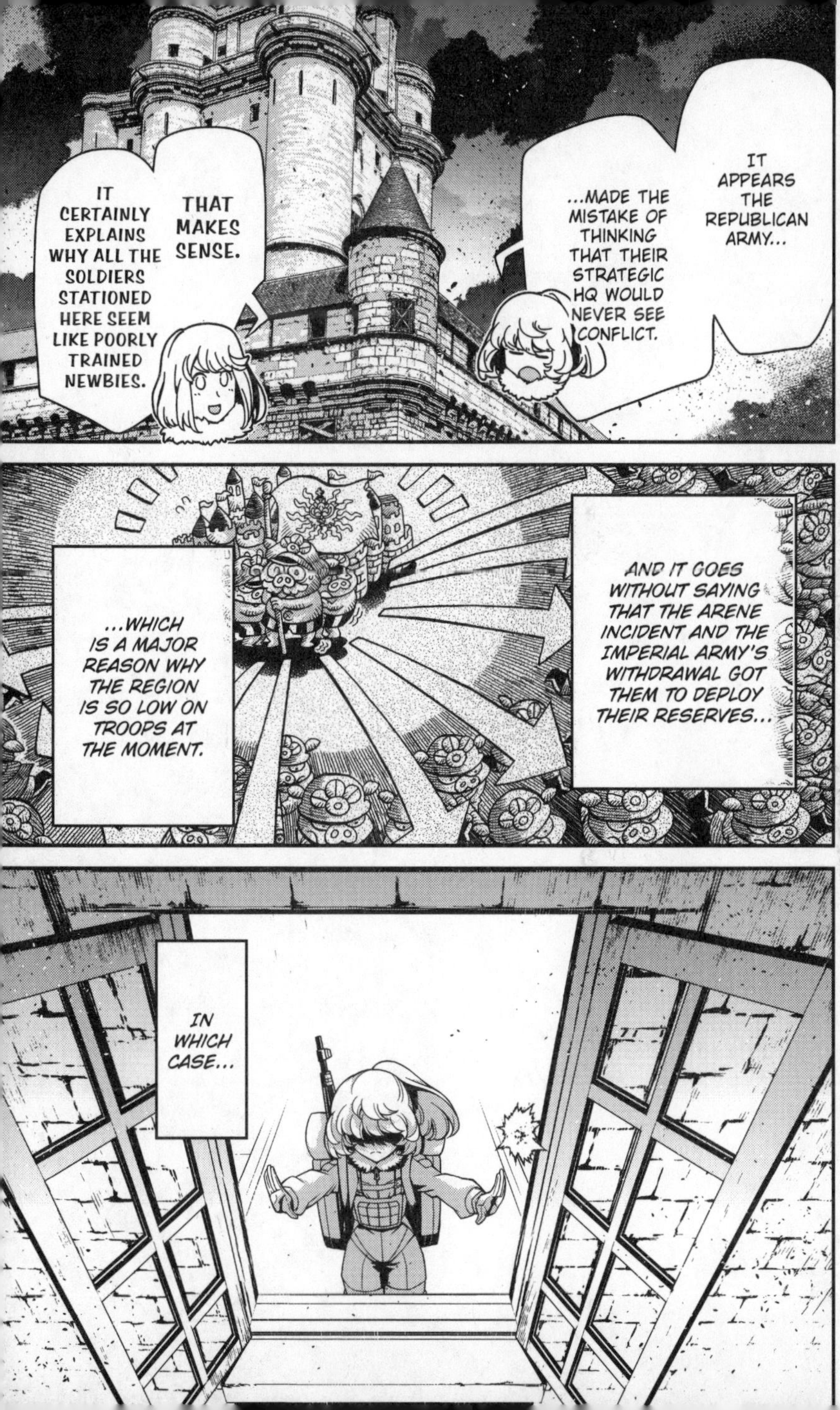
IT APPEARS THE REPUBLICAN ARMY...
...MADE THE MISTAKE OF THINKING THAT THEIR STRATEGIC HQ WOULD NEVER SEE CONFLICT.
THAT MAKES SENSE.
IT CERTAINLY EXPLAINS WHY ALL THE SOLDIERS STATIONED HERE SEEM LIKE POORLY TRAINED NEWBIES.
AND IT GOES WITHOUT SAYING THAT THE ARENE INCIDENT AND THE IMPERIAL ARMY'S WITHDRAWAL GOT THEM TO DEPLOY THEIR RESERVES...
...WHICH IS A MAJOR REASON WHY THE REGION IS SO LOW ON TROOPS AT THE MOMENT.
IN WHICH CASE...

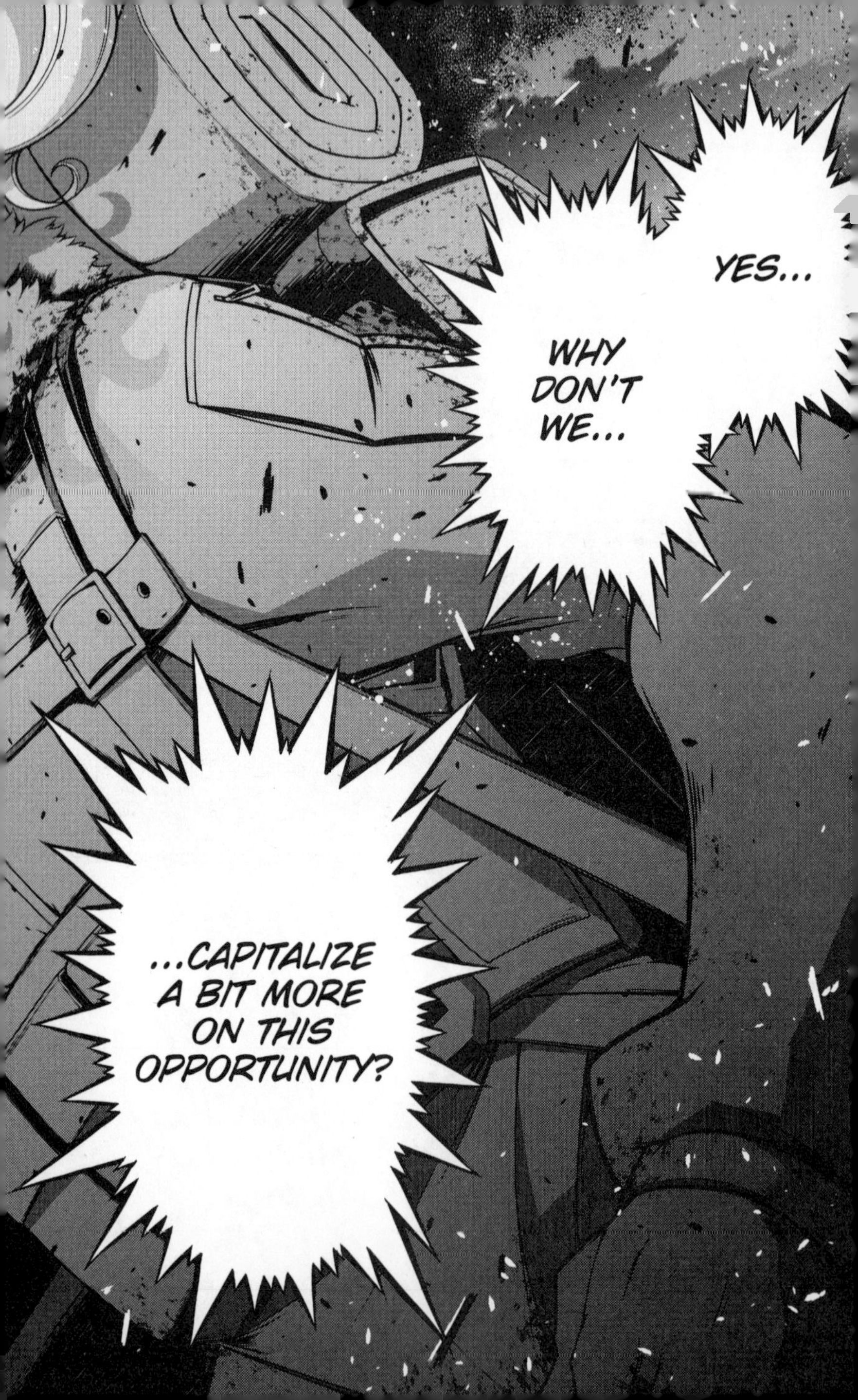
YES...
WHY DON'T WE...
...CAPITALIZE A BIT MORE ON THIS OPPORTUNITY?

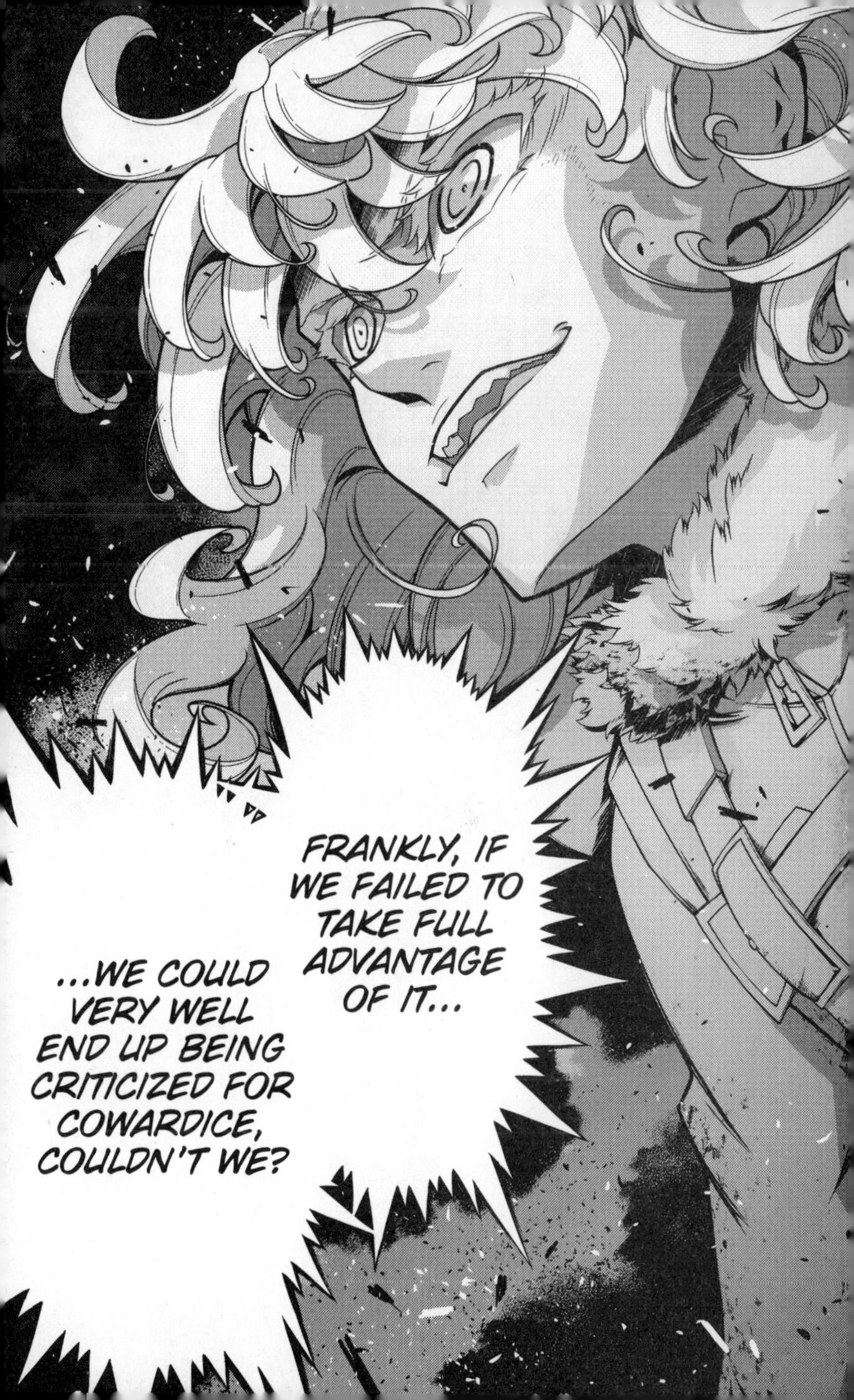
FRANKLY, IF WE FAILED TO TAKE FULL ADVANTAGE OF IT...
...WE COULD VERY WELL END UP BEING CRITICIZED FOR COWARDICE, COULDN'T WE?

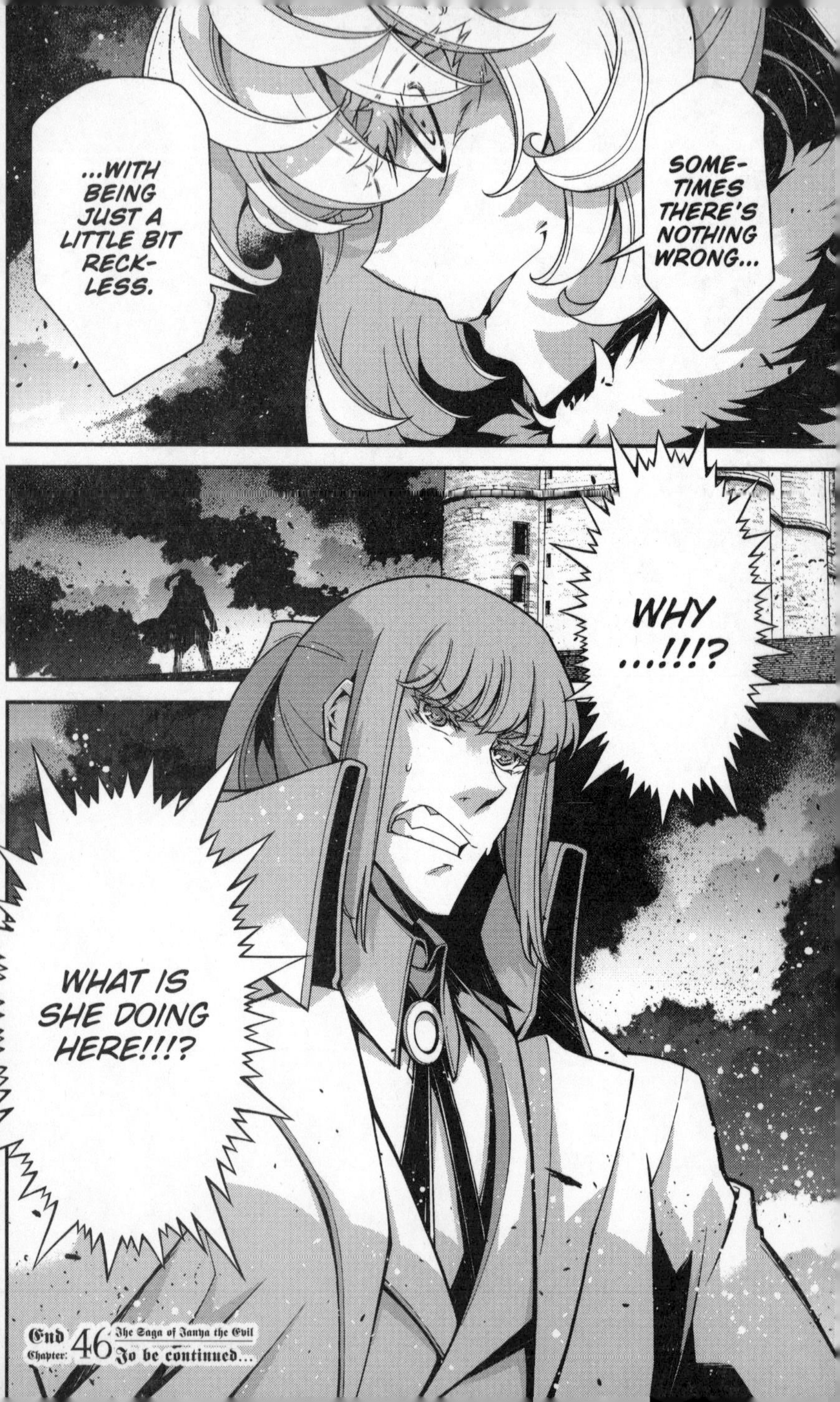
SOME-TIMES THERE'S NOTHING WRONG...
...WITH BEING JUST A LITTLE BIT RECK-LESS.
WHY ...!!!?
WHAT IS SHE DOING HERE!!!?
End Chapter: 46 The Saga of Tanya the Evil
To be continued...

The Saga of
Tanya the Evil

16

Original Story: Carlo Zen   Art: Chika Tojo
Character Design: Shinobu Shinotsuki

Special Thanks

Carlo Zen

Shinobu Shinotsuki

Takamaru

KURI

Miira

Yamatatsu

Agatha

Kuuko

Shinno Himegami

Yoshitsuki Toyama

Figurine sales and production
Plabbit

THE SAGA OF TANYA THE EVIL 16

ORIGINAL STORY: Carlo Zen

ART: Chika Tojo ❧ CHARACTER DESIGN: Shinobu Shinotsuki

Translation: Richard William Tobin II ⚔ Lettering: Chiho Christie

YOJO SENKI Vol. 16
©Chika Tojo 2019
©Carlo Zen
First published in Japan in 2019 by KADOKAWA CORPORATION, Tokyo.
English translation rights arranged with KADOKAWA CORPORATION, Tokyo
through TUTTLE-MORI AGENCY, INC., Tokyo.

English translation © 2022 by Yen Press, LLC

Yen Press
150 West 30th Street, 19th Floor
New York, NY 10001

Visit us at yenpress.com
facebook.com/yenpress
twitter.com/yenpress
yenpress.tumblr.com
instagram.com/yenpress

First Yen Press Edition: May 2022

Yen Press is an imprint of Yen Press, LLC.
The Yen Press name and logo are trademarks of Yen Press, LLC.

Library of Congress Control Number: 2017954161

ISBNs: 978-1-9753-4258-6 (paperback)
978-1-9753-4259-3 (ebook)

1 3 5 7 9 10 8 6 4 2

WOR

Printed in the United States of America